PRACTICUM AND INTERNSHIP

Completely revised and updated, the sixth edition of *Practicum and Internship* is a practical resource that provides students and supervisors with thorough coverage of all stages and aspects of the practicum and internship process.

New to this edition are:

- Downloadable, customizable online forms, contracts, and other materials
- Across-the-board updates that reflect 2016 CACREP standards
- Incorporation of contemporary research and literature that addresses recommended practices and ethical considerations regarding the use of technology in counseling
- New information on preparing students to run their first counseling and therapy groups
- A review of ethical standards and current perspectives on working with culturally diverse clients
- Current perspectives on managing self-care during practicum and internship and beyond
- A thoughtful presentation of trauma-informed approaches to counseling
- A revised final chapter including guidelines for preparing for licensure exams and for longevity in the profession

With comprehensive information that spans across therapeutic approaches, concerns, and topics, this remains an essential foundational text for counseling and psychotherapy students and their supervisors.

Christin M. Jungers, PhD, LPCC-S, is a professor and clinical supervisor in the Clinical Mental Health Counseling Program at Franciscan University of Steubenville. She is a licensed professional clinical counselor with 20 years of clinical experience.

Judith Scott, PhD, is a professor emeritus at the University of Pittsburgh, and was previously the internship coordinator in the counselor education program. She is a licensed psychologist with 40 years of clinical experience currently in private practice in Pittsburgh, Pennsylvania.

PRACTICUM AND INTERNSHIP

Textbook and Resource Guide for Counseling and Psychotherapy

Sixth Edition

Christin M. Jungers and Judith Scott

Routledge
Taylor & Francis Group

NEW YORK AND LONDON

Sixth edition published 2019
by Routledge
52 Vanderbilt Avenue, New York, NY 10017

and by Routledge
2 Park Square, Milton Park, Abingdon, Oxon, OX14 4RN

Routledge is an imprint of the Taylor & Francis Group, an informa business

First edition published by Accelerated Development, 2008
Fifth edition published by Routledge, 2014

Library of Congress Cataloging-in-Publication Data
Names: Jungers, Christin M., author. | Scott, Judith, 1940– author.
Title: Practicum and internship : textbook and resource guide for counseling and psychotherapy / Christin M. Jungers, Judith Scott.
Description: 6th edition. | New York, NY : Routledge, 2019. | Previous edition cataloged under John Charles Boylan. | Includes bibliographical references and index.
Identifiers: LCCN 2019004725 (print) | LCCN 2019006842 (ebook) | ISBN 9780429506307 (eBook) | ISBN 9781138492615 (hardback) | ISBN 9781138492608 (pbk.)
Subjects: LCSH: Psychotherapy—Study and teaching (Internship)—Outlines, syllabi, etc. | Psychotherapy—Study and teaching—Supervision—Outlines, syllabi, etc. | Psychotherapy—Study and teaching (Internship)—Forms. | Psychotherapy—Study and teaching—Supervision—Forms.
Classification: LCC RC459 (ebook) | LCC RC459 .B68 2019 (print) | DDC 616.89/140076—dc23
LC record available at https://lccn.loc.gov/2019004725

ISBN: 978-1-138-49261-5 (hbk)
ISBN: 978-1-138-49260-8 (pbk)
ISBN: 978-0-429-50630-7 (ebk)

Typeset in Stone Serif
by Apex CoVantage, LLC

Visit the eResources: www.routledge.com/9781138492608

To my children and their spouses: Kristin and Bill Pardini; Troy and Kristin Scott; Megan and Adam Swift; and Neil and Shannon Scott for their loving support of my life and work.

To my grandchildren: Brenna, Katrina, and Nate Scott; Josie and Mica Swift; Riley, Aiden (AJ), and Ellie Scott; and Roman and Levi Pardini, who bring me constant joy and hope for the future.

Judith Scott

To my family, who have brought so much happiness to my life; and especially to my nieces, Natalie, Rebecca, Eleanor, and my nephews, Nicholas and Benjamin. May you grow up to know how special each one of you is and how much you have to offer this world.

Christin M. Jungers

CONTENTS

About the Authors   xix
Preface   xxi
Acknowledgments   xxiii
Overview of the Book   xxv

SECTION I   PRE-PRACTICUM

CHAPTER 1   Preparing for Practicum and Internship   3

The Professional Counselor   3
   Steps to Becoming a Professional Counselor   4
Accreditation Standards for Practicum and Internship   4
   CACREP/CORE Standards for Practicum and Internship   6
   CACEP Standards for Initial and Final Practicum   6
   MPCAC Standards for Practicum and Internship in Counseling   7
Counselor Certification   7
   National Certified Counselor (NCC) and Board Certification   7
   NBCC Specialty Certification   8
   Certified Rehabilitation Counselor (CRC)   8
   Canadian Certified Counsellor (CCC): Canadian Counsellors and
     Psychologists Association   8
   Registered Professional Counsellor (RPC): Canadian Professional
     Counsellors Association   9
   Other Specialty Counseling Certifications   9
State Licensure for Counselors and Psychologists   9
Pre-Practicum Considerations   10
   Checklist of Questions to Be Researched and Answered Before Practicum
     Site Selection   10
Phases of Practicum and Internship   11

Development Reflected in the Program Structure   11

Development Reflected in the Learning Process   12

Development Reflected in Supervisor Interaction   12

Implications   12

Summary   12

References   13

■ **CHAPTER 2** Securing a Practicum and Internship Site   15

Guidelines for Choosing a Practicum and Internship Site   15

Criteria for Site Selection   16

Professional Staff and Supervisor   16

Professional Affiliations of the Site   16

Professional Practices of the Site   16

Site Administration   17

Training and Supervision Values   17

Theoretical Orientation of the Site and Supervisor   17

Client Population   17

Negotiating the Practicum and Internship Placement   19

Typical Questions Asked at the Interview   19

Getting Oriented to Your Field Site   21

Role and Function of the Practicum and Internship Student   21

Summary   22

References   22

SECTION II BEGINNING TO WORK WITH CLIENTS

■ **CHAPTER 3** Starting the Practicum   25

Beginning the Practicum Experience   25

Getting Started: Where Do I Begin?   25

I Have Taken the Classes, but Do I Really Know What to Do?   26

What If I Say Something Wrong?   26

How Do I Know When to Use the Right Techniques?   27

But I'm Just a Rookie! (Learning to Trust Yourself and Your Inner Voice)   27

When in Doubt, Consult! (Your Faculty and Site Supervisors Are
There to Help You)   28

Becoming Part of the Professional Counseling Team   28

Preparing to Meet With Your First Client   29

The Health Insurance Portability and Accountability Act (HIPAA)   29

Informed Consent   31

Sample Informed Consent and Disclosure Statement   32

Establishing a Therapeutic Alliance   35

The Initial Session With the Client   35

Structured and Unstructured Interviews   36

Basic and Advanced Helping Skills   36

Procedural and Issue-Specific Skills   37

Structuring the Initial Session   38

Closing the Initial Session   39

Pretherapy Intake Information   40

Intake Summary   40

Preparing to Lead Your First Group   40

What Does It Take to Be an Effective Group Counselor?   41

Things to Know About Running Groups   41

Skills to Practice Implementing When Running Groups   42

Dispositions Suited to Running Groups   42

Tips for Co-Leading a Group   43

Client Record Keeping   43

Progress Notes   44

The DAP Format   44

The SOAP Notes Format   44

Sample SOAP Note   45

Record Keeping and the School Counselor   45

Documenting Practicum Hours   48

Summary   48

Note   48

References   48

CHAPTER 4 Assessment and Case Conceptualization   51

Initial Assessment   52

Gathering Family History Data   52

Gathering Personal History Data   53

Assessing the Client's Mental Status   54

Mental Status Categories of Assessment   54

Gathering Additional Data Through Tests and Inventories   55

Obtaining Information From Others   55

Goals of Assessment   56

Processes and Categories for Assessing Client Problems   56

Diagnosis in Counseling   58

DSM-5	58
Subtypes and Specifiers	59
Other Specified and Unspecified Designation	60
DSM-5 Codes and Classification	60
Case Conceptualization	60
Case Conceptualization Models	61
The "Linchpin" Model	61
The Inverted Pyramid Model	62
The Integrative Model	63
Sharing Assessment Information With the Client	63
Assessing the Client's Progress	64
Reporting Therapeutic Progress	66
Summary	67
References	67

CHAPTER 5 Goal Setting, Treatment Planning, and Treatment Modalities 71

Goal Setting in Counseling	71
Goals and the Stages of Change Model	71
Types of Goals	72
Developing a Treatment Plan	73
A Review of Philosophy, Theories, and Theory-Based Techniques of Counseling	76
Identifying Your Theory and Technique Preferences	76
Extending the Counselor's Theory-Based Approaches: Brief Therapies and Evidence-Based Practices	84
Brief Therapies	85
Solution-Focused Brief Therapy	85
Strategic Solution-Focused Therapy	86
Cognitive Restructuring Brief Therapy	87
Rational Emotive Behavior Therapy	88
Coping Skills Brief Therapy	88
Evidence-Based Practices and Third Wave Therapies	88
Mindfulness-Based Therapy (MBT)	88
Mindfulness-Based Stress Reduction (MBSR)	89
Mindfulness-Based Cognitive Therapy (MBCT)	90
Acceptance and Commitment Therapy (ACT)	90
Dialectical Behavior Therapy (DBT)	91
Summary	91
References	92

SECTION III   SUPERVISION IN PRACTICUM AND INTERNSHIP

CHAPTER 6   Group Supervision in Practicum and Internship   97

Identifying Counseling Skill Areas   97

    Skill Area One: Counseling Performance Skills   97

        Basic and Advanced Counseling Skills   97

        Theory-Based Techniques   98

        Procedural Skills   98

        Professional and Issue-Specific Skills   98

    Skill Area Two: Cognitive Counseling Skills   98

    Skill Area Three: Self-Awareness/Multicultural Awareness Skills   98

        Self-Awareness Skills   99

        Multicultural Awareness Skills   99

    Skill Area Four: Developmental Level   99

Self-Assessment in the Skill Areas   100

    Sample Supervisee Goal Statement   100

Concepts in Group Supervision   101

Group Supervision in Practicum   103

    Sample of Course Objectives and Assignments in Group Practicum   105

Activities in Group Supervision   106

    Peer Consultation   106

Evaluation of Practicum in Group Supervision   108

    Formative Evaluation   108

    Summative Evaluation   108

Transitioning Into Internship   109

    Recommended Skill Levels for Transitioning Into Internship   109

Group Supervision in Internship   109

Group Supervision Models in Internship   111

    The SPGS Model   111

    The Structured Group Supervision (SGS) Model   112

Evaluation in Group Supervision of Internship   112

Summary   113

References   113

CHAPTER 7   Individual Supervision in Practicum and Internship   115

Role and Function of the Supervisor in Practicum and Internship   115

Administrative and Clinical Supervision   116

The Supervisor–Supervisee Relationship   116
What Is "Lousy" Supervision?   117
    Overarching Principles   118
    General Spheres   118
Models and Methods of Individual Supervision   118
    Models Grounded in Psychotherapy Theory: The Psychodynamic
      Model   119
    Developmental Models: The Integrated Developmental Model   119
    Process Models: The Discrimination Model   120
    The Triadic Method of Supervision   121
The Clinical Supervision Process   123
    Informed Consent in Supervision   123
    Sample of a Supervisor Informed Consent and Disclosure Statement 123
    Forming a Supervision Contract   125
    Sample Supervision Contract   126
    The Supervision Session Format   128
    Supervising the Developing Counselor-in-Training   128
Evaluation of Counseling Performance in Individual Supervision   130
    Midpoint and Summative Evaluation in Practicum   130
    Sample of a Midpoint Narrative Evaluation of a Practicum Student 130
    Midpoint and Summative Evaluation in Internship   132
    Supervisee's Evaluation of the Supervisor and of the Site Experience 133
Documenting Internship Hours   133
Summary   134
References   134

SECTION IV   PROFESSIONAL PRACTICE TOPICS

▪ CHAPTER 8   Selected Topics Surrounding Ethical Issues in Counseling   139

Definitions: Morality, Ethics, and Law   139
Ethical Codes for Counselors   140
    Websites for Ethical Codes and Related Standards for Professional
      Organizations   140
Codes of Ethics: Similarities Across Disciplines and Specialties   141
Ethical Decision Making   142
    Principle-Based Ethics   142
    Virtue-Based Ethics and Ethical Decision Making   145

Self-Tests After Resolving an Ethical Dilemma   146

Selected Ethical Issues for Consideration by Beginning Counselors   147

    Ethics of Counseling Culturally Diverse Clients   147

        Building Awareness   147

        Becoming Knowledgeable   148

        Choosing Culturally Appropriate Strategies   149

    Managing Issues Related to Self-Care   150

    The Ethical Use of Distance Counseling, Technology, and Social Media   151

        Telephones and Technologies Related to Telephone Use   151

        Electronic Mail and Digital Communication   151

        Distance Counseling   152

        Social Media   153

        Web-Based Professional Discussion Groups   153

Summary   153

References   154

CHAPTER 9 Selected Topics Surrounding Legal Issues in Counseling   157

The Law   157

Classifications of the Law   157

Types of Laws   158

The Steps in a Lawsuit   158

Elements of Malpractice   159

Why Clients Sue   160

Risk Management and the Counselor   161

Liability Insurance   162

Privacy, Confidentiality, and Privileged Communication   163

Release of Information   165

When the Counselor Must Breach Confidentiality   165

    The Law and the Duty to Protect: The Suicidal Client   165

    The Law and the Duty to Warn: The Potentially Dangerous Client   166

    Mandatory Reporting: Suspected Child Abuse and Neglect   166

    Mandatory Reporting: Suspected Harm to Vulnerable Adults   167

    The Law and the Practice of Counselor–Client Confidentiality in Canada   168

Managed Care and the Counselor   168

Client Records   169

Summary   171

References   171

■ **CHAPTER 10** Working With Clients in Crisis and Other Special Populations — 175

Understanding Crisis and Trauma — 175

Approaches to Crisis Intervention in the Community — 176

    The Kanel Model of Crisis Intervention — 176

    The James and Gilliland Model of Crisis Intervention — 177

Approaches to Trauma Counseling — 178

    Evidence-Based Treatments — 179

        Prolonged Exposure Therapy — 179

        Cognitive Processing Therapy — 180

    Cross-Cutting Ingredients for Effective Trauma Counseling — 180

Crisis Intervention and Trauma Response in Schools — 181

    School Counselor as Crisis and Trauma Specialist — 181

    Tasks of the School Counselor in Preventing and Responding to Crisis — 182

    Practical Recommendations for Limiting School Violence — 183

    Post-Crisis: Understanding Children's Responses — 183

The High-Risk Client: Understanding and Assessing Harm to Self — 184

    Defining Suicide and Debunking Common Myths — 184

    Risk Assessment for Suicide — 185

        Assessment Point 1: Desire to Die — 185

        Assessment Point 2: Capacity to Commit Suicide — 186

        Assessment Point 3: Suicidal Intent — 186

        Assessment Point 4: Buffers Against Suicide — 187

        Evaluating Suicide Risk: Putting It All Together — 187

    Suicide Risk Assessment Instruments — 188

    Intervention and Planning — 188

    Ethical and Legal Mandates Relating to Danger to Self — 189

        Professional School Counselors — 189

        Professional Counselors — 190

    Suicide Risk Assessment and Prevention in Schools — 191

        Basics of Suicide Prevention Programs in Schools — 191

        Learning About and Responding to Potentially Suicidal Students — 192

        Suicide Risk Assessment for Students — 192

The High-Risk Client: Potential Harm to Others — 193

    The *Tarasoff* Case: The Events — 194

        Implications of the *Tarasoff* Case — 194

        What *Tarasoff* Did Not Require — 195

        Post-*Tarasoff* — 195

    Risk Assessment for Potentially Dangerous Clients — 195

Task I: Risk Assessment 196

Task II: Selecting a Course of Action 197

Task III: Monitoring the Situation 198

Clients' Past Criminal Acts 198

The Client Who Is Being Abused: Responding, Reporting, and Intervening 198

Risk and Mediating Factors for Child Abuse 199

Legal Issues Related to Reporting Child Abuse 200

Making a Report Related to Child Abuse 200

Interviewing Children Who May Have Been Sexually Abused 201

Before the Interview 201

Interviewing the Child 201

Counseling the Sexually Abused 202

The Client Who Is Dealing With Addiction 204

Understanding Addiction 204

Diagnosing Alcohol and Drug Use 204

What Is Treatment? 205

What Is Recovery? 206

Stages of Recovery 206

Counseling Recommendations for Clients With Addiction 207

Preventing Relapse 208

Summary 209

References 209

CHAPTER 11 Consultation in the Schools and Mental Health Agencies 215

What Is Consultation? 215

Types of Mental Health Consultation 216

Characteristics of Mental Health Consultation 216

Assumptions Behind and Metaphors for Consultation 218

The Purchase-of-Expertise Model 218

The Doctor–Patient Model 219

The Process Consultation Model 219

Cultural Issues in Consultation 219

School Consultation 220

Consultation Models and Practices in Schools 222

Developmental Counseling and Therapy-Based Consultation 223

Sensorimotor 223

Concrete 223

Formal-Operational 224

Dialectic/Systemic	224
Solution-Focused Consultation	224
Positive Psychology Approaches to Consultation	225
Emerging Evidence-Based Approaches to Consultation in Schools	225
General Guidelines for Consultation	226
Preentry	226
Entry Into the System	227
Orientation to Consultation	227
Problem Identification	228
Consultation Intervention	228
Assessing the Impact of Consultation	229
Resistance to Consultation	230
Contracting and the Forces of Change in the Organization	231
Summary	231
References	232

CHAPTER 12 Looking Ahead to a Career in Professional Counseling — **235**

The First Steps Towards Licensure	235
Licensure Law	235
Licensure and Certification Exams	236
Securing a Supervisor for Post-Graduate Training Supervision	237
Longevity in the Profession	238
Self-Care, Wellness, and Burnout	238
Recommendations for Sustaining Personal and Professional Excellence	239
References	239

Appendix I: Psychiatric Medications — **241**

Appendix II: Forms — **251**

Form 2.1	Practicum Contract	253
Form 2.2	Internship Contract	255
Form 2.3	Student Profile Sheet	257
Form 2.4	Student Practicum/Internship Agreement	258
Form 3.1a	Parental Release Form: Secondary School Counseling	259
Form 3.1b	Elementary School Counseling Permission Form	260
Form 3.2	Client Permission to Record Counseling Session for Supervision Purposes	261
Form 3.3	Initial Intake Form	262
Form 3.4	Psychosocial History	264
Form 3.5	Case Notes	268

Form 3.6   Weekly Schedule/Practicum Log   270
Form 3.7   Monthly Practicum Log   271
Form 4.1   Mental Status Checklist   272
Form 4.2   Elementary School Counseling Referral Form   275
Form 4.3   Secondary School Counseling Referral Form   276
Form 4.4   Therapeutic Progress Report   278
Form 5.1   Counseling Techniques List   279
Form 6.1   Self-Assessment of Counseling Performance Skills   283
Form 6.2   Self-Awareness/Multicultural Awareness Rating Scale   285
Form 6.3   Directed Reflection Exercise on Supervision   286
Form 6.4   Supervisee Goal Statement   287
Form 6.5   Recording Critique Form   288
Form 6.6   Peer Rating Form   289
Form 6.7   Interviewer Rating Form   290
Form 7.1   Supervision Contract   292
Form 7.2   Supervisor Notes   294
Form 7.3   Supervisee Notes on Individual Supervision   295
Form 7.4   Supervisor's Formative Evaluation of Supervisee's Counseling Practice 296
Form 7.5   Supervisor's Final Evaluation of Practicum Student   298
Form 7.6   Supervisor's Final Evaluation of Intern   299
Form 7.7   Evaluation of Intern's Practice in Site Activities   301
Form 7.8   Client's Assessment of the Counseling Experience   302
Form 7.9   Supervisee Evaluation of Supervisor   303
Form 7.10 Site Evaluation Form   305
Form 7.11 Weekly Internship Log   306
Form 7.12 Summary Internship Log   307
Form 10.1 Suicide Consultation Form   308
Form 10.2 Harm to Others Form   311
Form 10.3 Child Abuse Reporting Form   314
Form 10.4 Substance Abuse Assessment Form   315

Index   319

ABOUT THE AUTHORS

Judith Scott, PhD, is a licensed psychologist, certified school counselor, National Certified Counselor, and professor emeritus of the Department of Psychology in Education at the University of Pittsburgh. During her tenure at the University of Pittsburgh she served as director of doctoral studies and as field site coordinator in the CACREP-accredited counseling programs. She is a past president of Pennsylvania ACES and was awarded Counselor Educator of the Year by the Pennsylvania School Counselors Association. Dr. Scott maintains a private practice that specializes in outpatient individual psychotherapy in women's issues and infertility counseling. Her research focuses on counseling supervision and women's adult development.

Christin M. Jungers, PhD, LPCC-S, is a professor at Franciscan University of Steubenville in the Clinical Mental Health Counseling Program. She also is the Dean of the School of Professional Programs at Franciscan University. She is a licensed professional clinical counselor who has experience working with a variety of life span issues faced by individuals and couples. Dr. Jungers has co-authored two other books and numerous articles. She served two terms as a governor-appointed member of the Counselor, Social Worker, and Marriage and Family Therapist Licensure Board in Ohio.

PREFACE

Since the publication of the first edition of this text in 1988, each new edition has evolved to provide materials that support the many changes and developments in the counseling profession and the preparation of professional counselors. In particular, the experiences and competencies required of counselors-in-training while involved in their practicum and internship placement have been and continue to be the focus of this book. As counselor educators, it has been exciting and our privilege to have been a part of participating in a process that enhances the quality of those who become licensed and certified as professional counselors. This sixth edition has benefited greatly from new views and new voices that reflect the evolving nature and areas of study within the profession. We are excited about the new additions to this text, respectful of the maturation of our profession, and hopeful about the many contributions of the new professional counselors.

Christin M. Jungers and Judith Scott

ACKNOWLEDGMENTS

The authors gratefully appreciate the efforts of the following individuals, who were instrumental in the development of the sixth edition of this textbook:

The graduate counseling students at Marywood University, the University of Pittsburgh, and Franciscan University of Steubenville for all they have contributed to our professional growth and enhancement;

Anna Moore, editor at Routledge, whose understanding and editorial suggestions were invaluable in the development of the textbook;

our reviewers who provided valuable recommendations about how to update and streamline the text, as well as thoughtful insight into new topics that might be addressed;

John Boylan, PhD and Patrick Malley, PhD, for their many contributions to the development of this text, especially the first four editions, and for the many conversations regarding essential elements that contribute to the preparation of competent counselors; and

Claire Richard, graduate assistant for the Clinical Mental Health Counseling Program at Franciscan University, for her careful review of the references, citations, and headings, among other things in the manuscript.

OVERVIEW OF THE BOOK

The sixth edition of this text guides students through the important pre-professional training experiences, from the selection of an appropriate practicum site to the final evaluation of the internship. The text is organized according to a skill-based approach to the practicum and internship experience. Separate chapters are related to counseling performance, cognitive skills, and group and individual supervision. Selected topics in professional practice include related professional resource materials; practical self-assessment instruments; and guidelines, formats, and forms to assist in applied counseling and supervision practices.

The first part of the text focuses on the preparation, identification, and application process to secure a field site placement. Chapter 1 provides foundational information that students must consider as they prepare to identify their practicum/internship placements. Chapter 2 guides students through the process of selecting, applying for, securing, and orienting to a site appropriate to their professional goals and specializations.

The second part of the text emphasizes counseling performance skills and cognitive counseling skills. Chapter 3 emphasizes starting the practicum and initiating contact with clients in both individual and group settings. It includes a sample informed consent statement and current HIPAA (Health Insurance Portability and Accountability Act) guidelines. Chapter 4 includes assessment and case conceptualization practices, references, and models to be used in practice with clients. An overview of the *Diagnostic and Statistical Manual of Mental Disorders* (*DSM*, 5th ed.) coding and classification system is included. Chapter 5 content areas include goal setting, treatment planning, and theory-related approaches to treatment. An updated section reviews the "New Wave" theories of mindfulness-based practices, acceptance and commitment therapy, and dialectical behavior therapy and provides an introduction to well-known evidence-based practices in the counseling field.

The third section of the text focuses on group and individual supervision. Chapter 6, on group supervision, begins with a full description of the skill-based model and includes self-assessment exercises for the supervision group to use to become more familiar with the model. Chapter 7, on individual supervision, describes several regularly applied models of individual supervision that students may encounter, as well as an expanded section about the triadic model of supervision. A sample informed consent and disclosure statement for supervisors and a sample supervision contract consistent with the Association for Counselor Education and Supervision's best practices guidelines are included. Forms that support the application of best practices, such as supervisor notes, supervisee notes, and evaluation checklists and formats are included.

The fourth section of the text includes Chapters 8–12 on selected topics related to professional practices in ethics, law, and assessment of and response to crisis and trauma-causing situations, and consultation. An overview of ethical decision-making models, including principle-based, virtue-based, and self-review approaches are included. New sections on the ethics of working with diverse populations and counselor self-care have been added to the discussion of ethics, as has updated information about the use of technology in counseling. In addition, new content related to trauma, trauma treatments in clinical and school settings, and risk and mediating factors for child abuse have been added. Information on crisis intervention and response as well as risk assessment tools and revised content related to substance abuse assessment and related forms have been updated. A more explicit inclusion of material related to evidence-based practices is incorporated across the text. Finally, an entirely new approach to the book's final chapter has been included, with an emphasis on practical information about licensure and certification, tips for seeking supervision post-graduation, and recommendations for how to enhance longevity in the profession.

Forms and samples of completed forms have been referenced throughout the text. A complete set of available forms is provided in the Forms section at the end of the text. They can now be accessed for download on the website for this edition of the text at www.routledge.com/9781138492608.

We are very pleased with this new edition and hope that the information, materials, and resources included will provide the student, counselor, and supervisor with a useful and reader-friendly approach to the practicum and internship experience.

SECTION I

PRE-PRACTICUM

CHAPTER 1

PREPARING FOR PRACTICUM AND INTERNSHIP

The focus of this book is on fostering the development of qualified, competent professional counselors. The text provides information and guidelines concerning practicum and internship for students enrolled in master's degree programs in professional counseling and psychology in the United States and Canada. It is also a useful reference book for doctoral-level students and site supervisors who supervise master's degree students in their practicum/internships. Required practicum and internship experiences have been increasingly influenced by evolving accreditation standards for professional counseling programs and by changing licensing requirements in the states and provinces. The first two chapters of the book are designed to provide the counselor-in-training with foundational information about what the professional accreditation requirements are for practicum and internship and how to identify, apply for, and secure a field placement. The emphasis in practicum and internship is on the application of basic knowledge in the practice of counseling at the field site of choice. It is possible for the professional counselor to practice in a variety of settings (i.e., schools, colleges, and universities, mental health agencies, rehabilitation counseling agencies, government agencies, and career centers). Counselor education and psychology training programs, national associations, and the accrediting bodies related to these specializations continue to clarify and solidify the definitions of practicum and internship, along with their field experience requirements. They also specify activities, experiences, and knowledge base requirements that are appropriate to each component of training. Similarly, national accrediting bodies specify the qualifications and levels of experience of both field- and campus-based supervisors. Information about practicum and internship accreditation standards for the Council for the Accreditation of Counseling and related Education Programs and its affiliate Council on Rehabilitation Education (CACREP/CORE), The Canadian Council on Accreditation of Counselling Education Programs (CACEP), and the Masters in Psychology and Counseling Accreditation Council (MPCAC) is provided. Having a degree from an accredited program is becoming increasingly important and even is required by some states to become a licensed professional counselor.

The Professional Counselor

A current consensus definition of counseling is that "[c]ounseling is a professional relationship that empowers diverse individuals, families, and groups to accomplish mental health, wellness, education, and career goals" (Kaplan, Tarvydos, & Gladding, 2014, p. 366). Over the last 75 years, counseling has achieved a recognized professional status. Professionalization has been accomplished through forming associations, changing names to reduce identification with its previous occupational status, developing a code of ethics, and obtaining public sanction through the passage of licensure laws in all 50 states. Changes taking place in counselor preparation in the last 30 years include increases in the credit hours required in training, the establishment of accreditation and certification standards, increases in the body of knowledge in counseling as distinguished from psychology, and the passage of state laws granting privilege in interactions between counselors and clients (Remley & Herlihy, 2016).

Professional counselors apply a wellness model of mental health in their work that emphasizes helping people maximize their potential rather than curing their illness. Counselors emphasize prevention and early intervention rather than remediation. In addition, the training of counselors focuses on teaching counseling skills rather than physical health care and psychopathology (Remley & Herlihy, 2016). It is important that the student identifies a field site setting that understands and respects the foundational values of the professional counselor.

Steps to Becoming a Professional Counselor

Schweiger, Henderson, McKaskill, Clawson, and Collins (2012) have reviewed the steps one must take in order to become certified and recognized as a professional counselor. These include:

1. Completing a master's degree program in counseling. The program may or may not be a nationally accredited program.
2. Completing a practicum.
3. Completing a supervised clinical internship with clients in your specialty area.
4. Graduating from a master's degree (or higher) counseling program.
5. Applying to the national certification board or the appropriate credentialing association to obtain certification. (Completion of a CACREP-accredited program allows one to sit for certification exams just prior to or immediately following graduation.)
6. Applying to the state board and obtaining state licensure.

Because of changes in accreditation standards, requirements for sitting for professional exams and changes in state licensure requirements, students should check that their master's degree program meets state requirements for licensure as a professional counselor. Students should also check with the appropriate credentialing association about requirements to sit for credentialing exams.

Accreditation Standards for Practicum and Internship

Accreditation of counselor preparation programs in the United States and Canada largely is a voluntary process. The accreditation bodies are independent from federal and state and provincial governments. However, some states in the US (e.g., Ohio and Kentucky) have recently opted to require through legislation that counselor preparation programs in their states be CACREP accredited. In most cases, the accreditation bodies were initially established by a professional association. For example, the American Counseling Association's division on counselor education and supervision developed educational standards that eventually led to the establishment of the Council for the Accreditation of Counseling and Related Educational Programs

(CACREP). The Council on Rehabilitation Education (CORE) became the accrediting body for rehabilitation counselors (CACREP and CORE merged in July 2017 to become CACREP/CORE). The American Psychological Association Commission on Accreditation (APA-CoA) became the accrediting body for psychologists. The Council of Applied Masters Programs in Psychology formed the Masters in Psychology and Counseling Accreditation Council (MPCAC), and the Canadian Counselling and Psychotherapy Association (CCPA) established the Council on Accreditation of Counsellor Education Programs (CACEP). Each accrediting body established program and educational criteria to be met by programs before they would be granted accreditation. If a department offers more than one specialty program in counseling (e.g., school counseling and clinical mental health counseling), each program must be evaluated separately for accreditation. Thus, a department may have some programs that are accredited and others that are not. Graduation from an accredited program has a number of significant advantages for students. For example, accreditation:

- provides assurance that programs meets high professional standards;
- provides periodic review of programs;
- offers enrolled students some advantages, such as sitting for the national certification exams prior to graduation; and
- provides a source of pride for faculty, students, and the college or university as they become involved in a nationally recognized program (Schweiger et al., 2012).

The major applied components in counselor preparation are practicum and internship. Professional practice provides for the development of counseling skills under supervision. Practicum and internship students counsel clients in their specialty who represent the ethnic and demographic diversity of the community. Their hours of direct service are with actual clients, which contributes to the development of core counseling skills. The internship begins after successful completion of the practicum. The internship should reflect the comprehensive work of a professional in the designated program specialty and include individual and group counseling.

Practicum and internship requirements have undergone four major changes in recent years: (a) the amount of time spent in practicum and internship has increased, (b) the setting in which the experience occurs has changed, (c) the specifications for the supervisor doing the clinical supervision of practicum and internship have become more stringent, and (d) the number of hours spent in supervision has increased. These four aspects could make major differences in the job opportunities, types of practice, clientele, philosophical orientation, and techniques emphasized throughout the student's professional life. For these reasons, as well as others (e.g., personalities involved, practicum and internship sites available), each student needs to give considerable attention to practicum and internship, especially under whose clinical supervision it occurs and for what period of time.

If a student is attending a counselor preparation program that has not sought accreditation, it may be wise to consider standards established by the appropriate national credentialing association regarding practicum and internship when fulfilling the professional practice requirements of the counselor preparation program. The student is encouraged to keep careful records of total practicum and internship hours, client contact hours, supervision hours, and supervisor credentials—both on-site and on campus. The forms in this textbook can be helpful for such record keeping.

CACREP/CORE Standards for Practicum and Internship

CACREP/CORE accredits entry-level programs at the master's degree level. Program graduates are prepared as counseling practitioners and for respective credentials (e.g., certification and/or licensure) in eight specialty areas:

- Addictions Counseling (60 credit hours)
- Career Counseling (48 credit hours)
- Clinical Mental Health Counseling (60 credit hours)
- Clinical Rehabilitation Counseling (60 credit hours)
- Marriage, Couple, and Family Counseling (60 credit hours)
- Rehabilitation Counseling (48 credit hours)
- School Counseling (48 credit hours)
- Student Affairs and College Counseling (48 credit hours)

CACREP guidelines are expected to increase the total semester hours required in each of these specialties to 60 semester hours by 2023. The following summarizes information about the primary aspects of practicum and internship in each of the above specializations:

Setting: An agency, institution, or organization appropriate to the specialization in one of the above identified specialties.

Practicum: Minimum of 100 clock hours over a minimum 10-week academic term with 40 hours of direct contact with actual clients in the area of specialty; weekly average of 1 hour of individual or triadic supervision with site and/or faculty supervisor; and weekly average of 1.5 hours of group supervision by faculty.

Internship: Minimum of 600 clock hours with at least 240 clock hours of direct service, including leading groups; weekly average of 1 hour per week of individual or triadic supervision, usually by site supervisor; and weekly average of 1.5 hours per week of group supervision by a faculty supervisor.

Supervisor: Faculty supervisors must have relevant experience, professional credentials and counseling supervision training and experience. *Site supervisors* must have a minimum of a master's degree, preferably in counseling or a related profession; relevant certifications and/or licenses; a minimum of 2 years of pertinent professional experience in the specialty area in which the student is enrolled and/or appropriate counseling preparation; knowledge of the program's expectations, requirements, and evaluation procedures; and relevant training in counseling supervision. *Graduate student supervisors* of entry-level programs must have completed CACREP entry-level requirements; have completed or are receiving training in counseling supervision; and be under the supervision of counselor education program faculty (CACREP, 2016).

CACEP Standards for Initial and Final Practicum

The Council on Accreditation of Counsellor Education Programs (CACEP) is the accreditation body established by the Canadian Counsellors and Psychologists Association (CCPA). CACEP established standards for accrediting master's degree programs in School Counseling, Counseling in Higher Education, Community/Agency Counseling, Rehabilitation Counseling, and Family

Counseling, each of which requires a minimum of 48 credit hours. A summary of the requirements for the initial and final practicum in these programs follows (CCPA, 2003).

Setting: An agency, institution, or organization appropriate to the specialization and career goals of the student.

Initial practicum: 100 hours of supervised practice with 50 hours of direct service with clients (40 hours with individual clients and 10 hours in group work), an average of 1 hour per week of individual or joint supervision, and 1.5 hours per week of group supervision by a faculty member or a supervisor under the supervision of a faculty member.

Final practicum: 400 hours of supervised practice with 200 hours of direct client contact (160 hours with individual clients and 40 hours of group work) under the supervision of the site supervisor in collaboration with a faculty member.

Supervisor: The site supervisor must have a minimum of 4 years of experience as a counselor, recognized competence, and knowledge of program expectations, requirements, and evaluation procedures. Doctoral students in counseling may supervise under the supervision of a faculty member.

MPCAC Standards for Practicum and Internship in Counseling

The Masters in Psychology and Counseling Accreditation Council (MPCAC) accredits counseling and psychology programs located in regionally accredited colleges and universities in the United States. Master's degree students are educated in the science-based practice of counseling and psychological services. MPCAC accredits entry-level programs that prepare graduates to practice in a variety of settings (schools, community and mental health agencies, pastoral care, and others). Programs are required to consist of a minimum of 48 credit hours while considering licensure and certification requirements in their state. Many accredited programs require 60 credits (MPCAC, 2017).

Setting: Schools and agencies that provide mental health counseling services.

Internship: A minimum of 600 hours across 2 semesters. At least 40% of the supervised experiences should be direct contact hours.

Supervisor: Supervisor must be appropriately credentialed (commensurate with program goals and relevant state requirements).

Counselor Certification

National Certified Counselor (NCC) and Board Certification

Counselor certification indicates to the public that the counselor has met national standards established by the counseling profession. This is not a license to practice, although in some states national certification can help with getting a state license. The National Board of Certified Counselors (NBCC) administers two exams for which the designation of National Certified Counselor (NCC) is currently awarded: the National Counselor Exam for Licensure and Certification (NCE) and the National Clinical Mental Health Counseling Exam (NCMHCE).

Applicants who have graduated from a CACREP-accredited program in any of the eight specialty areas may sit for the National Counseling Exam for Licensure and Certification (NCE) or the National Clinical Mental Health Counseling Exam (NCMHCE) immediately upon or even in the last semester prior to graduation. After passing the exam and submitting a final transcript indicating conferral of degree, they will be awarded the status of National Certified Counselor (NCC). Beginning January 1, 2022, NCC status will require graduation from a CACREP-accredited program. Counselors who did not graduate from a CACREP-accredited institution who have or will receive their NCC before 2022 will continue to be recognized by NBCC after this change occurs. This change was formally announced in November of 2014 (ACA, 2014).

Applicants graduating from programs that are not CACREP approved must complete a master's degree in counseling or master's degree with a major focus in counseling from a regionally accredited institution. Their program must meet specified course requirements within their master's degree program. For course requirements, go to http://nbcc.org/Assets/NCCRequiredCoursework.pdf. They also must complete 3,000 hours of counseling experience and 100 hours of supervision by a supervisor who holds a master's degree (or higher) in a counseling field in their specialty or a related mental health field. These hours must be completed in a 2-year post-master's time frame (NBCC, 2018). Individuals who complete these requirements may then be approved to sit for the NCE or the NCMHCE.

NBCC Specialty Certification

NBCC awards specialty counseling credentials in three areas: addictions, clinical mental health, and school. The requirements for specialty certification require additional post–master's degree coursework, supervised experience, and the completion of an exam. With any NBCC specialty certification, the general counseling practice certification is a prerequisite. For more information regarding specialty certification, access www.nbcc.org.

Certified Rehabilitation Counselor (CRC)

Rehabilitation counselors may sit for the CRC exam upon completion of a CACREP/CORE accredited master's degree program to be awarded the credential of CRC. For information regarding additional requirements if one is completing a master's degree in a program that is not accredited by CACREP/CORE, access www.crccertification.com/about-crc-certification.

Canadian Certified Counsellor (CCC): Canadian Counsellors and Psychologists Association

The CCPA offers the credential of CCC after one has met specified training and practice standards. One must become a member of CCPA before being eligible to apply for certification. Certification is different from membership. Certification represents a successful evaluation of a member's qualifications to practice. A member of CCPA must apply for certification and go through an evaluation process; if approved, one will be permitted to use the CCC when practicing as a counselor. Those graduating from a CCPA-accredited program can apply for the CCC certification immediately upon graduation. Those graduating from other degree programs in counseling or a related field must meet specific course and direct practice experience requirements (CCPA, 2017). For more information, access www.ccpa.ca/en/certificationrequirements.

Registered Professional Counsellor (RPC): Canadian Professional Counsellors Association

The Canadian Professional Counsellors Association, as part of its membership, offers the designation of RPC upon attaining the level of Full Member (CPCA, 2018). The levels of membership are Student Member, Intern (RPC-C) candidate, Full Member (RPC), and Master Practitioner Practicing Counselling Psychology (MPPCP). Each level of membership specifies coursework, direct practice, and supervision requirements. To progress to the Intern level, you must complete and pass an exam package consisting of a qualifying exam. At the Intern level, you must complete supervision requirements in a 24-month period, whereupon you can become a Full Member (RPC).

Other Specialty Counseling Certifications

The American Association for Marriage and Family Therapy offers a specialty professional counseling credential entitled Clinical Member Status. For more information regarding this designation of membership, access www.aamft.org/membership/levels.

The National Career Development Association offers specialty professional credentials entitled Fellow, Master Career Counselor, or Master Career Development Specialist. For more information, access www.ncda.org/aws/NCDA/pt/sp/credentialing.

State Licensure for Counselors and Psychologists

Government-sanctioned credentialing is usually called licensure. Passage of a state licensure law for a given profession restricts or prohibits the practice of the profession by individuals not meeting the state-determined qualification standards (American Counseling Association, 2013). In the United States, all 50 states and Washington, DC, Puerto Rico, and Guam have passed licensing laws for counselors. The laws, however, are not consistent from state to state, so you must go to the website of the state in which you intend to practice to become informed of the requirements for licensing in that state. Currently, school counselors are certified but not licensed by each state. In Canada, there is no licensing law, but the practice of counseling is variously regulated by the provinces.

To learn about standards established by state licensure laws and provincial regulations within specified counseling or psychology professions, the following websites are recommended:

Addictions Counselor: Access www.naadac.org/certification, then click on "state licensing boards."

Canadian regulation standards for counselling and school counselling: Access www.ccpa-accp.ca/en/pathways.

Clinical Mental Health Counselor or Licensed Professional Counselor: Access www.nbcc.org/Search/StateBoardDirectory.

Marriage, Couple, and Family Therapist: Access www.aamft.org/Directories/MFT_Licensing_Boards.aspx.

In the United States, all states require psychologist licensure in order to practice as a psychologist, and a doctoral degree is required. About half of the states and the Canadian provinces have a category for licensure for the practice of psychology under the supervision of a doctoral-level licensed psychologist. A person practicing at this level is called a psychological associate, which usually requires a master's degree in psychology (ASPPB, 2009). For more information, access http://asppb.net/page/BdContactNewPG.

Pre-Practicum Considerations

All individuals involved in the applied training components of counseling and psychology need to carefully examine the expectations they bring to the practicum and internship. The practicum professor, practicum student, site supervisor, and professional accreditation agencies all have expectations about practicum and internship, which may vary. We are providing a list of questions that counseling students should research and answer for themselves before proceeding to select a field site for a practicum and/or internship. Students should modify and adapt this list in keeping with their own training program and specific practicum situations.

Checklist of Questions to Be Researched and Answered Before Practicum Site Selection

- What are the practicum and internship (or final practicum) requirements to become credentialed in my specialty?
- What are the practicum and internship (or final practicum) requirements for securing certification and/or licensure in the state or province where I intend to be employed?
- What are the basic skills and content areas that are necessary to begin the practicum experience in my program?
- What are the prerequisites for the practicum?
- What number of credit hours are devoted to the practicum and internship (or final practicum)? Do practicum hours include class on campus?
- Will I be retained in practicum until minimal competencies are demonstrated?
- How will I be expected to demonstrate identified competencies, and how are they to be evaluated?
- How much time will be spent in direct service with individual clients? With groups? With other professional activities?
- What is the role of the faculty supervisor in the field site experience? Instructional leader? Liaison? Role model? Evaluator?
- What is my responsibility for site placement?
- What are the guidelines and procedures for practicum and internship placement?
- What field site placements are recommended and available? Is there a list of approved field sites? If I want to go to a previously unknown field site, how do I know if they have an approved supervisor?
- How does the site supervisor communicate with the university training program?
- Who are the other students in my practicum group? How many? Will we have the same counseling specializations?
- Who gives me a grade and recommends that I have met the expected standards to complete my practice requirements?

In some cases, you may have to do website searches to get information regarding state and provincial requirements. In other cases, you may have to check your student handbook or program procedures and syllabi for the needed information.

Phases of Practicum and Internship

The phases of practicum and internship can be described from a variety of perspectives. For example, one might describe the practicum and internship from the categories of level of skill, such as beginning, intermediate, or advanced. Another way of categorizing phases of practicum might be according to functions, such as structuring, stating goals, acquiring knowledge, and refining skills and interventions. We prefer to describe practicum/internship phases from a developmental perspective. Several principles regarding development can be identified within practicum and internship:

1. *Movement is directional and hierarchical.* Early learning in the program establishes a foundation (knowledge base) for later development in the program (applied skills).
2. *Differentiation occurs with new learning.* Learning proceeds from the more simplistic and straightforward (content) toward the more complex and subtle (process).
3. *Separation or individuation can be observed.* The learning process leads to progressively more independent and separate functioning on the part of the counselor or therapist.

These developmental principles can be identified within the specific program structure, the learning process, and the supervisory interaction encountered by the student.

Development Reflected in the Program Structure

Students in a counseling or psychology training program can expect to proceed through a well-thought-out experiential component of their programs. Generally, experiences are orderly and sequentially planned. A typical sequence begins with pre-practicum and moves to practicum, internship, and full professional status (obtained after graduation and after receiving post-graduate supervision hours).

Some variations exist in counseling and psychology programs regarding the number of clinical hours required in each component of training. Some variations also exist in training programs regarding the range and depth of expected skills and competencies that are necessary before a student can move to the next component in the program. Generally, programs begin with courses that orient the student to the profession. The history of the profession and its current status, including ethics issues, might well be a beginning point. Early courses tend to be more didactic and straightforward. As the student enters the pre-practicum phase of the program, he/she can generally expect more interaction and active participation with the professor. In this stage, the focus is on basic skill development, role playing, peer interaction and feedback, and observation activities in a classroom or counseling laboratory. In the practicum component, the student is likely to be functioning at a field site with supervision and on campus in a practicum class with university faculty. The focus in both of these settings is on observation by functioning professionals as well as on initial interactions with clients. As time progresses, the student becomes more actively involved with a range of clients and is given increased opportunities to expand and develop the full range of professional behaviors. At the internship end of the continuum, the student is expected to be able to participate in the full range of professional counseling activities within the field site under the supervision of an approved field site supervisor.

Development Reflected in the Learning Process

As students progress in their training, they tend to progress across several stages or steps of learning. Initially, counselors-in-training often lack confidence in their skills and tend to imitate the type of supervision they receive. They look to others for an indication of how they should function in the setting. Counselors-in-training also tend to question their level of skill development. As time passes, they tend to fluctuate between feeling competent and professional and feeling inadequate. At this point, most students see the need to develop an internalized theoretical framework, to give them a sense of "grounding" and to help them to develop their own approach to counseling. Further learning helps counselors-in-training to develop confidence in their skills and an awareness of their strengths, weaknesses, and motivations. Finally, students internalize and integrate their personal theories with their counseling practice.

Development Reflected in Supervisor Interaction

Supervisory interaction between supervisor and student begins with a high level of dependence on the supervisor for instruction, feedback, and support. This interaction is modified as skill, personal awareness, and confidence increase for the student. The student becomes more likely to explore new modes of practice that reflect his/her own unique style. The interaction continues to move more gradually toward a higher level of independent judgment by the student and a more collegial and consultative stance on the part of the supervisor.

Implications

The implications for students in professional counselor training are becoming quite clear. In addition to requirements for practicum and internship as stipulated by the counselor preparation program, each student will need to give careful consideration to (a) the selection of sites where practicum and internship are experienced, (b) a review of required supervisory credentials, (c) a determination of the amount of supervisory time available, (d) the identification of a site that provides opportunities to work with one's chosen population, (e) an understanding of program accreditation or its equivalent, (f) an understanding of the credentialing requirements of organizations with which the student hopes to affiliate, and (g) a knowledge of state licensure requirements in the state where you intend to practice.

Summary

In this chapter, we described the current accreditation, certification, and licensing standards that apply to students in a variety of counseling and psychology training programs in the United States and Canada. Specific attention was directed to the CACREP/CORE, CACEP, and MPCAC guidelines for practicum and internship. In addition, we provided students with a checklist of questions to be answered prior to selecting and procuring a field site for the applied supervised practice component of their master's degree program. We hope that the information in this chapter will help the beginning counseling student to gain a fuller understanding of the professional training and certification requirements for counseling specializations as they relate to the practicum and internship experience.

References

American Counseling Association. (2013). *Licensure and certification.* Retrieved from www.counseling.org/knowledge-center/licensure-requirements

American Counseling Association. (2014). *NCC status will require graduation from a CACREP accredited program beginning in 2022.* Retrieved October 2018 from www.Counseling.org/news/news-release-archives/by-year/2014

Association of State and Provincial Psychology Boards (ASPPB). (2009). *Guidelines on practicum experience for licensure.* Peachtree, GA: Author.

Canadian Counselling and Psychotherapy Association (CCPA). (2003). *CCPA Accreditation procedures & standards for counsellor education programs at the master's level.* Retrieved October 2018 from www.acpa-accp.ca/wp-content/uploads/2018/01/AccreditationProcedures_en.pdf

Canadian Counselling and Psychotherapy Association (CCPA). (2017). *Certification guide.* Retrieved October 2018 from www.ccpa-acpa.ca/2018/(05)/CertificationGuide_EN_2017.pdf

Canadian Professional Counsellors Association. (2018). *Membership designations.* Retrieved October 2018 from www.cpca-rpc.ca/designations-criteria-aspx

Council for Accreditation of Counseling and Related Educational Programs (CACREP). (2016). *CACREP standards.* Alexandria, VA: Author

Kaplan, D. M., Tarvydos, V. M., & Gladding, S. T. (2014). A vision for the future of counseling: The new consensus definition of counseling. *Journal of Counseling & Development, 92,* 366–372.

Master's in Psychology and Counseling Accreditation Council. (2017). *Accreditation manual.* Retrieved October 2018 from www.mpcacaccreditation.org/wp-content/uploads/2017/11/MPCAC2017AccreditationManual.pdf

National Board of Certified Counselors. (2017–2018). *Understanding board certification and licensure.* Retrieved October 2018 from www.nbcc.org/certification

Remley, T. P., Jr., & Herlihy, B. (2016). *Ethical, legal and professional issues in counseling* (5th ed.). Upper Saddle River, NJ: Pearson.

Schweiger, W. K., Henderson, D. A., McKaskill, K., Clawson, T. W., & Collins, D. R. (2012). *Counselor preparation: Programs, faculty, trends* (13th ed.). New York, NY: Routledge.

CHAPTER 2

SECURING A PRACTICUM AND INTERNSHIP SITE

Chapter 2 has as its focus the process of selecting and negotiating a site placement. We provide you with guidelines for choosing a field site, recommendations for interviewing with the site coordinator, and specific orientation information that will allow you to make a smooth transition into the role of counselor-in-training at the site.

Guidelines for Choosing a Practicum and Internship Site

The practicum placement is often the first opportunity that a student has to gain experience working with a client population. Approval to proceed to a field site placement usually occurs after the completion of academic prerequisites and pre-practicum or practicum lab situations with volunteers or with peer counseling interactions where students can demonstrate and practice basic counseling skills. Many counselor preparation programs offer the student an opportunity to have some say in determining practicum placement. For example, you may prefer to complete your initial practicum at one site and move to a different site for your internship. Or, you may wish to do half of your internship hours at one site and the rest at a different site. Some school counseling training sites prefer that you split your internship between the elementary or middle school and the high school. Some mental health agencies provide both outpatient services and partial hospitalization treatment programs, and you may wish to have experience in both settings. Your career and specialization goals, the expectations of the university program, as well as the flexibility of the training site all can influence how you may wish to pursue these options. Variations of your site hours and patient population are best accomplished by negotiating for different placements in one system.

Although some programs may assign students to a site that fits their career goals, it is more often students' responsibility to identify and secure their own field placement. Students are required to contact the appropriate person at the site and go through a formal interviewing process at the field site of their choice. The field site coordinators are responsible for selecting students who they believe will benefit from the placement and who will best serve the needs of the site's client population. The student is responsible for obtaining a field site, but the training program establishes the guidelines and procedures for approval of the site. Most counselor training programs have established guidelines and procedures for procuring a field placement that can be approved by the program, and they provide a list of possible sites where previous students have successfully completed practicum and internship. If you identify a possible practicum/internship site that meets your career and specialization goals but the site has no previous connection to your university program, check with your university coordinator about how and whether to proceed. An important consideration is always the credentials of the site and those of the proposed site supervisor, as well as the site supervisor's knowledge of the university's practicum and internship course requirements.

Identifying and applying for a field placement normally begins in the semester before the student begins the practicum. At this time, the student should purchase malpractice insurance if the university has not purchased it as part of course enrollment. Your professional counseling organization can provide you with information regarding insurance options. The student must also obtain appropriate state or provincial clearances prior to beginning the placement, including a criminal background check. These clearances are managed through state regulatory agencies in the United States and through the Royal Canadian Mounted Police in Canada. Clearances can take as long as a month to process. Be sure to obtain these clearances before applying to your practicum site.

Prior to applying to the site, the student should thoroughly research each field placement of interest. Some of this information can be obtained by reviewing the website of the school or agency. Other information can come from informal sources, such as students who are further along in the program or other professional counselors. The selection and application process for practicum/internship sites can be confusing and at times overwhelming. To alleviate some of the frustration, the student might find it helpful to have a set of criteria in mind.

Criteria for Site Selection

In the sections that follow, we list questions pertaining to important categories that may be helpful in determining the selection of a practicum site.

Professional Staff and Supervisor

- What are the professional credentials of the site personnel?
- Do their credentials meet the standards of your professional credentialing bodies?

Professional Affiliations of the Site

- In what association does the site hold membership?
- Does the site hold the approval of national certifying agencies?
- What is the reputation of the site among other organizations?
- Does the site have affiliations or working relationships with other institutions?

Professional Practices of the Site

- Does the site follow the ethical guidelines of the appropriate profession (e.g., American Counseling Association [ACA], American Psychological Association [APA], Canadian Psychological Association [CPA], Canadian Counselling and Psychotherapy Association [CCPA], etc.)?
- What kinds of resources are available to personnel (e.g., a library, computer programs, ongoing research, professional consultation)?
- What are the client procedures, treatment modalities, and staffing and outreach practices? How are these practices consistent with the goals of the practicum/internship?

- What are the policies and procedures regarding recording (audio/video) and other practicum support activities?
- Do the staff members regularly update their skills and participate in continuing education?
- Are continuing education opportunities available to counselor trainees?

Site Administration

- What resources, if any, are directed toward staff development?
- Does the administration of the site provide in-house funds for staff training or reinforcement for college credit?
- How is policy developed and approved (corporate structure, board of directors, contributions)?
- How stable is the site? (Does the site receive hard money or soft money support? What is the length of service of the director and staff? What is the site's mission statement or purpose?)

Training and Supervision Values

- What values regarding training and supervision are verbalized and demonstrated?
- Will the supervisor be available for individual supervision for a minimum of 1 hour per week?
- Will practicum/internship students have opportunities for full participation?
- What kinds of counseling and professional services are offered by the site, such as individual counseling and/or therapy, group counseling and therapy, couples/family therapy, psycho-educational group guidance or workshops, consultation with professionals or families, career counseling, proposal writing, or student advising?
- Are adequate facilities available for practicum/internship students?

Theoretical Orientation of the Site and Supervisor

- What are the special counseling or therapy interests of the site supervisor(s)?

Many therapists are eclectic in their counseling practice, but many may also favor a particular therapeutic approach over others. Thus, if students are exposed to a supervisor who favors and supports the use of a particular theoretical approach, it requires the student to have grounding in the knowledge base of that theory. Naturally, the advantage of having one approach to counseling is that it affords the student the opportunity to become more proficient at it. Also, in mastering one approach, the student begins to develop a clearer, firmer professional identity regarding his/her goals in counseling practice. Conversely, the disadvantage of learning only one approach is that it limits the student's opportunity to measure other approaches that could be more in keeping with his/her own style and personality.

Client Population

- What are the client demographics in the placement site?
- Who is the client population served? For example, is it a restricted or open group? Is the age range narrow or wide? Are clients predominantly of a low, middle, or high socioeconomic level?

- Do clients require remedial, preventive, and/or developmental services?
- What opportunities exist for multicultural counseling?
- Do the site and its professional staff demonstrate high regard for human dignity and support the civil rights of clients?

Multicultural counseling skills have become increasingly important for the practicing professional counselor. The American Counseling Association's *Code of Ethics* (2014) under Section F.11.c asserts that "Counselor educators actively infuse multicultural/diversity competency in their training and supervision programs. They actively train students to gain awareness, knowledge, and skills in the competencies of multicultural practice." The American Mental Health Counselors Association's *Code of Ethics* (2015) and the American School Counselor Association's *Ethical Standards for School Counselors* (2016) similarly emphasize the importance of multicultural competency in the practice of counseling. Sections A10, B9, and D10 of the Canadian Counselling and Psychotherapy Association's *Code of Ethics* (2007) emphasize that counselors respect and understand diversity, do not condone or engage in discrimination, and demonstrate sensitivity to diversity when assessing and evaluating clients.

The demographic composition of clients is and will be of a different nature than it was not long ago in the United States. The projected changes from 2012 through 2060 indicate that the United States is set to become a more diverse nation (US Census Bureau, 2012). The non-Hispanic white population is expected to peak in 2024 at 199.6 million and then slowly decrease, falling nearly 20.6 million by 2060. The Hispanic population is projected to increase from 17% in 2012 to 31.3% in 2060. By 2060, nearly one in three US residents is expected to be Hispanic. The black population is projected to increase from 41.2 million to 61.8 million over the same period; this is a population increase from 13.1% to 14.7% of total US residents by 2060. The Asian population is projected to more than double, increasing from 15.9 million in 2012 to 34.4 million in 2060 (8.2% of the US population). Other remaining racial groups and those people identifying as being of two or more races will continue to grow. Minorities, now 37% of the US population, are projected to become 57% of the population by 2060 (US Census Bureau, 2012).

The demographic composition of clients is also changing in Canada. Statistics Canada (2010) projects that by 2031 approximately 28% of the population will be foreign born. The number of people belonging to "visible minority" groups will double and make up the majority of the population in Toronto and Vancouver. The Southeast Asian population is expected to double to between 3.2 and 4.1 million in the next 20 years. The Chinese population is expected to grow from 1.3 million to between 2.4 and 4 million in the next 20 years.

Constantine and Gloria (1999, p. 21) noted that studies have suggested that counseling students' "exposure to multicultural issues may increase their sensitivity to and effectiveness with racially and ethnically diverse clients." It is important to realize that race and ethnicity are only two of the important variables about which you must be aware when considering diversity. Culture must be defined broadly to include many other variables. Other variables that are visible are social class, gender, age, and disability status. Those variables that may not be visible are educational attainment, geographic origin, marital status, sexual orientation, language, religion, and citizenship status (Remley & Herlihy, 2016, p. 65).

Sue and Sue (2016) described multicultural competence as consisting of three areas:

- *Attitudes and beliefs*—awareness of one's own cultural conditioning and how this conditioning affects the personal beliefs, values, and attitudes of a culturally diverse population.

- *Knowledge*—understanding the *worldview* of culturally diverse individuals and groups.
- *Skills*—an ability to determine and use culturally appropriate intervention strategies. (All areas of diversity must be addressed as you develop these skills.)

It is clear that the majority of counselor education and professional psychology programs have responded to multicultural imperatives by examining their curricular offerings and reacting positively to the need for counselors to develop cultural competence. Some training programs recommend that trainees have caseloads of at least 30% minority clients or other clients who represent diversity. As a practicum or internship student, you might want to consider the client population of the field site you choose in order to ensure you will have the opportunity to increase your understanding and application of multicultural counseling skills. It is also important to consider the practices and policies of schools and agencies where you will be doing your training to determine how these practices and policies support culturally competent practice. Considering client systems is important particularly when problems are outside rather than inside the client (i.e., racism, sexism, homophobia).

Negotiating the Practicum and Internship Placement

After reviewing the resources available from your university with regard to practicum and internship sites, and after considering the points of reflection offered here, you likely will want to identify two or three field sites where you will apply. In many instances, several students may be applying for the same practicum/internship site, which may have only a limited number of openings. Consequently, you must approach the application process the same as you would in applying for a job in the profession. Start by preparing a résumé that identifies your objectives and the relevant educational, work, and volunteer experiences that support your application as a counselor-in-training at that site. You may also prepare a cover letter including a description of what training opportunities specific to that site make you especially interested in doing your practicum/internship there. Thinking this through will prepare you for a face-to-face interview with the contact person who will be making the decision about whether or not your background, goals, and personal impression seem to be a good fit with their site. The cover letter, with your résumé as an attached document, can be sent to the contact person at the site. Next, call the identified contact person to set up an interview. The contact person may be a supervisor of outpatient services at an agency, a director of counseling or student services, an administrator at a school district, or a specific supervisor at the site. When you go to the interview, dress as other professionals do at that site. Remember, you are the one who is to be interviewed at the site. Be prepared to answer questions about the skills, interests, and experiences that make you a good fit for the site.

Typical Questions Asked at the Interview

Be prepared to answer the following kinds of questions at your interview. You may want to work with some of your peers to brainstorm other possible questions and give thought to how you may respond.

- Tell me what you know about the students/clients we serve? What makes you want to work with them?
- What do you hope to gain from training at this site?

- What is your comfort level working with diverse clients?
- How would you describe your role as counselor to a student/client?
- Is there a theory that influences your practice as a counselor?
- Have you had any life experiences that help you relate to the concerns that students/clients may have?
- What student/client concerns are you ready to begin seeing now?
- Are there any problems that a student/client might present in counseling that would be challenging for you to work with?
- Describe your strengths as a counselor.
- How can a supervisor support your development as a counselor?
- Why did you choose our agency/school to do a practicum/internship?
- What types of professional experiences are you most/least interested in?
- What do you consider to be a rewarding practicum/internship experience?

In addition to answering questions, you may also ask questions to clarify information you have gotten from your research about the site.

- You may need more information about how audio or video recording of sessions is permitted and managed.
- Are there any releases to be signed or guidelines to follow, and how is confidentiality safeguarded? This can be a concern if you are required to bring recorded session material to university-based supervision.
- You could ask about what population of students/clients you would begin working with and how will you make initial contact with them. In a school setting, counselors sometimes do outreach by introducing themselves through classroom guidance activities, or they shadow another counselor before seeing students one-to-one.
- In general, what kind of applied experience occurs at the beginning of the placement, and what range of practices are gradually added to the trainee's responsibilities? What kinds of groups are offered at the site?

When you are accepted as a counselor-in-training at the site, a written exchange of agreement is made so that all parties involved in the practicum/internship placement understand the roles and responsibilities involved. With regard to written contracts, most counselor or psychology training programs have developed their own contracts. Specific guidelines followed in the practicum or internship are part of the agreement. Guidelines identified by national accrediting agencies are often used or referenced in formalizing the practicum/internship placement.

In the guidelines of the Council on the Accreditation of Counseling and Related Educational Programs (CACREP, 2016) and the Canadian Counselling and Psychotherapy Association's Council on the Accreditation of Counselling Education Programs (CACEP, 2002), the development of counseling skills is emphasized. We suggest that the counselor preparation program identify the guidelines and standards that it follows and include these in the contract. An example of a formal contract between the university and the practicum/internship field sites is included in the Forms section at the end of the book for your review. The sample Practicum Contract and Internship Contract (Forms 2.1 and 2.2) can be adapted to the specific needs of your training program. The contract includes a statement concerning guidelines to be followed, conditions agreed on by the field site, conditions agreed on by the counselor preparation program, student responsibilities, and a list of suggested practicum/internship activities. Form 2.3 is a Student Profile Sheet, which can be submitted to the field site supervisor. The profile sheet guides the documentation of the student counselor's academic preparation and relevant experience prior to practicum. Form 2.4 is a Student Practicum/Internship Agreement, which the student submits to the university practicum/internship coordinator. The agreement form demonstrates the formal agreement entered into by the student at the commencement of practicum and internship.

Getting Oriented to Your Field Site

Some field sites have a specific orientation for all new personnel to acquaint them with policy and procedures for working with clients/students. Other sites have no formal orientation, and you must seek out needed information. When you meet with your site supervisor, start by asking what you need to know about operations at the site in order to begin. Information about site operations is related to space (offices, study areas); support people (receptionists, secretaries); and access to resources (computer, phone, fax, forms). Site operations also specify how client records are kept (what is in the record, what notes and in what form, where and how records are kept and secured).

It would be helpful to know about the process a client/student follows when coming for counseling. How does a client/student get an appointment, how are they assigned to a particular counselor, what is the intake process, and how and with whom do they schedule a next appointment? Inquire about site policy regarding phone, e-mail, or other media-related contact with clients/students.

You will want to know what a typical day's schedule looks like for a counselor at the site. Often, a new practicum/internship student will shadow the supervisor or another staff member as an orientation. This gives the student an opportunity to experience the range of professional practices at the site and the procedures associated with them. Finally, you will need information about policy and protocols related to managing crisis situations or dealing with client/student behaviors of concern.

Role and Function of the Practicum and Internship Student

The student who has been accepted to the field site will start as a novice in the counseling profession but at the same time is a representative of his/her university training program and of other student counselors. The student is working in the setting as a guest of the practicum/internship site. The site personnel have agreed to provide the student with appropriate counseling experiences with the clientele they serve.

Although the individual freedom of the student counselor is understood and respected, the overriding concern of the site personnel is to provide role-appropriate services to the client population. The role of the practicum/internship student is to obtain practice in counseling or psychotherapy in the manner in which it is provided in the field site setting. The student counselor is expected to adhere to any dress code or expected behaviors that are existent at the field site. In some instances, the student may disagree with some of the site requirements; however, the role of the student counselor is not to change the system but to develop his/her own abilities in counseling practice.

Occasionally, tension or conflict may arise between the student and site personnel. Although such events are upsetting to all involved, these events can provide an opportunity for the student to develop personal insight into and understanding of the problem. After all, practicum/internship placement is real-life exposure to the realities of the counseling profession; however, should the tension or conflict persist, the student should consult with the faculty liaison, who is available to assist the student in the process of understanding his/her role within the system and to facilitate the student's ability to function in the setting.

Summary

The information presented in this chapter is designed to assist the counseling student in the process of choosing and negotiating a practicum and/or an internship placement. Several aspects of the practicum/internship experience need to be carefully considered by the student prior to making this important decision, and to this end, we have provided a number of questions that warrant attention. We recommend that the student make an effort to answer these questions to understand fully the benefits and disadvantages of a particular site. We have discussed additional information concerning the role and function of the practicum/internship student. Finally, we have included sample forms for use in preselection planning and ongoing practicum/internship activities; the student can adapt these to fit his/her own needs.

References

American Counseling Association. (2014). *Code of ethics*. Alexandria, VA: Author.

American Mental Health Counselors Association. (2015). *Code of ethics*. Alexandria, VA: Author.

American School Counselors Association. (2016). *Ethical standards for school counselors*. Alexandria, VA: Author.

Canadian Counselling and Psychotherapy Association. (2002). *Accreditation manual*. Retrieved from www.ccpa.accp.ca/en/accreditation/standards

Canadian Counselling and Psychotherapy Association. (2007). *Code of ethics*. Retrieved from www.ccpa-accp.ca/_documents?CodeofEthics_en_new.pdf

Constantine, M. G., & Gloria, A. M. (1999). Multicultural issues in predoctoral internship programs: A national survey. *Journal of Multicultural Counseling and Development, 27*, 42–53.

Council on the Accreditation of Counseling and Related Educational Programs. (2016). *CACREP standards*. Alexandria, VA: Author.

Remley, Jr., T. P., & Herlihy, B. (2016). *Ethical, legal, and professional issues in counseling*. New York, NY: Pearson.

Statistics Canada. (2010). *Study: Projections of the diversity of the Canadian population*. Retrieved from www.statcan.gc.ca/daily-quotidien/100309/dq100309a-eng.htm

Sue, D. W., & Sue, D. (2016). *Counseling the culturally diverse: Theory and practice* (7th ed.). New York, NY: Wiley.

US Census Bureau. (2012). *US Census Bureau projections show a slower growing older, more diverse nation a half century from now*. Washington, DC: Author.

SECTION II

BEGINNING TO WORK WITH CLIENTS

CHAPTER 3

STARTING THE PRACTICUM

This chapter is designed to assist the counseling student in understanding the importance of developing a therapeutic alliance with the client and how to proceed with privacy and informed consent requirements in the initial interview. The emphasis is on how the counselor-in-training develops and applies counseling performance skills with clients at the field site. A review of basic and advanced helping skills, the initial intake, and suggestions for opening and closing the initial session with individuals and groups of clients have been included. Formats for taking case notes in clinical and school settings also will be reviewed.

Beginning the Practicum Experience[1]

Getting Started: Where Do I Begin?

The practicum course tends to bring out the most anxiety in students. Prior to the start, most students have not had the experience of interacting one-on-one with "real" clients, or, at the least, their exposure has been very limited. By this time, most students have completed several foundational classes including theory, techniques, and very structured applied work but have not yet begun a true ongoing counseling relationship. This can make students feel very apprehensive and anxious about their upcoming practicum experience.

It is also the case that once students break down the requirements and begin to work, the anxiety does begin to slowly decline. As with most things, the anticipation is often much worse than the actual event. The key is to take things one step at a time so as not to become overwhelmed by details. Some common tips to consider prior to beginning the practicum course include the following:

1. *Choose an appropriate field site.* Students tend to choose the field site that they are most familiar with, which is not always the best option. It is better to investigate possible field sites (whether in a school or an agency) to see what best fits with their personal style and learning goals. The field site should be a place where you believe you will gain the most valuable experience and where you will get the best support in mentoring and supervision. If your university program chooses your site for you, it is best to arm yourself with as much information as possible about the mission, objectives, and goals of the field site. Find out everything you can so you are as prepared as possible and show your site supervisor that you are prepared to hit the ground running.

2. *Be aware of course requirements*. Practicum course requirements can vary considerably from school to school and program to program. Some requirements are based on accreditation standards and others on professional ideology. For example, some programs may require sessions to be recorded and monitored by a third party. A prospective practicum site supervisor needs to be aware of this requirement in the event the field site does not permit such practices. Most programs require a specific amount of direct contact hours and one-on-one sessions. These requirements must be communicated early in the process so that the field site supervisor can make provisions for these types of tasks to be available to the counselor trainee. It is imperative that you make the site supervisor aware of all class requirements so you can be sure that all course objectives and requirements are attainable during the field placement.

3. *Plan your time wisely*. After you have been given all the specific requirements for your practicum course, be sure to create a realistic schedule to make the most of your time. Do not try to do too much in too short a period of time. We all know that unforeseen circumstances can arise, so be sure to give yourself room for unplanned situations. For example, if your course requires 100 on-site hours, you may want to plan for 120 hours of fieldwork so you have room in your schedule to accommodate a variety of occurrences (illness, holidays, missed appointments, etc.) that may affect your scheduled time at the field site. Plan for extra time, and if you do not need it, be happy that you have completed your requirements without any difficulty.

I Have Taken the Classes, but Do I Really Know What to Do?

Now that you have taken all the classes you need prior to moving on to your practicum experience, you are ready, confident, and completely sure of yourself, right? Most likely you are experiencing the exact opposite emotions as you get ready to begin your on-site hours. Most students at this stage are feeling anxious, frightened, incompetent, and unsure of their skills. You would not be alone by any means if this description fits you at this point in your academic career, but hold on—there is hope!

So how do you deal with these feelings and jitters? First of all, take a long, deep breath and relax (and feel free to repeat this as often as you deem necessary). You would not have gotten this far if you did not *successfully* complete the critical components of your program. Remember, you chose this college or university for a reason, so have confidence in your training and in your professors' and instructors' support as you begin your field site experience.

What If I Say Something Wrong?

One of the greatest fears of many students is doing or saying the wrong thing to a client and not knowing when or how to use the appropriate techniques. One of the most frightening aspects is that this may depend to a large degree on the client's needs. In addition, there is no cookie-cutter way to perform successfully in a counseling session.

So what happens if you say something wrong? In most situations, honesty is the best policy. If it is a minor offense and you feel you may have slightly offended the client, apologize ("I'm very sorry. It appears that I may have offended you by asking that question. Please permit me to rephrase the question."). It is important that your clients know you are being authentic and are tuned into them and their needs. Remember, the counseling relationship is a two-way street. You need to be genuine with your clients if you expect them to reciprocate.

If you feel you have made an egregious error, consult with your faculty or site supervisor and have him/her assist you in coming up with a plan to deal with the situation. Remember, first and foremost, "do no harm," and if you feel that somehow you have crossed into that territory, you need to deal with the issue as quickly and thoroughly as possible. Do not be afraid to ask for help if you need it. Recognizing when this has happened and seeking appropriate help are signs of a competent counselor.

How Do I Know When to Use the Right Techniques?

Finding the appropriate techniques can be difficult for beginning counselors. It is best if you review a prospective technique or intervention before using it and consult with your supervisor to get his/her input as to its suitability for the client and your ability to execute it properly. Chances are you have the capability to implement the technique but need some extra support and feedback as to how to use it and ensure its appropriateness.

As stated before, there is no perfect way to proceed in your treatment of clients. However, one of the greatest benefits of your practicum experience is knowing that you have experienced professors and supervisors who are willing to provide you with the needed support in your efforts to implement the appropriate techniques and strategies in your counseling session.

But I'm Just a Rookie! (Learning to Trust Yourself and Your Inner Voice)

When students are first beginning to work with clients in live sessions, it is common for them to try to recall all of the knowledge and skills they have learned in the classroom. Although this can be beneficial in some ways, it may actually stifle the session and the client.

If you are distracted by attempting to recall all of the information learned in coursework, you may not be fully present with the client. It is critical to the counseling process that you are as completely present with the client as possible to ensure that the correct information is taken in and also to assure the client that you are listening attentively. The client should be encouraged by the fact that you are attentive and feel that what he/she is saying has value. In addition, the counseling process cannot proceed if you are not authentic to yourself. In other words, be yourself. If the client senses that you are not being genuine, he/she may reciprocate in kind. If you want the client to truly be himself/herself and to be open to you, you must be open yourself. The process becomes easier if you have the confidence in the knowledge and skills learned in your training program.

So how does one go about doing this? Of course, it does take time and experience to relax and be yourself. The goal of the practicum experience is to assist student counselors in honing their therapeutic skills and building a level of confidence and comfort in their counseling. It is important to note that the field site experience is the most appropriate setting for honing skills in a clinically supervised environment.

One of the most difficult aspects of counseling is learning to trust one's own instincts or inner voice. This does occur over time, but like many other aspects of counseling, it often needs some tweaking in the beginning stages of the counseling experience. To accomplish trust in oneself, you must first listen to your inner voice and instincts, trust them, and then observe the outcome. As when you are learning techniques and interventions, there are trials and errors, but if you can learn to trust yourself and that inner voice, you will be more genuine in your counseling relationships, which will serve to greatly enhance the counseling process. It is only when you learn to listen to and use your inner voice that you can truly see the counseling process at work—and it can be really wonderful when you do.

When in Doubt, Consult! (Your Faculty and Site Supervisors Are There to Help You)

One of the most important aspects of counseling is knowing when to seek professional or supervisory assistance. Throughout your coursework, you have been taught to recognize your strengths and weaknesses. This is vital to your success as a counselor. As mentioned previously, your instinct or inner voice plays a large part in knowing when to seek assistance, because it can let you know when you are in over your head or if you are unsure of your boundaries.

If you are not certain of how to proceed with a client, if you feel your ethics may be at risk, or if you are dealing with an issue you know is a difficult one for you, it is important to seek consultation with another professional. Your practicum experience will help you with these issues because you are already receiving close supervision and support. When you are finished with your school requirements and are on your own, you will find it is still critical to seek consultation when you deem it necessary. This is always the best practice to be sure that you are helping your clients appropriately and professionally.

Consultation happens at all levels, not just at the novice level. Professionals who have been in the field for many years often consult with others when they feel it is necessary. It is a process that ensures that you have your client's best interest at heart. Consultation should never be seen as a sign of weakness or incompetence but rather as the hallmark of a professional working ethically and responsibly. It is a truly professional counselor who realizes and accepts his/her limitations and is not too proud or overzealous to seek assistance and consultation from another professional. If you need to consult, it is important to be sure to consult with a trusted and ethical professional.

Becoming Part of the Professional Counseling Team

One of the organizational structures that can support your need for consultation is the professional counseling team. As you begin your practicum/internship experience, you will be joining an existing team of mental health and other professionals who are concerned with the health and well-being of students and/or clients. In a school setting, you are likely to attend meetings where teachers, social workers, school psychologists, school nurses, administrators, and others meet to review concerns and make recommendations about students of concern. If your field site is in a mental health agency, regularly scheduled team meetings, which can include psychiatrists, mental health counselors, psychiatric nurses, social workers, and others, are the venue for discussing and reviewing the status of identified clients.

The ACA *Code of Ethics* (2014) directs counselors to develop positive working relationships with colleagues within and outside the field of counseling. The counselor acknowledges and respects the expertise of team members who represent other helping professions (ACA, 2014, D.1.a., D.1.c.). The counselor is also required to respect clients' rights, including those regarding confidentiality, in interdisciplinary contexts (ACA, 2014, A.2.b., p. 4; B.3.b.). How then do you approach this collaboration?

- First, review and clarify for yourself your developing identity as a professional counselor (Atieno Okech & Geroski, 2015). What are the philosophical underpinnings and your understanding of the scope of practice? What does a wellness and developmental approach mean for you?

■ Second, learn about the language, scope of practice, and roles of the other professionals with whom you will be working (Miller & Katz, 2014). Actively research how other mental health professionals describe their values and practices as mental health professionals.

■ Third, keep an open mind. Be flexible and open to the professional orientation of others. Remember that one professional orientation/approach is not the only valid approach (Bemak, 1998).

■ Finally, discuss your collaboration activities and skills with your site supervisor and in your group supervision sessions on campus.

Preparing to Meet With Your First Client

Several things must be accomplished in the first session with your client. Most important, from your initial contact with your client you are establishing a warm and genuine helping relationship. The importance of establishing a therapeutic alliance cannot be overstated. In clinical settings, clients come to counseling with concerns, vulnerabilities, and apprehensions about what kinds of responses they are likely to receive. In school, career, or post-secondary settings, clients can come to counseling with similar dynamics, but many of their concerns can be of a developmental or life transition nature. Although they may be experiencing emotional discomfort or confusion, they are often functioning adequately in their life circumstances but require support, clarification, and assistance with their concerns. The counselor must greet each client with empathy for his/her unique situation and make every effort to reduce any discomfort. The counselor must establish himself/herself as someone who can be both approachable and helpful.

Specifics that must be accomplished in the first session are:

■ making certain that clients are informed of their privacy rights as required by federal law in settings where health information is managed electronically;

■ providing the client with informed consent about the counseling process they are about to begin; and

■ helping the client talk about the concerns and life situations that motivated them to seek counseling.

Prior to meeting with your first client, it is necessary to review required federal guidelines that mental health practitioners and others who provide health services to clients must review with clients about the privacy practices at the site. These requirements must be posted in a prominent place at the site. Counselors must be prepared to answer any questions a client may have regarding these guidelines. In the United States, the Health Insurance Portability and Accountability Act (HIPAA) informs these guidelines. Any site that transmits records electronically is required to comply with this law. We are including information about the law so that you will be able to answer questions clients may have regarding this process.

The Health Insurance Portability and Accountability Act (HIPAA)

HIPAA is the first federal privacy standards law in the United States intended to protect patients' health information and medical records. It took effect in 2003, and after some changes, revised standards were enacted in September 2013. HIPAA rules apply to therapists (sites) who transmit records electronically in carrying out financial transactions or administrative activity such as claims submission. This includes the internet, e-mail transmissions, and the use of electronic media such as CDs. HIPAA is a federal law that applies throughout the United States and overrides state laws unless state laws are stricter in protecting consumer health care privacy. Civil penalties for violation of HIPAA rules have been identified. Criminal penalties for providers who knowingly and improperly disclose information include fines and prison terms.

HIPAA identifies three core compliance areas:

1. *The privacy rule* restricts use and disclosure of an individual's "protected health information" (PHI). The privacy rule provides for individual rights such as a patient's rights to access their PHI, restrict disclosures, request amendments or an accounting disclosure, and complain without retaliation.
2. *The security rule* requires covered practices to implement a number of administrative, technical, and physical safeguards to ensure confidentiality, integrity, and availability of electronic PHI. "Electronic PHI" refers to all individually identifiable health information a covered entity creates, receives, maintains, or transmits in electronic form.
3. *The breach notification rule* requires covered practices to notify affected individuals, the secretary of the US Department of Health and Human Services, and, in some cases, the media when they discover a breach of a patient's PHI (American Medical Association, 2013).

The Notice of Privacy Practices (NPP) must be made available to existing clients on request and must be posted in a prominent location or on the therapist's (site's) website. Therapists (sites) must have a documented procedure to handle patients' requests regarding:

- medical record access, inspection, and copy requests;
- disclosure restriction requests—when a client asks you to limit sharing of his/her medical information with other covered entities;
- amendment requests—when a client asks you to make a change to information in his/her medical record;
- accounting or disclosure requests; and
- confidential communication channel requests—when a client asks to receive information in a specific way or at a specific location; for example, he/she may request not to be called at home for an appointment reminder (American Medical Association, 2013).

Counselors may wish to customize their Notice of Privacy Practices (NPP) to include a broader discussion of the limits of confidentiality, privilege, and privacy, including issues of imminent harm to self or others and other mandatory reporting duties. They may also wish to include a statement in the section related to psychotherapy notes that states that PHI and psychotherapy notes may be released in response to a complaint filed against the counselor. Another option is to use the model but cross-reference to the counselor's informed consent document (Wheeler, 2013).

For students preparing to become professional counselors in Canada, health information privacy is protected under the Personal Information Protection and Electronics Documents Act (Office of the Privacy Commissioner of Canada, May, 2014). Since January 1, 2002, this act has applied to personal health information and the ways it is collected, used, or disclosed. Several provinces also have enacted laws in matters related to health care information, and these laws are substantially similar to the federal law.

Informed Consent

In counseling and psychology professions, ethical guidelines require that we disclose to clients some information about the benefits and risks of, and alternatives to, treatment procedures. Clients have a right to know what they are getting into when they are coming for counseling. In addition to being a proper and ethical way to begin counseling, there are legal concepts that require that informed consent be obtained from clients before counseling begins. A written informed consent form is a contract and a promise made by the mental health professional to perform therapy competently. There are three basic legal elements of informed consent:

1. The client must be competent. Competence refers to the legal capacity to give consent. If, because of age or mental ability, a client does not have the capacity to give consent, the therapist should consult another person or a judicial body who can legally assume responsibility for the client.
2. Both the substance of the information regarding therapy and the manner in which it is given are important. The substance of the information should include the relevant facts about therapy. This information should be presented to the client in a manner that is easily understood.
3. The client must volunteer for therapy and must not be forced or coerced to participate. Some state licensing laws or regulations require that counselors provide written documents to clients (Remley & Herlihy, 2016).

The American Counseling Association *Code of Ethics* (2014) in Standard A.2.b details the elements that should be included in securing informed consent. These elements include the following:

- the purposes, goals, techniques, procedures, limitations, potential risks, and benefits of the counseling services;
- the counselor's qualifications, arrangements for continuation of services if necessary;
- the implications of diagnosis and the intended use of tests and reports;
- the role of technology and other pertinent information;
- fees and billing information;
- confidentiality and its limitations;
- clients' right to obtain information about their records and counseling plans; and
- clients' right to refuse any recommended services and be advised of the consequences of refusal.

In addition, Remley and Herlihy (2016) have identified elements that have been suggested by other writers. Some of these elements are summarized here:

- a description of the counselor's theoretical orientation or how the counselor sees the counseling process (Corey, Corey, Corey, & Callanan, 2014);
- information about the length and frequency of sessions, procedures for making and canceling appointments, policies regarding contact between sessions, and ways to reach the counselor or an alternative service in an emergency (Corey et al., 2014);
- information about insurance, including that any diagnosis assigned will become a part of the client's permanent health record; what information will be provided to insurance carriers and how this limits confidentiality (Welfel, 2010); and a description of how the managed care system may affect the counseling process; and

■ if applicable, a statement that sessions will be video or audio recorded, along with information that the client's case may be discussed with a supervisor (Corey et al., 2014).

Each field site should have in place written guidelines regarding informed consent, confidentiality, and privacy. The counseling student should review these with the client at the first session. Guidelines may vary somewhat because of different legal requirements in each state. They may also vary depending on whether the client is a minor or an adult. Consistent with our earlier statements about the importance of establishing and sustaining a therapeutic alliance, reviewing information in informed consent should be done in a manner that assists the client in the decision to proceed with the counseling. Counselors must achieve a balance between giving needed information and establishing rapport. Written disclosure statements can assist in the process of providing the detailed information needed. Many agencies have a written brochure that explains the counseling relationship and any limits to confidentiality and provide this to clients before their first appointment. This gives clients the opportunity to ask questions face-to-face with the counselor after they have received and thought about the information. Counselors should focus on developing rapport in a first session and, at the end, go over important details regarding the counseling relationship). A sample of an informed consent document (disclosure statement) is provided here.

SAMPLE INFORMED CONSENT AND DISCLOSURE STATEMENT

This form is intended to inform you about my background and to help you understand our professional relationship. I am a master's degree student in the Department of Counseling and Psychology at Blank University studying to be a professional counselor. I am not yet licensed by the state as a professional counselor. However, I am working under the direct supervision of a university faculty member and a site supervisor who are both licensed/certified by the state. The following information is provided about the site and my supervisors.

My internship placement is: Community Mental Health Center
1234 First St., Butler, PA
Phone number: 724-654-3210

Site Supervisor:	Dr. John Smith	Phone number: 724-654-3211
University Supervisor:	Dr. Elizabeth Jones	Phone number: 412-687-8675

Please read and understand this Informed Consent and Disclosure Statement and ask me about any parts that may be unclear to you. My university department requires that I have you sign this to acknowledge that I have provided you with this information. Please understand that you may end this agreement at any time.

My Background and Experience

I graduated from the University of Pittsburgh in 2009 with a bachelor of arts degree in sociology. I worked as the student coordinator of freshman orientation during my junior and senior years. I worked as a college admissions and financial aid counselor for 2 years after earning my BA and began my graduate studies in counseling in 2011. I have enjoyed working with adolescents, adults, and families.

Counseling Philosophy

A counseling relationship between a professional counselor and client is a professional relationship where the professional counselor assists the client in exploring and resolving difficult life issues. I believe in a collaborative approach while working with clients and will help each client develop his/her own individual counseling goals and plan to reach those goals. I follow a wellness model of mental health where the goal is to achieve positive mental health to the degree it is possible. I will adjust counseling techniques to best meet the needs of each client. I do align myself with cognitive behavioral theory and person-centered counseling theory.

Counseling may have both benefits and risks. Since counseling may involve unpleasant parts of your life, you may experience uncomfortable feelings. However, counseling has been shown to have many benefits. It can lead to better relationships, help solve certain problems, and decrease feelings of distress. Please understand there are no guarantees of what you will experience. I can assure you that my services will be conducted in a professional manner consistent with accepted ethical standards. Sessions are 50 minutes in duration. Some clients resolve their concerns after relatively few sessions, while others require many months or more to improve their life situations.

Clients are in complete control, and you may end our counseling relationship at any time, and I will be supportive of that decision. If you have questions about procedures, please discuss them with me. You have the right to ask about any aspect of counseling or to decline any part of your counseling. You also have the right to request another counselor. If you are dissatisfied with my services, please let me know. If I am unable to resolve your concern, you may report your complaint to my supervisor here at the agency.

In an Emergency

You may need help at a time when I am not available or cannot return your call. If you find yourself in a mental health emergency, please contact the agency or go to the emergency room and ask for the mental health professional on call. In the event that I become incapacitated and am unable to work, the agency will provide you with another counselor.

Confidentiality

I will keep confidential anything you say to me with the following exceptions: You direct me to tell someone else; I determine you are a danger to yourself or others; I have reason to believe that a child or vulnerable adult is being neglected or abused; or I am ordered by a court to disclose information. Psychotherapy notes may also be released in the event of a complaint being filed against the counselor. Because of my training my supervisor may need information or audiotapes of my counseling for confidential supervision and training purposes. You have the right to refuse the taping of sessions.

Diagnosis

If a third party such as an insurance agency is paying for part of your bill, I am normally required to give a diagnosis to that third party. Diagnoses are technical terms that describe the nature of your problems and indicate whether they are short-term or long-term problems. If I do use a diagnosis, it will be from a book titled the *Diagnostic and Statistical Manual of Mental Disorders* (5th ed.; *DSM-5*).

I have this book in my office and will be glad to make it available to you to learn more about what it says about your diagnosis.

The agency has provided you with information regarding privacy practices that comply with the Health Information Portability and Accountability Act (HIPAA); it outlines your rights to review, correct, and request transfer of files to other health care providers as well as keep your records secure.

Fees

Information about policies and procedures regarding fees and any responsibilities you have regarding payment has been discussed with the mental health services coordinator at the agency prior to this appointment. Some managed care insurance policies limit the number of sessions they will pay for each year. If you exceed that limit, you may still receive services from me, but your plan will not reimburse you for the services, and you will be responsible for any fees. Please refer to the materials that were provided to you for more information.

Signed Acknowledgment

I have read and understand the statement and have had the opportunity to discuss it before revealing any personal information.

Client Signature: _____ Date: _____

Parent/Guardian Signature: _____ Date: _____

Informed consent and confidentiality guidelines are handled differently in school settings. Most school-based field placements consider that school counseling services are an integral part of the educational program. Information about the counseling program is disseminated in a variety of ways so that parents and students understand the services provided and the confidentiality guidelines for school counselors. Some school districts have policies that require the counselors to obtain parents' permission before beginning counseling with students; others require counselors to obtain parents' permission if they see students for more than a specified number of sessions (Glosoff & Pate, 2002).

Before the school year begins, the school's guidelines are typically posted in the student handbook, on the counseling department's web page, and in brochures in the counseling office. They also are discussed at the first meeting between the counselor and the student. Hanson (2009) has developed a sample of a counseling confidentiality guidelines brochure and a sign-off sheet that the student counselor can review if the field site does not have one available.

Counseling students should review the guidelines in place in their field placement and be prepared to review these with the client in the initial session. Some field sites will include an authorization for student counselors or psychologists to see clients while being supervised and will include permission to audio- or videotape sessions for supervision. Other settings require a separate authorization for practice under supervision. Examples of authorization forms are included in the Forms section at the end of the book. The Parental Release Form (Forms 3.1a and 3.1b) can be used when initiating counseling with a child in a school, and the Client Permission to Record

Counseling Session for Supervision Purposes (Form 3.2) should be used when initiating counseling with adults or children. These forms should be adapted for use by the counseling student according to the specific field site and university requirements.

Establishing a Therapeutic Alliance

The formation of a relationship with the client is the critical initial step in the therapeutic process. Essentially, it involves the processes of developing trust, caring, and respect between the counselor and client to foster the client's motivation to actively engage in the work of counseling. Building rapport and collaboration begins the moment the counselor and client make contact. In your initial session, make sure that you greet the client warmly, introduce yourself, and walk to your office or counseling space with the student/client. Carl Rogers (1951) suggested that the core conditions for personality change to occur include accurate empathy, unconditional positive regard, and congruence. A more recent study of relationship variables in therapy suggests that the therapeutic relationship variables contribute to successful outcomes in counseling regardless of the theoretical approach and intervention strategies used by the practitioner (Norcross, 2002). These core conditions are important because they help clients feel safe, and clients who feel safe are trusting and free to be open. Clients who feel unsafe are often self-protective, guarded, and subdued (Cormier, 2016). A summary of procedures and interventions that can promote rapport and the development of a positive therapeutic alliance follows:

- Facilitate the client's effort to begin treatment by clarifying how treatment will proceed and the roles of clinician and client.
- Support the client's decision to seek treatment, offer support and encouragement.
- Establish and consistently follow session guidelines (i.e., starting times, client participation, homework assignments, etc.).
- Discuss the client expectations for treatment, encouraging realistic hope.
- Develop with the client goals that reflect those hopes and expectations.
- Understand and value the client's perspective on the world.
- Communicate warmth, genuineness, and empathy for the client's concerns.
- Demonstrate congruence and genuineness in verbal and nonverbal messages.
- Engage the client in the therapeutic process.
- Acknowledge and build on successes and support networks that the person has already established (Seligman, 2004).

The Initial Session With the Client

In the initial contact with the client, the counselor sets the tone for the counseling work by attending to important relationship conditions. The student counselor must also collect needed information from the client and help the client know what to expect in the ongoing counseling process. Counselors can proceed in two ways. Some counselors choose to start with a focus on relationship dynamics and focus solely on gaining an accurate sense of the client's world and communicating that understanding to the client. Other counselors use the first session as an intake to collect needed information about the client. With either choice of beginning emphasis, information or relationship dynamics must soon be attended to. Cormier (2016) identified these as an underlying set of objectives for the initial session:

1. reducing the client's initial anxiety to facilitate his/her talking;
2. listening more than you talk;
3. listening carefully and imagining the world he/she is describing; and
4. being aware that your client's choice of topics gives insight into his/her priorities.

Structured and Unstructured Interviews

The initial interview with the client requires the counselor to make a determination as to the type of interview to conduct. Will it be a structured interview, an unstructured interview, or a semi-structured interview? According to Whiston (2017), there are advantages to all three types of interviews. The structured interview is one where the counselor has an established set of questions that he/she asks in the same manner with each client. This format is often used in agencies that require the same structure with each client. Furthermore, if the purpose of the interview is to screen clients to see if they are appropriate for the agency or clinic, then the structured interview is preferred.

The advantage of the unstructured interview is that it can be adapted to respond to the unique needs of the client. Similarly, if the purpose of the interview is to better understand the specifics of the individual client, the unstructured interview may be preferred. Finally, the semi-structured interview is a combination of the structured and unstructured interviews, wherein certain questions are always asked but there is room for exploration and additional questioning. Whiston (2017) suggested several common guidelines for an initial interview:

- Assure the client of confidentiality and specify any limitations.
- Ask questions in a courteous and accepting manner.
- Use open-ended questions.
- Avoid leading questions.
- Listen attentively.
- Consider the client's cultural and ethnic background in structuring the interview.
- Adjust your approach to the individual client and be attuned to their comfort level.
- Avoid "chatting."
- Encourage clients to express feelings, thoughts, and behaviors openly.
- Avoid psychological jargon.
- Use voice tones that are warm and inviting yet professional.
- Do not rush clients to finish complex questions.
- If client responses drift from pertinent topics, gently redirect them.
- Vary your posture.

Basic and Advanced Helping Skills

Egan and Reese (2019) presented a three-stage structured, solution-focused approach to helping that can frame the counseling approach from the initial phases through to termination.

Stage 1—focuses on the current scenario: What is the client's story? What are the blind spots? What does the client want to change?

Stage 2—focuses on the preferred scenario: What are the possibilities? What are the priorities? To what does the client commit?

Stage 3—focuses on the strategy or getting-there phase: What strategies are possible? What strategies are the best fit? What is the plan to get there? What specific measurable change will happen in thoughts, feelings, and behaviors?

The basic skills of attending, active listening, making appropriate use of probes, and conveying empathy are used to explore the thoughts, feelings, and behaviors related to the client's current scenario. The skills of paraphrasing, reflecting feelings, clarifying, and summarizing also facilitate the counseling communication. The more advanced skills involve presenting a greater degree of challenge to the client. Advanced helping skills presented in the Egan and Reese model (2019) are interpretation, pointing out of patterns and connections, identification of blind spots and discrepancies, self-disclosure, confrontation, and immediacy. At each level, the movement is from exploring to challenging to focusing and committing to change.

Another useful model for conceptualizing counseling performance skills is the microskills training model (Ivey, Ivey, & Zalaquett, 2014). This model identifies basic and advanced skills ranging from attending behaviors to skill integration and the development of one's own style and theory. Ivey and colleagues (2014) represent the microskills as hierarchy in which the base of a pyramid of skills is ethics, multicultural competence, and wellness. Each skill level builds on this foundation and on each new level of microskills that is presented. The skill levels progress from attending behaviors to the basic listening sequence of open and closed questions, client observation, encouraging, paraphrasing and summarizing, and reflection of feeling. The next level includes influencing skills, which help clients explore personal and interpersonal conflicts. The skills of confrontation, focusing, reflection of meaning, interpretation, and reframing are at this level. The key skills of interpersonal influence—self-disclosure, feedback, logical consequences, information/psychoeducation, and directives—further build on the range of skills needed to successfully move the client from problem disclosure to goals to action. The microskills are intentionally used to enable the client to move through an interview process that begins with relationship building, transitions to telling of one's story, and proceeds to goal setting. Skillful use of attending behaviors and the basic listening sequence can guide the client through these stages. The fourth and fifth stages are "restorying" or helping the client describe a preferred story and action that will help them accomplish the story (Ivey et al., 2014). This five-stage interview structure (relationship—story and strengths—goals—restory—action) can be applied to a wide range of theoretical approaches in counseling and psychotherapy. We have extrapolated specific basic and advanced skills from this model to help prepare counselors-in-training become conscious of the range of skills implemented in their counseling sessions.

Procedural and Issue-Specific Skills

Procedural skills refer to the way the counselor manages the opening and closing of sessions. Does the session open easily and proceed to the ongoing work of the counseling? Or, does it begin with chitchat about the weather or other content unrelated to the focus of the counseling work? Once the relationship with the client is established, ongoing interviews require that the counselor reinstate the relationship. This can be done with short statements helping the client to connect with the counseling work rather than spend too much time detailing how the week has gone. Middle sessions in a counseling relationship thus are characterized by more clinical information gathering and focusing in depth (Cormier, 2016).

Procedural skills also refer to the way the counselor ends the session. A general guideline is to limit the session to a certain amount of time. With children, sessions may be 20 to 30 minutes, with adults 45 to 50 minutes. Sessions rarely need to exceed an hour. Sommers-Flanagan and Sommers-Flanagan (2003) recommended (a) leaving enough time to close the session, (b) validating any concerns or self-disclosures the client has made during the session, (c) solidifying a follow-up appointment, and (d) giving the client a chance to ask questions or make a comment as the session ends. The counselor also sets the boundaries for ending the session, even though some clients may challenge these boundaries. For example, a client may abruptly end a session saying, "I'm done for today," or bring up a crisis just prior to the end of a session. Sommers-Flanagan and Sommers-Flanagan (2003) asserted that maintaining time boundaries is in the best interest of the client in the long run. In the first case, the counselor acknowledges the client concern but is available for the full session, and in the second case, he/she notes the timing of the crisis disclosure and reschedules the next session based on the agreed-on timing for the next appointment. The rare exception to this is if the client is desperately anxious to leave and when a client brings up a recent traumatic event or a serious threat against self or others.

Structuring the Initial Session

You may wish to open the counseling interview by structuring what the client can expect in the session. An example is:

> Hi Jane. We will have about an hour together today for you to let me know what brings you to counseling and some of the concerns you have and want to discuss. Whatever you discuss with me will be kept between you and me. This is called confidentiality. This is a very important part of the counseling. However, I must tell you that there are some exceptions to this. For example, if you tell me you are abusing a child or a vulnerable person, I'm mandated to report this as these actions are against the law in this state. Or if I was ordered by a court of law to provide information or if you were in a legal proceeding and requested I share information, I would have to comply. Finally, if you gave me information that gave me reason to think that there was a serious risk of harm to you or someone else, there would be some limits to the complete confidentiality of what we have discussed. Since I am a counselor-in-training, I will be reviewing my work with my supervisor, who is also obligated to honor the confidentiality of what you talk about. Before we go on with our session and you let me know about your concerns, I want to be sure you understand this. Your safety and your privacy are important to me and to you. . . . The rest of the session is for you to let me know about your concerns. I'm happy to answer any questions you may have. This is your time to talk about whatever you wish.

The initial contact with the client is a crucial point in the process of counseling. It provides the counselor with the opportunity to begin structuring the therapeutic relationship. Methods of structuring vary according to the counselor's style and theoretical approach to counseling. Ivey (1999) suggested a five-step process for the purpose of structuring the counseling relationship:

1. *Rapport and structuring* is a process that has as its purpose the building of a working alliance with the client to enable the client to become comfortable with the interviewer. Structuring is needed to explain the purpose of the interview and to keep the sessions on task. Structuring informs the client about what the counselor can and cannot do in therapy.

2. *Gathering information, defining the problem, and identifying the client's assets* is a process designed to assist the counselor in learning why the client has come for counseling and how he/she views the problem. Skillful problem definition and knowledge of the client's assets give the session purpose and direction.

3. *Determining outcomes* enables the counselor to plan therapy based on what the client is seeking in therapy and to understand, from the client's viewpoint, what life would be like without the existing problem(s).

4. *Exploring alternatives and confronting incongruities* is purposeful behavior on the part of the counselor to work toward resolution of the client's problems. Generating alternatives and confronting incongruities with the client assists the counselor in understanding more about client dynamics.

5. *Generalization and transfer of learning* is the process whereby changes in the client's thoughts, feelings, and behaviors are carried out in everyday life by the client.

Hutchins and Cole (1992) suggested that structuring also includes explaining to the client the kinds of events that can be expected to occur during the process of helping, from the initial interview through the termination and follow-up process. Some aspects of structuring will occur in the initial phase of the helping process (initial greeting; discussion of time constraints, roles, confidentiality), whereas other aspects of structuring may take place throughout the remainder of the helping process (clarification of expectations and actions both inside and outside the interview setting).

In summary, structuring the relationship entails defining for the client the nature, purpose, and goals of the counseling process and provides the client with information regarding confidentiality guidelines for their informed consent. Critical to the structuring process is the counselor's ability to create an atmosphere that enables the client to know that the counselor is genuine, sincere, and empathic in his/her desire to assist the client.

Closing the Initial Session

Remember that your goal in this first session is to understand, as fully as possible, the client's concerns from the client's point of view. Using the basic skills you have practiced in your classes facilitate the telling of the story that the client brings about his/her circumstances. Understand the feelings, thoughts, and behaviors that are part of the client's concerns and communicate this understanding. At the same time that you are attuned to the concerns that the client presents, you are also observing how the client sees himself/herself in his/her world—what are the challenges, the strengths, the supports, the areas of confusion and intensity, and the client's interpretation of his/her experiences with others. In reflecting on the process through which the client tells of his/her concerns, you may have some hunches about the client's dynamics. How does the client present a picture of himself/herself as someone who can get his/her needs met in the world? Is the client likely to present one face to the world and feel quite differently on the inside? Is the client's narrative focused on how others have failed or misled him/her? By the completion of the first session, you will have formed the beginnings of a therapeutic relationship; you will be attuned to the client's concerns as he/she presents them; and you will have some tentative hunches about the client's dynamics and how this may assist or complicate a healthy resolution to his/her concerns.

Allow time before the end of the session to review additional informed consent information. Also allow time for the client to ask questions about the consent and/or about the session. You can end the session with a question about whether the client felt that his/her concerns had been understood. Or, if there is an issue that needs further exploration, you can ask the client to think further about this and you can begin the next session with this topic. You can also thank clients for being open to the counseling process and encourage them for being willing to look at their concerns and for being open to the changes they may need to consider to improve their situation.

Pretherapy Intake Information

Many agencies gather pretherapy intake information prior to the first counseling session. Typically, this will include medical, psychological, and psychiatric data that focus on the history and outcomes of treatment. The Initial Intake Form (Form 3.3) is designed to provide the counselor with identifying data about the client. The Psychosocial History Form (Form 3.4) provides information to assess developmental history and the acuteness or chronicity of the current concerns. Data about the client are obtained directly from the client by the counselor at the initial interview in settings where a structured interview is preferred. Other agencies ask that the client fill in forms prior to the beginning of treatment, and this information is made available to the therapist prior to the initial session. Still other agencies have a separate intake interview by someone other than the counselor who will be providing the ongoing therapy. The counselor can refer to the pretherapy assessment information prior to writing an intake summary. Further assessment processes may be recommended based on the pretherapy information and the needs that were determined based on the initial session. Chapter 4 will provide a more extensive review of the intake interview that focuses on data collection. Other information regarding overall assessment and diagnosis procedures will also be found in that chapter.

Intake Summary

At the conclusion of the initial interview and intake process, the counseling student should include a brief description of the client during the session. Observations can include the client's physical appearance; ease in the session, the way the problems were verbalized; and the client's response to you (warmth, distance, eye contact, facial expressions). What are the ways, if any, that the client's race, ethnicity, and general cultural background may influence your perception and understanding? Finally, a summary of the initial session and pretherapy assessment should be written. Remember, this summary should be brief and represents your clinical hunches at this point. Cormier (2016) identified several elements that can be included in the summary:

1. How do you understand the problem, and what outcome might you expect?
2. How does the intake information relate to the problem?
3. What strengths does the client bring to the counseling work?
4. What internal and external factors might complicate achieving the desired outcome?
5. What techniques and approaches to counseling might be helpful to this client?

Preparing to Lead Your First Group

The same thoughtfulness that accompanies meeting with your first individual client also should be part of preparing to lead or co-lead your first counseling group. It is not uncommon for practicum and even internship students to be asked by site supervisors to spend some time observing existing groups at the placement site. This can be a valuable opportunity for you to become familiar with the client population and clinical issues at the site, as well as to learn about the leadership style of therapists with whom you may be asked to co-lead a group. Being an observer-participant of the group process thus should not be viewed as an unimportant experience; rather, it is a chance to attend to group member interactions; reflect on the kinds of clinical interventions (e.g., questions, statements of empathy, etc.) that you might use; and even to get to know group members before formally taking on the role of leader.

Eventually, practicum and internship students will be expected to assume increasingly active roles in group development and group leadership. Many sites, including drug and alcohol rehabilitation centers and therapeutic centers for children and adolescents, deliver services through programs with a structured set of group experiences and topics relevant to the clients' needs. If you are working at such a site, you may not be tasked with beginning a group from scratch; rather, you likely will be asked to facilitate pre-existing psychoeducation and process groups. If this is the case, there is still plenty of opportunity to develop your leadership skills and style.

Other sites, such as elementary, middle, and high schools; university counseling centers; and some community mental health facilities, may offer you a chance to develop your own group. These groups could have open or closed membership and likely will be time limited to the duration of your contract with the site. Proposing and developing a group requires that you have a clear purpose and rationale for the group you would like to create, as well as measurable objectives and global outcomes for clients (Corey et al., 2014). The proposal that you develop should be done in conjunction with the site supervisor or other counselors at your field placement because they can influence the success of your proposed group, as well as help you refine your ideas for the group you plan to offer. If you are planning a new group, you will need to consider things such as:

- the composition of the group membership,
- the size of the group that is best suited to the group's purpose and goals,
- how frequently the group will meet,
- where the group will meet,
- the content and/or activities associated with the group sessions, and
- how you will assess the effectiveness of the group throughout the process and at its completion (Corey et al., 2014).

What Does It Take to Be an Effective Group Counselor?

Working with groups requires that you have knowledge about groups (sometimes called group dynamics) and clients' clinical issues; skills that help you to advance clients' therapeutic goals; and a learner's disposition, values, and habits suited to the counseling profession (e.g., open-mindedness, reflectivity, and compassion). Because working with groups involves balancing the needs and experiences of many clients at once, the knowledge and skills for working with groups at your practicum or internship site are specialized to this method of delivery of services. Many students find their first experiences working with groups to be challenging. This is very normal, and you are encouraged to persistently observe your work, solicit feedback from supervisors, and be willing to take risks to step outside of your comfort zone. Having a baseline level of knowledge and skills can contribute to your success.

Things to Know About Running Groups

Group leadership involves knowledge about the academic, personal, mental health, and social concerns of the group members. However, you also benefit from knowing about group dynamics as they apply to all groups. Groups have been described as having the elements of content and process (Gladding, 2015). The content refers to the information that group members and the leader share with one another, and it reflects the purpose of the group. The content of a group on social skills for students may revolve around members sharing or learning about how to express interest and accurate empathy in others' experiences, how to engage nonverbally with others, and how to regulate their emotions. The group process refers to the style of interaction among members and the energy of the group (Jacobs, Schimmel, Masson, & Harvill, 2016); process can include group anxiety, conflict, validation of others, and feelings of hope and connectedness. Although different types of groups may emphasize either content (e.g., a psychoeducation group) or process (e.g., a personal growth counseling group), you should strive to balance your attention and skill at observing and working with both content and process. Indeed, students can find that developing skills around managing and supporting process to be more challenging; thus, you are recommended to practice intervening at the level of as often as possible. Jacobs et al. (2016) noted that, at the process level, counselors have to be aware of the therapeutic forces at play in a group that go beyond what is shared verbally. These include members' desire to know that they are accepted, feel a sense of belonging, feel safe, and know what to expect. Some of the skills described in the next section can help you practice enhancing therapeutic factors.

Skills to Practice Implementing When Running Groups

Gladding (2015) described various skills necessary to running groups that counselors cultivate over their careers. Some of these are the same foundational techniques that you would use with individual clients; they include rapport building, active listening, restating, paraphrasing, reflection of feelings, and challenging. Other skills are unique to group counseling. Several are noted here:

- *Facilitating:* The counselor's use of communication skills that help the communication process to unfold for and among members of the group.
- *Protecting:* A counselor's intentional intervention aimed at ensuring that one or more group members are not attacked by others in the group or that a member does not disclose information the group is not ready to handle
- *Blocking:* A counselor's interventions that are aimed at stopping unproductive behavior or tangential conversation that distracts from an effective group interaction. It might include, for example, stopping a client who monopolizes the conversation in order to allow other members to participate.
- *Linking:* Involves the counselor in pointing out similar experiences, feelings, thought patterns, and the like among members in order to help build rapport, compassion, interest, and empathy.
- *Delegating:* A counselor's request that a group member take on a particular task in the group process (Gladding, 2015).

Dispositions Suited to Running Groups

Knowledge about groups and skills in working with groups are two components that will help you when you are getting ready to run your first group. Similar to working with individual clients, a third element is needed, and that is your attitude and disposition. Disposition touches on the very personal component of being a good helper. Corey and colleagues (2014) described effective group counselors as having courage to be vulnerable when needed yet being willing to confront members as required. They also suggested that of importance is:

- a disposition of goodwill, care, and genuineness that lets members know they are valuable as persons;
- sensitivity to cultural issues that honors clients' differences;
- an ability to identify with and appreciate others' pain and suffering; and
- a sense of one's authority as a leader that is used to help facilitate what group members want.

Tips for Co-Leading a Group

Much more common to group counseling than to individual counseling is co-leadership. Successfully leading a group with another student or with a counselor at the site takes preparation, shared vision, flexibility, and knowledge of your co-leader's style. When done well, co-led groups have the advantage of having two helpers working collectively to help clients use the group for their personal growth. It can be challenging for one person to attend to the content and process of the group at the same time; having a partner to share these responsibilities is helpful. At the same time, you might notice that not all co-leaders work well together, and if this is the case, co-leadership can be a detriment to the counseling process. We therefore recommend that, when co-leading, you minimally:

- get to know your co-leader and evidence respect for him or her within the group;
- discuss group goals and leadership approaches with your co-leader prior to group sessions;
- avoid power struggles with your co-leader during counseling groups;
- possibly negotiate specific roles to leading with your partner in order to enhance effectiveness and avoid cross-purposes during the group; and
- debrief with your co-leader after groups with regard group content, group process, and the shared leading experience (Corey et al., 2014).

Client Record Keeping

The keeping of client records is essential to professional and ethical practice. What is contained in a client's record is oftentimes unclear to the beginning counselor. Of utmost importance for counselors is learning how to write a clinical case note or progress note. However, you also may be asked by your site to complete administrative records, such as informed consent documents, intake and release of information forms, and update appointment calendars. While these are not as critical to the consistent, professional service of clients, they are important business records that should be treated with privacy and confidentiality. Increasingly, agencies are managing and storing client records electronically; thus, your site might give you access to a computer or other electronic device on which to track client records. You should find out from the site's records manager what policies surround the responsible handling of data and data entry devices. Some sites also may use some version of case management software that collects and coordinates client information, including information that would be included in a progress note. In such a case, the information in your clinical note may be pre-determined by the agency and its software package. If this is not the case, we are providing you with two formats for progress notes that are used frequently in agency and other settings.

Progress Notes

The specifics of the progress notes required may differ depending on whether the setting is clinical or nonclinical. The progress notes may also differ to reflect the counseling specialty pursued (addictions; career; college; marriage, couple, and family; mental health; school).

In clinical settings, the notes kept as part of the ongoing work of the agency are referred to as progress notes. First and foremost, progress notes are used to ensure that professional, consistent service is rendered to the client. These notes become part of the client's medical records and are protected by HIPAA federal guidelines (Remley & Herlihy, 2016). This information belongs to the client, and the client has the privilege that his/her information be kept confidential. Client records are a legal document that can be subpoenaed. Clinical records kept in agency or clinical settings typically include the counseling start and stop times; medications; modalities and frequency of treatment; results of tests; and progress notes that summarize diagnoses, functional states, symptoms, prognoses, and progress made. The two most frequently used formats for progress notes are DAP notes and SOAP notes (Gehart, 2013).

The DAP Format

DAP is an acronym for "data, assessment, and plan." The notes are divided into three sections:

1. *The data or description section:* This section includes what happened in the session: interventions, clinical observations, symptom diagnosis, and stressors. This can include both subjective and objective information. Subjective information includes themes of what the clients say about themselves, others, and their environment and situation. Objective information is what the counselor observes about the client's behavior and appearance. The counselor also records the interaction with the client, describing what took place and how it relates to the client's goals (Gehart, 2013).
2. *Assessment:* This is the interpretation section and includes the counselor's analysis and conclusion about the data. What do the data mean or suggest? Wiger (2013) identified the following areas and types of information for this section: effects or results of this session, therapeutic progress, client's level of cooperation, client progress and setbacks, areas requiring more work, effectiveness of treatment strategies, completion of treatment plan objectives, changes needed to keep therapy on target, and need for diagnostic revision.
3. *Plan:* What happens next, or what is the follow-up (i.e., scheduled next session, homework, referral, change in treatment plan, or interventions for next session)?

The SOAP Notes Format

SOAP is an acronym for "subjective, objective, assessment, and plan" (Cameron & Turtle-Song, 2002). The data collection is divided into subjective (S) and objective (O) parts.

The subjective part (S) contains information about the problem from the client's perspective or that of significant others. The entries here should be brief and concise. The client's perception of the problem should be clear to the outside reader when reading this section.

The objective part (O) consists of observations made by the counselor. The counselor's observations should be precise, descriptive, and factual. Report what can be seen, heard, smelled, counted, or measured. The phrase "is evidenced by" is helpful here.

The assessment (A) section demonstrates how the data are being interpreted and reflected on. This is a summary of the counselor's clinical thinking about the client's problem. This usually includes a *DSM* diagnosis. The counselor needs to have sufficient data to support the diagnosis.

The plan (P) section summarizes the treatment direction. This includes both the action plan and a prognosis (Cameron & Turtle-Song, 2002).

SAMPLE SOAP NOTE

The following is an example of the kind of content that comprises a SOAP note that would be used in a clinical setting.

Subjective: Maria is a 16-year-old in active rebellion against her parents' efforts to control her. She resists their pressure for her to go church and rejects their disapproval of her friendship group. Her parents believe she is ruining her life because she hangs out with friends who have a reputation for drinking and run-ins with the law. She strongly defends her friends. She admitted to regular drinking, though she is unwilling to say specifically how much or how often she does drink. She wants to be independent from her parents and their conflict has escalated to the point where she ran away from home.

Objective: Maria is angry and dug-in to her opposition to her parents' point of view. Because she came for counseling, she is perhaps open to other solutions to achieve more independence. She identifies strongly with this friendship group and goes to great lengths to preserve her connection to them. Running away from home and regular drinking are behaviors of concern.

Assessment: Z60.0 phase of life problem.

Z62.82 parent-child relational problem
Recommend substance abuse evaluation
Get school performance information

Plan: Continue weekly individual counseling sessions with focus on identity issues and problem solving. Recommend family therapy sessions to deescalate the conflict.

Record Keeping and the School Counselor

Record keeping for the school counselor presents some complications that are different from those encountered by mental health counselors and psychologists. Merlone (2005), in a thorough review of laws regarding confidentiality and privilege, noted that most states do not grant privilege to school counselors. This has major implications for record keeping. The contradiction is that confidentiality is needed to properly assist students, but there is no legal protection of confidentiality. The Family Education Rights and Privacy Act, passed in 1979, defined the rights of parents and students age 18 and older regarding access to student records. Student records were defined as a record maintained by the educational institution containing information directly related to the student. This definition does not include counselors' personal files if they are entirely private and not made available to others (Fischer & Sorenson, 1996). Common practice has become maintaining anecdotal notes in a personal notebook or folder securely kept on one's own person and not kept in the school. Swanson (1983) cautioned that, even though counselors' notes are not part of the school's record, they are subject to subpoena. Notes should be written in behavioral terms and avoid defamatory statements. We have provided a Case Notes Form (Form 3.5) for practicum/internship students in school counseling to use to maintain their private notes about their clients. Other students who prefer a notes format other than DAP or SOAP notes may use the Case Notes format to monitor the progress of their clients and to prepare for supervision. Categories included in this format are presenting/current concern, key issues addressed, interventions, progress/setbacks, assessment, and objectives and plan.

American School Counselors Association's *Ethical Standards for School Counselors* (2010) provide both a rationale for student record keeping that protects student confidentiality and a rationale for organizing data about the scope of counseling practice. Documentation serves two major functions. First, accurate documentation is an integral part of providing professional counseling services that allow the counselor to keep track of pertinent information about specific students. These serve as a memory aid about the progress of the counseling, assist in any necessary referral processes, and meet the best practice guidelines of the professional school counselor. Second, documentation of all school counseling-related activities with students, teachers, and parents; prevention programing; consulting; and non-counseling-related duties provides evidence to support the need for a school counseling program. This is a method of accountability and allows the school counselor to track the school counseling program's progress from year to year (Wehrman, Williams, Field, & Schroeder, 2010).

The practicum/internship student in school counseling will be documenting all counseling-related activities on the Weekly Schedule/Practicum Log and Monthly Practicum Log (Forms 3.6 and 3.7). The Case Notes Form (Form 3.5) provides a structure for personal notes to aid in keeping track of work with specific students. Remember, case notes are considered your personal property and must not be shown to anyone or they become public property and can no longer be considered confidential. You can take your notes to court and read from them, but do not visually show them or turn them over to anyone (Hanson, 2009). If you are working with a student at risk, you should take more detailed notes separate from your case notes summary. These situations usually occur when the student's safety is in question and you must inform others, such as parents, the administration, the school nurse, or someone in the legal system. Consult with your supervisor regarding the procedures in place at your practicum/internship site. Your more detailed notes should contain the following:

■ the time and date you spoke to the student;
■ exactly what the student said, "in quotes";
■ interventions you did at the time—be specific;
■ recommendations or suggestions you made to the student;
■ follow-up calls you had with anyone—be specific (i.e., who, when, content of call, quote when significant);
■ recommendations, referrals, and resources offered to parents; and
■ other details you want in writing for future reference (Hanson, 2009–2012).

Hanson (2009) provided other useful forms such as the Record of All Students Seen, Individual Student Contact Sheet, Parent Contact Log, and a Support Group Log.

The taking of progress notes and case notes is an invaluable aid to the counselor-in-training. Session notes assist the counselor in focusing his/her attention on the most salient aspects of the

Day of week	Location	Time	Practicum activity	Comment
Mon	UUC	9–10	Intake interview	1st session
			John W.	Problem exploration
		10–11	Individual counseling	5th session, taped
			Jane D.	Personal/social
		11–12	Ind. supervision	Reviewed reports
				Tape critique
		1–3	Group counseling	Eating disorder
			Co-lead	Group 3rd session
		3–4	Report writing	
		4–5	Testing	Interpreted
			Mary B.	Strong/Campbell
Wed	University	6–8	Group	Case presentation
			Supervision	Jane D.

Student counselor name _____

Week beginning _____ Ending _____

Figure 3.1 Weekly Practicum Schedule

counseling session. In addition, session notes can help the counselor to review significant developments from session to session.

Documenting Practicum Hours

Because of national accreditation guidelines and state and university requirements, it is necessary to document both the total number of hours spent in practicum and the total number of hours spent in particular practicum activities. Two forms are provided here for your use in tracking the time spent on various activities. The Weekly Schedule/Practicum Log (Form 3.6) can be used in two ways. First, the weekly schedule can be used by the practicum student and the practicum supervisor to plan the activities in which the student will participate from week to week. Second, the weekly schedule can be used to document the weekly activities the student has already completed. An example of a completed Weekly Schedule is provided in Figure 3.1. The Monthly Practicum Log (Form 3.7) provides a summary of the number of hours of work per month in which the student has engaged in the activity categories established in the practicum contract. The student will calculate the number of hours spent in direct client contact and in indirect service and the total practicum hours. A file should be kept for each student for the duration of the practicum experience and turned in to the faculty supervisor after being signed by the site supervisor.

Summary

This chapter has presented a review of basic information and practices required to begin working with clients at your field site. Information regarding HIPAA and informed consent guidelines, as well as a sample informed consent and disclosure statement, was included. Forms for getting proper authorizations for recording sessions for supervision purposes are included in the Forms section at the end of the book. Basic and advanced counseling skills and procedural and structuring practices were reviewed. Guidelines for writing progress notes in clinical practice as well as guidelines for record keeping in a school setting were provided. The counselor-in-training must make certain that professional practices consistent with field site policies and procedures and the ethics of the counseling profession are followed when initiating counseling relationships.

Note

1. These sections were contributed by Megan Crucianni, MA, NCC, LPC, part-time faculty in the graduate program in counseling at Marywood University, Scranton, Pennsylvania.

References

American Counseling Association. (2014). *Code of ethics*. Alexandria, VA: Author.

American Medical Association. (2013). *HIPAA privacy and security toolkit: Helping your practice meet new compliance guidelines*. Retrieved from www.ama-assn.org/resources/doc/washington/hipaa.toolkit.pdf

American School Counselors Association. (2010). *Ethical standards for school counselors*. Retrieved from www.schoolcounselor.org/asca/Media/asca/Resource%20Center/Legal%20and%20Ethical%20Issues/Sample%20Documents/EthicalStandards2010.pdf

Atieno Okech, J. E., & Geroski, A. M. (2015). Interdisciplinary training: Preparing counselors for collaborative practice. *The Professional Counselor, 5*(4), 458–472.

Bemak, F. (1998). Interdisciplinary collaboration for social change: Refining the counseling Profession. In C. C. Lee & G. R. Walz (Eds.), *Social action: A mandate for counselors* (pp. 279–292). Greensboro, NC: ERIC/CASS.

Cameron, S., & Turtle-Song, I. (2002). Learning to write case notes using the SOAP format. *Journal of Counseling and Development, 80*(3), 286–292.

Corey, G., Corey, M. S., Corey, C., & Callanan, P. (2014). *Issues and ethics in the helping professions* (9th ed.). Belmont, CA: Brooks/Cole/Cengage.

Cormier, S. (2016). *Counseling strategies and interventions* (9th ed.). Upper Saddle River, NJ: Pearson Education.

Egan, G., & Reese, R. (2019). *The skilled helper: A problem management and opportunity development approach to helping* (11th ed.). Belmont, CA: Brooks/Cole.

Fischer, L., & Sorenson, G. P. (1996). *School law for counselors, psychologists and social workers* (3rd ed.). White Plains, NY: Longman.

Gehart, D. R. (2013). *Mastering competencies in family therapy: A practical approach to theory and case documentation*. Belmont, CA: Brooks/Cole.

Gladding, S. (2015). *Groups: A counseling specialty* (7th ed.). New York: Pearson.

Glosoff, H. L., & Pate, R. H., Jr. (2002). Privacy and confidentiality in school counseling. *Journal of School Counseling, 6*(1), 20–27.

Hanson, S. (2009). *Confidentiality and the school counselor*. Retrieved from www.school-counseling-zone.com/confidentiality.html

Hutchins, D. E., & Cole, C. G. (1992). *Helping relationships and strategies*. Monterey, CA: Brooks/Cole.

Ivey, A. E. (1999). *Intentional interviewing and counseling*. Pacific Grove, CA: Brooks/Cole.

Ivey, A. E., Ivey, M. B., & Zalaquett, C. P. (2014). *Intentional interviewing and counseling* (7th ed.). Belmont, CA: Brooks/Cole.

Jacobs, E., Schimmel, R., Masson, R., & Harvill, C. (2016). *Group counseling: Strategies and Skills* (8th ed.). Belmont, CA: Cengage.

Merlone, L. (2005). Record keeping and the school counselor. *Professional School Counseling, 8*(4), 372–376.

Miller, F. A., & Katz, J. H. (2014). 4 keys to accelerating collaboration. *OD Practitioner, 46*, 6–11. Retrieved from http://c.ymcdn.com/sites/odnetwork.siteym.com/resources/resmgr/2015Awards/ODP-Vol46.No1-MillerandKatz.pdf

Norcross, J. C. (Ed.). (2002). *Psychotherapy relationships that work*. New York, NY: Oxford University Press.

Office of the Privacy Commissioner of Canada. (2014, May). *A basic overview of privacy legislation in Canada*. Retrieved from www.priv.gc.ca/resources/fs-fi02_05_d_15_e.asp

Remley, T. P., Jr., & Herlihy, B. (2016). *Ethical, legal, and professional issues in counseling* (5th ed.). Upper Saddle River, NJ: Pearson.

Rogers, C. (1951). *Client-centered therapy: Its current practice, implications and theory*. Boston, MA: Houghton Mifflin.

Seligman, L. (2004). *Systems, strategies, and skills of counseling and psychotherapy*. Upper Saddle River, NJ: Merrill/Prentice Hall.

Sommers-Flanagan, J., & Sommers-Flanagan, R. (2003). *Clinical interviewing* (3rd ed.). New York, NY: Wiley.

Swanson, C. D. (1983). The law and the counselor. In J. A. Brown & R. H. Pate, Jr. (Eds.), *Being a counselor: Directions and challenges* (pp. 26–41). Monterey, CA: Brooks/Cole.

Wehrman, J. D., Williams, R., Field, J., & Schroeder, S. D. (2010). Accountability through documentation: What are best practices for school counselors? *Journal of School Counseling, 8*(38), 2–21. Retrieved from www.jsc.montana.edu/articles/v8n38.pdf

Welfel, E. (2010). *Ethics in counseling and psychotherapy* (4th ed.). Belmont, CA: Brooks/Cole, Cengage.

Wheeler, A. M. (2013). *Tick tock . . . beat the HIPAA/HITECH clock: American Counseling Association.* Retrieved from www.counseling.org/docs/ethics/aca-hipaa-hitech-9-23-13-compliance-date.pdf?sfv

Whiston, S. C. (2017). *Principles and applications of assessment in counseling* (5th ed.). Belmont, CA: Brooks/Cole, Cengage.

Wiger, D. E. (2013). *Psychotherapy documentation primer* (3rd ed.). Hoboken, NJ: Wiley.

CHAPTER 4

ASSESSMENT AND CASE CONCEPTUALIZATION

The implementation of assessment practices appropriate to the counselor's specialization is a central skill in the practice of professional counseling. The standards of the Council for Accreditation of Counseling and Related Educational Programs (CACREP, 2016) require as part of the core curriculum that all specializations include instruction in basic concepts of standardized and non-standardized testing, validity and reliability, environmental assessment, individual and group assessment, personality testing and behavioral observation, assessment for diagnosing, and basic ethics of providing a psychological assessment. The specializations of addictions counseling and clinical mental health counseling also require instruction in the use of the diagnostic classifications of the *Diagnostic and Statistical Manual of Mental Disorders* (*DSM*). The practicum and internship experience provides the counselor-in-training with the opportunity to implement assessment and testing practices under supervision.

The task of counselors during the assessment process requires that they know what information to obtain and how to obtain it and that they have both the ability to put it together in some meaningful way and the capacity to use it to generate clinical hunches. Such hunches, or hypotheses about client's problems, can then allow counselors to develop tentative ideas for planning and treatment. In the process of preparing the client for data-gathering and assessment activities, the therapist employs attending skills and facilitative therapeutic techniques. Balkin and Juhnke (2014) describe assessment as a collaborative process between the counselor and the client that is used to identify, analyze, understand, and address the client's problems. During assessment, clients have the right to understand what the process will involve, what its purposes are, and how the assessment will be used.

It is through this initial contact and data-gathering process that the counselor is challenged to demonstrate skills that evidence an understanding of self and others in an attempt to gather relevant data about the client and his/her concerns. Like all other counseling skills, effective questioning requires the counselor to be sensitive to the client's emotional state, to demonstrate proper timing of questions, and to contain the questioning in an attempt to control the flow of information from the client. Questioning enables the counselor to gather information and to deepen the level of discussion with the client or to broaden its focus. Questioning should always be balanced, however, with empathetic interest and concern, particularly because sensitive information can be revealed through intake and assessment processes. The following is a description and format of typical assessment activities occurring prior to and during the initial stages of counseling.

Initial Assessment

Many agencies gather assessment information about the client prior to the beginning of the first counseling session. Sometimes, clients are asked to complete intake questionnaires and psychosocial history questionnaires on their own to bring with them to the initial counseling session. The Initial Intake Form (Form 3.3) and the Psychosocial History (Form 3.4) are examples. The psychosocial history provides more data than the initial intake and is invaluable in examining the acuteness or chronicity of the client's problem. Specific attention is directed toward the milestones or benchmarks in the client's developmental history that have implications for the treatment strategies to be employed in therapy. Other agencies conduct an initial intake assessment prior to assigning a client to a counselor. The intake interview is an information-gathering process rather than a therapeutic process. However, the use of basic counseling skills to create a facilitative interaction remains a priority. Frequently, someone other than the counselor conducts the interview and passes critical information on to the counselor. Regardless of who does the interview, it is essential that certain data be collected to provide the counselor with the information necessary to understanding the client's presenting problem(s) and current life issues. Cormier (2016) and Balkin and Juhnke (2014) proposed helpful guides outlining the core content of an intake interview, including:

- *Identifying data:* Name, address, phone number where client can be reached; age, gender and sexual orientation; ethnic origin, race; partnered status; occupational and educational status; languages spoken; citizenship status.
- *Presenting issues—both primary and secondary:* The counselor helps the client describe the purpose for seeking services, including the presenting problem. It is important to understand, if the concern has interfered with everyday functioning, how long it has existed and why the client decided to seek counseling at this time.
- *Client's current life setting:* The client's typical day or week, living environment, important current relationships, financial stressors, current work or educational situation.
- *Relevant family and personal history:* Discussion of past life events can help to put the presenting problem into focus. History gathering can include information about whether the client has a family of choice or biological family; age, order, and names of siblings and relationships between them; and family distress or stability. It also can include a personal history, especially of any crisis or trauma-causing events.
- *Description of the client during the interview:* This description includes appearance; the way the client related to you; areas of comfort or discomfort, warmth, or distance; language use; and mental status.
- *Suicidal and homicidal risk:* It is important to assess whether or not the client has suicidal or homicidal intentions. If so, is there a plan? Are there factors in the client's past and current life situation that elevate risk for harm to self and others?
- *Summary and recommendations:* The summary is the counselor's conceptualization of the client's needs and problem in light of all of the intake data. It culminates in a recommendation for treatment approach and goals.

We will describe a number of these assessment points in greater depth in the following sections.

Gathering Family History Data

When the client presents for counseling, he/she can bring concerns about emotional distress, overwhelming life circumstances, struggles to make complex life transitions, or any number of emotion-laden situations in which he/she is seeking help. Whatever the nature of the presenting concern, the situation occurs in the context of the client's whole life and worldview. Consequently, gathering information about family and personal history and contextual information about the client's current life can help both the counselor and the client become aware of some of the antecedents of the problem and of the possible complications in making the necessary changes for a healthy resolution. The counselor should be able to reassure the client about the benefits of reviewing this information. Some of the questions about family and personal history may elicit painful or emotionally uncomfortable memories. It is important to let clients know that they have choices about how much they want to disclose. Because this is a great deal of information to obtain, the counselor must move through the questions in a timely fashion but also be sensitive to areas of questioning that may be uncomfortable for the client. It is helpful to let the client know that the counseling process will occur over time, and any areas of concern that may be revealed in this intake process can be discussed with the counselor if the client so chooses.

Remember when you are gathering family history data that we live in a pluralistic society and there are many forms of family in our culture. There are many blended families, families of choice rather than biological families, single-parent families, and multigenerational families. When gathering family data, the counselor should pursue the following information:

- Begin by having the client let you know about the kind of family he/she grew up in. Then, proceed to ask about the names, ages, and order of any brothers or sisters and, if siblings were present, whether they were biological, blended, or adopted.
- Inquire about parents and their relationship with one another and with the client and siblings. Ask about a history of distress or substance abuse.
- Ask about the stability of the family. Check about frequent moves, significant losses, and level of conflict, if any.
- Inquire about the client's current relationship with family members.

Gathering Personal History Data

In addition to gaining an accurate picture of family history, Cormier (2016) suggested addressing the following categories of information to gather relevant data regarding personal history:

- *Medical and psychiatric history:* Are there any significant or mental health illnesses? Any accidents, treatment for substance abuse, or prior hospitalizations?
- *Sexual orientation and gender identification:* How does the client describe his or her sexual desires or attractions? With what gender does the client identify?
- *Educational history:* What is the progress through grade school, high school, and post–high school, including extracurricular and peer relationships?
- *Military service:* Were there any active duty tours in the service and was there involvement in combat situations?
- *Work history:* Where, when, what type, and for how long did the client work? Any job termination or job losses?
- *Spiritual and religious history:* Any current beliefs and practices?
- *Legal history:* Is there any history of speeding tickets, fights, violence, bankruptcy, or other legal issues?
- *Substance use history:* Has there been previous or current use of alcohol, drugs, or prescription drugs? How much and how often?

- *Relationship history:* When did client receive sexual information? Dating history? Any engagements and/or marriages and/or partnerships? Other serious emotional involvements prior to the present? Reasons previous relationships ended? Are there any children?
- *Traumatic experiences:* Has the client been neglected or abused sexually, physically, or emotionally by anyone? Natural disasters? Oppression? Discrimination? Military service?

Assessing the Client's Mental Status

Mental health professionals routinely use the mental status examination in the initial assessment to gain insight into the client's presenting condition. The mental status examination is designed to provide the therapist with signs that indicate the "functional" nature of the person's psychiatric condition. In addition, the mental status examination can be used to provide counselors with a current view of the client's mental capabilities and deficits prior to and during the course of treatment. Many formats can be used to obtain a client's mental status. However, all formats have common areas that are routinely assessed. The following is an example of items fairly typically covered in a mental status exam. You can use the Mental Status Checklist (Form 4.1) to evaluate core areas of functioning.

Mental Status Categories of Assessment

Appearance and behavior: This category consists of data gathered throughout the interview so that the person reading the narrative can develop a visual of the client during the interview. Data are gathered by direct observation of the client. To assess a client's appearance and behavior, the counselor or therapist might use the following questions: Is the client's appearance appropriate? Does the client appear to be his/her stated age? Is the client's behavior appropriate to the surroundings? Is the behavior overactive or underactive? Is the behavior agitated or retarded? Is speech pressured? Retarded? Logical? Clear? What is the content of speech?

Attention and alertness: Is the client aware of his/her surroundings? Can the client focus attention on the therapist? Is the client highly distractible? Is the client scanning the environment? Is he/she hypervigilant?

Affect and mood: What is the quality of the client's affect? Is the client's affect expressive? Expansive? Blunted? Flat? Agitated? Fearful? Is the client's affect appropriate to the current situation? Though related, affect and mood are distinct, with mood referring to the client's internal emotional state and affect referring to the external expression of mood.

Perception, thought processes, and thought content: Does the client have false ideas or delusions? Does the client experience his/her own thoughts as being controlled? Does the client experience people putting thoughts in his/her head? Does the client experience his/her own thoughts as being withdrawn or taken away? Does the client think that people are watching him/her? Out to get him/her? Does the client experience grandiose or bizarre delusions? The counselor also will want to observe if the client hallucinates or experiences visual, auditory, tactile, or gustatory false perceptions.

Orientation: Is the client oriented to persons, place, and time? Does the client know with whom he/she is dealing? Where he/she is? What day and time it is?

Judgment: Can the client act appropriately in typical social, personal, and occupational situations? Can the client show good judgment in conducting his/her own life?

Attention and concentration: Does the client have any memory disturbance?

Recent memory: Can the client remember information given a few minutes ago? (For example, give the client three or four things to remember and ask him/her to repeat back after several minutes.)

Long-term memory: Can the client remember or recall information from yesterday? From childhood? Can the client concentrate on facts given to him/her?

Abstract ability: Can the client recognize and handle similarities? Absurdities? Proverbs?

Insight: Is the client aware that he/she has a problem? Is he/she aware of possible causes? Possible solutions?

Gathering Additional Data Through Tests and Inventories

Many counselors supplement the intake information by administering additional structured assessments. These are usually related to the client's stated concerns such as substance abuse, depression, or anxiety. The use of these formalized questionnaires and instruments can be helpful in providing information about potential diagnoses (Cormier, 2016). Examples of several widely used assessments are the Beck Depression Inventory II (BDI-II), the Zung Self-Rating Anxiety Scale, the Beck Anxiety Inventory (BAI), the Michigan Alcohol Screening Test (MAST), and the Alcohol Use Disorders Identification Test (AUDIT). When using tests in the assessment process, the student counselor should have completed formal coursework on testing and use the tests under the supervision of a qualified supervisor. Anastasi (1992) and Gregory (2011) caution counselors about their ethical responsibility to use multiple criteria for any decision making. Counselors should never use one test as the only criterion for making a clinical or educational decision. The counselor should also consider his/her clinical impressions and the client's reported behaviors and should consult the diagnostic criteria references before coming to any decision about treatment directions.

Obtaining Information From Others

Occasionally, client information must be obtained from others (parents, therapists, teachers). The Initial Intake and Psychosocial History forms can be used for this purpose. The Elementary School Counseling Referral Form (Form 4.2) and the Secondary School Counseling Referral Form (Form 4.3) tend to include more data regarding the academic history of the student and his/her behavior and demeanor in school. The Elementary and Secondary School Counseling Referral Forms are designed to obtain appropriate precounseling data from sources other than the client. Typically, the professional making a referral of a school-age child for counseling or therapy is asked to describe and comment on his/her perceptions and knowledge of the pupil's current academic and social functioning.

At the completion of the intake assessment and the initial counseling session, the counselor should be prepared to write a summary of the presenting concerns and any connections that are noted that may connect the presenting problems with the background information that has been gathered. You may have recommendations for gathering additional assessment information; you may note whether anything in the client's history seems like a red flag, how you understand the problem, and how will you proceed. Be as concise as possible. Avoid elaborate inferences. Include only information that is directly relevant to the client and the counseling services to be recommended. Make sure the assessment report is kept *confidential.*

Goals of Assessment

Howatt (2000) suggested that a number of goals need to be kept in mind when conducting an assessment interview. As the counselor is forming impressions of the client and his/her family background and personal history, the counselor is also developing a working relationship with the client and is making connections between the information and the problems and possible interventions. Additional probes and requests for more detail or examples should be consistent with the suggested goals of any assessment process. A summary of these goals includes the following:

1. to gather consistent and comprehensive information,
2. to identify a person's major strengths,
3. to identify the problem(s) that bring the client to counseling,
4. to prioritize problems,
5. to teach the inadequacy of a quick fix to problems,
6. to clarify diagnostic uncertainty,
7. to measure cognitive functioning,
8. to differentiate treatment assignments,
9. to develop rapport and create a healthy working environment, and
10. to focus on the therapeutic interventions.

In prioritizing problems that clients bring to counseling, Guo, Wang, and Johnson (2012) noted that, very early on in the assessment process, counselors must identify the presence of any crisis issues that pose a potential threat to a client's or others' well-being. If these concerns are present, counselors, and especially those in training, should consult with supervisors in order to determine the next course of action, including referrals for hospitalization or other appropriate treatment settings.

Processes and Categories for Assessing Client Problems

When the intake interview and initial assessment is concluded, the counselor shifts the focus of continuing assessment to obtaining a fuller understanding of the scope and degree of the problem/s the client is presenting. Cormier and Nurius (2003) suggested a variety of processes and categories that can be addressed when fully assessing the client's problems. This focus allows both the counselor and the client to appreciate and acknowledge the full range of concerns that the client brings and to prioritize the work of the therapy. An overview of these processes and categories for assessing a client's problems follows:

1. *Explanation of the purpose of assessment:* rationale provided to the client;
2. *Identification of a range of problems:* identify relevant issues to get "the big picture";
3. *Prioritization and selection of issues and problems:* selecting the area of focus;
4. *Identification of present problem behaviors:* affective, somatic, behavioral, cognitive, contextual, and relational;
5. *Identification of antecedents:* sources of antecedents and effect on the problem;
6. *Identification of consequences:* identify sources of consequences and their effect on problem behavior;
7. *Identification of secondary gains:* variables that serve as "payoffs" to maintain problem behavior;

8. *Identification of previous solutions:* identify previous solutions and their effect on the problem;
9. *Identification of client coping skills:* identify past and present coping behaviors;
10. *Identification of the client's perception of the problem:* describe the client's understanding of the problem; and
11. *Identification of problem intensity:* client self-monitoring to identify the impact of the problem on the client's life.

Remley and Herlihy (2016) suggested an approach to assessment from the perspective of the wellness model of mental health. As the scope of the problem is explored and clarified, the counselor can view the problem/s in terms of how this may affect the client's level of functioning in important areas of the client's life. In this model, the goal is for each person to achieve positive mental health to the degree possible. Mental health is seen as occurring on a continuum (Smith, 2001). The wellness orientation views mental health as including a number of scales of mental and emotional wellness in important areas of living. Counselors assess a client's functioning on a continuum ranging from dysfunction (very mentally ill) to highly functioning (self-actualizing) in the areas of

- family relationships, friendships, and other relationships (work/church, etc.);
- career/job;
- spirituality;
- leisure activities;
- physical health;
- living environment;
- financial status; and
- sexuality.

Counselors assess clients' current life situations and help determine which factors are interfering with the goal of reaching their maximum potential. Many persons are limited by physical or other disabilities or environmental conditions that cannot be changed. Consequently, counselors assist their clients in becoming as autonomous and successful in their lives as possible. Although counselors understand and use the *DSM* in diagnosis, the goal of counseling is to help the client accomplish wellness rather than to cure an illness.

Other approaches to assessment may include more emphasis on elements such as psychopathology, problem complexity, and resistance. Nelson (2002) suggested an eclectic selection model based on the premise that a single, one-dimensional approach is simply not appropriate for all clients who present for counseling and that individual clients can benefit from strategies that honor their particular needs and difficulties. As a result, Nelson (2002) suggested the following:

1. *Identify initial counseling goals:* How does the client want to benefit from counseling? What are the counselor's and client's time constraints for counseling?
2. *Identify or rule out psychopathology:* Does the client have a biological illness? Does the client demonstrate signs of clinical depression or other disorders that require a consultation with a physician or psychiatrist?
3. *Determine problem complexity:* Simple problems are often present when clients have had adequate support throughout life and need to address unwanted cognitive or behavioral symptoms related to situational life events. Complex problems stem from family-of-origin

difficulties and often involve long-standing, complicated interpersonal difficulties that require greater analysis and time to address.

4. *Assess resistance level:* To what degree does the client resist the counselor's suggestions? Is it simply resistance to influence by an authority figure? Is it depression and a sense of hopelessness that trigger resistance?

5. *Assess capacity and desire for insight:* The counselor must assess the degree of insight a client is either capable or desirous of pursuing.

Thorough assessment of the potential interference or limitation in resolving the problems that the client brings to therapy helps both the counselor and the client to understand the boundaries, patterns, and intensity of those problems in the client's life.

Diagnosis in Counseling

The use of diagnosis by counselors has been a controversial issue in the training of counselors (Eriksen & Kress, 2005). In part, the controversy stems from a belief that diagnosis contradicts some of the more accepted and foundational models of counseling (i.e., client-centered, humanistic, etc.). However, it remains a fact that practicing counselors in agencies and mental health facilities are routinely asked to diagnose and treat clients who have severe mental health issues. This is especially true for counselors in private practice, who are regularly confronted with a managed care environment that requires the use of diagnosis for treatment consideration, as well as for insurance coverage. Moreover, the scope of practice for counselors in many states includes and allows for diagnosis and treatment. In reality, diagnosis is nothing new. Every time a counselor treats a client, he/she is making a diagnosis when choosing and implementing therapeutic interventions. Whether it is through the use of the *DSM*, the highly formalized diagnostic system, or some other system, diagnosis is a reality for trained counselors.

Counselors are frequently asked to participate in collaborative mental health service teams that work together in planning, coordinating, evaluating, and providing direct service to clients. Geroski and Rodgers (1997) suggested that, because school counselors interact with a large number of children and adolescents on a daily basis, they are uniquely able to identify students who manifest particularly worrisome behaviors possibly consistent with significant mental health issues. The counselor is able to provide direct interventions and support services for some of these students. To become a viable member of a collaborative mental health system, the counselor must at the very least become familiar with the language of the *DSM*. Remley and Herlihy (2016) agree that in today's world counselors must be knowledgeable of the current *DSM* and be able to talk with other mental health professionals about its contents.

DSM-5

Information on the *DSM-5* is included here to provide an overview of this classification and coding system. We believe that school, agency, college, career, and mental health counselors must become familiar with the *DSM-5*. The *DSM-5* was published in May 2013, culminating a 12-year process of review. It has a goal of providing the best available description of how mental disorders are expressed and can be recognized by trained clinicians. It also has a goal of harmonizing two classification systems: the *DSM* and the International Classification of Diseases (ICD). The *DSM* is the diagnostic manual used by most clinicians in the United States, while the ICD is the diagnostic tool used by the World Health Organization. Obviously, knowledge about the classification and coding system is not a substitute for formal training and supervised practice with the *DSM-5* or the ICD.

Classifications in the *DSM-5* are ordered according to developmental and life span considerations. (The order of diagnoses within classifications also follows developmental and life span considerations.) Classifications begin with diagnoses that manifest early in life (e.g., neurodevelopmental, schizophrenic spectrum, and other psychotic disorders); move on to diagnoses likely to manifest in adolescence and young adulthood (e.g., bipolar, depressive, and anxiety disorders); and then to those appearing in adulthood and later (e.g., neurocognitive disorders). The sections (diagnostic classifications) are also ordered to begin with neurological disorders, then groups of internalizing disorders, groups of externalizing disorders, and other disorders (American Psychiatric Association, 2013).

An element that assists in the harmonization of the *DSM-5* with the ICD is the coding system. In the United States, the Health Insurance Portability and Accountability Act (HIPAA) requires the use of ICD codes in diagnoses, and insurance companies also require this coding. The International Classification of Diseases, 9th Edition, Clinical Modification (ICD-9-CM) codes correspond closely to the *DSM-IV* codes. However, ICD-10-CM codes are quite different and were required to be in use beginning in October 2015. Therefore, the *DSM-5* codes include both the ICD-9-CM and the corresponding ICD-10-CM codes. ICD-10-CM codes are indicated in parentheses, for example, [309.0 (F43.21)].

The *DSM-5* uses a nonaxial documentation of diagnoses (formerly axes I, II, and III in the *DSM IV-TR*), with separate notations for psychosocial and contextual factors and disability. Psychosocial and environmental problems use a selected set of Z codes contained in the ICD-10-CM. To provide a global measure of disability, the World Health Organization Disability Assessment Schedule (WHODAS) is included for further study. Clinicians list medical conditions that are important to the understanding of the individual's mental disorders.

Subtypes and Specifiers

In the formation of a diagnosis, first the diagnostic criteria are offered as guidelines. When the full criteria for a diagnosis are met, the application of disorder subtypes and/or specifiers are considered when appropriate. Subtypes and specifiers provide for increased specificity. *Subtypes* define mutually exclusive subgroupings within a diagnosis (American Psychiatric Association, 2013). An example of a diagnosis with a disorder subtype would be Adjustment Disorder with Depressed Mood [309.0 (F43.21)]. *Specifiers* are not intended to be mutually exclusive; therefore, more than one can be given. Specifiers can indicate severity (mild, moderate, severe, extreme); course (in partial remission, in full remission, recurrent); descriptive features (good/fair insight, poor insight, absent insight); and other specifiers as indicated in the manual. Subtypes and specifiers can be coded in the fourth, fifth, or sixth digit of the diagnostic code. However, the majority of subtypes and specifiers included in the *DSM-5* cannot be coded in the ICD-9-CM and ICD-10-CM systems. They are indicated by including the subtype after the name of the disorder (e.g., social anxiety disorder/social phobia, performance type is coded as [300.23 (F40.10)/performance type]. Not all disorders include the course, severity, or descriptive features as specifiers.

Other Specified and Unspecified Designation

The *DSM-5* offers two options for diagnoses not otherwise specified: *other specified disorder* and *unspecified disorder*. The "other specified/unspecified" disorder options allow for presentations that do not exactly fit the diagnostic criteria for disorders in each chapter. The "other specified" category indicates that the full criteria for a diagnosis within a diagnostic class are not met. The "other specified" designation is used when the clinician wants to indicate the specific reason that the presentation doesn't meet the criteria (American Psychiatric Association, 2013). An example of this diagnosis would be Other specified trauma-and stressor-related disorder [309.89 (F43.8)]. *If the clinician chooses not to specify the reason* that the criteria are not met for the disorder, then Unspecified trauma- and stressor-related disorder would be the diagnosis [309.9 (F43.9)].

DSM-5 *Codes and Classification*

The following codes are intended to be used in conjunction with the text descriptions for each disorder found in the *DSM-5*:

- Before each disorder name, ICD-9-CM codes are provided, followed by ICD-10-CM codes in parentheses.
- Blank lines indicate that either the ICD-9-CM or the ICD-10-CM code is not applicable.
- ICD-9-CM codes were to be used for coding purposes in the United States through September 30, 2014. ICD-10-CM codes have been used since October 1, 2014 (American Psychiatric Association, 2013).

The final section (Section III) of the *DSM-5* is titled "Emerging Measures and Models" and includes the WHODAS 2.0, information and interview guidelines about cultural formulation, and a glossary of cultural concepts of distress.

The revision of criteria for the diagnosis and classification of mental disorders was completed in May 2013. The revised criteria for mental disorders is now used regularly for diagnosing mental disorders. Clinicians base their diagnostic decisions on the *DSM-5* criteria and then crosswalk their decisions to the appropriate ICD-10-CM codes. There will be some instances where the *DSM-5* name of a disorder will be crosswalked to an ICD-10-CM code that has a different name. The new *DSM-5* disorders were assigned to the best available ICD codes. Because *DSM-5* and ICD disorder names may be different, the *DSM-5* diagnosis should always be recorded by name in the medical records in addition to listing the codes. The American Psychiatric Association has worked with the appropriate organizations to include new *DSM-5* terms in the ICD-10-CM and will inform clinicians and insurance companies when modifications are made.

We urge counselors-in-training to attend training opportunities to become informed and current in their understanding and application of the *DSM-5* criteria and classification revisions. Proper coding requirements for *DSM-5* and ICD-10-CM will be in place at the time of your internships and entry into full professional practice.

Case Conceptualization

The process of case conceptualization can be a daunting task for beginning counselors. Determining how best to conceptualize a case and following through with an appropriate treatment plan requires the counselor to thoughtfully consider the development of his/her own strategy. To assist in that process, we now provide a variety of methods and models of case conceptualization for your consideration.

Case Conceptualization Models

A case conceptualization or case formulation represents the clinical understanding of a client's concerns. It provides the counselor with a rationale and a framework for his/her work with a client (Sperry, 2010). Beton and Binder (2010, p. 43) consider the conceptual frame to be the "linchpin of clinical practice." A conceptualization is a framework through which the counselor organizes his/her understanding of self, client, therapeutic interaction, and the process of helping that will be engaged. Counselors "observe, think and act based on the conceptual frame they are using" (Reiter, 2014, p. 4). Eels, Kendjelic, and Lucas (1998), in a study on case formulation skills, reviewed several systematic methods for constructing case formulations. A case formulation is a hypothesis about the causes, precipitants, and maintaining influences of a person's psychological, interpersonal, and behavioral problems. The authors assumed that the primary function of a case formulation was to integrate rather than summarize descriptive information about the client. Four broad categories of information are found in most case formulation methods:

1. *Symptoms or problems:* This includes the patient's presenting concerns as well as problems apparent to the counselor but not to the client.
2. *Precipitating stressors:* This includes what triggered the current symptom or problems or increased the severity of a pre-existing problem (i.e., divorce, job loss, illness, loss of social support).
3. *Predisposing life events:* This includes traumatic events or stressors occurring in the client's past that may have led to increased vulnerability.
4. *Inferred mechanisms:* This links together the information in the first three sections. This is the counselor's hypothesis about how psychological, biological, or sociocultural mechanisms contribute to the client's difficulties.

We are presenting the counseling student with three different conceptualization models that can facilitate the development of their clinical thinking skills. Each model brings a different focus in its application to understanding the counseling work. The first model, the "linchpin" model, requires that the counselor organize the case around one central underlying causal source. Another, the inverted pyramid model requires that the analysis begins with identifying a broad array of client concerns and then progresses to the deepest level of motivation (from a theoretical perspective) that fuels and sustains the concerns. The final model, the integrative model, frames the symptom and diagnosis within the context of social and cultural elements that influence and sustain the dysfunction and how these elements can be effected by selected interventions.

The "Linchpin" Model

Bergner (1998) suggested that using a linchpin concept would ideally culminate in the construction of an empirically grounded, comprehensive formulation for case conceptualization that (a) organizes all of the key factors of a case around one causal, explanatory source; (b) frames this source in terms of factors amenable to direct intervention; and (c) lends itself to being shared with the client to his/her considerable benefit. According to Bergner (1998), a clinical case formulation has the following characteristics:

1. *Organize facts around a linchpin:* Clients generally tend to provide a great deal of information about themselves, often above and beyond the data initially sought by the counselor. In addition to the presenting complaint, clients provide a wealth of information about their problem, including their emotional state, personal history, goals, expectations, and history of their concerns. However, in most cases, clients have not organized these data into a theory of their problem(s). Similarly, relevant information about such factors as personal beliefs and values, which can create problems, has been left out of their discussion. Organizing around a linchpin helps to collect all the information obtained around a core state of affairs from which all the client's difficulties spring. According to Bergner (1998), a linchpin, as the meta-phor implies, is what holds everything together; it is what, if removed, might cause destructive consequences.

2. *Target factors amenable to intervention:* It is essential that the counselor look at factors that are currently maintaining the client's dysfunctional state and that are directly amenable to therapeutic intervention. The focus is to target the factors that currently maintain the problem and that permit translation into therapeutic factors.

3. *Share the data with the client:* The case formulation shared with the client results in (a) the client organizing his/her thinking about the problem; (b) the client identifying key or central maintaining factors in his/her dysfunction and making them the focal point of change efforts; and/or (c) maximizing the client's sense of control or power over what he/she is doing, sensing, and feeling. As a result, case formulation becomes a collaborative effort between the therapist and the client in an attempt to work through the client's problems.

The Inverted Pyramid Model

The inverted pyramid model was proposed by Schwitzer in 1996 and has been refined over a period of years. The purpose of this method is to identify and understand client concerns and to provide a diagram that visually guides the conceptualization process. Four steps are identified that proceed from theory-neutral clinical observations to systematically deeper theoretical understandings (Schwitzer & Rubin, 2012; Neukrig & Schwitzer, 2006; Schwitzer, 1996, 1997):

Step I: Problem identification. The first step involves the exploration of the client's functioning, with emphasis on the inclusion of any potentially useful descriptive information about the client's particular difficulty. The clinician is advised to cast a wide net in listing client concerns.

Step II: Thematic grouping. The second step involves the process of organizing the client's problems into intuitively logical groupings or constellations. Thematic grouping entails grouping together those of the client's problems that seem to serve similar functions or that operate in similar ways.

Step III: Theoretical inference about client concerns. This moves from thematic groupings to theoretically inferred areas of difficulty (Schwitzer & Rubin, 2012). The third step requires that the counselor make inferences by applying selective general principles to his/her reasoning about a client's situation. Previously identified symptom constellations are refined further, as the inverted pyramid implies, allowing the counselor to progress down to deeper aspects of the client's problems. This honing-down process emphasizes a smaller number of themes that are unifying, central, explanatory, causal, or underlying in nature (Schwitzer, 1996). As a result, these themes can then be made a focus of treatment.

Step IV: Narrowed inferences about client difficulties. Finally, the unifying, causal, or interpretive themes inferred from the previous process are honed into existential, fundamental, or underlying questions of life and death (suicidal ideation or behavior), deep-rooted shame, or other relevant themes. This step will help the beginning counselor to apply a theoretical framework to the client's most threatening or disruptive difficulties.

Steps I and II use a pragmatic approach using theory-neutral clinical judgment. In Steps III and IV, the same theoretical orientation is applied to interpret or explain information collected in Steps I and II. This model can use any theoretical orientation chosen as appropriate by the counselor.

The Integrative Model

The integrative model (Sperry & Sperry, 2012; Sperry, 2005a, 2005b, 2010) provides the theoretical understanding of the client and links the client's problem to an appropriate treatment plan. An important element in this case conceptualization model is the inclusion of the impact of culture on the client's symptoms and solutions. The integrative model has four components:

1. *What is the diagnostic formulation?* This phase focuses on the symptoms the client presents with in therapy and includes consideration of whether or not there is an emergency or an issue that requires inpatient or outpatient treatment.
2. *What is the clinical formulation?* How did the symptoms develop, and how are they maintained? What is your understanding of the pattern of the client's symptoms?
3. *What is the cultural formulation?* How does the client's culture impact the symptom pattern? Culture can be based on ethnicity, gender, socioeconomic status, geographic region, religious beliefs, and any other factors that impact how people develop a sense of self.
4. *What is the plan of action?* What is the therapeutic model of the problem formation, and what is the theory of change to resolve the problem?

The therapist has a picture of what the symptom is and how it developed, as well as the larger systems influencing the client, and then develops a plan of action with the client. Approaching a case from a behavioral perspective would differ from approaching it from an existential or other theoretical perspective.

Each of these models can be applied to a variety of theoretical approaches, which provide an understanding of how the process of development and change can be engaged. This way of thinking influences the selection of interventions, which may result in healthier functioning for the client.

Sharing Assessment Information With the Client

The process of assessment centers on gathering information from the client for the purpose of identifying the problem or problems that the client brings to the counseling session. The results of assessment activities enable the counselor to integrate the information he/she has gathered into the treatment planning process. It should be noted that assessment activities are primarily for the benefit of the client, enabling him/her to come to an understanding of his/her problems and to cope with real-life concerns. Patterson and Welfel (2000) discussed five components to the data-gathering and hypothesis-testing process of assessment, which can be followed in assessment discussions with the client. The following is a summary of those components:

1. *Understanding of the boundaries of the problem:* Both the counselor and the client need to recognize the scope and limits of the difficulty the client is experiencing. It is important to know the problem boundaries in current functioning as well as the history and duration of the problem.
2. *Mutual understanding of the patterns and intensity of the problem:* Recognition on the part of the counselor and client that problems are not expressed at a uniform level all the time helps the client realize that understanding the pattern of the problem makes its causation clearer. Understanding the intensity of the problem helps the client to get a clearer sense of the dimensions of feelings and associated behavior.
3. *Understanding of the degree to which the presenting problem influences functioning in other parts of the client's life:* The aim is to learn how circumscribed or diffused the difficulty is and to clarify the degree to which it is compromising other unrelated parts of the client's experience.
4. *Examination of the ways of solving the client's problem that he/she has already tried before entering counseling:* This process aids understanding of the impact of the problem's history on the current status of the problem. It is also helpful in the selection of strategies for change.
5. *Understanding of the strengths and coping skills of the client:* This process helps in keeping a balanced perspective on the problem and aids in the client's realization that he/she has the resources to bring about the resolution of problems.

Assessing the Client's Progress

Assessment activities in counseling can take many forms. Regardless of the approach taken by the counselor, assessment needs to be viewed as an ongoing process that begins with the initial intake and culminates with the termination of counseling. All too often, the counselor learns that the presenting problem is only the tip of the iceberg, and new or more urgent needs arise during the therapy process. Viewing assessment as a continuous process enables the counselor to modify and adjust treatment plans, therapeutic goals, and intervention strategies as needed.

Counselors are encouraged to consider a variety of data sources and information as they make continuous assessments of progress. Continuous assessment should include qualitative and behavioral tools and the review of clients' records. Qualitative assessment activities can include role playing, simulations, and games. These methods are employed for the purpose of gathering additional data from the client. The use of qualitative methods in sessions provides for the processing of information and feedback to the client. Behavioral assessment examines the overt behavior of the client. According to Galassi and Perot (1992), behavioral assessment emphasizes the identification of antecedents to problem behaviors and of consequences that reduce their frequency or eliminate them. Indirect methods of behavior assessment might include talking to significant others about the client's issues and problems. Direct behavioral methods involve observing the client, administering behavioral checklists, and having the client self-monitor his/her behavior. A review of the client's records affords the counselor the opportunity to examine possible patterns of behavior. Likewise, it can provide the counselor with a history of the past therapy experiences of the client, as well as an understanding of the client's history in light of the client's presenting concerns. Assessment is not restricted to the use of objective, standardized, quantifiable procedures; rather, it includes interviewing, behavioral observation, and other qualitative methods.

Ongoing assessment also assists the counselor in evaluating the effectiveness of strategies used in the counseling process. Cormier, Nurius, and Osborne (2009) acknowledged the role and function of assessment in counseling as a crucial component in the selection of appropriate strategies for intervention. They assert that it is naïve to think that a single theoretical framework or strategy is appropriate for all clients. Interventions that are based on specific client needs and problems, rather than on the preferred strategy of the counselor, tend to lead to better outcomes. Patterson (1997) argued that counseling would be beneficial when cases are conceptualized through a useful theory and when carefully selected techniques are used to address client-specific difficulties. The emergence of evidence-based treatment approaches is consistent with these points of view. Thus, the areas of assessment are expanded to include an outcome-oriented review of client progress in relationship to selected interventions.

Monitoring the client in therapy is a continuous process, beginning with the initial contact with the client and ending with therapy termination. Monitoring allows the therapist to understand how the goals and objectives of the therapy are being met, as well as the direction of the therapy and the progress taking place during therapy. A cornerstone in assessment skills is the awareness, observation, and recognition of relevant data from which to formulate an accurate description and then an explanation of the client. Relevant data refer not only to specific content gleaned through a review of the records; the client's self-report; and anecdotes, incidents, and interaction shared by the client or others but also to process data, such as how the client relates a story, what kind of affect is revealed, and what the client avoids talking about.

The counseling student must observe the emotions of the client and identify what would be relevant information in understanding the client's personal dynamic. This may include observations and inferences from the client's nonverbal behaviors. It may include the client's labeled or expressed emotions or the counselor's impression of the client's overall emotional state. The counseling student's ability to elicit, observe, and note relevant emotional data in the process of the counseling session contributes to the ability to formulate an accurate description of the client, which can then lead to potential explanations and hypotheses about the emotional development of the client and possible strength or problem areas.

As the counselor facilitates the client's work with his/her concerns, he/she is noticing patterns and themes in the way that the client describes himself/herself in relationship to the world, the recurring range of behaviors and thoughts chosen when confronted with problems, and the strengths in coping with a variety of situations. The counselor is also noting how the client interacts with the counselor over time; that is, is the client expansive or monosyllabic, selective or evasive in responses, emotionally responsive and open or cautious and suspicious?

This commentary emphasizes that a major element in establishing assessment skills is the recognition and selection of relevant data when beginning to form an impression and then when monitoring the client's progress and sticking points as the counseling process unfolds. A helpful practice after each counseling session is to write brief notes about the client, in which you ask yourself the following questions:

1. What do I know about my client at this point in the counseling process? How does she/he think, act, and feel about who she/he is in the world as she/he sees it?
2. What would it be like to be in my client's shoes?

3. What are the influences that are currently contributing to my client's being who she/he is at this time in this circumstance?
4. What other information or observation would be helpful for me to understand this client?
5. What additional interventions, if any, may help my client progress toward healthier choices and actions?

The practice of writing such notes after each session helps the counseling student to develop assessment skills by regularly focusing on questions that will help in formulating a comprehensive explanation of the client and his/her issues. These questions can be incorporated into the assessment and plan sections of the Case Notes (Form 3.5). These notes can also be used in individual, group, or peer supervision, and the questions can be expanded or discussed as appropriate.

An adaptation of Kanfer and Schefft's (1988) approach suggests

■ monitoring and evaluating the client's behavior and environment from session to session;
■ assessing improvement in coping skills by noting the client's use of the skills in relation to behavior and other activities;
■ evaluating any change in the client's status or in his/her relationships to significant others that resulted from treatment;
■ utilizing available data to review progress, to strengthen gains, and to maintain the client's motivation for completing the change process;
■ negotiating new treatment objectives or changes in methods or the rate of progress if the evidence suggests the need for such changes; and
■ attending to new conditions that have been created by the client's change and that may promote or defeat further change efforts.

Furthermore, Kanfer and Schefft (1988), in examining treatment effectiveness, suggest that therapists ask themselves the following questions:

■ Are the treatment interventions working? The therapist should note the client's progress with respect to therapeutic objectives, as compared to the baseline data gathered at the beginning of treatment (initial assessment).
■ Have other treatment targets been overlooked? By monitoring other changes and emergent problems, the therapist obtains cues for the necessity of renegotiating treatment objectives or treatment methods.
■ Is the therapeutic process on course? Individuals differ in their rate of progress, and plateaus may occur at various phases of therapy; these need to be scrutinized.
■ Are subsidiary methods needed to enhance progress or to handle newly emerged problems? Are there gaps in the client's basic skill level that need to be filled to make progress?
■ Are the client's problems and the treatment program being formulated effectively? Monitoring and evaluation by the therapist in process is crucial to successful treatment. Consultation with other professionals and colleagues is recommended (pp. 255–258)

Reporting Therapeutic Progress

The counselor-in-training may receive requests from other professionals to provide diagnostic information and reports of therapeutic progress, and to make recommendations regarding a client.

The format for reporting the data will vary according to the specific requests that are made. Each progress report needs to be prepared in keeping with the request, the client, ethical standards regarding release of information, and the person to whom the report is sent. Therapeutic progress reports are often used by the agency or institution for the purpose of assisting in the development of treatment plans for placement of clients into appropriate programs and for providing information for the final disposition of a therapy case. A Therapeutic Progress Report (Form 4.4 at the end of the book) needs to include pertinent data about the method of treatment employed as well as the client's current status. Treatment recommendations are especially helpful to those who must make a final disposition of the case.

Summary

This chapter has presented the practicum/internship student with a review of assessment guidelines, diagnosis, and several case conceptualization models. The assessment of the client and the way in which the counselor conceptualizes the problem are key aspects of any approach to counseling the individual. You have now begun working with clients. You are becoming more experienced in helping your clients disclose the problems that brought them to counseling and to understand, with them, the context in which they are trying to resolve their concerns. As a professional counselor, you then frame the work based on your clinical understanding of how one can come to have these concerns and how one can accomplish the changes that allow healthier and more satisfying choices and behaviors. The counselor-in-training may find one case conceptualization model to be more useful during the practicum and may find another, perhaps more complex model to be appropriate once he/she has more experience. We assume that the counselor-in-training is working toward developing his/her own personal theory of counseling, which may be eclectic or focused on a particular theory. The application of these case conceptualization models will assist the student in the process of refining his/her own approach to the practice of professional counseling. The variety of case conceptualization models presented should enable counselors to choose a model that best fits their view of counseling. In addition, the models presented can be adapted to serve as a starting point for the development of the counselor's own way of viewing clients and their problems and then determining the best course of treatment. Following the completion of the case conceptualization process, the counselor must decide how to set goals and plan effectively for the treatment of his/her client. Thoughtful, thorough, ongoing assessment contributes to the counselor's ability to think through the case conceptualization and treatment planning process so that the client receives optimal benefit from the counseling services.

References

American Psychiatric Association. (2013). *Diagnostic and statistical model of mental disorders* (5th ed.) (DSM-5). Washington, DC: Author.

Anastasi, A. (1992). What counselors should know about the use and interpretation of psychological tests. *Journal of Counseling and Development, 70*(2), 610–615.

Balkin, R. S., & Juhnke, G. A. (2014). *The theory and practice of assessment in counseling.* New York, NY: Pearson.

Bergner, R. (1998). Characteristics of optimal clinical case formulations: The linchpin concept. *American Journal of Psychotherapy, 52*(3), 287–301.

Beton, E. J., & Binder, J. L. (2010). Clinical expertise in psychotherapy: How expert therapists use theory in generating case conceptualizations in interventions. *Journal of Contemporary Psychotherapy, 40*, 141–152.

Cormier, S. (2016). *Counseling strategies and interventions* (9th ed.). Upper Saddle River, NJ: Pearson Education.

Cormier, S., & Nurius, P. S. (2003). *Interviewing and change strategies for helpers*. Belmont, CA: Brooks/Cole.

Cormier, S., Nurius, P. S., & Osborne, C. (2009). *Interviewing and change strategies for helpers: Fundamental skills and cognitive behavioral interventions* (6th ed.). Belmont, CA: Brooks/Cole.

Council for Accreditation of Counseling and Related Educational Programs (CACREP). (2016). *CACREP standards*. Alexandria, VA: Author.

Eels, T. D., Kendjelic, E. M., & Lucas, C. P. (1998). What's in a case formulation? Development and use of a content coding manual. *Journal of Psychotherapy Practice and Research, 7*(2), 144–153.

Eriksen, K., & Kress, V. E. (2005). *Beyond the DSM story: Ethical quandaries, challenges, and best practices*. Thousand Oaks, CA: Sage.

Galassi, J. P., & Perot, A. P. (1992). What should we know about behavioral assessment: An approach for counselors. *Journal of Counseling and Development, 75*(5), 634–641.

Geroski, A. M., & Rodgers, K. A. (1997). Using the DSM IV to enhance collaboration among school counselors, clinical counselors and primary care physicians. *Journal of Counseling and Development, 75*(3), 231–239.

Gregory, R. J. (2011). *Psychological testing: History, principles, and applications* (6th ed.). New York, NY: Allyn & Bacon.

Guo, Y. J., Wang, S. C., & Johnson, V. (2012). *Clinical assessment in the counseling process: A teaching model*. Retrieved from www.counseling.org/knowledge-center/vistas/by-subject2/vistas-education-and-supervision/docs/default-source/vistas/vistas_2012_article_10

Howatt, W. A. (2000). *The human services counseling toolbox*. Pacific Grove, CA: Brooks/Cole.

Kanfer, F. H., & Schefft, B. K. (1988). *Guiding the process of therapeutic change*. Champaign, IL: Research Press.

Nelson, M. L. (2002). An assessment based model for counseling selection strategy. *Journal of Counseling and Development, 84*(4), 416–422.

Neukrig, E. S., & Schwitzer, A. (2006). *Skills and tools for today's professional counselors and psychotherapists: From natural helping to professional counseling*. Belmont, CA: Brooks/Cole.

Patterson, T. (1997). Theoretical unity and technical eclecticism: Pathways to coherence in family therapy. *American Journal of Family Therapy, 25*, 97–109.

Patterson, T., & Welfel, E. (2000). *The counseling process* (5th ed.). Pacific Grove, CA: Brooks/Cole.

Reiter, M. (2014). *Case conceptualization in family therapy*. Upper Saddle River, NJ: Pearson.

Remley, T. P., Jr., & Herlihy, B. (2016). *Ethical, legal, and professional issues in counseling* (5th ed.). Upper Saddle River, NJ: Pearson.

Schwitzer, A. M. (1996). Using the inverted pyramid heuristic. *Counselor Education and Supervision, 35*(4), 258–268.

Schwitzer, A. M. (1997). Using the inverted pyramid framework applying self psychology constructs to conceptualizing college student psychotherapy. *Journal of College Student Psychotherapy, 20*(2), 29–52.

Schwitzer, A. M., & Rubin, L. C. (2012). *Diagnosis and treatment skills for mental health counselors: A popular culture casebook approach*. Thousand Oaks, CA: Sage.

Smith, H. B. (2001). Counseling: Professional identity for counselors. In D. C. Locke, J. E. Myers, & E. L. Herr (Eds.), *The handbook of counseling* (pp. 569–579). Thousand Oaks, CA: Sage.

Sperry, L. (2005a). Case conceptualization: A strategy for incorporating individual, couple and family dynamics in the treatment process. *American Journal of Family Therapy, 33*, 189–194.

Sperry, L. (2005b). Case conceptualization: The missing link between theory and practice. *Family Journal: Counseling and Therapy for Couples and Families, 13*(1), 71–76.

Sperry, L. (2010). *Core competencies in counseling and psychotherapy: Becoming a highly competent and effective therapist.* New York, NY: Taylor and Francis.

Sperry, L., & Sperry, J. (2012). *Case conceptualizing: Mastering the competency with ease and confidence.* New York, NY: Taylor and Francis.

CHAPTER 5

GOAL SETTING, TREATMENT PLANNING, AND TREATMENT MODALITIES

This chapter focuses on cognitive skills, which represent the next step in forming an overall structure for the counseling process. Goal setting, treatment planning, and treatment modalities represent the action strategies the counselor intends to use to help the client move toward a healthier level of functioning. These two processes are interrelated.

Goal Setting in Counseling

Setting goals is a basic component of the treatment planning process. Failure to set goals inhibits the ability of the counselor and client to determine the direction of counseling, to assess the success of counseling, and to know when counseling should be concluded. Counselors and clients together mutually determine appropriate goals. The counselor's training and experience coupled with the client's experience of the issues and personal insight into problems enable the process of goal setting to provide direction to the counselor and client. Often, the goals that are chosen are affected by the client's openness to making the changes that might be necessary to achieve the desired outcome. In Chapter 3, both the Egan and Reese and the Ivey models of practice emphasized a progression beyond understanding clients' initial presentation of problems and concerns to identifying their preferred scenario or story. Clients are encouraged to work with counselors to identify the kinds of changes that will help them move toward their preferred circumstances.

Goals and the Stages of Change Model

Prochaska and Norcross (2010) provided a useful model for understanding a client's motivation for or hesitancy for change and goal setting. Their stages of change model also provides useful information for planning treatment strategies that encourage the client to move forward with making targeted personal changes. An overview of the model's six stages and the implication each stage may have for treatment goals and the counseling process provides the counselor with a useful frame of reference when working with clients.

1. *Precontemplation:* The client is unaware of a need to change or does not want to change. Goals for those in this stage are process oriented and emphasize helping the client acknowledge the limitations of the current behaviors and identify elements that may be open to change.

2. *Contemplation:* The client is aware of a need to change and thinks about it but cannot decide what to do. Clients can stay in this stage for years. Their ambivalence about a job change, a relationship change, an education change, or any number of important life issues keeps them stuck. At this phase, the counselor can encourage little action-steps in the desired direction. Sometimes, unexpected circumstances force a life change. Often, clients stay stuck because they fear change, and they must work on reducing the amount of anxiety they experience at the thought of doing something different.

3. *Preparation:* The client has decided to take some action in the near future and may have tried some action unsuccessfully. This is the time to set action goals with clients. Clients stuck in the previous stages benefit more from process goals than do clients in the preparation phase.

4. *Action:* Clients are motivated to do something new or different and take action toward their goals. They also are likely to recognize the forces that may undermine the changes they are attempting. Some clients may terminate counseling when they reach this phase. Clients may be encouraged to return to therapy when anticipated undermining forces begin to surface or the counselor may suggest that clients reduce the frequency of sessions.

5. *Maintenance:* The client reaches his/her goals based on a solid action plan and maintains the change for at least 6 months. The focus is now on maintaining gains and preventing relapse.

6. *Relapse and Recycling:* Those with serious clinical disorders and even some types of wellness issues often have difficulty maintaining changes and may make several attempts to achieve maintenance. It is helpful for people to know that relapse and recycling through behaviors aimed at achieving personal change is quite normal (Prochaska & Norcross, 2010).

The change model is characterized as a cyclical model where clients spiral through change rather than move through each stage in progression. When clients relapse, they may recycle back to a much earlier stage and require more process-type goals until they progress again toward maintenance. Prochaska and Norcross state, "each time relapsers recycle through the stages, they potentially learn from their mistakes and try something different the next time around" (2010, p. 496). Identifying where your client falls in the process of change can help you work with the client to choose goals that are appropriate to your client's motivation level and help you encourage the client to commit fully to the counseling process.

Types of Goals

The helping process involves two types of goals: process goals and outcome goals. Process goals relate to establishing the necessary conditions for change to occur. These include establishing rapport, providing a safe environment, and helping the client reveal his/her concerns. These goals are the responsibility of the counselor. Outcome goals are different for each client and directly related to the client's life circumstances and personal issues. It is important to remember that goal setting is a flexible process open to modification and refinement. Defining outcome goals can be a joint venture between counselors and clients, but the goals always relate to the reasons the clients sought counseling and the changes he/she wants to accomplish. In this view, outcome goals form the basis for treatment plans in counseling. A summary of the elements to be considered when identifying treatment goals is offered for your consideration.

- The goals are culturally appropriate (Sue & Sue, 2016).
- The goals identify the behavior to be changed. What will the client do differently?

- The goals identify the conditions under which the change will occur. What are the situations in which the client will try the new behavior?
- The goals identify the level or amount of new behavior. What is a realistic amount of change (Cormier, 2016)?

The effectiveness of goal setting is determined to a large part by the ability of the counselor and client to choose goals that are relevant, realistic, attainable, and owned by the client.

Goal setting is important to counseling from all theoretical perspectives, but it is particularly central to brief therapies that emphasize targeted behavioral or cognitive changes. For example, solution-focused therapists believe people have the ability to define meaningful personal goals and that they have the resources required to solve their problems. In solution-focused therapy, the sessions begin with identifying what the client chooses to do in order to improve his/her situation (de Shazer, 1990). Prochaska and Norcross (2010) emphasize that goals are unique to each client and are constructed by the client as he/she defines a more satisfying future. From the first contact with clients, the counselor works to create a climate that will facilitate change and encourage clients to think about a range of possibilities for change. In solution-focused therapy, the emphasis is on small, realistic, achievable changes that can lead to additional positive outcomes within a short period of time. It is important for the beginning counselor to understand that structured goal setting aids the client in translating his/her concerns into specific steps needed to accomplish change. Beginning counselors are cautioned to make sure that initial goals are modest and capable of being attained by the client.

Developing a Treatment Plan

Treatment planning is an essential part of the overall process of developing a coherent approach to counseling. The presenting problem (or problems) has been explored and placed into the context of the client's life situation. Client strengths and limitations have been assessed. A conceptual frame for understanding the client's case has been hypothesized. Treatment goals have been identified. Now, it is time to identify the range of interventions that will help the client move forward to achieve a healthier resolution of his/her problem(s). A treatment plan can include interventions specific to the individual counseling process. It can also include interventions such as a psychiatric assessment for needed medications, participation in a support or therapy group, getting a full medical check-up, and/or completion of homework outside of the counseling sessions. Treatment planning in counseling is a method of plotting out the counseling process so that both counselor and client have a road map that delineates how they will proceed from the point of origin (the client's presenting problem) to resolution, thus alleviating troubling and dysfunctional symptoms and patterns and establishing improved coping mechanisms and self-esteem. Seligman (1993) explained how treatment planning plays many important roles in the counseling process, for instance, in the following ways:

- A carefully developed treatment plan, fully grounded in research on treatment effectiveness, provides assurance that treatment with a high likelihood of success is being provided.
- Written treatment plans allow counselors to demonstrate accountability.
- Treatment plans can substantiate the value of the work being done by a single counselor or by an agency and can assist in obtaining funding.

- Use of treatment plans that specify goals and procedures can help counselors and clients to track their progress and determine whether or not goals are being met as planned. If they are not, counselors and clients can reassess the treatment plan.
- Treatment plans also provide a sense of structure and direction to the counseling process and help counselors and clients develop shared and realistic expectations for the process.

Gehart (2013) proposed a treatment planning process that establishes treatment across three phases of therapy: the initial phase (sessions 1–3), the working phase (sessions 4 and beyond), and the termination phase (the final sessions). She also described both therapeutic tasks and interventions as key components of the plan across all phases. The therapeutic tasks are process tasks that are the responsibility of the counselor and include things such as developing rapport and confronting. The goals and interventions are mutually determined by the counselor and the client and flow from the counselor's theoretical orientation as well as the client's stated purpose for coming to counseling. This model also includes a point at which therapy will conclude and allows the client to respond to the close of therapy with comments and concerns. This format may be used with the stages of change model, which also specifies the process goals associated with initiating therapy and identifies the action and maintenance stages as points where therapy may be concluded. Each of the three phases in the Gehart (2013) model include identifying and implementing:

- therapeutic tasks, which are treatment tasks across therapeutic models (i.e., establish therapeutic relationship, assess intra- and interpersonal dynamics, sustain working relationship);
- client goals, which are stated as behavioral goals specific to the client; and
- interventions, which are the specific theory or evidenced-based techniques that fit with each client goal.

In this treatment planning approach, goals are an integral part of the treatment plan and allow for continued assessment of treatment effectiveness.

Jongsma and Peterson (2006) identified six specific steps for developing a treatment plan. A summary of their steps includes the following:

1. *Problem selection:* During assessment procedures, a primary problem will usually emerge. Secondary problems may also become evident. When the problem selection becomes clear to the clinician, it is essential that the opinion of the client (his/her prioritization of issues) be carefully considered. Client motivation to participate in treatment can depend, to some extent, on the degree to which treatment addresses his/her needs.
2. *Problem definition:* Each problem selected for treatment focus requires a specific definition of how it is evidenced for the client. The *Diagnostic and Statistical Manual of Mental Disorders (DSM)* offers specific definitions and statements to choose from or to serve as an example for the counselor to develop his/her own personally developed statements.
3. *Goal development:* The goal statements need not be crafted in measurable terms but can be global, long-term goals that indicate a desired positive outcome to the treatment procedures.
4. *Objective construction:* Objectives must be stated in behaviorally measurable terms. Each objective should be developed as a step toward attaining the broad treatment goal. Generally, there should be two objectives for each problem, but the clinician can construct

them as needed for goal attainment. Target attainment dates should be listed for each objective.

5. *Intervention creation:* Interventions are designed to help the client complete the objectives. There should be one intervention for every objective. Interventions are selected on the basis of client needs, evidence-based approaches the fit the problem, and the treatment provider's full repertoire of skills.

6. *Diagnosis determination:* Determination of an appropriate diagnosis is based on an evaluation of the client's complete clinical presentation. The clinician must compare the behavioral, emotional, cognitive, and interpersonal symptoms that the client presents to the criteria for diagnosis of mental illness conditions as described in the *DSM*. The clinician's knowledge of *DSM* criteria and his/her complete understanding of the client's assessment data contribute to the most reliable and valid diagnosis.

Finally, Cormier, Nurius, and Osborne (2009) provided six guiding principles for use in the preparation of treatment plans that reflect client characteristics. These principles require attending to the cultural needs and preferences of the client, which are important elements to be considered in treatment planning.

- Make sure the treatment plan is culturally as well as clinically literate and relevant; that is, the plan should reflect the values and worldview of the client's cultural identity, not the counselor's.
- Make sure your treatment plan addresses the needs and impact of the client's social system as well as of the individual client, including (but not limited to) oppressive conditions within the client's system.
- Make sure the treatment plan considers the roles of important subsystems and resources in the client's life, such as family structure and external support systems.
- Make sure the treatment plan addresses the client's view of health and recovery and ways of solving problems. The client's spirituality may play a role in this regard.
- Consider the client's level of acculturation and language dominance and preference in planning treatment.
- Make sure the length of treatment matches the time perspective held by the client.

We have provided a number of different formats for preparing a treatment plan. Some of the formats include a broad-brush approach and include interventions outside the one-to-one counseling process that can enhance and support the client's progress. This type of treatment plan would be appropriate when working with a client who has experienced chronic emotional distress or with a client who has multiple concerns, limited coping skills, and uncertain social support. For clients who are experiencing distress that is more a function of a current life situation, a treatment plan may focus more on the counselor–client process. You may wish to follow one of the previous mentioned guidelines for treatment planning or you decide to combine elements of a variety of approaches. For example, you may first decide to determine if a broad-brush approach or counselor–client process approach is appropriate. Then, you may sequence the treatment across three distinct phases as suggested by Gehart (2013). Both process goals and outcome goals may be identified. Several interventions related to each goal can be identified and consideration of how the treatment approach may impact and be impacted by the client's cultural and social worldview and identity can be discussed with the client.

A Review of Philosophy, Theories, and Theory-Based Techniques of Counseling

Beginning counselors are confronted with the struggle to integrate the knowledge base of their training program into a coherent method of counseling. From the very beginning of their training programs, students are encouraged to examine their own values and beliefs as they are exposed to the various philosophical and theoretical approaches to counseling. The necessity for you to develop your own "theoretical approach" to working with clients is stressed for the purpose of sensitizing you to a consistent, well-thought-out approach to counseling. Spruill and Benshoff (2000) viewed the process of developing a personal theory of counseling as sequential. The initial phase emphasizes the examination of personal beliefs. Phase 2 emphasizes increasing the knowledge of counseling theories while integrating this knowledge with personal beliefs. Phase 3 focuses on the development of a personal theory of counseling.

The following section will present an overview of critical questions, theory components, and techniques that will assist you in developing a personal theory. This review also provides a framework for further refining case conceptualizations, goal setting, and treatment planning skills.

Murdock (1991) proposed the following foundational questions to be considered when reviewing theories, and you can apply these questions to your own personal beliefs and philosophy:

- What is the core motivation of human existence?
- How is this core motivation expressed in healthy ways? What are the characteristics of a healthy personality?
- How does the process of development get derailed or stuck? What are the factors that contribute to psychological dysfunction?
- What stages of an individual's life are considered key to the development process?
- Does the theory restrict the focus to the individual, or does it include family, culture, and others?
- What is the relative importance of affect, cognition, and behavior in the theory?

Answering these questions aids you in examining the key issues addressed in theories of counseling. An important element in counseling practice is to have a way in which you explain how change toward healthier functioning can occur in relationship to the intervention strategies you choose to implement in the treatment plan.

Table 5.1 provides a basic overview of the key points addressed in several theories of counseling and psychotherapy. Emphasis in this review section should focus on intervention strategies and goals and the ways your answers to the above questions are consistent with any of these theories.

Identifying Your Theory and Technique Preferences

In the previous section of this chapter, you were asked to answer a number of questions regarding your values, beliefs, and views of humankind. Similarly, you have read over the above review of several major theories of counseling and psychotherapy. To extend your review process, we are providing a Counseling Techniques List (Table 5.2), which can assist you in identifying the techniques with which you are familiar and those you would like to learn more about. Connecting the techniques to your theory base can also provide direction to your own developing personal or guiding theory.

Table 5.1 Overview of Theories of Counseling and Psychotherapy

Human Nature	Key Concepts	Intervention	Goals
Freud			
Person as biological organism, motivated to fulfill bodily needs; ruled by unconscious; instincts driving forces behind personality	id, ego, superego; conscious, unconscious, preconscious; ego defense mechanisms; psychosexual stages; transference and free association	analysis of transference, countertransference and resistance; dream interpretation	make unconscious conscious; apply appropriate defenses
Jung			
Person as motivated to grow and develop toward individuation; growth as lifelong process; tendency toward wholeness; unification of opposing aspects in the psyche	principle of entropy and equivalence; personal and collective unconscious; extraversion and introversion; thinking, sensing, feeling, intuiting	dream interpretation; use of symbols; word association	understand data from personal unconscious; resolve inner conflict; balance and integrate
Adler			
Inferiority feelings; free will to shape forces; unique style of life; strive for perfection, social interest	style of life; strive for superiority; birth order; early recollections	analysis of birth order; understanding style of life	development of socially useful goals; fostering social interest
Erikson			
Potential to direct our growth throughout our lives; personality affected by learning, experience over heredity	psychosocial stages of development; epigenetic principle of maturation; personality development throughout the life span; identity crisis in adolescence	analyzing basic weaknesses caused by ineffectual resolution of developmental crisis; adaptation	correct unbalance; develop a creative balance; positive ego identity
Kelly			
Optimistic; free to choose direction of our lives; development of constructs to view the world	anticipation of events; psychological processes directed by our constructs, ways of anticipating life events	assessment interview; self-characterization sketch; role construct repertory test	formulate new constructs and discard old ones

(continued)

Table 5.1 (continued)

Human Nature	Key Concepts	Intervention	Goals
Skinner			
People shaped more by external variables than genetic factors; behavior controlled by reinforcement; responsible for developing our own environment	functional analysis; assessing frequency of behavior, situation in which it occurs, and reinforcement associated with the behavior	direct observation of behavior; reinforcement schedules, operant conditioning	behavior and environmental change
Bandura			
Behavior controlled by the person through cognitive processes and environment through external social situations	process of observational learning; attention, retention, production, and motivation	direct observation of behavior; self-report inventories; physiological measures	change the learned behaviors seen as undesirable
Ellis			
Tendency to think both rationally and irrationally; ability to develop self-enhancing thoughts, feelings, and behaviors	development of rational philosophy of life; testing one's assumptions and validity of beliefs	ABCD theory of change; cognitive, affective, and behavioral interventions	reduction of emotional stress and self-defeating behaviors
Allport			
Uniqueness of the individual personality; people guided by the present and future; conscious control of life	traits are consistent and determine behavior; personal dispositions; functional autonomy; stages of development	personal document technique; study of values	identify personal traits; cope with the present, plan for the future
Fromm			
People can shape their own nature and destiny; innate ability to grow, develop, and reach their full potential	freedom versus security; interpersonal relatedness; basic psychological needs; character types	dream analysis, free association; interpretation of history, culture, and social events; clinical observation	realization of goals and potential; meaning in life; escape isolation and loneliness
Maslow			
Humanistic and free will to choose how we satisfy needs and fulfill potential	hierarchy of needs; peak experiences; self-actualization	physiological needs, safety needs, esteem needs, belongingness, and love	realization and fulfillment of potential, talents, and abilities

Table 5.1 (continued)

Human Nature	Key Concepts	Intervention	Goals
Rogers			
Optimistic; free will in determining, understanding, and improving oneself; innate tendency to grow and enhance	self-actualization tendency; organismic valuing process; conditions of worth; incongruency	unconditional positive regard; supportive dialogue; nonjudgmental therapeutic environment	to move toward self-actualization; responsibility for behavior
Existentialists			
Optimistic, freedom, choice, self-determination; creation of meaningful life	self-awareness, uniqueness and identity; being in the world; anxiety as a fact of life	understand client's current experience; techniques to increase client's awareness; choosing for oneself	accept freedom and responsibility for actions; live an authentic life
Post-Modernists/Solution Focused			
People formed in and through language; person is always in process of becoming; who one can become is emphasized over one's past	look for what is working; emphasis on the positive; future focused; causal understanding not necessary for change	identify past success in light of problem as probable "solution"; miracle question; scaling; applying skeleton keys or common solutions to broad range of problems	Strengthen resilience; make targeted changes
Narrative Therapy			
There is no pre-determined reality or truth that forms a structure of human nature; self is formed in context and community, through language, and in meaning-making process	language; de-construction and construction of story; externalizing of problems; unique outcomes; exception questions	diagnosis is de-emphasized; externalization of the problem; de-construction of oppressive narratives; clients empowered to name their own problem; unique outcomes used to create life sustaining stories	empower clients to re-write positive life stories; challenge oppressive, dominant cultural narratives that limit individual potential

Table 5.2 Counseling Techniques List

Directions

1. First, examine the techniques listed in the first column. Then, technique by technique, decide the extent to which you use or would be competent to use each. Indicate the extent of use or competency by circling the appropriate letter in the second column. If you do not know the technique, then mark an "X" through the "N" to indicate that the technique is unknown. Space is available at the end of the techniques list in the first column to add other techniques.
2. Second, after examining the list and indicating your extent of use or competency, go through the techniques list again and circle in the third column the theory or theories with which each technique is appropriate. The third column, of course, can be marked only for those techniques with which you are familiar.
3. The third task is to become more knowledgeable about the techniques that you do not know— the ones marked with an "X." As you gain knowledge relating to each technique, you can decide whether you will use it and, if so, with which kinds of clients and under what conditions.
4. The final task is to review the second and third columns and determine whether the techniques in which you have competencies are within one or two specific theories. If so, are these theories the ones that best reflect your self-concept? Do those techniques marked reflect those that are most appropriate, as revealed in the literature, for the clients with whom you want to work?

Extent of Use Key			
N = None	M = Minimal	A = Average	E = Extensive

Theory for Technique Key	
Ad = Adlerian (Adler, Dreikurs)	Ge = Gestalt (Perls)
Be = Behavioral (Skinner, Bandura, Lazarus)	PC = Person centered (Rogers)
CBT = Cognitive behavioral (Beck, Ellis, Meichenbaum)	Ps = Psychodynamic (Freud, Erikson)
Ex = Existential (May, Frankl)	Re = Reality (Glasser, Wubbolding)
FS = Family systems (Bowen, Satir, Minuchin)	SF = Solution focused (Berg, de Shazer)

Technique	Extent of Use	Theory for Technique
ABC model	N M A E	Ad Be CBT Ex FS Ge PC Ps Re SF
Acceptance	N M A E	Ad Be CBT Ex FS Ge PC Ps Re SF
Accurate empathic understanding	N M A E	Ad Be CBT Ex FS Ge PC Ps Re SF
Analysis of resistance	N M A E	Ad Be CBT Ex FS Ge PC Ps Re SF
Analysis of transference	N M A E	Ad Be CBT Ex FS Ge PC Ps Re SF
Analyze cognitive triad	N M A E	Ad Be CBT Ex FS Ge PC Ps Re SF
Analyze defense mechanisms	N M A E	Ad Be CBT Ex FS Ge PC Ps Re SF
Analyzing cognitive distortions	N M A E	Ad Be CBT Ex FS Ge PC Ps Re SF

Table 5.2 (continued)

Assertiveness training	N M A E	Ad Be CBT Ex FS Ge PC Ps Re SF
Assignment of tasks	N M A E	Ad Be CBT Ex FS Ge PC Ps Re SF
Avoid focus on symptoms	N M A E	Ad Be CBT Ex FS Ge PC Ps Re SF
Behavioral tasks	N M A E	Ad Be CBT Ex FS Ge PC Ps Re SF
Bibliotherapy	N M A E	Ad Be CBT Ex FS Ge PC Ps Re SF
Birth order	N M A E	Ad Be CBT Ex FS Ge PC Ps Re SF
Boundary setting	N M A E	Ad Be CBT Ex FS Ge PC Ps Re SF
Bridging compliments to tasks	N M A E	Ad Be CBT Ex FS Ge PC Ps Re SF
Change faulty motivation	N M A E	Ad Be CBT Ex FS Ge PC Ps Re SF
Change focused questions	N M A E	Ad Be CBT Ex FS Ge PC Ps Re SF
Change maladaptive beliefs	N M A E	Ad Be CBT Ex FS Ge PC Ps Re SF
Changing language	N M A E	Ad Be CBT Ex FS Ge PC Ps Re SF
Clarify personal views on life and living	N M A E	Ad Be CBT Ex FS Ge PC Ps Re SF
Classical conditioning	N M A E	Ad Be CBT Ex FS Ge PC Ps Re SF
Cognitive homework	N M A E	Ad Be CBT Ex FS Ge PC Ps Re SF
Cognitive restructuring	N M A E	Ad Be CBT Ex FS Ge PC Ps Re SF
Commitment to change	N M A E	Ad Be CBT Ex FS Ge PC Ps Re SF
Communication analysis	N M A E	Ad Be CBT Ex FS Ge PC Ps Re SF
Communication training	N M A E	Ad Be CBT Ex FS Ge PC Ps Re SF
Compliments	N M A E	Ad Be CBT Ex FS Ge PC Ps Re SF
Confrontation	N M A E	Ad Be CBT Ex FS Ge PC Ps Re SF
Co-therapy	N M A E	Ad Be CBT Ex FS Ge PC Ps Re SF
Detriangulation	N M A E	Ad Be CBT Ex FS Ge PC Ps Re SF
Disputing irrational beliefs	N M A E	Ad Be CBT Ex FS Ge PC Ps Re SF
Dramatization	N M A E	Ad Be CBT Ex FS Ge PC Ps Re SF
Dream analysis	N M A E	Ad Be CBT Ex FS Ge PC Ps Re SF
Dreamwork	N M A E	Ad Be CBT Ex FS Ge PC Ps Re SF
Early recollections	N M A E	Ad Be CBT Ex FS Ge PC Ps Re SF
Empty chair	N M A E	Ad Be CBT Ex FS Ge PC Ps Re SF
Enactments	N M A E	Ad Be CBT Ex FS Ge PC Ps Re SF
Encouragement	N M A E	Ad Be CBT Ex FS Ge PC Ps Re SF

(continued)

Table 5.2   (continued)

Exaggeration exercise	N M A E	Ad Be CBT Ex FS Ge PC Ps Re SF
Examine source of present value system	N M A E	Ad Be CBT Ex FS Ge PC Ps Re SF
Examining automatic thoughts	N M A E	Ad Be CBT Ex FS Ge PC Ps Re SF
Exception questions	N M A E	Ad Be CBT Ex FS Ge PC Ps Re SF
Experiential learning	N M A E	Ad Be CBT Ex FS Ge PC Ps Re SF
Experiments	N M A E	Ad Be CBT Ex FS Ge PC Ps Re SF
Explore quality world	N M A E	Ad Be CBT Ex FS Ge PC Ps Re SF
Explore subjective reality	N M A E	Ad Be CBT Ex FS Ge PC Ps Re SF
Exposing faulty thinking	N M A E	Ad Be CBT Ex FS Ge PC Ps Re SF
Family constellation	N M A E	Ad Be CBT Ex FS Ge PC Ps Re SF
Family-life chronology	N M A E	Ad Be CBT Ex FS Ge PC Ps Re SF
Finding alternative interpretations	N M A E	Ad Be CBT Ex FS Ge PC Ps Re SF
Flooding	N M A E	Ad Be CBT Ex FS Ge PC Ps Re SF
Focus on choice	N M A E	Ad Be CBT Ex FS Ge PC Ps Re SF
Focus on personal responsibility	N M A E	Ad Be CBT Ex FS Ge PC Ps Re SF
Focus on present problems	N M A E	Ad Be CBT Ex FS Ge PC Ps Re SF
Focus on what client can control	N M A E	Ad Be CBT Ex FS Ge PC Ps Re SF
Formulate first-session task	N M A E	Ad Be CBT Ex FS Ge PC Ps Re SF
Foster social interest	N M A E	Ad Be CBT Ex FS Ge PC Ps Re SF
Free association	N M A E	Ad Be CBT Ex FS Ge PC Ps Re SF
Genogram	N M A E	Ad Be CBT Ex FS Ge PC Ps Re SF
Genuineness	N M A E	Ad Be CBT Ex FS Ge PC Ps Re SF
Guided imagery	N M A E	Ad Be CBT Ex FS Ge PC Ps Re SF
Hypothesizing systemic roots of problems	N M A E	Ad Be CBT Ex FS Ge PC Ps Re SF
Identify and define wants and needs	N M A E	Ad Be CBT Ex FS Ge PC Ps Re SF
Identify basic mistakes	N M A E	Ad Be CBT Ex FS Ge PC Ps Re SF
Immediacy	N M A E	Ad Be CBT Ex FS Ge PC Ps Re SF
Internal dialogue	N M A E	Ad Be CBT Ex FS Ge PC Ps Re SF
Interpersonal empathy	N M A E	Ad Be CBT Ex FS Ge PC Ps Re SF
Interpretation	N M A E	Ad Be CBT Ex FS Ge PC Ps Re SF
In vivo exposure	N M A E	Ad Be CBT Ex FS Ge PC Ps Re SF
Keep therapy in the present	N M A E	Ad Be CBT Ex FS Ge PC Ps Re SF

Table 5.2 (continued)

Lifestyle assessment	N M A E	Ad Be CBT Ex FS Ge PC Ps Re SF
Logotherapy	N M A E	Ad Be CBT Ex FS Ge PC Ps Re SF
Maintain analytic framework	N M A E	Ad Be CBT Ex FS Ge PC Ps Re SF
Making the rounds	N M A E	Ad Be CBT Ex FS Ge PC Ps Re SF
Miracle question	N M A E	Ad Be CBT Ex FS Ge PC Ps Re SF
Natural consequences	N M A E	Ad Be CBT Ex FS Ge PC Ps Re SF
Negative reinforcement	N M A E	Ad Be CBT Ex FS Ge PC Ps Re SF
Objective empathy	N M A E	Ad Be CBT Ex FS Ge PC Ps Re SF
Objective interview	N M A E	Ad Be CBT Ex FS Ge PC Ps Re SF
Observational tasks	N M A E	Ad Be CBT Ex FS Ge PC Ps Re SF
Operant conditioning	N M A E	Ad Be CBT Ex FS Ge PC Ps Re SF
Plan for acting	N M A E	Ad Be CBT Ex FS Ge PC Ps Re SF
Positive reinforcement	N M A E	Ad Be CBT Ex FS Ge PC Ps Re SF
Progressive muscle relaxation	N M A E	Ad Be CBT Ex FS Ge PC Ps Re SF
Psychoeducation	N M A E	Ad Be CBT Ex FS Ge PC Ps Re SF
Recognizing and changing unrealistic negative thoughts	N M A E	Ad Be CBT Ex FS Ge PC Ps Re SF
Reflection of feeling	N M A E	Ad Be CBT Ex FS Ge PC Ps Re SF
Reframing	N M A E	Ad Be CBT Ex FS Ge PC Ps Re SF
Rehearsal exercise	N M A E	Ad Be CBT Ex FS Ge PC Ps Re SF
Reject transference	N M A E	Ad Be CBT Ex FS Ge PC Ps Re SF
Reorientation	N M A E	Ad Be CBT Ex FS Ge PC Ps Re SF
Reversal exercise	N M A E	Ad Be CBT Ex FS Ge PC Ps Re SF
Scaling questions	N M A E	Ad Be CBT Ex FS Ge PC Ps Re SF
Sculpting	N M A E	Ad Be CBT Ex FS Ge PC Ps Re SF
Self-evaluation	N M A E	Ad Be CBT Ex FS Ge PC Ps Re SF
Self-monitoring	N M A E	Ad Be CBT Ex FS Ge PC Ps Re SF
Shame-attacking exercises	N M A E	Ad Be CBT Ex FS Ge PC Ps Re SF
Social skills training	N M A E	Ad Be CBT Ex FS Ge PC Ps Re SF
Staying with the feeling	N M A E	Ad Be CBT Ex FS Ge PC Ps Re SF
Stress inoculation training	N M A E	Ad Be CBT Ex FS Ge PC Ps Re SF

(continued)

Table 5.2 (continued)

Subjective empathy	N M A E	Ad Be CBT Ex FS Ge PC Ps Re SF
Subjective interview	N M A E	Ad Be CBT Ex FS Ge PC Ps Re SF
Systematic desensitization	N M A E	Ad Be CBT Ex FS Ge PC Ps Re SF
Unbalancing	N M A E	Ad Be CBT Ex FS Ge PC Ps Re SF
Unconditional positive regard	N M A E	Ad Be CBT Ex FS Ge PC Ps Re SF

Source: Adapted from Hollis, Joseph W. (1980). Techniques used in counseling and psychotherapy. In K. M. Dimick and F. H. Krause (Eds.), *Practicum manual in counseling and psychotherapy* (4th ed., pp. 77–80). Muncie, IN: Accelerated Development. Theories and techniques listed have been updated and drawn from Corey, G. (2013). *Theory and practice of counseling and psychotherapy* (9th ed.). Belmont, CA: Brooks/Cole.

The Counseling Techniques List (Table 5.2) provides a list of counseling and psychotherapy techniques that, while not all-inclusive, does represent techniques used by a broad spectrum of philosophical bases. The number of counseling techniques used by any one counselor varies. If a counselor reviews his/her tape recordings from several sessions with different clients, 10 to 15 different techniques may be identified that were used frequently with competence. An additional 10 to 15 may be identified that were used but with less frequency or, in some cases, with less professional competence. Suggestions for using the accompanying Counseling Techniques List are dependent on one's professional development. However, students have used the list primarily in two ways:

1. to check out and expand their knowledge about counseling techniques and
2. to introspect into their own counseling, philosophical bases, and treatment approaches.

Please read the directions for completing Table 5.2. These directions should be read in their entirety before proceeding with the completion of the form.

Be sure to reflect on the connections you have noticed between your answers to the questions posed about your values related to theory, the theories or aspects of theories you preferred on Table 5.1, and the techniques and theories you have identified on Table 5.2.

Extending the Counselor's Theory-Based Approaches: Brief Therapies and Evidence-Based Practices

The practicum/internship student in mental health agencies frequently is confronted with the reality of having to use treatment methods capable of delivering low-cost, quality mental health services. The need to employ brief therapeutic strategies in counseling has exploded onto the scene as a result of our present-day managed care environment. Most health care companies today limit the number of outpatient visits for mental health concerns that members are allowed each year (Remley & Herlihy, 2016). School counselors as well may find some brief therapies that are appropriate to use with students, as students who require long-term counseling are usually referred to mental health agencies. Similarly, it is increasingly expected that counselors will have knowledge of and skill in employing some evidence-based therapies (EBTs). Many of the EBTs spring from a cognitive-behavioral base and are sometimes called third wave cognitive behavioral approaches. They focus on helping clients adjust not just the content of their thoughts, but the process of thinking, as well.

Brief Therapies

The following sections of the text are designed to provide counseling students with a sampling of the varied approaches to brief therapy. In some cases, students will be familiar with and have training in these models. In other cases, this section might provide students with their first exposure to models of brief therapy. In any case, students need to become familiar with and skilled in the implementation of brief therapeutic interventions and strategies.

Solution-Focused Brief Therapy

Solution-focused brief therapy is based on the work of de Shazer and associates (de Shazer, 1989, 1990; de Shazer & Berg, 1985), who developed a model of therapy that was brief by design and was based on focused solution development. Some of the guiding principles of solution-focused therapy include the following:

1. the notion that the power of resistance need not be a part of effective therapy but can be replaced by cooperation;
2. the principle that solution-focused therapy is intended to help clients become more competent at living their lives day by day; accordingly, this conception involves normalizing behavior and the constructing of new meaning from behavior; and
3. the belief that client–therapist interactions are directed by three rules: (a) if it ain't broke, don't fix it; (b) once you know what works, do more of it; and (c) if it doesn't work, don't do it again; do something else (de Shazer, 1990).

Solution-focused brief therapy differs from traditional approaches to therapy in a number of ways. The focus is not on the past but on the present and future. Behavior change is seen as the most effective approach to helping clients. De Shazer (1989, 1990) asserts that it is not necessary to know the cause of a problem to solve it and there is no necessary relationship between what caused the problem and how to solve it. Little attention is given to making a diagnosis, taking the client's history, or exploring the emergence of the problem (O'Hanlon & Weiner-Davis, 2003). An underlying assumption of solution-focused therapy is that people have the ability to resolve life's challenges but at times have lost their sense of direction or awareness of their competencies. Treatment planning in solution-focused therapy is based on the understanding that clients must be customers for change and come to the realization of the existence of exceptions to their problems when they occur. Treatment plans become a source of documentation of treatment appropriateness, efficacy, and accountability.

The client–therapist relationship is essential for the development of therapeutic interventions in solution-focused therapy. The therapeutic process works best when clients become involved, when they experience a positive relationship with the counselor, and when counseling addresses what clients see as being important (Murphy, 2008). According to de Shazer (1990), clients can be visitors, complainants, or customers, depending on both their views of themselves in relation to their problem and their willingness to take an active part in doing something to solve the problem. Customers are usually those individuals who are willing to do something about their problems. Customers are asked to do something and follow through by taking an active part in their own improvement. Similarly, what clients do to improve their situation between the time of the telephone call for an appointment and the first session can be important to the therapist in his/her search for exceptions to the problem. A client who is a complainant is one who describes a problem but is not able or willing to assume a role in constructing a solution. He/she generally expects the therapist to change some other person to whom he/she attributes the problem. The visitor client comes to therapy because someone else thinks the client has a problem. Both complainant and visitor clients have the potential to become customers based on skilled questioning and intervention (Corey, 2013). The underlying assumption of the solution-focused model is that clients come to therapy because they have a complaint, a problem, or both. Problems do not occur all the time. When clients choose to do something differently, in a way that does not involve the problem, problem behavior is less likely to occur, and exception behavior is more likely to be observed (de Shazer & Berg, 1985). It can be helpful to conceptualize the visitor, complainant, and customer in light of the stages of change described earlier in this chapter.

Both the client and the therapist construct exception behavior while exploring what happens when the problem does not occur (Gingerich, de Shazer, & Weiner-Davis, 1988). Another guiding principle of solution-focused therapy is to help the client become more competent at living life day by day. Using the EARS (elicit, amplify, reinforce, and start again) approach, the therapist elicits dialogue about exception behavior and positive thoughts and behaviors that the client reports about himself/herself and others. This process helps the client progress toward goal attainment. Reinforcing what the client has done to improve the situation by attaching positive thoughts and behaviors to his/her goals helps the client realize that his/her action makes a difference.

De Shazer (1990) employed what he called the miracle question: "Let's suppose tonight while you're asleep a miracle happens that solves all the problems that brought you here. How would you know that this miracle really happened? What would be different?" The miracle question helps the client to attain the future-focus and positive mindset that are central to solution-focused therapy. The therapist also uses exception questions and coping questions to get the client to examine his/her attempts at coping. The therapist believes that asking solution-focused questions helps clients become more aware of their resources and strengths and use them to make better choices for themselves. Finally, the focus of brief therapy is centered on specific, concrete, behavioral goals. Talking about goals and the steps taken to achieve them is essential for positive outcomes. Both the client and the therapist need to know where they are going and how they are going to get there for brief therapy to be successful. The therapy process involves five steps:

1. The client describes the problems.
2. The therapist and client develop goals as soon as possible.
3. The therapist and client explore the times when problems were less severe. They explore these exceptions and how they happened.
4. After each solution-building conversation, the therapist provides feedback, encouragement, and suggestions about what to do before the next session to further solve the problem.
5. The therapist and client evaluate the progress made by using a rating scale, and the client identifies what the next step will be (De Jong & Berg, 2008).

Strategic Solution-Focused Therapy

"What's the trouble?" "If it works, do more of it." "If it doesn't work, don't do it anymore. Do something different." These are some of the guiding principles of strategic solution-focused therapy. This method, developed by Quick (1998), combines the theories and procedures of brief strategic therapy (Fisch, Weakland, & Segal, 1982) and solution-focused therapy (de Shazer, 1985).

"What's the trouble?" and "Do something different" are principles derived from brief strategic therapy, a model developed at the Mental Research Institute in Palo Alto, California, in the 1960s and 1970s, which stressed the idea that people generally attempt to solve problems by doing what makes sense to them. In contrast, the "If it works, do more of it" principle comes from a model developed at the Brief Family Therapy Center in Milwaukee, Wisconsin, in the 1970s and 1980s.

The strategic solution-focused model integrates these parent models in two main ways: (a) by combining brief strategies of focusing on clarification of the problem with the solution-focused emphasis on elaboration of the solution and (b) by blending the solution-focused emphasis on maintaining what works with the strategic emphasis on interrupting what does not work. Strategic solution-focused therapy is always tailored to the needs of the client. The following is a summary of some of the major principles and techniques of strategic solution-focused therapy.

The initial step in strategic solution-focused therapy is clarifying the client's complaint and identifying the highest-priority problem. The highest-priority problem is the problem to resolve to make the biggest positive difference in the client's life. The therapist wants to know the who, what, when, and where of what happened. Does the client's complaint result in a behavioral excess or deficit? The therapist's focus is to try to clarify what happened at this particular time that makes this problem an immediate issue. The therapist wants to clarify the client's expectations of how therapy is supposed to be helpful. Clarification of the primary problem is an important consideration throughout therapy. It is the therapist's job to find out from the client what problems or issues should be the focus in sessions.

The next step is the elaboration of the solution. "What will be different in the client's life?" "What will let the client know that things are moving in the right direction?" "What will be the first signs of change?" A focused inquiry invites the client to amplify the solution scenario, elaborating on what will be different as a result of lasting changes. When the solution has been elaborated, the therapist invites the client to describe how he/she has begun to make the positive changes happen. If the primary problem has been identified, the focus shifts to what will be different when that specific issue is resolved.

The next step is assessing what has already been done and suggested in previous attempts to solve the problem. With questions like "What has been done?" and "What have you tried?" the therapist focuses on specific attempts at problem solution. The therapist looks for main themes among attempted solutions, particularly unsuccessful ones, in an attempt to avoid trying them again (Quick, 1998).

Near the end of the session, the therapist asks if the client wants feedback or input. The therapist will also compliment the client on realizations that he/she has made in the session. This suggestion component of therapy depends on what has or has not worked for the client. If things are working out, the suggestion may be to continue and amplify existing behaviors. On the other hand, if attempted solutions are not working, the suggestion may be designed to interrupt the behavior. General or specific suggestions may be offered to the client by the therapist.

"Keep doing what works for you, or do something different." It is important to remember that the needs of the client and the intervals between sessions are highly variable. Termination might include encouragement to continue doing what works or to slowly make additional changes (Quick, 1998).

Cognitive Restructuring Brief Therapy

Cognitive restructuring brief therapy emphasizes the acquisition of new beliefs and thought patterns. The central notion is that clients build internal "schemas" of self and the world to organize their perceptions (Goldfried, 1988; Moretti, Feldman, & Shaw, 1990). Early experiences can lead to the development of negative schemas, which can affect one's perception of the self, world, and future. According to Beck (Beck, Rush, Shaw, & Emery, 1979), the counselor collaboratively helps the client to marshal evidence that disconfirms negative schemas.

Rational Emotive Behavior Therapy

According to Steenbarger (1992), Albert Ellis, the founder of rational emotive therapy, took a different restructuring approach to brief therapy. The focus in rational emotive therapy is on identifying faulty beliefs as a link between activating events and emotional and behavioral consequences. Challenging, confronting, and disputing irrational beliefs is an attempt to reshape irrational thought patterns. Ellis, unlike Beck, relied on confrontation rather than on collaborative helping to get at the client's irrational thoughts.

Coping Skills Brief Therapy

This method represents a teaching approach to counseling in which clients learn to solve difficult life problems and cope with anticipated stresses (Steenbarger, 1992). The focus of this approach to brief therapy is on the use of cognition and behavioral methods in the development of life skills that promote self-efficacy (Bandura, 1977). Coping skills brief therapy relies heavily on in-session and between-session exercises.

Evidence-Based Practices and Third Wave Therapies

Evidence-based practices or third wave therapies were born from the behavioral school of therapy. The first generation was traditional behaviorism. The second generation was cognitive behavioral therapy. The current "third wave" generation includes contextual approaches to behavior change (Hayes, 2005; Hayes & Hofmann, 2017). The third wave of cognitive behavioral therapy has an existential component that assumes that suffering is a basic characteristic of human life. The change from behaviorism and cognitive behavioral therapy includes acceptance and mindfulness-based techniques. This third wave includes mindfulness-based therapy (MBT), mindfulness-based stress reduction (MBSR), mindfulness-based cognitive therapy (MBCT), acceptance and commitment therapy (ACT), and dialectical behavioral therapy (DBT). Many of these approaches are identified as evidence-based approaches to therapeutic care.

Mindfulness-Based Therapy (MBT)

Mindfulness refers to a process that leads to a mental state of nonjudgmental awareness of the present-moment experience including one's sensations, thoughts, bodily states, consciousness, and the environment, while encouraging openness, curiosity, and acceptance (Bishop et al., 2004; Kabat-Zinn, 2003). The basic premise underlying mindfulness practices is that experiencing the present moment nonjudgmentally can counter the effects of stressors because excessive orientation to the past or future can be related to feelings of depression and anxiety (Hofman, Sawyer, Witt, & Oh, 2010). Some approaches to MBT, such as MBSR and MBCT, require that the therapist practice mindfulness meditation both personally and as part of the treatment protocol. However, to introduce into therapy mindfulness techniques such as watching the breath or labeling emotions, the therapist needs suitable instruction and supervision to try the techniques. Germer, Siegel, and Fulton (2005) identify the key elements in mindfulness techniques as (a) awareness, (b) of present moment, (c) with acceptance.

Awareness: Awareness techniques involve a stopping or slowing down of our activity. For example, one can stop arguing on the phone by stopping and taking a deep conscious breath. Or one can slow down any activity to observe the activity in more detail such as mindful eating or mindful walking while attending to each detail. One can stop talking and remain silent. One can sit still, close one's eyes, and allow the mind to settle.

Awareness techniques involve observing. Observing as a mindful practice is not observing in an objective, detached manner but rather "calmly abiding" as a participant observer. In order to turn one's attention from any rumination to be able to observe, it is effective to focus on a particular object. The most common object of focus in mindfulness is the breath. As one shifts the focus of attention to the breath, you can begin to note the sensations, feelings, and thoughts that naturally arise. You can notice that your heart is pounding or that you forgot to make a doctor's appointment. Each mental event is there to be noted without judging, analyzing, or suppressing it. One notes only what it is that takes attention away from the breath. In the beginning, noticing the moment-to-moment experience is facilitated by labeling the experience, such as "thinking," "feeling," "fear," "anger," or "worry."

Awareness techniques include a return to awareness of the breath. Returning is the final awareness technique. When you notice you are distracted or absorbed by a thought, you "wake up," note what took your attention, and gently return awareness to the breath. Then, watch where the mind wanders next. Waking up is a moment of mindfulness. Whenever necessary, you can return to the breath and anchor your attention.

Present moment: All mindfulness activities bring attention to the present. However, there are times when we need to focus on our goals to avoid making errors. An example would be if you feel angry while operating dangerous machinery. It would be dangerous to attend to your emotions. You must pour all your attention into the task at hand. Wise direction of attention to an activity in the present moment is a core mindfulness exercise. Mindfulness practice is training the attention to focus on present experience. If you are peeling an orange, notice the juice, the smell, the feel of the skin. If you are sitting with a young child as he/she plays, be there fully in the moment, attending to all your senses. Sometimes, you will continue to think of other things, such as a work dilemma. A question for yourself is "Do you know where your attention is now?" Any instruction to return to the present moment is a mindfulness exercise.

Acceptance: Acceptance means to accept our experience without judgment or preference, with curiosity and kindness. Our acceptance is always incomplete and must be cultivated because we never really stop judging. A client can be encouraged to "relax into" or "soften into" an experience. One can "breathe into" an aversive experience such as pain. Goldstein (1993) suggests using a mantra such as "It's OK, just let me feel this" or "Let it be."

Therapists can design mindfulness exercises by prescribing momentary breaks from activities, directing the client to anchor attention in the breath and notice the sensations, thoughts, and feelings that arise.

Mindfulness-Based Stress Reduction (MBSR)

MBSR is an approach developed by Jon Kabat-Zinn. It consists of several forms of mindfulness practice including formal and informal meditation practice as well as hatha yoga (Kabat-Zinn, 1990).

Formal meditation practice consists of breathing-focused attention, body scan–based attention, shifting of the attention across sensory modalities, open monitoring of moment-to-moment experience, walking meditation, or eating meditation. Informal practice includes brief pauses involving shifting the attention to present-moment awareness. This package of mindfulness practices aims to enhance the ability to observe the immediate content of experience (Goldin & Gross, 2000). MBSR is provided in eight weekly group classes and one full day of mindfulness.

Mindfulness-Based Cognitive Therapy (MBCT)

MBCT is based on an integration of aspects of cognitive behavioral therapy for depression and components of the MBSR program. The focus of MBCT is to teach clients to become more aware of thoughts and feelings and to relate to them in a decentered perspective as "mental events" rather than as aspects of the self or as accurate reflections of reality (Teasdale et al., 2002). Mindfulness components from MBSR are combined with aspects of cognitive behavioral therapy that are designed to facilitate decentered views such as "Thoughts are not facts" and "I am not my thoughts." MBCT helps one see the patterns of the mind and know how to recognize when your mood begins to go down. It helps to break the connection between negative mood and negative thinking. In this approach, clients are taught to develop the ability to disengage from distressing moods and negative thoughts. MBCT has been demonstrated as effective in relapse prevention for patients in remission following three major depressive episodes, and it is used as a treatment method for a variety of other clinical issues, including insomnia, chronic pain, anxiety, and trauma symptoms among others (Eisendrath, 2016). MBCT is provided in eight weekly group classes and one full day of mindfulness practice between weeks 5 and 7. Much of the work also is done at home between classes.

Acceptance and Commitment Therapy (ACT)

A basic assumption in ACT is that a person can take action without first changing or eliminating feelings. Acceptance-based approaches state that instead of only opting for change, a more effective approach is to accept and change. ACT suggests that both behavior and emotion can exist simultaneously and independently. For example, a patient may say, "I can't work today because I am too anxious about what the boss may say about my work evaluation." However, it is possible to go to work while feeling anxious. The goal of ACT is to help clients choose to act effectively (concrete behaviors as defined by their values) in the presence of difficult or disruptive "private" (cognitive or psychological) events (Dewane, 2008). In ACT, the client accepts the effects of life's hardships, chooses directional values, and takes action. The theory holds that much of what we call psychopathology is the result of the human tendency to avoid negatively valued private events (what we think and feel). This is called *psychological inflexibility*. The goal of ACT is to "increase psychological flexibility—the ability to contact the present moment more fully as a conscious human being and to change or persist in behavior when doing so serves valued ends" (Hayes, Luoma, Bond, Misuka, & Lillis, 2006, p. 8). In ACT, the aim is to transform our relationship with our difficult thoughts and feelings so that we no longer perceive them as symptoms. Instead, we learn to perceive them as harmless, even if uncomfortable, transient psychological events (Harris, 2006). ACT can be used with individuals, couples, and groups, as brief or long-term therapy with a wide range of clinical populations.

Psychological flexibility is achieved through six core processes:

Acceptance: This is taught as an alternative to experiential avoidance; for example, anxiety patients are taught to feel anxiety as a feeling, fully and without defense.

Cognitive diffusion: ACT attempts to change the way a person interacts with or relates to thoughts. For example, a person could thank his/her mind for such an interesting thought or label the process of thinking ("I am thinking that I am no good").

Being present: ACT promotes ongoing nonjudgmental contact with psychological and environmental events as they occur. Language is used more as a tool to note and describe events than to predict and judge them.

Self as context: Self is a context for verbal knowing, not the content of that knowing. One can be aware of one's own flow of experiences without an attachment to them or an investment in what experiences occur. Mindfulness exercises and metaphors are used to foster this process.

Values: Values are chosen qualities of purposive action. ACT uses exercises to help clients choose life directions in family, career, spirituality, and other domains. Verbal processes that lead to choices based on avoidance, social compliance, and fusion are discouraged.

Committed action: This requires setting goals, guided by your values, and taking effective action to achieve them (Hayes et al., 2006).

Dialectical Behavior Therapy (DBT)

DBT is a combination of group skills training and individual therapy designed for the treatment of complex, difficult-to-treat borderline personality disorder (BPD; Linehan, 1993a, 1993b) and is currently used to treat other severe mental disorders such as substance dependence in persons with BPD; depressed, suicidal adolescents; and depressed elderly (Dimeff & Linehan, 2001). DBT is based on a motivational model that states "that (1) people with BPD lack important interpersonal self-regulation (including emotional regulation) and distress tolerance skills; and (2) personal and environmental factors often block and/or inhibit the use of behavioral skills that clients do have and reinforce dysfunctional behaviors" (p. 10). DBT combines basic behavioral strategies with Eastern mindfulness practices. The fundamental dialectic is between the radical acceptance and validation of the client's current capabilities and behavioral functioning and simultaneous attempts to help them change. Treatment includes structured skills-training group sessions, individual psychotherapy to address motivation and skills training, and regular phone contact with the therapist to support the use of coping skills. Therapists working with this client population often experience burnout; consequently, therapist consultation and support are included in the model.

Acceptance strategies in DBT include mindfulness (attention to the present moment, a nonjudgmental stance, focus on effectiveness) and validation. Change strategies include behavioral analysis of maladaptive behaviors and problem-solving techniques such as skills training, use of reinforcers and punishment, cognitive modification, and exposure-based strategies. Weekly group sessions emphasize skills in mindfulness, interpersonal effectiveness, distress tolerance/reality acceptance, and emotional regulation. Therapists who are DBT practitioners require extensive training and support in the use of this therapeutic approach.

Summary

This chapter has added to the development of cognitive counseling skills for the counselor-in-training by reviewing resources focused on goal setting, treatment planning, and theory-based approaches to treatment. Several models and formats for applied practice in these cognitive areas have been presented as well as self-assessment questionnaires concerning theory and theory-based techniques to guide your progress toward developing your own theoretical approach to your counseling practice.

References

Bandura, A. (1977). Self-efficacy: Toward a unifying theory of behavioral change. *Psychological Review, 84*(2), 191–215.

Beck, A. T., Rush, A. J., Shaw, B. E., & Emery, G. (1979). *Cognitive therapy for depression.* New York, NY: Guilford.

Bishop, S., Lau, M., Shapiro, S., Carlson, L., Anderson, N., & Carmody, J. (2004). Mindfulness: A proposed operational definition. *Clinical Psychology: Science and Practice, 11*(3), 230–241.

Corey, G. (2013). *Theory and practice of counseling and psychotherapy* (9th ed.). Belmont, CA: Brooks/Cole.

Cormier, S. (2016). *Counseling strategies and interventions* (9th ed.). Upper Saddle River, NJ: Pearson.

Cormier, S., Nurius, P. S., & Osborne, C. J. (2009). *Interviewing and change strategies for helpers* (6th ed.). Belmont, CA: Brooks/Cole.

De Jong, P., & Berg, I. K. (2008). *Interviewing for solutions* (3rd ed.). Belmont, CA: Brooks/Cole.

de Shazer, S. (1985). *Keys to solution in brief therapy.* New York, NY: Norton.

de Shazer, S. (1989). Resistance revisited. *Contemporary Family Therapy, 11*(4), 227–233.

de Shazer, S. (1990). What is it about brief therapy that works? In J. K. Zeig & S. G. Gillian (Eds.), *Brief therapy: Myths, methods, and metaphors* (pp. 120–150). New York, NY: Brunner/Mazel.

de Shazer, S., & Berg, I. K. (1985). A part is not apart: Working with only one of the partners present. In A. S. Gurman (Ed.), *Casebook of marital therapy* (pp. 97–110). New York, NY: Guilford.

Dewane, C. (2008). ABC's of ACT. *Social Work Today, 8*(5), 34.

Dimeff, L., & Linehan, M. M. (2001). Dialectical behavior therapy in a nutshell. *California Psychologist, 34,* 10–13.

Dimick, K., & Krause, F. (Eds.). (1980). *Practicum manual for counseling and psychotherapy.* Muncie, IN: Accelerated Development.

Eisendrath, S. J. (2016). Introduction. In S. Eisendrath (Ed.), *In Mindfulness-based cognitive therapy: Innovative applications* (pp. 1–6). Basel, Switzerland: Springer.

Fisch, R., Weakland, J. H., & Segal, L. (1982). *The tactics of change.* San Francisco, CA: Jossey/Bass.

Gehart, D. R. (2013). *Theory and treatment planning in counseling and psychotherapy.* Belmont, CA: Brooks/Cole, Cengage.

Germer, C. K., Siegel, R. D., & Fulton, P. R. (Eds.). (2005). *Mindfulness and psychotherapy.* New York, NY: Guilford.

Gingerich, W. J., de Shazer, S., & Weiner-Davis, D. (1988). Constructing change: A research view of interviewing. In E. Lipchik (Ed.), *Interviewing* (pp. 21–32). Rockville, MD: Aspen.

Goldfried, M. R. (1988). Application of rational restructuring to anxiety disorders. *Counseling Psychologist, 16,* 50–68.

Goldin, P. R., & Gross, J. J. (2000). Effects of MBSR in emotion regulation in social anxiety disorder. *Emotion, 10*(1), 83–91.

Goldstein, J. (1993). *Insight meditation: The practice of freedom.* Boston, MA: Shambhala.

Harris, R. (2006). Embracing your demons. *Psychotherapy in Australia, 12*(4), 1–8.

Hayes, S. C. (2005). *Get out of your mind and into your life: The new acceptance and commitment therapy*. Oakland, CA: New Harbinger Publishing.

Hayes, S. C., & Hofmann, S. G. (2017). The third wave of cognitive behavioral therapy and the rise of process-based care. *World Psychiatry*, *16*(3), 245–246.

Hayes, S. C., Luoma, J. B., Bond, F. W., Misuka, A., & Lillis, J. (2006). Acceptance and commitment therapy: Model, processes and outcomes. *Behavior Research and Therapy*, *44*, 1–25.

Hofman, S. G., Sawyer, A. T., Witt, A. A., & Oh, D. (2010). The effect of mindfulness-based therapy on anxiety and depression: A meta-analytic review. *Journal of Consulting in Clinical Psychology*, *78*(2), 169–183.

Jongsma, A. E., & Peterson, M. (2006). *The complete psychotherapy treatment planner* (4th ed.). New York, NY: Wiley.

Kabat-Zinn, J. (1990). *Full catastrophe living: Using the wisdom of your body and mind to face stress, pain and illness*. New York, NY: Dell.

Kabat-Zinn, J. (2003). Mindfulness-based interventions in context: Past, present and future. *Clinical Psychology: Science and Practice*, *10*(2), 144–156.

Linehan, M. M. (1993a). *Cognitive behavioral therapy of borderline personality disorder*. New York, NY: Guilford.

Linehan, M. M. (1993b). *Skills training manual for treating borderline personality disorder*. New York, NY: Guilford.

Moretti, M. M., Feldman, L. A., & Shaw, B. (1990). Cognitive therapy: Current issues in theory and practice. In R. A. Wells & V. J. Giametti (Eds.), *Handbook of psychotherapy* (pp. 217–238). New York, NY: Plenum.

Murdock, N. (1991). Case conceptualization: Applying theory to individuals. *Counselor Education and Supervision*, *30*, 355–365.

Murphy, J. J. (2008). *Solution-focused counseling in schools* (2nd ed.). Alexandria, VA: American Counseling Association.

O'Hanlon, B., & Weiner-Davis, M. (2003). *In search of solutions: A new direction in psychotherapy*. New York, NY: Norton.

Prochaska, J. O., & Norcross, J. C. (2010). *Systems of psychotherapy: A transtheoretical analysis* (7th ed.). Belmont, CA: Brooks/Cole.

Quick, E. (1998). Doing what works in brief and intermittent therapy. *Journal of Mental Health*, *7*, 527–534.

Remley, T. P., Jr., & Herlihy, B. (2016). *Ethical, legal, and professional issues in counseling* (8th ed.) Upper Saddle River, NJ: Pearson.

Seligman, L. (1993). Teaching treatment planning. *Counselor Education and Supervision*, *35*(4), 287–298.

Spruill, D. A., & Benshoff, J. M. (2000). Helping beginning counselors develop a personal theory of counseling. *Counselor Education and Supervision*, *40*(1), 70–80.

Steenbarger, B. N. (1992). Toward science-practice integration in brief counseling and therapy. *Counseling Psychologist*, *20*(3), 403–451.

Sue, D. W., & Sue, D. (2016). *Counseling the culturally diverse: Theory and practice* (6th ed.). New York, NY: Wiley.

Teasdale, J., Moore, R., Hayhurst, H., Pope, M., Williams, S., & Segal, Z. (2002). Metacognitive awareness and prevention of relapse in depression: Empirical evidence. *Journal of Consulting and Clinical Psychology*, *70*(2), 275–287.

SECTION III

SUPERVISION IN PRACTICUM AND INTERNSHIP

CHAPTER 6

GROUP SUPERVISION IN PRACTICUM AND INTERNSHIP

The accreditation requirements of the Council for Accreditation of Counseling and Related Educational Programs (CACREP, 2016) for practicum and internship require that counseling students receive both individual and group supervision throughout the course of their field site–based experiences. Although these supervision processes may be conducted both by university-based faculty and field site–based supervisors, the focus on understanding and applying identified counseling skills is a common goal. In this chapter, we focus on the practices and activities that are likely to be included in group supervision classes during the practicum and internship.

Identifying Counseling Skill Areas

In this section, we address the need for, the categories of, and the skills necessary for professional counselor development. Remley and Herlihy (2016) emphasize that a primary focus on counseling skills forms the basis for master's degree programs in professional counseling. Development of those skills happens most intensely during the practicum and internship, and evaluation of counselor competencies is often best assessed by supervisors who provide individual and group supervision. The skill development framework presented here has been adapted from the work of Borders and Leddick (1997) and Borders and Brown (2005) on clinical supervision. Four broad skill areas have been identified as those within which self-assessment, peer consultation, supervisor assessment, goal identification, and evaluation can be implemented.

Skill Area One: Counseling Performance Skills

Counseling performance skills refers to "what the counselor does during the session" (Borders & Brown, 2005, p. 8) or his/her counseling behaviors. Performance skills are one primary area in which group supervisors in practicum and internship evaluate supervisees. These skills include the student supervisee's use of basic and advanced counseling skills, theory-based techniques, procedural skills, and professional and issue-specific skills.

Basic and Advanced Counseling Skills

The basic skills identified in the Egan and Reese model (Egan & Reese, 2019) established the core conditions of genuineness, respect and empathy, attending, active listening, appropriate use of probes, paraphrasing, reflecting feelings, clarifying, and summarizing. The more advanced skills involve presenting a greater degree of challenge to the client. Advanced helping skills presented in the model are interpretation, pointing out patterns and connections, identifying blind spots and discrepancies, self-disclosure, confrontation, and immediacy (Egan & Reese, 2019).

In the Ivey microskills model, the basic skill levels progress from attending behaviors to the basic listening sequence of open and closed questions, client observation, encouraging, paraphrasing and summarizing, and reflection of feeling. At the next level, the skills of confrontation, focusing, reflection of meaning, interpretation, and reframing are added. Finally, the key skills of interpersonal influence—self-disclosure, feedback, logical consequences, information/psychoeducation, and directives—further build on the range of skills (Ivey, Ivey, & Zalaquett, 2014).

Theory-Based Techniques

Theory-based techniques refer to the use of intervention techniques and strategies consistent with a chosen theoretical approach to case conceptualization and treatment planning. Examples might include such things as behavioral charts that coincide with cognitive behavioral therapy, the empty chair technique that comes out of Gestalt therapy, and the miracle question that corresponds with solution-focused therapy.

Procedural Skills

Procedural skills are those skills the counselor uses to manage the opening and closing of sessions and to provide a transition from session to session. These skills are especially important for new counselors to master as they help to suggest the counselor's competence and confidence to clients, create continuity between sessions, solidify key elements of sessions, allow for check-in with regard to homework, and advance counselors' ethical practices. Learning how to terminate with clients appropriately is particularly important as improper termination is a frequently cited ethical sanction for non-independently licensed counselors.

Professional and Issue-Specific Skills

Professional and issue-specific skills refer to the way the counselor understands, integrates, and responds to issues related to professional ethics and the law, as well as the way the counselor responds to crisis-related situations. In supervision, the university or site-based supervisor often focus attention on a trainee's recognition of ethics issues and dilemmas, and ability to respond to ethics issues with professionalism and in keeping with standard of care expectations.

Skill Area Two: Cognitive Counseling Skills

Cognitive counseling skills refer to the counselor's ability to think about the counseling session and to form a comprehensive sense of the client's presenting problems and issues (Borders & Brown, 2005). Related skills include the writing of intake summaries and case notes; assessment, diagnosis, and case conceptualization; and goal setting, treatment planning, and theory orientation.

Skill Area Three: Self-Awareness/Multicultural Awareness Skills

Self-awareness involves a counselor's recognition of how personal issues, beliefs, and motivations may influence in-session behavior, as well as case conceptualization (Borders & Brown, 2005).

Similarly, multicultural awareness involves a counselor's recognition of how personal issues, beliefs, and motivations may influence the worldview of the counselor and the worldview of clients from diverse cultures. We have adapted Skill Area Three to include multicultural awareness because it deeply influences the counseling process. Corey (2013) asserted that counselors have an ethical obligation to develop sensitivity to cultural differences and to help clients make decisions that are congruent with their own worldviews. Goals must be defined that are consistent with the life experiences and cultural values of the client, not the therapist.

Self-Awareness Skills

This skill area starts with the recognition of how personal values and biases affect the counseling process and progresses toward a counselor's ability to integrate this awareness into the counseling process. These skills sometimes are referred to as reflective skills and are defined as "the ability to examine and consider one's own motives, attitudes and behaviors and one's effect on others" (Hatcher & Lassiter, 2007, p. 53). Self-awareness skills help counselors to become aware of how their personal unresolved issues may get projected onto the client. This is called countertransference. Countertransference influences the way a counselor perceives and reacts to the client. Counselors can become emotionally reactive, respond defensively, or be unable to be truly present because their own issues are involved.

Multicultural Awareness Skills

The interrelationship between self-awareness and multicultural awareness may seem obvious; however, both these processes require ongoing work and focus as you develop as a counselor. The area of multicultural awareness and competency continues to be emphasized strongly in training programs as the profession has recognized the importance of understanding how diversity influences the counseling relationship. Culture impacts gender relationships, authority relationships, communication patterns, expressions of formality/informality, family dynamics and expectations, ideas of power and privilege, and ideas about economic differences, to name a few. Cormier (2016) noted that achieving cultural competency does not happen overnight but is a long-term process. She recommended the following actions to develop multicultural awareness and skills:

- Become aware of your own culture and the impact it has on the counseling relationship.
- Become involved in cultures of people different from you.
- Be realistic and honest about your own range of experience and issues of power, privilege, and poverty.
- Educate yourself about dimensions of culture.
- Be aware of your own biases and prejudices.
- Broach cultural issues with the client and be willing to explore issues of diversity.

Skill Area Four: Developmental Level

Developmental level refers to the process of moving from being a novice counselor to becoming a professional counselor. This level is inferred based on how supervisees function on a continuum from dependence on the supervisor and the supervision process toward functioning at a collegial level with the supervisor. Developmental level as a skill area addresses the following elements:

- the ability to establish a working alliance with your supervisor,
- the ability to participate in an evaluation of your counseling practice,
- the ability to examine your work in a non-defensive manner,
- an openness to new learning and a continuing practice of refining your clinical thinking,
- an openness to reflecting on and examining your own dynamics as they relate to clients,
- an ability to reflect on and examine multicultural issues appropriate to your counseling practice,
- the ability to identify the strengths and weaknesses in your counseling practice, and
- an understanding of what you might need from supervision.

Self-Assessment in the Skill Areas

We suggest that the group supervision class in practicum begin with reviewing the skill areas and conducting a number of self-assessment activities. This allows the counseling student to become familiar with the skill development model that will form the framework for supervision processes throughout the practicum and internship. It also facilitates the process of forming specific goals for the counseling student to bring to the supervisor as they negotiate a supervision contract that will be the basis for both formative and summative evaluation. We have provided a number of self-assessment instruments and exercises in the Forms section at the back of the text. Other self-assessment instruments and exercises that focus on individual skill areas are the Counseling Techniques List (Form 5.1), the Self-Assessment of Counseling Performance Skills (Form 6.1), the Self-Awareness/Multicultural Awareness Rating Scale (Form 6.2), and the Directed Reflection Exercise on Supervision (Form 6.3).

At the completion of this self-assessment process, the counseling student should be able to identify specific goals in each skill area that will become the initial focus for both group and individual supervision. A sample of a goal statement that can give focus and direction to the supervision process is provided below. The Supervisee Goal Statement (Form 6.4) can be completed each time you reassess and move toward increased skill levels during practicum and internship.

SAMPLE SUPERVISEE GOAL STATEMENT (FORM 6.4)

Directions: You should complete this and provide a copy to your individual and/or group supervisor at the beginning of supervision. This will assist you in forming the supervisory contract with your supervisor.

Student's name: _____

Supervisor's name: _____   Date submitted: _____

Counseling Performance Skills

1. Demonstrate the application of facilitative and challenging skills in client interviews.
2. In initial sessions with clients, be able to integrate giving informed consent and privacy information.

3. Be able to help client form goals about changes needed to improve and move toward healthier choices, behaviors, or feelings.

Cognitive Counseling Skills

1. Complete initial intake processes and be able to write an intake summary.
2. Perform appropriate assessment and understand how this can be helpful in identifying the client's strengths and weaknesses.
3. Become skilled in writing case notes.

Self-Awareness/Multicultural Awareness Skills

1. Actively examine any biases that would affect my counseling—especially in setting goals that are consistent with my client's worldview.
2. Increase my understanding and awareness of countertransference as it affects my counseling practice.
3. Increase my contact with clients and others whose culture I am not familiar with.

Developmental Level

1. Decrease my self-consciousness about reviewing tapes of my counseling sessions.
2. Increase my confidence about asking questions (don't worry about seeming unskilled).
3. Be open to my supervisor's suggestions.

As the counseling student progresses from pre-practicum to practicum to internship the focus of skill development in supervision shifts as the counseling student becomes more skilled in the practice of counseling. Figure 6.1 provides a visual schematic of this progression.

Concepts in Group Supervision

Concepts about the group supervision experience influence the kinds and range of activities, the process of supervisory and consulting interaction, and the nature of the teaching contract between the counseling student and the university professor. Such concepts provide the foundation of this experiential component of professional training.

   This section presents a typical conceptual framework for group supervision that can be used as a reference for the student who is beginning the practicum and internship experience. Some concepts may be used as a point of departure for discussion, and others may be modified and/or challenged.

1. *Group supervision in counseling is a highly individualized learning experience* in which the counseling student is met at the level of personal development, knowledge, and skills that he/she brings to the experience. The student has the responsibility to bring in material about his/her counseling practice and to share any concerns related to practice.
2. *Group supervision facilitates an understanding of one's self, one's biases, and one's impact on others.* Whatever the theoretical orientation of counseling, practicum and internship students must personally examine those qualities about themselves that may enhance or impede their counseling. The group supervision experience provides the setting in which personal

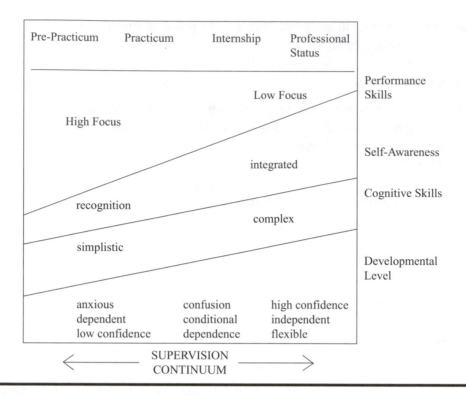

Figure 6.1   Schematic Representation of Relative Goal Emphasis in Supervision and the Shift in Goal Emphasis as the Student Progresses From Pre-practicum to Completion of Internship

qualities related to counseling practice can be examined. Focus in supervision is directed not only toward determining the dynamics and personal meaning of the client but also toward examining how the student views others and how his/her behaviors and attitudes affect others. Counseling students must also examine the cultural biases and assumptions they, knowingly or unknowingly, may be imposing on the understandings and goals being established for the client.

3. *Each member of a practicum and internship supervision group is capable of and responsible for facilitating professional growth and development.* The group supervision experience usually involves dyadic, individual, and group activities designed to enhance the quality of counseling practice. Each member of the supervision group participates not only as a student but also as someone who is able to provide valuable feedback to others regarding the impact particular responses and attitudes can have on clients.

4. *Group supervision is composed of varied experiences*, which are determined by the particular needs, abilities, and concerns of the group members and the professor. These may be personal concerns of the student or concerns related to client needs brought back to the group supervision class for discussion. Therefore, group supervision, by necessity, must have a flexible and formative approach to planning learning activities.

5. *Supervision and consultation form the central core of the practicum/internship experience.* Intensive supervision and consultation allow the student to move more quickly toward competence and mastery in counseling or therapy. The supervisory interaction can help make the student more aware of obstacles to the counseling process so that they can be examined and modified. The supervisory interaction also provides the opportunity for the role-modeling process to be strengthened.

6. *Self-assessment by the student and professor is essential.* Because of the flexible and formative nature of group supervision in practicum and internship, regular reviews need to be made of how the group supervision experiences are meeting the learning needs of the student. Self-assessment allows the student to be consciously aware of and responsible for his/her own development and also provides information for the professor in collaborating on appropriate group supervision activities.

7. *Evaluation is an integral and ongoing part of the practicum/internship.* Evaluation in group supervision provides both formative information and summative information about how the counseling development goals of the student and professor are being reached. A variety of activities support this evaluation process. Among these are self-assessment, peer evaluations, regular feedback activities, site supervisor ratings, and audio and video recording review. The attitude from which evaluations are offered is characterized by a "constructive" coaching perspective rather than a "critical" judgmental perspective.

Group Supervision in Practicum

Group supervision course requirements are designed to support and monitor the evolving skill and knowledge base of the student. Practicum students are expected to spend a minimum of 1.5 hours per week in a group session with the university supervisor. This time can include didactic and experiential activities and will include some form of review of counseling practices.

In addition to attending the weekly group meetings, students are required to engage in a specified number of counseling sessions each week. These may be both individual and group sessions. Early in the course, the typical amount of required sessions would be fewer in number than in the middle and final phases of the course. A specific minimum number of sessions is required for the course. Moreover, accreditation guidelines require that students receive both individual and group supervision during the practicum. Guidelines and reference materials regarding individual supervision in practicum and internship will be reviewed in Chapter 7. Practicum students are expected to record (audio and video) their counseling sessions. Of course, permission must be obtained from each client prior to recording the session (see Forms 3.1a, 3.1b, and 3.2 at the end of the book). The practicum site will have policies and procedures that must be followed to ensure the informed consent of the client. The recordings are to be submitted regularly to the university supervisor who is providing individual supervision to allow for sharing and evaluation. In some programs, the same university supervisor provides both group and individual supervision. In other programs, the student will have different university supervisors for group and individual supervision. Recorded sessions can be reviewed in either group or individual supervision sessions, or both. Each recording should be reviewed by the student prior to submission and be accompanied by a written or typed critique (Form 6.5).

Every effort must be made to ensure the confidentiality of the counseling session. Be sure to check about the procedures at your field site regarding recording of sessions and the required safeguards and consents with regard to recording sessions for supervision purposes. When the recording has been reviewed and discussed with the student counselor, appropriate notes regarding counseling performance can be made for the counseling student's records. The recordings should then be erased.

A blank copy of a Recording Critique Form (Form 6.5) has been included in the Forms section for students' use. This form can be used to guide the student in developing a written review and analysis of recorded therapy sessions. A sample of a completed Recording Critique Form is provided in Figure 6.2.

Jean Smith
_____

Student counselor's name

Tom D. Session #3
_____

Client I.D. & no. of session

Brief summary of session content:

Tom is citing his reasons for being unhappy in his job situation and reviewing all he has

attempted to do to make his boss like and respect his work.
_____

_____

Intended goals:

1. To help Tom explore all of his feelings and experiences related to the job situation.
_____

2. To help Tom be able to assess and value his work from his own frame of reference

rather than his boss's.
_____

Comment on positive counseling behaviors:

I was able to accurately identify Tom's feelings and to clarify the connection of feelings

to specific content.
_____

_____

Comments on areas of counseling practice needing improvement:

I sometimes became hooked into Tom's thinking about how to please his boss and would

work with him about problem solving in this way.
_____

_____

Concerns or comments regarding client dynamics:
_____

_____

_____

Plans for further counseling with this client:

Continue weekly appointments; move focus back onto the client and try to identify other

ways he worries about approval.
_____

_____

Recording submitted to _____

Date _____

Figure 6.2   Sample Completed Recording Critique Form (Form 6.5)

We are providing excerpts from a practicum syllabus to the counselor-in-training as a representative sample of course objectives and assignments in group practicum. Students should note that additional and varied requirements may be included in the practicum experience.

SAMPLE OF COURSE OBJECTIVES AND ASSIGNMENTS IN GROUP PRACTICUM

Course Objectives

- To develop expertise in counseling, consulting, and guidance experiences
- To demonstrate an understanding of various counseling theories, techniques, and procedures
- To establish a facilitative and ongoing relationship with clients and on-site staff
- To demonstrate competence and skill in record keeping and case reporting
- To provide a safe place to share information about and reactions to your practicum experiences
- To define your professional identity as a counselor
- To develop skills in identifying and monitoring your strengths and growth edges
- To identify and examine personal issues that affect your work with clients
- To improve understanding of how multicultural issues interact with counseling practice
- To demonstrate an understanding of the ethical standards of the American Counseling Association (ACA) with respect to counseling practice.

Course Assignments

- This course is a supervised practicum experience that focuses on case conceptualization, client assessment and evaluation, oral and written case reporting, and evaluation of counseling performance in individual intervention. Each section of the practicum uses a concerns-based developmental group supervision model. In this model, students are expected to openly discuss current cases and professional issues in counseling, develop their own personal counseling styles, and participate in giving and receiving feedback. The methods of instruction will include minilectures, demonstrations, group discussions, and student presentations.
- *Precourse self-assessment:* Write a 4- to 5-page paper assessing yourself as a developing counselor. The paper should include the following: (a) your strengths as a counselor-in-training, (b) growth edges, (c) learning goals for the semester, (d) countertransference issues requiring additional examination and work, and (e) theoretical orientation(s) to which you subscribe. The paper must be written using APA style.
- *Clinical case presentation:* Each student will make one major case presentation. An oral description of the client should briefly address the information listed below. The focus of the presentation should be on discussing the unanswered questions. For the case presentation, students must bring the most recent video- or audiotaped session cued for viewing. The case presentation should be 20 to 30 minutes. Furthermore, a case conceptualization paper summarizing the information on Intake Summary, Background Information, Clinical Impressions, Client–Therapist Match, Treatment, Client's Progress to Date, and Unanswered Questions will be submitted to the instructor on the assigned due date. The paper should be 8 to 10 pages in length. Grading will focus on relevance of content, depth of reflection, and quality of writing. The paper must be written using APA style.
- *Postcourse self-assessment:* Write a 4- to 5-page paper reassessing yourself since you have completed your first semester as a counselor trainee. Please make note of areas that are simi-

lar to and different from your initial assessment. The paper should include the following: (a) strengths, (b) growth edges, (c) learning goals for future training, (d) countertransference issues, and (e) theoretical orientation(s).

* Adapted from a syllabus by Megan Curcianni, MS, NCC, LPC, and Janet Muse-Burke, PhD, Department of Psychology and Counseling, Marywood University, Scranton, PA. Reprinted with permission.

Activities in Group Supervision

A typical class session in group supervision would begin by addressing any specific concerns a student has regarding his/her practicum. After immediate concerns are addressed, the practicum student might engage in any of the following:

- doing self-assessment and skill development orientation;
- role-playing problem situations with clients encountered at the practicum site;
- listening to and discussing various recorded counseling sessions;
- reviewing previously recorded counseling sessions made by class members;
- discussing theories and techniques related to common problems and client work of concern to group members;
- giving and receiving feedback with peers regarding personal and professional interactions, including legal, ethical, and multicultural issues;
- participating in peer consultation group activities; and
- preparing and doing case presentations including assessments, case conceptualizations, goal setting, and treatment planning.

Peer Consultation

Peer supervision and consultation have been identified as a valuable adjunct to the supervision process (Bernard & Goodyear, 2014). This modality is, however, recommended with some precautions. Peer supervision should be used only as a supplement to regular supervision in practicum. The peer consultant can promote skill development through ratings and shared perceptions, but it is important to make sure that any peer supervision activities that are initiated occur after group supervision has provided sufficient training and practice. Peer supervision/consulting within the group supervision class with assigned peer dyads or small group consultation activities outside of class prepare counseling students to incorporate peer consultation activities into their ongoing work as a professional counselor. Peer collaboration has been referred to by a number of different terms in the literature (i.e., peer supervision, reflecting teams, peer consulting). For our purposes we will use the term *peer consulting*. The benefits of incorporating peer consultation into the group supervision process are that it

- fosters collegial supervision relationships;
- prepares the counseling student for continued use of peer consultation after the completion of training;
- fosters reciprocal learning, increased skills, and responsibility for self-assessment;
- decreases dependence on expert supervisors;

- emphasizes helping each other achieve self-determined goals rather than focusing on evaluation; and
- challenges the counselor to consider alternate perspectives (Benhoff & Paisley, 1996).

When involved in peer consultation activities, peers must assume a greater responsibility for providing critical feedback, challenge, and support to colleagues. As practicum students function as peer consultants, they are strengthening their own abilities to review their own work. A goal of peer consultation is enhanced self-awareness and a deeper understanding of the complexities of counseling (Granilla, Granilla, Kinsvetter, Underfer-Babulis, & Hartwood Moorhead, 2008). Suggested guidelines for peer consulting activities are as follows:

1. Comment on the case rather than solving it or giving advice.
2. Speak tentatively and speculatively about possible meanings or interpretations.
3. Ask questions and express curiosity.
4. Avoid judgment (Winslade & Monk, 2007).

Peer consultation can use directed feedback for client recordings, goal setting, case conceptualization, and theoretical orientation. It works best when applying structured supervision tools. After a particular counseling skill has been introduced, modeled, and practiced within the group context, peer rating of recordings can be implemented. We suggest that the peer critique of recordings be structured to focus on the rating of specific skills. For instance, the target skills might be identified as one or more of the facilitative skills such as basic empathy, use of open-ended questions, or concreteness. Other target skills could be the recognition and handling of positive or negative affect or the effective use of probes. The Peer Rating Form (Form 6.6) and the Interviewer Rating Form (Form 6.7) used to structure peer rating activities have been included in the Forms section.

Another approach to improving the use of functional basic skills is to teach students to identify their dysfunctional counseling behaviors and then to minimize those behaviors (Collins, 1990). Instead of rating functional skills, peer reviewers can measure the incidence of dysfunctional skills such as premature problem solving or excessive questioning in their review of counseling tapes. The goal would be for the counselor to decrease or eliminate dysfunctional counseling behaviors in actual sessions. Collins (1990), in a study of the occurrence of dysfunctional counseling behaviors in both role playing and real client interviews of social work students, identified the following as dysfunctional behaviors:

- *Poor beginning statements:* The session starts with casual talk or chitchat instead of engagement skills.
- *Utterances:* The counselor's responses consist of short utterances or one-word responses such as "uh-huh," "yeah," "okay," or "sure"; two different types of utterance responses rated were utterances (alone) and utterances (preceding a statement).
- *Closed questions:* The counselor asks questions that require one-word answers by clients, such as "yes" or "no" or their age or number of children.
- *Why questions:* The counselor asks statements starting with the word "why."
- *Excessive questioning:* The counselor asks three or more questions in a row without any clear reflective component to the questions (reflective component refers to restating content the client has expressed in his/her statements to the counselor).

- *Premature advice or premature problem solving:* The counselor gives advice that is considered premature, that is, advice given in the first 10 minutes of the session or after the first interview, judgmental statements, or problem solving where the counselor is doing the work for the client.
- *Minimization:* The counselor downplays the client's problem, gives glib responses, or offers inappropriate comments such as "Life can't be all that bad."

Another structured peer reviewing process could be implemented using Form 6.1, the Self-Assessment of Counseling Performance Skills. Instead of applying this to a self-assessment, the peer consultant group could use these items to rate counseling recordings presented by members of the group supervision class. The student who has a recording under review could choose the items for which he/she wants to receive feedback.

Borders (1991) presented a structured peer group supervision model (SPGS), which is based on a case presentation approach. In this model, the counselor provides a brief summary of a client and therapy issues. The counselor then provides a sample of a counseling session (audio or video recording). The counselor then identifies questions about the client or the recorded session and requests feedback. The peers are assigned roles, perspectives, or tasks for reviewing the recorded session.

The peers may perform *focused observations* on a skill, such as how well the counselor performs a confrontation, or on one aspect of a session, or on the relationship between the counselor and the client. Another assigned task may be *role taking*. Peers may be asked to take the perspective of the counselor, the client, or some significant person in the client's life.

Similarly, structured learning activities could focus instead on self-awareness or multicultural awareness questions posed by the counseling student who is requesting feedback. Several other strategies that may be included using the SPGS model will be suggested for use in the internship seminar.

Evaluation of Practicum in Group Supervision

Formative Evaluation

Assessment is provided by the supervisor at various times throughout the practicum. Continuing assessment of the student's work occurs regularly during weekly individual and/or group supervision sessions both at the field site and in the university setting. A mid-semester evaluation also often is incorporated into ongoing assessment. This regularly occurring feedback to the practicum student about his/her work is called formative assessment (Bernard & Goodyear, 2014). The supervisor is constantly assessing the student on a variety of skills, abilities, and cognitions. These evaluations can range from comments about a counseling technique to dialogue about a case conceptualization. Formative evaluations are usually verbal, and the supervisor often keeps notes on the content and process of the supervision. In group supervision, a number of assignments, both written and verbal, are assigned and evaluated as completed. Group interaction, which involves peer consultation and audio or video recording review, is observed and assessed related to the appropriate skill areas that were the focus. Evaluations from individual supervision are integrated into group supervision evaluations to determine the final grade in practicum.

Summative Evaluation

Summative evaluation occurs at the completion of practicum. The supervisor can give a narrative report of the student's progress, but more often the supervisor uses a standardized assessment instrument.

Form 7.5 (Supervisor's Final Evaluation of Practicum Student) offers a template for rating the student on recommended skill levels for transitioning into internship.

Transitioning Into Internship

The final evaluation in practicum serves two purposes. First, it serves as a decision point about whether or not the student is recommended to proceed into the internship phase of training. We must note that if there is a concern about the student's abilities to practice counseling with clients, the student should have been receiving supportive and honest formative assessments along the way. The student's group and individual supervisors would have collaborated and met with the student to discuss any ways that the situation could be remedied. Most programs have a procedure in place to address this situation. Second, summative evaluation in practicum provides the opportunity for the student to advance into the internship with a clearer identification of the skill development goals that he/she will pursue at the next level of training. Group supervision and individual supervision evaluations are both reviewed as part of the practicum student's final grade and evaluation.

Recommended Skill Levels for Transitioning Into Internship

Each training program will have considered the criteria related to the skill levels that must be met in order to recommend that the counselor-in-training proceed on to the internship. We are proposing the following skill levels as a guide for making this recommendation. The practicum student:

1. consistently demonstrates the use of basic and advanced helping skills;
2. has the ability to appropriately use additional theory-based techniques consistent with at least one theoretical framework;
3. demonstrates skill in opening and closing sessions and managing continuity between sessions;
4. demonstrates knowledge and integration of ethical standards into practice;
5. has cognitive skills of awareness, observation, and recognition of relevant data to explain some client dynamics;
6. writes accurate case notes, intake summaries, and case conceptualizations;
7. recognizes how several of his/her personal dynamics may impact a client and the counseling session and demonstrates sensitivity to cultural differences; and
8. demonstrates moderate to low levels of anxiety and moderate to low levels of dependency on supervisor direction during supervision sessions.

Group Supervision in Internship

CACREP accreditation guidelines stipulate that the internship student have an opportunity to become familiar with a variety of professional activities and resources in addition to direct service. They further require that the internship student receive an average of 1.5 hours per week of group supervision throughout the internship by program faculty or a student supervisor under the supervision of a faculty member. The student's counseling performance and ability to integrate and apply knowledge are subject to formative and summative evaluation as part of the internship

(CACREP, 2016). The guidelines of the Canadian Counselling and Psychotherapy Association's Council on Accreditation of Counsellor Education Programs require that students complete a 400-hour final practicum where students receive regularly scheduled individual supervision by qualified field site supervisors in collaboration with program faculty. A group supervision experience is not stipulated (Canadian Counselling and Psychotherapy Association, 2003). At the internship (final practicum) level, students will be further refining and progressing in their counseling practice of understanding and analyzing client concerns and implementing appropriate counseling interventions.

Hatcher and Lassiter (2007), in their article on practicum competencies in professional psychology, identified several levels of competence that apply to the progression of developing competencies in training. They proposed the following levels:

1. *Novice (N):* Novices have limited knowledge, understanding, and abilities in analyzing problems and implementing intervention skills. Distinguishing patterns and differentiating between important and unimportant details are limited. They do not yet have well-formed concepts about how clients change toward healthier functioning.

2. *Intermediate (I):* Students at this level have gained enough experience to recognize important patterns and can select interventions to respond to the presenting concerns. They understand and intervene beyond the surface level more typical of those at the Novice level, but generalizing diagnosis and intervention skills to new situations and clients is limited, and supervisory support is needed.

3. *Advanced (A):* At this level, the student has more integrated knowledge and understanding of client processes and can recognize recurring patterns and select appropriate intervention strategies. Treatment plans and case conceptualization are based on more integrated knowledge, and this understanding influences treatment actions taken. The student is less flexible than the proficient practitioner (the next level of competence) but has mastery and can cope with and manage a broader range of clinical work.

Internship students can reflect on this description of progressing toward proficiency when reviewing their own skill levels as they complete their practicum experience. In general, most students will have developed some confidence and skills in establishing therapeutic relationships with their clients, and they will be seeking a broader range of theory-based techniques that are consistent with their concepts of how people change to become healthier in their emotional and functional life situations. The focus of group supervision in internship shifts toward cognitive counseling skills with a concurrent integration of self-awareness/multicultural awareness and professional understanding into the counseling process.

The group supervision seminar in internship generally includes assignments that allow counselors-in-training to demonstrate how their clinical thinking skills are applied to their counseling practice. A typical seminar includes assignments such as the following:

- *Case Conceptualization Presentation and Paper:* Students are to present a case from their internship practice that outlines the presenting problem, psychiatric history, medical history, family history, educational/occupational history, mental status, assessment, diagnostic impressions, and treatment plan and goals and includes a sample of progress notes.
- *Integrative Paper:* Students will write a double-spaced, typewritten paper presenting their integrated approach to counseling. The paper is to be written in two parts. In Part I, students are

to cover their philosophical, theoretical, and practical view of (a) human health and dysfunction, (b) the role of the counselor, (c) the goals and methods of therapeutic change, and (d) the process of therapeutic change. In Part II, students are to present an illustrative case from their internship practice. A counseling case presentation is to be written, including a description of the case from intake through termination (including a prognostic statement).

■ The student will demonstrate the application of cultural diversity skills by showing the following competencies in counseling practice reviews:

Awareness of and respect for clients' cultural differences

Orientation to learning more about the client's culture as needed

Application of multicultural competencies to case conceptualization, diagnosis, interventions, and prevention work

Group Supervision Models in Internship

Bernard and Goodyear (2014, p. 181) define group supervision as

the regular meeting of a group of supervisees (a) with a designated supervisor; (b) to monitor the quality of their work; and (c) to further their understandings of themselves as clinicians, of the clients with whom they work, and of service delivery in general.

As the members of the supervision group move from novice to more advanced levels of skill, they typically interact at first with a focus on conceptualization and intervention and slowly move to more sharing regarding personalization.

The SPGS Model

We reviewed the SPGS model (Borders, 1991) in the section on peer consultation groups in practicum; the approach is similarly effective at the internship level. When using the SPGS model with novice counselors, the supervisor provides more direction and structure. When using this model with more advanced supervisees, the supervisees take on more responsibility. The supervisor serves as the moderator for the group and assures they stay on task. Then, the supervisor takes on the role of process commentator and offers feedback about group dynamics. The supervisor then summarizes the initial feedback and discussion and asks the presenting counselor if his/her supervision needs were met.

Lassiter, Napolitano, Culbreth, and Ng (2008) proposed an expansion of Borders's format to include a multicultural-intensive observer role for a peer responder. This person focuses on cultural matters represented in the session, including issues of cultural differences and assumptions, privilege, and power differentials. Another variation is to ask an observer to watch a recorded session by developing a *descriptive metaphor*. Borders found this useful when the supervision issue was the interpersonal dynamics between the counselor and the client, or when the counselor felt "stuck." A suggestion is for the observer to think of a road map and describe the direction the counselor is taking, or to think of the session as a movie and describe each actor's part in the drama.

For a focus on cognitive counseling skills, the counselor question and the peer assignment are on theoretical perspectives regarding

1. the assessment of the client,
2. the conceptualization of the issue or problem,
3. the goals of counseling,
4. the choice of intervention, and
5. the evaluation of progress (Borders & Brown, 2005).

After the counselor presents the taped segment of the counseling session, the group members give feedback from their theoretical perspectives. The presenting counselor then summarizes the feedback. This process facilitates the development of cognitive counseling skills and gives the supervisor the opportunity to observe the complexity and accuracy of the theoretical perspectives that are offered.

The Structured Group Supervision (SGS) Model

The SGS Model (Wilbur, Roberts-Wilbur, Hart, Morris, & Betz, 1994) begins with a supervisee making a "plea for help." This plea includes information about the case and often a sample from the session. The supervisee specifically states what he/she needs help with. The supervision group members then ask questions about the information presented to clear up any faulty assumptions or missing information. These are informational and clarifying questions. The supervisor monitors the dialogue so that group members do not offer premature feedback. The group members are given a few moments to think about how they would handle whatever was sought in the plea for help. Then, in orderly fashion, each member offers what he/she would do "if this were my client" or "if I had your concern." The supervisee remains silent but may take notes. This continues until there is no more feedback. At the conclusion of this feedback process, there is a 10- to 15-minute break in which the supervisee can think about the feedback. Group members do not converse with the supervisee during this break. After the break, the supervisee responds to the group by addressing each member to say what feedback was helpful and what feedback was not helpful and why. This is presented in a way that does not infer that the feedback was right or wrong but focuses more on the cultural fit, style of therapy, or history with the case. Depending on the needs of the group, the supervisor may summarize or discuss the process or reframe an issue to invite the group to look at it in another possible way. Comments on the group process or comments about the case are offered as "something to think about." Supervisees are affirmed for being open and taking the risk in allowing themselves to be vulnerable.

Evaluation in Group Supervision of Internship

Your internship grade is determined by your university supervisor in collaboration with your field site supervisor and given upon the completion of your internship contract. Certification of your internship hours is done by the site supervisor. Evaluations from your individual supervisor are an important part of your final evaluation because they reflect how you integrate and put into practice with clients the various elements in the skill areas. Several evaluation instruments have been provided in the Forms section for use by the site supervisor. The collaboration between your faculty supervisors and your site supervisor is essential for summative evaluation of your progress toward the completion of the internship. Your faculty group supervisor will be evaluating your cognitive performance skills based on weekly group counseling participation and completion of cognitive counseling skill assignments. Formative evaluations will be based on observations of performance in the four identified skill areas that were the focus of peer group interactions. Students in internship should be practicing at the intermediate, advanced, or professional levels of performance. Students performing at the novice level in any skill area would require notification and appropriate remediation action.

For summative evaluations, the group supervision faculty supervisor will review and evaluate the intern's case conceptualization presentations; review and evaluate the Integrative Paper, which articulates the guiding theory used by the intern; and observe how the intern integrates cognitive skills and self-awareness/multicultural awareness skills into practice during the seminar. Supervisor's Final Evaluation of Intern (Form 7.6) can also be used by the group supervisor to evaluate counseling practice.

Evaluations from your individual site supervisor and/or your individual faculty supervisor are an important part of your midpoint and final evaluations because they reflect how you integrate and put into practice with clients the various elements in the skill areas. Several evaluation instruments have been provided in the Forms section for use by your individual supervisor(s). The collaboration between your group supervisor and your individual supervisor(s) is essential for summative evaluation of your progress toward the completion of the internship. A successful completion of the internship indicates that the intern has demonstrated adequate competency in counseling performance and professional skills, cognitive counseling, self-awareness/multicultural awareness, and collaboration in supervision to be recommended for certification as an entry-level professional counselor.

Summary

In this chapter, we have presented a skill-based model to be used as a framework for both group and individual supervision during practicum and internship. The skill development areas of counseling performance and professional skills, cognitive counseling skills, self-awareness/multicultural awareness skills, and developmental level in supervision were reviewed. Self-assessment activities were presented to guide counselors-in-training in the articulation of their supervision goals. Sample course objectives and assignments that are typically included in both group practicum and group internship seminars were included. A variety of learning activities and peer consultation approaches that could be included in the group supervision process were suggested. Finally, we reviewed formative and summative evaluation practices.

References

Benhoff, J. M., & Paisley, P. O. (1996). The structured peer consultation model for school counselors. *Journal of Counseling and Development, 74*(3), 304–318.

Bernard, J. M., & Goodyear, R. K. (2014). *Fundamentals of clinical supervision* (5th ed.). Upper Saddle River, NJ: Pearson.

Borders, L. D. (1991). A systematic approach to peer group supervision. *Clinical Supervision, 10*(2), 248–252.

Borders, L. D., & Brown, L. L. (2005). *The new handbook of counseling supervision*. Mahwah, NJ: Lahaska.

Borders, L. D., & Leddick, G. R. (1997). *Handbook of counseling supervision*. Alexandria, VA: Association for Counselor Education and Supervision.

Canadian Counselling and Psychotherapy Association. (2003). *Accreditation manual.* Retrieved October 2013 from www.ccpa.accp.ca/en/accreditation/standards

Collins, D. (1990). Identifying counseling dysfunctional skills and behaviors. *Clinical Supervisor, 8*(1), 67–69.

Corey, G. (2013). *Theory and practice of counseling and therapy* (9th ed.). Belmont, CA: Brooks/Cole, Cengage Learning.

Cormier, S. (2016). *Counseling strategies and interventions* (9th ed.). Upper Saddle River, NJ: Pearson.

Council for Accreditation of Counseling and Related Educational Programs (CACREP). (2016). *CACREP standards.* Alexandria, VA: Author.

Egan, G., & Reese, R. (2019). *The skilled helper: A problem management and opportunity development approach to helping* (11th ed.). Belmont, CA: Brooks/Cole.

Fall, M., & Sutton, J. M., Jr. (2004). *Clinical supervision: A handbook for practitioners.* Boston, MA: Allyn and Bacon/Pearson.

Granilla, D. H., Granilla, P., Kinsvetter, A., Underfer-Babulis, J., & Hartwood Moorhead, H. J. (2008). The structured peer consulting model for school counselors. *Counselor Education and Supervision, 48*(1), 32–47.

Hatcher, R. L., & Lassiter, K. D. (2007). Initial training in professional psychology: The practicum competencies outline. *Training & Education in Professional Psychology, 1*, 49–63.

Ivey, A. E., Ivey, M. B., & Zalaquett, C. P. (2014). *Intentional interviewing and counseling* (8th ed.). Belmont, CA: Brooks/Cole.

Lassiter, P. S., Napolitano, L., Culbreth, J. R., & Ng, K. M. (2008). Developing multicultural competence using the structured peer group supervision model. *Counselor Education and Supervision, 47*, 164–178.

Remley, T. P., Jr., & Herlihy, B. (2016). *Ethical, legal, and professional issues in counseling* (5th ed.). Upper Saddle River, NJ: Pearson.

Wilbur, M. P., Roberts-Wilbur, J., Hart, G., Morris, J. R., & Betz, R. L. (1994). Structured group supervision (SGS): A pilot study. *Counselor Education and Supervision, 33*, 262–279.

Winslade, J. M., & Monk, G. D. (2007). *Narrative counseling in schools.* Thousand Oaks, CA: Corwin.

CHAPTER 7

INDIVIDUAL SUPERVISION IN PRACTICUM AND INTERNSHIP

Role and Function of the Supervisor in Practicum and Internship

According to the American Counseling Association (ACA) *Code of Ethics*, "the primary obligation of the counseling supervisor is to monitor the services provided by other counselors or counselors in training. Counseling supervisors monitor client welfare and supervisee clinical performance and professional development" (ACA, 2014, F1.a). In addition, supervisors are trained in supervision methods and techniques and regularly pursue continuing education in supervision and counseling. Many regulating boards require that counseling professionals who provide supervision receive supervision training and certification. Bernard and Goodyear (2014) stated that supervision minimally has two purposes:

1. *to foster the supervisee's professional development*—a supportive and educational function; and
2. *to ensure client welfare*—the gatekeeping function that is part of the monitoring process.

Supervisors are considered to be seasoned practitioners who, because of their special clinical skills, training, and experience, have been identified by the field site to monitor and oversee the professional activities of the counseling student. University supervisors share a similar role in promoting applied skills but have an indirect or liaison relationship to the field site (Ronnestad & Skovholt, 1993). The function of the supervisor has been variously described in the literature. Dye (1994) suggested that supervision should provide high levels of encouragement, support, feedback, and structure. Psychotherapy supervisors undertake multiple levels of responsibility as teachers, mentors, and evaluators (Whitman & Jacobs, 1998). Supervisors also are described as role models for a specific theoretical approach, as agents of professional development as supervisees progress through the stages of acquiring advanced skills, and as teachers, counselors, or consultants in the supervisory process (Bernard & Goodyear, 2014). The role that the supervisor takes with the counselor-in-training depends, optimally, on the developmental level of the counselor (Pearson, 2000). Beginning-level counselors tend to be uncertain about their counseling effectiveness and skills and tend to need a great deal of support. Intermediate-level counselors tend to fluctuate in their levels of confidence. High-level counselors are more consistent in their confidence and skill level. Practicum students are likely to move through the developmental levels idiosyncratically, usually at the beginning or intermediate levels. Some move more rapidly than others. Some progress, reach a plateau, then progress again. Some stay at the beginning levels. Some progress, encounter a new situation and regress, then stabilize and progress again. The supervisor often structures the supervision in ways consistent with the developmental needs of the practicum student.

Administrative and Clinical Supervision

The most controversial area of supervision lies in the contrast between clinical functions and administrative supervision functions. Clinical supervision functions emphasize counseling, consultation, and training related to the direct service provided to the client by the counselor trainee. Administrative functions emphasize work assignments, evaluations, and institutional and professional accountability in services and programs. For example, when clinical supervision is the emphasis, the counselor trainee's development of clinical skills is the focus of the supervisor–supervisee interaction. Feedback is related to professional and ethical standards and the clinical literature. In contrast, when administrative supervision is the focus, issues such as keeping certain hours, meeting deadlines, following policies and procedures, and making judgments about whether work is to be accomplished at a minimally acceptable level are emphasized. Feedback is related to institutional standards. Ideally, it is recommended that the same person should not provide both clinical supervision and administrative supervision. Realistically, this is not always the case. Therefore, separate meetings should be scheduled for clinical and administrative supervision.

The counselor trainee can expect to receive both clinical and administrative feedback. However, the emphasis of this chapter is directed toward clinical supervision and the intervention, assessment, and evaluative techniques related to a clinical supervisory situation. The student may want to reflect on the proportion of clinical to administrative supervision that he/she is receiving in practicum and internship.

The Supervisor–Supervisee Relationship

In clinical supervision, the importance of developing a positive working relationship with the supervisor cannot be overstated. In many ways, it is similar to the process that goes on in good therapy (Majcher & Daniluk, 2009). The consensus of supervision researchers and theorists is that "good supervision is about the relationship" (Ellis, 2010, p. 106). Indeed, numerous scholars and research studies have related success in supervision to the quality of the relationship between the supervisor and the supervisee (Alpher, 1991; Freeman, 1993; Ladany, Ellis, & Friedlander, 1999).

Bordin (1983) was among the first to be credited with characterizing the supervisor–supervisee relationship as a working alliance or a "collaboration to change" that consists of an agreement on goals, an agreement on tasks necessary to achieve these goals, and an affective bond that develops between them. In good supervision, supervisors who are genuine, real, and present with their supervisees promote an affective bond with supervisees. Relationship qualities of warmth, acceptance, trust, and understanding also are fundamental to positive supervision.

Scott (1976) emphasized the importance of establishing a collegial relationship within the supervisor–supervisee interaction. The relationship is characterized by balance and a shared responsibility for understanding the counseling process. A disruption in this balance or an inability to establish collegiality should be open areas of discussion to identify learning problems. A general rule is that disruptions in the supervisor–supervisee relationship always take precedence.

Kaiser (1997), in discussing the supervisor–supervisee relationship, suggested that supervision takes place in the context of the relationship between the supervisor and supervisee. Kaiser cited the following three components of the relationship: "the use of power and authority, creation of shared meaning, and creation of trust" (p. 16). It is essential that the counselor trainees recognize that supervisors do operate from a position of power, primarily because they will be evaluating the trainees' work. Thus, trainees need to be open and honest with their supervisors to gain effective guidance and feedback. Similarly, the creation of shared meaning between supervisor and supervisee is related to understanding and agreement between the two parties. The degree to which understanding and agreement are obtained determines how the two parties can communicate. Finally, the creation of trust between supervisor and supervisee develops out of the creation of shared meaning and the building of confidence in the mutual understanding between the two parties.

More recently, Wade and Jones (2015) wrote about strength-based approaches to supervision informed by positive psychology. Grounded in the literature that confirms the central importance of a working alliance between supervisor and supervisee, they also suggested that supervisors are transformational leaders who inspire counselor trainees to new levels of development. Wade and Jones suggested that supervisors reflect supervisees' enthusiasm, ask about positive experiences, and specifically inquire about strengths of the supervisee that contributed to success with clients.

Supervision, thus, is more than a didactic experience. It includes intensive interpersonal interaction with all of the potential complications that such relationships can include. Good supervision must integrate both task and relationship-oriented behavior. In positive supervision experiences, a critical balance exists between relationship and task focus. In negative supervision experiences, the total emotional focus is on the negative relationship. The literature cited in the foregoing section may provide the counselor-in-training with sufficient rationale and motivation to consider the supervisor–supervisee relationship as an important area on which to focus during supervision. Relational concerns and conflicts clearly detract from the amount of learning in supervision. Therefore, counseling students should assess their own attitudes, biases, and expectations as they enter into the supervisory process.

The supervisee typically brings a number of predictable sources of discomfort to the supervision process and the working alliance. Common sources of discomfort are

- anxieties about evaluation by the supervisor;
- feelings related to negative self-evaluation (i.e., "I am flawed." "I have done something wrong"); and
- issues of transference (i.e., a negative transference in which he/she perceives the supervisor to be more critical or punitive than actually is the case; or a positive transference in which the supervisor is idealized) (Bernard & Goodyear, 2014).

Concerns over performance and evaluation by supervisors can lead to a defensive stance on the part of the student. It is not uncommon for trainees to react by criticizing their supervisors, and therefore becoming resistant to supervisory feedback and evaluation. Borders (2009) emphasized that a safe environment that demonstrates mutual respect is necessary for a supervisee to be open to feedback and be willing to learn and change.

What Is "Lousy" Supervision?

The literature on supervision is replete with articles that focus on the qualities and practices of good supervisors. However, there is a paucity of information dealing with ineffective supervision. Magnuson, Wilcoxon, and Norem (2000) published an article on the subject that reported the results of a study of ten experienced clinical supervisors who were asked to respond to a number of prompts (e.g., "I am interested in knowing about things you might have experienced in supervision that hindered your learning and professional development"). In addition, participants were asked to describe or characterize lousy supervision. The following is an overview and summary of that study. According to the authors, the data yielded two broad categories of findings: (a) overarching principles of lousy supervision and (b) general spheres of lousy supervision. The following are statements and comments that reflect the participants' opinions regarding lousy supervision.

Overarching Principles

- *Unbalanced:* Supervision overemphasizes some elements of supervisory experiences, while excluding others.
- *Developmentally inappropriate:* The supervisor fails to recognize or respond to the dynamics and changing needs of supervisees.
- *Intolerant of differences:* The supervisor does not allow the supervisee the opportunity to be innovative; supervisors were impatient, rigid, and inflexible.
- *Poor model of professional or personal attributes:* The supervisor struggles with enacting appropriate boundaries, is intrusive, and exploits the supervisee.
- *Untrained:* The supervisor has inadequate training and a lack of professional maturity and is uncomfortable assuming supervisory responsibilities.
- *Professionally apathetic:* The supervisors evidenced a lack of commitment to the growth of the supervisees.

General Spheres

- *Organization and administrative:* Supervision is characterized by a lack of supervisory guidelines, a neglect of initial assessment procedures to identify supervisees' needs, a lack of continuity between sessions, and ineffective group supervision.
- *Technically and cognitively unskilled practitioners, unskilled supervisors, and unreliable resources:* Supervisors show a lack of therapeutic and developmental skills, a reliance on a single model of supervision, and a disregard for supervisees' approach to counseling.
- *Rational/affective:* The supervisor shows an inability to humanize the supervisory process, is overly critical, provides little positive feedback, and is unable to address personal concerns that hampered supervision.

These characteristics of a lousy supervisor are important to consider when approaching supervision. Unfortunately, ineffective supervisory methods often become known after the supervision process has begun. However, it is important to note that supervisees who experience such inappropriate and nonprofessional supervisors should consult with their on-campus supervisor (or liaison), who can provide guidance in coping with the situation or reassign the supervisee to another supervisor.

Models and Methods of Individual Supervision

The counselor-in-training often approaches clinical supervision with mixed feelings. On the positive side, supervision can be regarded as a helpful, supportive interaction that focuses on validating some practices. On the negative side, supervision can be regarded as an interaction that will expose inadequacies and leave the student with even more feelings of incompetence. Both sets of expectations coexist as the student approaches supervision. The tendency, particularly in the early stages of supervision, is for the student to work at proving himself/herself as a counselor so that the negative feelings of inadequacy will diminish. Thus, the initial phases of supervision often are spent establishing a working alliance between the supervisor and supervisee as a way to address supervisee anxiety, as well as other process issues such as resistance to supervision, and the influence and role of culture and diversity factors in supervision (Bernard & Goodyear, 2014).

To help reduce the counseling student's anxieties about supervision and to facilitate the creation of a working alliance, we believe a preview of how supervision could be implemented is in order. Bernard and Goodyear (2014) identify three major categories of clinical supervision models: models grounded in psychotherapy theory, developmental models, and process models. Each of these categories contains several different approaches to supervision. We will present one model from each category to provide the counseling student with an overview of the models of supervision she/he might encounter.

Models Grounded in Psychotherapy Theory: The Psychodynamic Model

Psychodynamic supervision falls within the category of psychotherapy theory-based models. In this supervision approach, the supervisor models a key competence (relationship) that is considered foundational for psychodynamic therapy (Bernard & Goodyear, 2014). In the psychodynamic model, "counselor supervision is a therapeutic process focusing on the intrapersonal and interpersonal dynamics in the supervisee's relationship with client, supervisors, colleagues, and others" (Bradley & Ladany, 2001, p. 148). Goals in this approach are to attain awareness of and acquire skills in the use of dynamics in counseling. The supervisee might expect to focus on a parallel process, that is, the idea that similar dynamics occur in the counselor–client dyad and the supervisor–supervisee dyad. For example, a supervisee might be counseling a client who is facing a crisis that overwhelms him and for which he demands concrete direction. When the supervisee meets with her supervisor, she similarly might present as very overwhelmed by the client's issue and press the supervisor for solutions to the client's problems. Another focus might be on the interpersonal dynamics between the supervisee and the client, where the supervisor teaches the supervisee by modeling effective interpersonal dynamics. A third focus might be on the interpersonal dynamics occurring in the counseling situation. Here the supervisor brings attention to how internalized feelings, thoughts, and meanings are affecting the thoughts and meanings of the supervisee and the client.

Other psychotherapy theory-based models are cognitive-behavioral, humanistic-relational, or systemic models. The advantage of a supervisor using one of these theory-based models is the modeling provided to supervisees who wish to master a particular theoretical approach to counseling (Bernard & Goodyear, 2014). Even if supervisees do not espouse the same theory-informed supervisory approach as the supervisor, it nonetheless can present an opportunity for supervisees to expand their knowledge and skills in a counseling approach with which they have less familiarity.

Developmental Models: The Integrated Developmental Model

The integrated developmental model falls within the developmental category of supervisory approaches. Developmental models generally are organized around the needs of the supervisee based on his/her state of professional development. The integrated developmental model

(Stoltenberg, 1981; Stoltenberg & McNeill, 2010) describes counselor development as occurring through four phases:

Level 1. Supervisees have limited training or experience and have high motivation and anxiety.
Level 2. Supervisees are making the transition from dependent and imitative and needing structure and support to more independent functioning. This usually occurs after practicum.
Level 3. Supervisees are focusing on a more personalized approach to practice.
Level 4. Supervisees' focus is on integrating practice across the domains of treatment, assessment, and conceptualization.

Stoltenberg and McNeill (2010) identified eight domains of professional functioning: intervention skills competence, assessment techniques, interpersonal assessment, client conceptualization, individual differences, theoretical orientation, treatment plans and goals, and professional ethics. Counseling students can identify themselves as being at a specific level of professional development and anticipate the supervision focus within and across the eight domains. As the supervisee moves forward to each new level, the structures of self—other awareness (cognitive and affective); motivation as reflected in interest, investment, and effort expended in clinical training and practice; and autonomy as reflected in the degree of independence the supervisee shows—are characterized by changes. For example, at Level 1 the counselor focuses on himself/herself and what feelings, thoughts, and behaviors he/she is experiencing, with less focus on the client. Motivation is high, and autonomy is low. At Level 2 the focus shifts toward the dynamics of the client, and this shift moves back and forth, causing confusion and varying motivation levels; the counselor will show more autonomy but fall back into dependence on the supervisor. At Level 3 the fluctuations stabilize, and the counselor moves toward a more personalized approach with the self—other focus in balance, motivation consistent, and autonomy more prevalent. At Level 4, all domains of practice are integrated, and underlying structures are stable, with high levels of autonomy. The supervisor uses Facilitative Interventions, Authoritative Interventions, or Conceptual Interventions to facilitate progress to the next stage of development (Bernard & Goodyear, 2014).

Other developmental models are the Loganbill, Hardy, and Delworth model, which identifies the three recurring stages of stagnation, confusion, and integration as the supervisee deals with eight developmental issues; the reflective model; and the life span model.

Process Models: The Discrimination Model

The discrimination model (Bernard, 1979, 1997) is a widely used model of supervision and falls in the category of supervision process models. Models in this category can be used in any psychotherapy orientation and are compatible with developmental models. In the discrimination model, the supervisor can take the roles of teacher, counselor, or consultant. The teacher role is taken when the supervisee needs structure and includes instruction, modeling, and feedback. The counselor role is taken when the supervisor wants to enhance the supervisee's reflectivity about his/her own dynamics. The consultant role is more collegial and supports the supervisees' trust in their own work and in their ability to work on their own (Bernard & Goodyear, 2014). The focus can be on any one of three foci:

■ intervention, or what the supervisee is doing in the session, what skill levels are being demonstrated;

- conceptualization, or how the supervisee understands what is occurring in the session; and
- personalization, or how the supervisee practices a personal style of counseling while attempting to keep counseling free of his/her personal issues and countertransference responses.

In this model, the supervisor has great flexibility in how each focus area is approached. For example, the supervisor may take the role of teacher when addressing a situation where the discussion is about how an ethical standard such as the "duty to warn" may apply to a client. In another situation, the supervisor may take on the role of counselor when the focus is on self-awareness and the supervisor is helping the counselor identify his/her feelings of anxiety when a client talks about acting out. When the supervisor takes the role of consultant, the supervisor and counselor may discuss the benefits of a variety of intervention approaches as the counselor decides how best to proceed with treatment. The supervisor at any given moment may be responding in one of nine different ways. The supervisor may respond from any role within each area of focus depending on the needs of the supervisee. Supervisors are more likely to use the teacher role with novice supervisees. Supervisors of beginning supervisees might focus more on intervention and conceptual skills, while supervisors of more advanced students may focus more on personalization issues. Other process models of supervision include the events-based model and the systems approach to supervision model.

The approaches to supervision that have been reviewed are some that are likely to be experienced by the counseling student. Because the trainee will probably have more than one supervisor during the field experiences, he/she may be working with a university supervisor who utilizes the discrimination model approach to supervision while simultaneously working with a field site supervisor who utilizes a cognitive behavioral approach to supervision. The trainee is advised to be open to any one of the approaches to supervision by recognizing the goals and advantages of each type of supervision.

The Triadic Method of Supervision

Psychotherapy-based, developmental, and process models of supervision each are akin to theories of supervision that offer supervisors and supervisees a framework within which to understand supervision. In addition to these, there are many interventions or methods of structuring and delivering individual supervision. In its most traditional form, individual supervision takes place between one supervisor and one supervisee. An increasingly popular supervisory method that you might experience as a student, however, is triadic supervision. Triadic supervision has been described as being a bridge between individual and group supervision. It is the term for supervision with one supervisor and two supervisees. The model has received significant research since it was adopted as an acceptable form of individual supervision by the Council for Accreditation of Counseling and Related Educational Programs (CACREP) in 2001. It also is acceptable to many state licensing boards as a form of individual supervision.

In the triadic method of supervision, three roles are designated: the role of supervisor, the role of supervisee, and the role of observer/commentator. For supervision of practicum/internship students, the field site or university supervisor takes the role of supervisor. In this role the supervisor reviews the counseling student's work sample (a video or audio recording, case presentation, or clinical notes together with a recording). The supervisor then gives feedback to the supervisee regarding (a) what is particularly well done in the work sample, (b) what has need for improvement, and (c) what is unclear or confusing in the work sample. An example of this feedback is as follows: The supervisor states,

> Your use of the basic empathy skills and confrontation skills was excellent. I particularly liked the way you confronted the client about the contradiction between his values and his behaviors. It didn't come across as blameful. You do need to review your use of questions. Too many questions in a row sound more like an interrogation. What I'd really like to focus on in this supervisory session is the theoretical approach you have in mind in working with this client. It is not clear to me how you see his concerns in relationship to making better decisions and healthier choices.

Discussion then follows, with clarification and expansion of the possible ways of viewing the client as the topic.

The supervisee provides the work sample, and the peer observer/commentator focuses on the communication and interpersonal dynamics going on between the supervisor and the supervisee. Before the close of the supervisory session, the observer shares his/her comments about what he/she observed in the interaction. An example of the observer's comment is as follows: To the supervisee, "I noticed that you seemed a bit defensive when the supervisor asked you to clarify what you meant when describing better decisions." Or, "The two of you seemed to be going all around the subject of the client's concerns, but you never gave specifics."

The two supervisees can alternate taking the roles of supervisee or observer/commentator. When they alternate by taking the role of supervisee in one session and the role of observer/commentator at the next supervisory session, this is referred to as the single-focus form. If the session is in a 90-minute time frame, the supervisees may switch roles midway through the session so that each student has the opportunity to present his/her work for feedback. This is referred to as the split-focus form (Nguyen, 2004).

When using a split-focus, 90-minute time frame, Stinchfield, Hill, and Kleist (2010) describe a process where the role assigned to the peer is that of observer/reflector and the peer engages in silent reflection and inner dialogue while observing the supervisor–supervisee process. This is followed by the peer then engaging in outer dialogue with the supervisor about what was reflected on. At the same time, the presenting supervisee moves into the reflective role and must listen and reflect on the outer dialogue taking place. The session then continues with supervisees switching roles for the second half of the session.

Use of this framework can have many variations for supervision. For example, the peer can be asked to adopt the perspective of the client and track thoughts and feelings as the session is being presented and then share these observations with the supervisee. Or, the peer can role-play the client when the supervisor is demonstrating to the supervisee the use of a specific intervention (Lawson, Hein, & Getz, 2009). Bernard and Goodyear (2014) have identified factors that may enhance the success of triadic supervision:

- Allot 90 minutes each week so that a split-focus form can be used.
- Thoughtfully consider the pairing of supervisees. The success of this model depends on the compatibility of the supervisees paired together.
- Have a distinct role for the non-presenting supervisee.
- Orient the supervisees to the method.

- Supplement with individual supervision—particularly when addressing personal growth issues and evaluation.
- Train supervisors in the use of the model to allow the supervisor to be aware of the needs of more than one supervisee and to be flexible and creative with the choice of strategies (Oliver, Nelson, & Ybanez, 2010).

The use of the triadic method can facilitate a deepening of the supervisory process and provide an opportunity to summarize the interaction process. Benefits associated with the use of triadic supervision include reports that supervisees value the special relationship developed with their supervisee cohort, that it allows for more diversity of perspectives, and that supervisees report a benefit from vicarious learning when a peer is the focus of the session (Lawson, Hein, & Stuart, 2009). Practicing professional counselors can also use this method when meeting for collegial peer supervision in the workplace.

The Clinical Supervision Process

We have noted previously the parallels between clinical supervision and the counseling process. Clinical supervision, similar to counseling practices, begins with informed consent.

Informed Consent in Supervision

The ACA *Code of Ethics* (2014) offers standards regarding supervision practices in counseling. The Association for Counselor Education and Supervision (ACES), in response to counseling supervisors' requests for more specific guidelines regarding supervision practices, developed and approved *Best Practices in Clinical Supervision* (ACES, 2011). Many of the apprehensions and concerns about the clinical supervision process can be mitigated by providing a formal structure for the process. The supervisee should be informed about the structure, processes, and evaluation practices that will be offered by the supervisor. This formal structure is facilitated by providing a Supervisor Informed Consent and Disclosure Statement to the supervisee at the initial supervision session. The informed consent can facilitate the development of a professional relationship and rapport between the supervisor and supervisee. It provides the supervisee with the opportunity to understand the supervisor and, when possible, make a voluntary choice between supervisors. We are offering a sample statement that is consistent with the best practice guidelines and has been adapted from several sources (Haarman, 2009; Remley & Herlihy, 2016; Bernard & Goodyear, 2014; Kitchener & Anderson, 2011).

SAMPLE OF A SUPERVISOR INFORMED CONSENT AND DISCLOSURE STATEMENT

Jane Doe
Student Services Supervisor
Anywhere School District

Purpose: The purpose of this form is to provide you with essential information about the supervision process you are about to begin. The information provided conforms with best practices guidelines and ensures that you understand our professional relationship and my background.

Professional Disclosure

I earned my MEd in School Counseling from a CACREP-approved university program and am a certified K–12 counselor in my state and a National Certified School Counselor. I earned a post-master's Educational Specialist degree (EdS) in School Counseling and am a certified student services supervisor in my state. I am a member of ACA, ASCA, and ACES and practice according to the ethical codes of my profession. I have additional training in crisis response and solution-focused brief therapy. I have been a school counselor for 20 years—10 years as an elementary school counselor and the last 10 years as a high school counselor and counseling supervisor. My general areas of competence in school counseling include crisis response, intervention, referral, and follow-up; social skill development group leadership; short-term counseling for academic, personal, and career-related concerns; and psychoeducational guidance and consultation.

The Supervision Process

As your supervisor, I am responsible to meet your professional development needs as a counselor-in-training while protecting the welfare of clients. Although the focus of supervision will be on you and your professional skill development, a primary concern will be client care. The benefits of receiving individual supervision are the potential growth and development of your professional skills as a counselor. The risks are the feelings of discomfort you may experience as you disclose any deficits or personal concerns as they relate to your counseling practice. Ours is a professional supervisor–supervisee relationship, and I will honor and respect the boundaries of this relationship. Our relationship can be congenial and collegial, but private social interactions will be considered inappropriate.

As your supervisor I follow a supervision model that employs the roles of teacher, counselor, and consultant within a developmental context. In the teacher role, I will help you learn and practice counseling techniques and skills. In the counselor role, I will attend to the development of your reflective skills concerning the interaction between your personal dynamics and those of your clients. Your dynamics will be a focus as they relate to client concerns and cultural considerations. Ethically, I cannot provide you with therapy as part of supervision but will encourage and refer you to continue personal work in therapy when appropriate. The consultant role is used to discuss areas of uncertainty or approaches to case conceptualization. The skill areas we will focus on in supervision are (a) counseling performance skills, which includes professional and ethical components; (b) cognitive counseling skills, which include how you think about, gather information about, and analyze your cases; (c) self-awareness and multicultural awareness skills, which help you examine personal dynamics such as transference and countertransference and personal values and biases that may impact your counseling practice; and (d) developmental level, which relates to your response to supervision and the level of needs you bring to supervision.

You will be recording your counseling sessions for review in supervision. We will also be using case note review, live observation, role playing, case conceptualizations, and other modalities in our sessions. Supervision will require that you reflect on your counseling sessions, yourself as a counselor, and the profession of counseling.

Practical Issues

We will meet for 1 hour per week with regularly scheduled appointments. You should have a new recording available for review each week after the first two sessions of practicum/internship. If our appointment is canceled for any reason, you should call and reschedule for another time that same week.

I will keep a record of our weekly sessions and suggest that you do the same. The records belong to me, but they are available for you to review at any time. I will destroy them 1 month after the completion of your practicum/internship.

I will provide you with both formative and summative feedback and evaluation throughout your practicum/internship. I will regularly give you feedback concerning your strengths and weaknesses as a counselor. I will provide a written summative evaluation at the midpoint and end of your practicum/internship. Evaluation will be based on the responsibilities, goals, and objectives established in the supervisory contract and consistent with identified skill areas and the format of your university program. I will complete university-required forms that document your practice hours in practicum/supervision. I will make recommendations to your university supervisor that will be considered in the grade you receive from your university supervisor.

Legal and Ethical Issues

My services as your supervisor will be given in a professional manner consistent with accepted ethical standards. It is important that you agree to act in an ethical manner as outlined in ACA and ASCA ethical codes and follow laws and regulations related to confidentiality, reporting of abuse, and the duty to warn. You will inform me immediately if these situations become a concern. You will always act in a manner that will not jeopardize, harm, or be potentially damaging to clients.

All information that you share with me concerning yourself or your clients will be kept confidential with several important exceptions:

- You or your client are a danger to yourself or others.
- I have reason to suspect child, vulnerable adult, or elder abuse on the part of you or a child.
- You direct me to share information.
- I am ordered by a court or laws to disclose information.
- I must defend myself against a legal action or formal complaint that you or your client has filed against me.
- Your progress requires me to bring your name up to your university field site liaison.

If you are dissatisfied with the supervision, please let me know. If we can't resolve your complaints, you may follow procedures established by your university field site liaison.

If you must reach me by phone, you can call me at _____ Home (emergency only) _____ Office.

If it is an emergency and I can't be reached, please call Dr. _____, Director of Student Services, at _____.

If you have questions concerning the information in this statement or other questions about supervision, you may ask about them at any time.

Please sign and date this form.

Forming a Supervision Contract

A second formal structuring process is accomplished by negotiating a goals statement. ACES's best practices policy (2011) recommends developing a mutually negotiated goals statement when possible. In addition to an informed consent statement, Cobia and Boes (2000) recommend a second document that is a formal plan for supervision. They conceptualize this as an individualized learner plan. It would include mutually agreed-upon goals for supervision, competencies to be learned and evaluated, and the responsibilities of both the supervisor and supervisee. We are providing a Sample Supervision Contract consistent with best practices guidelines and recommendations from several sources (ACES, 2011; Kitchener & Anderson, 2011; Remley & Herlihy, 2016; Cobia & Boes, 2000; Haarman, 2009; Bernard & Goodyear, 2014).

SAMPLE SUPERVISION CONTRACT

Purpose: The purpose of the supervision is to monitor client services provided by the supervisee and to facilitate the professional development of the supervisee. This ensures the safety and well-being of our clients and satisfies the clinical supervision requirements of _____ University and _____ school/agency.

Supervisor's Responsibilities

- The supervisor agrees to provide face-to-face supervision to the supervisee for 1 hour per week at a regularly scheduled time for the fall/spring practicum/internship semester as required by _____ University.
- The supervisor will complete forms required by the university concerning hours, completion, verification, and evaluation of the supervisee's practicum/internship and make appropriate contact with the university liaison concerning the supervisee's progress.
- The supervisor will make a recommendation as to the student's grade, but responsibility for the final grade rests with the university.
- The supervisor will review audio recordings, case notes, and other written documents; do live observations; and co-lead groups as part of the supervision format.
- The supervision sessions will focus on professional development, teaching, mentoring, and the personal development of the supervisee.
- Skill areas will include counseling performance skills and professional practices, cognitive counseling skills, self-awareness/multicultural awareness, and developmental level in supervision.
- The supervisor will provide weekly formative evaluations, document supervision sessions, and provide summative evaluations based on mutually agreed-on supervision goals. Evaluation will be offered within the skill categories listed above and will be consistent with university guidelines.
- The supervisor will practice consistent with accepted ethical standards.

Supervisee's Responsibilities

- Uphold the ACA *Code of Ethics*.
- Prepare for weekly supervisions by reviewing audio recordings and framing concerns to be the focus of the supervision session.
- Be prepared to discuss and justify the case conceptualization made and the approach and techniques used.
- Reflect on your own personal dynamics and any multicultural issues that may surface in your sessions.

- Review any ethical dimensions that may be important in your sessions.
- Contact your supervisor immediately in any crisis situations involving harm to self or others or abuse of a child, vulnerable adult, or elder.
- Keep notes regarding the supervision sessions.
- Provide the supervisor with video recordings to be reviewed prior to the supervision session.

Supervision Goals and Objectives

Goal 1: Solidify my use of basic and advanced counseling skills in intake sessions and continuing sessions.

Objective: Demonstrate skill in doing initial sessions, including addressing HIPAA and informed consent components.

Objective: Close sessions well by summarizing and allowing time for questions and transitions into the next session.

Objective: Demonstrate skill in preparing initial intake summaries and writing case notes.

Goal 2: Use assessment information and components of the client's story to form case conceptualizations that can help me think clinically about my client's needs.

Objective: Integrate more assessment information into the intake summary to form accurate diagnoses.

Objective: Apply two different case conceptualization models to cases.

Objective: Apply a preferred theoretical approach to explaining how change may occur when thinking of intervention strategies and techniques with specific clients.

Goal 3: Increase my awareness of personal and multicultural dimensions in my practice.

Objective: Examine counseling sessions to recognize instances where my issues may be complicating how I understand the client's concerns.

Objective: Pay particular attention to how any goals identified for the client may be influenced by multicultural elements.

Goal 4: Decrease my level of anxiety and self-consciousness when being supervised.

Objective: Allow time at the end of supervision sessions to review the session and identify points of anxiety and self-consciousness.

Objective: Attend to developing a supervisor–supervisee working alliance by focusing on mutually identified tasks and techniques.

The supervision contract will be revised at specified times or as competencies are established and new goals and objectives become appropriate. Form 7.1 at the end of the text provides a form to be used for initial and subsequent supervision contracts. Supervisee self-assessment practices within the four skill areas have been presented in Chapter 6 as well as a sample goal statement (Form 6.4). The completed Supervisee Goal Statement should be brought to the initial individual supervision session to assist in identifying mutually agreed-on goals in the supervision contract.

The Supervision Session Format

There are probably as many supervision session formats as there are supervisors. However, most sessions include

- review of recorded sessions,
- a critical review of specific aspects of the counselor's practice,
- a focus on areas that could benefit from encouragement or redirection,
- a discussion of how the clinical thinking relates to techniques and interventions used,
- a focus on areas in which reflection on personal dynamics or multicultural elements may be needed, and
- attention to the ethical underpinnings of practice.

Fall and Sutton (2004) recommend that the supervisee be given guidelines about how to do advanced preparation for the supervision session. These guidelines include how to develop an agenda for what the supervisee would like to focus on during supervision. They suggest identifying:

What content will be the focus? New cases, previous cases, self-awareness/cultural awareness, ethical or crisis issues, personal theory, and technique development.

What process will be the focus? How is what you are doing with the client helpful? What am I not getting about this client? Are there resources I could research that may help me with this client? Why do I feel exasperated/relieved when the session with this client ends? Are the goals we have established really the client's goals? I am not comfortable with proceeding as you have advised me with this client.

What do you need from the supervisor, and what modality will you use (case notes, audio recordings, role playing, self-reports, etc.)?

The session proceeds with the supervisee taking responsibility for identifying his/her needs and the supervisor clarifying concerns and responding to the agenda as appropriate. The supervisor may want to add to or amend the agenda. The supervisor keeps notes of content, process, priority of supervisee needs, and modality and intervention (teacher, counselor, consultant) used. (See Form 7.2 at the end of the book.) The supervisee may take notes during or after the session. Form 7.3 at the end of the book provides a format for these notes. The supervisee can make note of any changes or new understandings that will be incorporated into work with a particular client or applied generally in his/her counseling practice. Form 6.5 can be used by the site supervisor to evaluate recorded sessions provided by the supervisee.

Supervising the Developing Counselor-in-Training

The individual supervisor helps counseling students evolve from beginning helpers to professional counselors who are prepared to accept the rights and responsibilities of the profession. The professional developmental sequence has been characterized as a slow transition from dependence on the supervisor and a need for direct instruction to collaborative consultation as the trainee deepens his or her understanding the counseling work. Counselor development further has been described as a progression through increasingly complex levels of practice in which the trainee is initially focused on his/her own implementation of skills and processes to practice levels in which the trainee can integrate multiple elements of counseling all within the framework of his/her own personal theory of counseling. At the proficient clinician level, the trainee is able to be flexible across multiple areas of functioning, and work is based on integrated knowledge, which guides therapeutic action.

Supervision goals and methods of supervisory intervention evolve to match and support the developmental phase of the counselor-in-training. For example, to advance from practicum to internship may require that the supervisee is functioning at level 2 (intermediate) in the integrated developmental model and showing less dependence on the supervisor in the teaching role. These descriptors are based on the supervisor's observations and clinical judgment about how the supervisee functions in the supervision process. Supervision in practicum tends to focus on learning and applying assessment, basic conceptualization, and basic and advanced counseling skills.

As the counselor-in-training progresses to internship, individual supervision serves the unique training function of facilitating the integration of the various components of counseling training. The supervisor introduces a variety of activities that intertwine the following components:

1. forming a therapeutic relationship;
2. facilitating the client's healthy emotional development;
3. viewing the client and the counseling process through the lens of several theoretical perspectives;
4. identifying personalization or self-awareness related to values, beliefs, understanding, and the internal trigger points related to the counseling process;
5. identifying cultural components that are part of the counseling process;
6. integrating ethical principles into the professional identity of the counselor;
7. fostering maturation of the supervision process;
8. encouraging the development of a personal theory of counseling; and
9. supporting the developmental and/or remedial goals of counseling by consulting with others who also influence the healthy development of the client.

What makes the focus on these various components powerful in the context of supervision is that the counselor trainee's awareness, understandings, and insights are examined in direct relationship to the counselor's actual behavior with clients. Managing the supervision process so that supervision goals are realized is quite complex. When the supervisor and counselor-in-training mutually understand the full range of components that are part of the supervisory process, less resistance is likely to occur when supervision moves beyond just focusing on learning diagnostic and interaction skills. The counseling student's self-assessment within each of the skill components provides a preparation for understanding the complexities and subtleties of professional counseling practice. When the counselor trainee is in the beginning phase of preparation—at the clinical practice level of pre-practicum and practicum—the trainee needs "an environment with large amounts of support, direct instruction, and structure, and minimal amount of challenge and personal exploration" (Pearson, 2001, p. 174). As the trainee progresses to internship, he/she is likely to be at the intermediate level of development. The needs of the intern fluctuate between feeling dependent and wanting autonomy, and focusing on his/her own practices while wanting to improve awareness of client relationship dynamics. The supervisor generally reduces the amount of direct instruction and the degree of structure, provides a challenge relative to support, and begins to examine the counselor's personal reactions to clients. The supervisee is encouraged to influence getting what he/she needs and wants from supervision by self-assessment, forming specific goals within the skill areas, and preparing for supervision sessions by forming an agenda related to his/her practice concerns. The supervisor prepares for the supervision session by reviewing any audio recordings, live observation, co-leading, or written case material that may be relevant to the session. The supervisor uses strategies that are appropriate to the developmental level of the supervisee.

Evaluation of Counseling Performance in Individual Supervision

Assessment is provided by the supervisor at various times throughout the practicum and internship. Continuing assessment of the student's work occurs regularly during weekly individual or triadic supervision sessions both at the field site and in the university settings.

Formative evaluation includes verbal commentary about the work accomplished within the supervision session and includes identifying strengths and areas that need improvement. Sessions are organized around specific goals and objectives in the supervision contract, and evaluations are based on observation, discussion, and evidence of improved performance within the goals and objectives. Feedback in supervision is based on regular observation of counseling sessions (via audio recording and live observation) and review of clinical documentation. Supervision notes can be shared with the supervisee when considered appropriate by the supervisor and at the request of the supervisee. The Supervisor's Formative Evaluation of Supervisee's Counseling Practice (Form 7.4) can also be used to provide feedback after several sessions if a structured format is preferred by the supervisor.

Summative evaluation is given at the end point of the practicum and internship semesters. These assessments are important because they influence major educational, regulatory, and credentialing consequences. The assessment requires thoughtful attention to identifying the forms and competencies that will be included. We are including examples and forms that could be considered for use by sites and programs. Our formats are organized around the skill areas identified in the text.

Midpoint and Summative Evaluation in Practicum

The midpoint evaluation should reflect the supervisor's assessment of overall progress halfway through the term. It is an important evaluation point because it allows the supervisor to identify whether or not there are any concerns about recommending that the supervisee to go on to internship or progress with the internship experience. It also provides an opportunity to identify remediating possibilities for those who are not progressing. For students who are meeting or exceeding expectations, this becomes an opportunity to affirm elements of their practice and to renegotiate aspects of the supervision contract as appropriate. We are providing a sample of a narrative evaluation that can be used for the midpoint evaluation.

SAMPLE OF A MIDPOINT NARRATIVE EVALUATION OF A PRACTICUM STUDENT

Supervisor Name: _____

Supervisee Name: _____   Date: _____

The purpose of this evaluation is to provide feedback about your progress toward becoming a professional counselor as demonstrated in the skill areas that have been the focus of our supervision.

The evaluation is based on my observations of your practice, the conversations about your work, and my notes about the content and process of our supervision sessions.

Counseling Performance Skills

Use of basic and advanced counseling, procedural, and professional skills: You are able to form solid therapeutic relationships with a variety of clients by your genuine warmth and accurate empathy toward understanding their concerns. You begin the session smoothly and integrate privacy and informed consent information into initial sessions. A variety of helping skills are appropriately used to assist the clients' framing of their story and identification of areas that need change. You sometimes hurry the process toward an action plan without fully exploring feelings associated with thoughts and actions that may be triggered. More attention to the stage of change in which the client presents may be helpful in directing your efforts to move the counseling progress forward. In all, being able to stay with and explore the client's feelings as they relate to thoughts and actions is an area for you to identify goals for your next supervision sequence. You may also want to identify theory-based techniques that would broaden your range of intervention possibilities.

Cognitive Counseling Skills

We have focused on the areas of writing an intake summary, clinical notes, assessment, and goal setting thus far in supervision. Initially it was difficult for you to identify and connect relevant information to become confident that you could do this in a professional manner. The goals and objectives set for these areas have been met, although you still depend on me for feedback and approval about these functions. I would recommend that you set goals for increasing your case conceptualization skills and attend to the interrelationship of how you view a case clinically and how you conduct your sessions and the documentation that supports your work.

Self-Awareness/Multicultural Awareness

You have become more attuned to how your personal background and values and unexamined biases may impact your counseling practice—particularly when setting goals and staying with feeling content. Continued attention to this aspect of your work is recommended. This site has many clients who come from life situations and cultural backgrounds that are very different from yours. Staying open to and aware of the worldview of these clients is an important part of being an effective and helpful counselor.

Developmental Level

Your comfort level in supervision has noticeably increased. You regularly review your work, come to supervision with appropriate concerns, and take personal risks in revealing counseling practices that need to be improved. You also examine how your personal issues impact the counseling process. You have become less self-focused about your counseling and are able to focus more on client dynamics.

For the final or summative evaluation of the practicum student, you may use any number of assessment formats. We are providing an evaluation tool for use at the end of the practicum experience that is based on the criteria suggested in Chapter 6 as required for proceeding into internship (see

Form 7.5, Supervisor's Final Evaluation of Practicum Student). Documentation of practicum hours on the Weekly Schedule/Practicum Log (Form 3.6) and the Monthly Practicum Log (Form 3.7) must be signed by the site supervisor and turned in to the university supervisor along with the final practicum supervision evaluation.

Midpoint and Summative Evaluation in Internship

We have provided a sample of a narrative midterm evaluation in practicum. A similarly organized narrative could be used for the midterm intern evaluation. The narrative is organized within each skill area, and progress as demonstrated in relationship to goals and objectives is noted. Comment should also include assessment about how this progress meets or exceeds expectations in progressing toward a successful completion of internship requirements for professional practice.

An alternative evaluation process could be implemented that is similar to a work performance review utilized in the corporate world. In this process, both the supervisor and supervisee prepare an evaluation of the supervisee's performance in each of the skill categories based on how the supervisee has made progress toward meeting the goals and objectives established in the supervision contract. Each goal or objective is evaluated based on the categories of 1 = no progress, 2 = does not meet expectations, 3 = meets expectations, 4 = exceeds expectations, and 5 = outstanding. After progress in the skill categories has been evaluated, comments are made about overall progress and new objectives are suggested. When the supervisor and supervisee meet for evaluation, they compare each review for areas of agreement and differences. Future goals and objectives are discussed in relationship to the evaluation. These goals are accepted or revised and committed to. In the case of a supervisee who is falling behind in a skill area, remedial recommendations are established. The site supervisor will have been in contact with the university site liaison person. These recommendations may include such things as additional on-campus supervision, formal writing about the personal theory of counseling in response to specific theory development questions, and/or personal counseling or therapy. The remedial necessities will be part of an overall policy of the university program and determined and implemented by the university supervisor.

The final or summative evaluation of the counseling intern assesses whether the supervisor believes that the supervisee has achieved entry-level status as a practicing professional counselor. The professional literature describes the necessary skills in a variety of ways. For example, Fouad et al. (2009) developed a list of competencies for psychologists that identified readiness for entry to practice in several skill areas. In the skill area of intervention, the essential component was "independent intervention planning, including conceptualization and intervention planning specific to case and context" (p. 19) with the behavior anchors of ability to establish rapport with a wide variety of clients, use of good judgment in crises, and effective delivery of interventions. Engels et al. (2010) have developed an extensive list of competencies that parallel the CACREP standards in that they are written to assess generic counseling competencies, as well as those specific to the specialization areas (e.g., clinical mental health counseling, school counseling). Many summative evaluation forms used by universities and others have chosen a representative sample of similar competency items within specific categories that have been identified as consistent with foundational counseling competencies. Form 7.6 (Supervisor's Final Evaluation of Intern) at the end of the text provides an evaluation instrument with a list of criteria within each skill area that can be rated using a 5-point Likert scale. A rating of 3 signifies that the intern possesses adequate competence on each item rated. Supervisors working with counselor trainees in a specialization (i.e., career counseling; marriage, couple, and family counseling) can add on items from the specialization by referring to items in the competency areas in the work of Engels et al. (2010). Form 7.7 (Evaluation of Intern's Practice in Site Activities) provides a shorter final evaluation form based on activities performed at the practicum site.

Finally, in making a summative evaluation of the intern's skill, supervisors may want to take into account the feedback and experience of clients with the supervisee. Some sites regularly ask their interns to invite clients to complete counselor performance ratings during and at the completion of a counseling relationship. In order to capture the impressions of clients regarding the supervisee's work, we offer an example of a client assessment that can be used. The Client's Assessment of the Counseling Experience (Form 7.8) allows the intern's clients to indicate their satisfaction with the counseling process; it is used when the counseling relationship is terminated.

Supervisee's Evaluation of the Supervisor and of the Site Experience

Evaluation in supervision most often refers to the supervisor's evaluation of the practicum or internship student, as the student is the individual engaged in the training experience. At the same time, we must recognize that supervision is relational and that most programs strive to supervise students from a somewhat collaborative perspective that indicates a value to students on their overall supervisory experience. A collaborative approach does not diminish the gatekeeping duties of the supervisor in which critical feedback must be offered to supervisees for their growth and for the protection of clients. Rather, the collaborative spirit is evidenced, at least minimally, in the opportunities that programs offer students to share feedback about their individual supervision, as well as their site experience. Supervisors can benefit from hearing their supervisees' assessment of their work, as it offers an opportunity to reflect on how to become a better supervisor. Counseling programs that are CACREP accredited are expected to engage in robust program assessment processes that incorporate input from various stakeholders, including students, who must be given an opportunity to evaluate their clinical supervisors. Thus, we have included two forms that can be used to allow the student supervisee to assess the quality of their supervision and training experiences. The Supervisee Evaluation of Supervisor (Form 7.9) is completed by the practicum student or intern at the midpoint and conclusion of the supervisory contract. Both the student and his/her supervisor should sign the form. The Site Evaluation Form (Form 7.10) is to be used so that site personnel and university program faculty can assess the quality of their training sites.

Documenting Internship Hours

CACREP standards require that the intern successfully complete a 600-hour supervised internship that provides the counselor-in-training the opportunity to perform under supervision a variety of activities that a regularly employed staff member in that setting would be expected to perform—with 240 hours of direct service to clients, including group work. The remaining 360 hours are in other professional activities including documentation and record keeping, assessment, information and referral, staff and professional development, planning, and others depending on the site and specialization. The Canadian Counselling and Psychotherapy Association (2003) requires a 400-hour advanced practicum with 200 hours of direct service (140 with individual clients and 40 with groups). The Weekly Internship Log (Form 7.11) parallels the function of the practicum log and is used by interns. The Summary Internship Log (Form 7.12) quantifies the total number of hours spent within the identified counseling activities during the internship. The site supervisor will sign these logs and submit them to the university field site coordinator or the university supervisor at the conclusion of the internship experience in order to provide evidence having completing the requirements of the internship course and so that they can be considered in the final supervisory evaluation.

Summary

In this chapter, we have described several approaches to supervision that the counselor-in-training may experience. We provided information about the triadic model of supervision with several examples of practice applications. Examples and formats for a supervisor's informed consent and disclosure statement and a supervision contract that are consistent with ACES best practice guidelines were included. Finally, a variety of formative and summative evaluation processes, samples, and forms were included. A review of this chapter should provide the counselor-in-training with an understanding of what to expect in the individual supervision component of the practicum/internship.

References

Alpher, V. (1991). Interdependence and parallel processes: A case study of structured analysis of social behavior in supervision and short term dynamic psychotherapy. *Psychotherapy, 29*(2), 218–231.

American Counseling Association. (2014). *Code of ethics.* Alexandria, VA: Author.

Association of Counselor Education and Supervision (ACES). (2011). *Best practices in clinical supervision.* Retrieved from www.acesonline.net/wp/content/uploads/2010/10/ACES-Best-Practices-inclinical-supervision-document-FINAL.pdf

Bernard, J. M. (1979). Supervision training: A discrimination model. *Counselor Education and Supervision, 19,* 60–68.

Bernard, J. M. (1997). The discrimination model. In C. E. Watkins (Ed.), *Handbook of psychotherapy supervision* (pp. 310–327). New York, NY: Wiley.

Bernard, J. M., & Goodyear, R. K. (2014). *Fundamentals of clinical supervision* (5th ed.). Upper Saddle River, NJ: Pearson.

Borders, L. D. (2009). Subtle messages in clinical supervision. *Clinical Supervisor, 28,* 200–209.

Bordin, E. S. (1983). The working alliance model of supervision. *Counseling Psychologist, 11,* 35–42.

Bradley, L. J., & Ladany, N. (2001). *Counselor supervision: Process and practice.* Philadelphia, PA: Brunner/Routledge.

Canadian Counselling and Psychotherapy Association. (2003). *Accreditation manual.* Retrieved from www.ccpa.accp.ca/en/accreditation standards

Cobia, D. C., & Boes, S. R. (2000). Professional disclosure statements and formal plans for supervision: Two strategies for minimizing risk of ethical conflicts in post-master's supervision. *Journal of Counseling and Development, 78,* 293–296.

Council for Accreditation of Counseling and Related Educational Programs (CACREP). (2001). *Accreditation manual* (2nd ed.). Alexandria, VA: Author.

Dye, A. (1994). Training doctoral student supervisors at Purdue University. In J. E. Myers (Ed.), *Developing and directing counselor education laboratories* (pp. 130–131). Alexandria, VA: American Counseling Association.

Ellis, M. V. (2010). Bridging the science and practice of clinical supervision: Some discoveries, some misconceptions. *Clinical Supervisor, 29*, 95–116.

Engels, D. W., Minton, C. A. B., Ray, D. C., Bratton, S. C., Chandler, C. K., & Edwards, N. A. (2010). *The professional counselor: Portfolio, competencies, performance guidelines, and assessment* (4th ed.). Alexandria, VA: American Counseling Association Press.

Fall, M., & Sutton, J. M. (2004). *Clinical supervision: A handbook for practitioners*. Boston, MA: Allyn & Bacon.

Fouad, N., Grus, C. L., Hatcher, R. L., Kaslow, N. J., Hutchings, P. S., & Madson, M. B. (2009). Competency benchmarks: A model for understanding and measuring competence in professional psychology across training levels. *Training and Education in Professional Psychology, 3*(4, Suppl.), S5–S26.

Freeman, S. C. (1993). Reiteration on client centered supervision. *Counselor Education and Supervision, 32*, 213–215.

Haarman, G. (2009). *Clinical supervision: Legal, ethical and risk management issues. Course workbook*. Brentwood, TN: Cross Country Education.

Kaiser, T. L. (1997). *Supervisory relationships*. Pacific Grove, CA: Brooks/Cole.

Kitchener, K. S., & Anderson, S. K. (2011). *Foundations of ethical practice, research, and teaching in psychology and counseling* (2nd ed.). New York, NY: Taylor & Francis/Routledge.

Ladany, N., Ellis, M. V., & Friedlander, M. L. (1999). The supervisory working alliance, trainee self-efficacy, and satisfaction. *Journal of Counseling and Development, 77*, 447–455.

Lawson, G., Hein, S. F., & Getz, H. (2009). A model for using triadic supervision in counselor preparation programs. *Counselor Education and Supervision, 48*, 257–270.

Lawson, G., Hein, S. F., & Stuart, C. L. (2009). A qualitative investigation of supervisees' experiences of triadic supervision. *Journal of Counseling and Development, 87*, 449–457.

Magnuson, S., Wilcoxon, S. A., & Norem, K. (2000). A profile of lousy supervision: Experienced counselors' perspectives. *Counselor Education and Supervision, 39*, 189–202.

Majcher, J. A., & Daniluk, J. C. (2009). The process of becoming a supervisor for students in a doctoral supervision training course. *Training and Education in Professional Psychology, 3*, 63–71.

Nguyen, T. V. (2004). A comparison of individual supervision and triadic supervision. *Dissertation Abstracts International, 64*(9), 3204A.

Oliver, M., Nelson, K., & Ybanez, K. (2010). Systemic processes in triadic supervision. *Clinical Supervisor, 29*, 51–67.

Pearson, Q. (2000). Opportunities and challenges in the supervisory relationship. *Journal of Mental Health Counseling, 22*, 283–294.

Pearson, Q. (2001). A case in clinical supervision: A framework for putting theory into practice. *Journal of Mental Health Counseling, 23*(2), 174–183.

Remley, T. P., Jr., & Herlihy, B. (2016). *Ethical, legal, and professional issues in counseling* (4th ed.). Upper Saddle River, NJ: Pearson.

Ronnestad, M. H., & Skovholt, T. M. (1993). Supervision of beginning and advanced graduate students of counseling and psychotherapy. *Journal of Counseling and Development, 71*, 396–405.

Scott, J. (1976). Process supervision. In J. Scott (Ed.), *A monograph on training supervisors in the helping professions* (pp. 1–10). Retrieved from www.eric.govcontentdelivery/servlet/ERICServlet?accno-ED126398

Stinchfield, T. A., Hill, N. R., & Kleist, D. M. (2010). Counselor trainees experiences in triadic supervision: A qualitative exploration of transcendent themes. *International Journal for the Advancement of Counselling, 32*, 225–239.

Stoltenberg, C. D. (1981). Approaching supervision from a developmental perspective: The counselor complexity model. *Journal of Counseling Psychology, 28*, 59–65.

Stoltenberg, C. D., & McNeill, B. W. (2010). *Supervision: An integrative developmental model for supervising counselors and therapists* (3rd ed.). New York, NY: Routledge.

Wade, J. C., & Jones, J. E. (2015). *Strength-based clinical supervision: A positive psychology approach to clinical training.* New York, NY: Springer Publishing Co.

Whitman, S. M., & Jacobs, E. G. (1998). Responsibility of the psychotherapy supervisor. *American Journal of Psychotherapy, 52*(2), 166–176.

SECTION IV

PROFESSIONAL PRACTICE TOPICS

CHAPTER 8

SELECTED TOPICS SURROUNDING ETHICAL ISSUES IN COUNSELING

The importance of ethics education in counselor training has been cited by all credentialing bodies in counselor training. It is required that counseling ethics be addressed in core and specialized areas of the curricula. Codes of ethics address a broad range of behavior in counseling and psychology. Most important, the codes serve to educate practitioners about the responsibilities inherent in their professional work and protect clients from unethical practices. Seligman (2004) suggested that having knowledge of and familiarity with ethical standards, and abiding by them, is essential to sound clinical practice. The many reasons to be an ethically informed counselor include the following:

■ Ethical standards give strength and credibility to the mental health profession and help clinicians make sound decisions.
■ Providing clients with information about when clinicians can and cannot maintain confidentiality, as well as other important ethical guidelines, affords clients safety and predictability and enables them to make informed choices about their treatment.
■ Practicing in accord with established ethical standards can protect clinicians in the event of malpractice suits or other challenges to their competence.
■ Demonstrated knowledge of relevant ethical and legal standards is required for licensing and certification in all mental health professions.

Fowers (2005) similarly stated that ethics codes serve four functions:

■ They establish integrity for the profession by providing an assessment of what is or is not professionally acceptable.
■ They serve an educational and role socialization function.
■ They incur public trust because professionals can be held accountable for actions that do not meet standards.
■ They serve an enforcement value in developing licensing requirements and legal sanctions.

Definitions: Morality, Ethics, and Law

The terms morality and ethics sometimes are used interchangeably. *Morality* often refers to the principles or the codes of conduct that people of a particular society accept and use to govern themselves (Gert, 2016). Morals help people to distinguish between right and wrong or good and bad behavior when making every day decisions. *Ethics* is the philosophical study of right and wrong, as well as the processes for how moral decisions are made (Sperry, 2007). The understanding of ethics and what constitutes an ethical decision can vary depending on an ethicist's philosophical perspective. Some perspectives suggest, for example, that there are identifiable, intrinsically right and wrong acts (i.e., deontology), while other perspectives posit that an act's moral quality is known only by looking at its consequences and evaluating how much good came from it (i.e., teleology). Various schools of philosophical ethics have informed the codes of ethics for the counseling and related professions as we know them today (Jungers & Gregoire, 2013). *Law* can be thought of as the codification of rules of conduct that members of a society agree are important to the good of their community. Law is informed both by morals and ethics, but it also is enforced by recognized authorities within societies.

Ethical Codes for Counselors

We suspect that, when you think about ethics with regard to the counseling profession, you first think about the ethical codes, such as the ACA (2014) or ASCA (2016) codes of ethics or any other similar code for your mental health specialty. As mentioned, ethics is a very broad body of knowledge developed by ancient and modern philosophers who try to answer the question of what is good and moral or bad and immoral. The codes are the practical guidelines, informed by philosophical ethics, that help counselors think about what is upright behavior in the professional counseling "world" and in its day-to-day tasks (Jungers & Gregoire, 2013). Corey, Corey, and Callahan (2011, p. 14) noted that ethical codes represent "aspirational goals, or the maximum or ideal standards set by the profession, and they are enforced by professional associations, national certifying boards and government boards that regulate professions." Interestingly, by stating that codes of ethics are aspirational, Corey et al. (2011) rightly suggest that the codes help to nudge counselors towards what many members of the profession see as good or preferred behavior for mental health practitioners. Similarly, there are elements of the codes of ethics that *oblige* professionals to act in certain ways for the welfare of clients (e.g., standards forbidding counselors to enter into sexual relationships with clients). In the end, you as a counseling student and soon-to-be professional will have to develop ethical autonomy, or the ability to make informed ethical decisions for which you take personal responsibility (Jungers & Gregoire, 2013).

Each helping profession (counseling, psychology, social work, etc.) has an ethical code specific to its particular discipline. The codes are both national, as they are developed by national associations, and regional, in that the codes are part of every state's licensure laws. Indeed, codes of ethics allow mental health professionals to "police" their own members, thus reducing the need for government regulation of the profession. Careful consideration and knowledge of codes of ethics thus is critical, as violations of the standards by a mental health worker can result in sanctions or loss of licensure. Before you begin your practicum and internships, we urge you to review again the codes of ethics relevant to your area of specialization. We are providing you with a list of websites to access these codes.

Websites for Ethical Codes and Related Standards for Professional Organizations

American Association of Marriage and Family Therapy: www.aamft.org
American Association of Pastoral Counselors: www.aapc.org

American Counseling Association: www.counseling.org

American Mental Health Counselors Association: www.amhca.org

American Psychological Association: www.apa.org

American School Counselors Association: www.schoolcounselor.org

Association for Multicultural Counseling and Development: www.amcdada.org/amcd/default.cfm

Canadian Counselling and Psychotherapy Association: www.ccpa.ca

Canadian Psychological Association: www.cpa.ca

Code of Professional Ethics for Rehabilitation Counselors: www.crccertification.com

NAADAC—The Association for Addiction Professionals: www.naadac.org

National Board for Certified Counselors: www.nbcc.org

National Career Development Association: www.ncda.org

Codes of Ethics: Similarities Across Disciplines and Specialties

Most national and some state professional organizations and certifying bodies for mental health professionals have their own codes of ethics, including the American Counseling Association (ACA) and its divisions, the American School Counselor Association (ASCA), the American Psychological Association (APA), and the Canadian Counselling and Psychotherapy Association and the Canadian Psychological Association. National certification boards such as the Commission for Rehabilitation Counselor Certification and the National Board of Certified Counselors publish codes of ethics for certified counselors. State licensure laws also all include codes of ethics within their rules and regulations. This proliferation of ethical standards and codes has the potential of creating confusion for professional counselors. However, similarities across the codes do exist:

- All major professional associations stipulate that clients have the right to confidentiality barring limitations in some situations. Limits to confidentiality are based on state laws, provincial laws, and the professional codes of ethics. Clients must be notified at the start of counseling of any exceptions to confidentiality.
- The issue of competence is addressed across ethical codes. You must practice within the areas for which you have received training and/or certification. Professionals are expected to seek supervision and training before trying an intervention on their own. As a student counselor, you should discuss and consult with your supervisor about when and how to incorporate a new technique into your practice.
- The practice of establishing multiple relationships is addressed across all professional associations' ethical codes. Most important, all ethical codes prohibit sexual intimacy of any kind with clients. When counselors have a "connection with a client in addition to the therapist-client relationship, a secondary relationship exists" (Welfel, 2010, p. 217). These have been referred to as dual relationships, multiple relationships, or nonprofessional relationships. None of the codes refers to nonsexual relationships as strictly unethical, but most warn against them. If counselors enter into such a relationship, they are advised to seek consultation with peers and/or supervisors. Discussions and consultations about the potential benefits and harms that could occur in such a relationship should be documented and placed into the counselor's records. If the potential benefits can be thoughtfully established, engaging in actions such as attending an important function that is culturally valued and expected can be justified. Counselors must always behave in a manner that protects the integrity of the counseling relationship.

- All professional codes address the importance of cultural issues. Counselors must work with clients from diverse cultures and backgrounds in an aware, knowledgeable, competent, and respectful way. Cultural meanings and the worldview of the client must be incorporated into all areas of practice.
- All professional codes address the necessity of using a systematic process of ethical decision making when encountering ethical dilemmas (Cormier, 2016).

Ethical Decision Making

Principle-Based Ethics

Ethical principles are norms that provide a rationale for the standards that comprise the ethical codes of most health professions. They are always considered in the process of ethical decision making (Meara, Schmidt, & Day, 1996). Kitchener and Anderson (2011) identified five foundational ethical principles upon which we ground our understanding of good and professional conduct in the helping professions. These principles are:

- *Nonmaleficence:* This refers to the duty to do no harm or not to engage in actions that risk harm to others. Harm means that the interests or well-being of another has been reduced in a substantial way. The ACA's *Code of Ethics* (2014) requires that counselors must minimize or remedy unavoidable or unanticipated harm. The risk of harm must also be balanced with other ethical principles, but it is often considered the first principle to meet when making an ethical decision.
- *Beneficence:* This principle refers to doing good or benefitting others, and it has two major aspects. First, one must provide benefits to others by acting in ways that increase their general well-being. Second, one must balance the potential benefit of an action against the potential harm (Beauchamp & Childress, 2001).
- *Respect for a person's autonomy:* This principle imposes the moral requirement that counselors respect others, including their choices and desires, regardless of their personality type or characteristics and regardless of our assessment of the person's decision. Respect for autonomy includes valuing others' freedom of action and freedom of self-directed choice. One can do what one wants to do with one's own life as long as it does not interfere with similar actions of others. Freedom of choice also entails making one's own judgments. However, it should be noted that respect for autonomy is not entirely boundless, as counselors are recognized to uphold the principle of doing no harm. In the case of a client's clear intent to harm themselves or others, most professionals recognize that the principle of autonomy must be subordinated in order that they can protect a client's or others' personal safety.
- *Fidelity:* Fidelity is at the core of the relationship between the counselor and the client. It includes the qualities of truthfulness and loyalty as well as honesty and trustworthiness—core components of human trust.
- *Justice:* Justice involves treating equals equally and unequals unequally but in proportion to their relative differences (Beauchamp & Childress, 2001). Justice implies that judging relevant and irrelevant characteristics in a particular case should be done impartially. Professionals in the helping professions are forbidden to unfairly discriminate on the basis of age, gender, race, ethnicity, national origin, religion, sexual orientation, socioeconomic status,

and so on. Counselors ought to have a commitment to being fair where they agree to promote the worth and dignity of each individual and work to ensure that people have access to a minimum of goods and services such as education and health care. Practitioners often contribute a portion of their work to help those with limited resources (Kitchener & Anderson, 2011).

In ethical decision making, the question arises about how decisions are made when ethical principles conflict. Kitchener and Kitchener (2008) support the process of using a balancing approach, which suggests that all principles are valuable and, in particular situations, must be weighed against each other to get the best overall outcome doing the least amount of harm.

The American Psychological Association (APA) identifies the principles of beneficence and nonmaleficence, fidelity and responsibility, integrity, justice, and respect for people's rights and dignity in its code of ethics (2017). The Canadian Counselling and Psychotherapy Association's (CCPA) *Code of Ethics* (2007) identifies the principles of beneficence, fidelity, nonmaleficence, autonomy, justice, and responsibility to society. The Canadian Psychological Association (2017) organizes the values and standards in its *Code of Ethics* based on the principles of respect for the dignity of persons and peoples, responsible caring, integrity in relationships, and responsibility to society. The American Counseling Association's *Code of Ethics* (2014), identifies the principles of autonomy, nonmaleficence, beneficence, justice, fidelity, and veracity. A great deal of similarity exists for the principles underlying these codes of ethics.

Should ethical codes not be specific or thorough enough to answer a question you encounter in your practice, you should employ ethical principles in evaluating the situation. Ethical principles are used to make decisions about the moral issues inherent in a particular dilemma. An ethical dilemma is a situation in which one must make a choice between competing and contradictory ethical mandates. Pope and Vasquez (2011), in their discussion about ethical dilemmas, stated that "ethical awareness is a continuous, active process that involves constant questioning and personal responsibility" (p. 2) and that "we often encounter ethical dilemmas without clear and easy answers" (p. 5). Ethical codes do not and cannot always provide solutions to the dilemmas we encounter.

Professional ethical behavior begins with the counselor's familiarity with the professional codes of ethics. These are the first source for standards regarding appropriate behaviors and responsibilities inherent in the counseling profession. Developing sensitivity to the ethical principles in the code enables the counselor to feel more secure when faced with situations that are ethically problematic. Ethical decision making is rarely an easy task for the counselor; it involves the application of the code of ethics coupled with one's own values and morals and one's own interpretation of what is in the best interest of the client.

Corey (2017) suggested that developing a sense of professional and ethical responsibility is never-ending. It demands that the professional must review a number of ethical issues during one's ongoing professional self-reflections. Some areas for regular consideration include the following:

1. Counselors need to be aware of what their own needs are, what they are getting from their work, and how their needs and behaviors influence their clients. It is essential that the therapist's own needs not be met at the client's expense.
2. Counselors should have the training and experience necessary for the assessments they make and the interventions they attempt. They also should be aware of cultural factors in

using assessment and diagnostic tools and apply those in determining outcomes of assessment and diagnosis.

3. Counselors need to become aware of the boundaries of their competence, and they should seek qualified supervision or refer clients to other professionals when they recognize that they have reached their limit with a given client. In particular, counselors carefully weigh their ability and skill to use evidence-based practices (EBP), whether an EBP is warranted in light of the clinical issue, and if it is culturally appropriate.

4. Although practitioners know the ethical standards of their professional organizations, they also must be aware that they must exercise their own judgment in applying these principles to particular cases. They realize that many problems have no clear-cut answers, and they accept the responsibility of searching for appropriate solutions.

5. It is important for counselors to have some theoretical framework of behavior change to guide them in their practice. They also regularly evaluate those theories for cultural relevance and consider how they do or do not meet the needs of diverse client groups.

6. Counselors need to recognize the importance of finding ways to update their knowledge and skills through various forms of continuing education.

7. Counselors should avoid any relationships with clients that are clearly a threat to therapy.

8. It is the counselor's responsibility to inform clients of any circumstances that are likely to affect the confidentiality of their relationship and other matters that are likely to negatively influence the relationship.

9. It is imperative that counselors be aware of their own values and attitudes, recognize the role that their belief system plays in their relationships with clients, and avoid imposing these beliefs, either subtly or directly.

10. It is important for counselors to inform their clients about matters such as the goals of counseling, techniques, and procedures that will be employed, possible risks associated with entering the relationship, and any other factors that are likely to affect the client's decision to begin therapy.

11. Counselors must realize that they teach their clients through a modeling process. Thus, they should attempt to practice in their own lives what they encourage in their clients.

12. Counseling takes place in the context of the interaction of cultural backgrounds. Counselors bring their culture to the counseling relationship, and clients' cultural values also operate in the process.

13. Counselors need to learn a process of thinking about and dealing with ethical dilemmas, realizing that most ethical issues are complex and defy simple solutions. The willingness to seek consultation is a sign of professional maturity (Corey, 2017).

Ethical codes provide general broad guidelines for ethical conduct. However, each client's situation is unique and does not always fit exactly into the guidelines. The American Counseling Association's *Code of Ethics* (2014) states that "when counselors are faced with ethical dilemmas that are difficult to resolve, they are expected to engage in a carefully considered ethical decision-making process" (p. 3). Resolving ethical issues is described in the code as a process that considers professional values, professional ethical principles, and ethical standards. An ethical counselor recognizes an ethical challenge and accepts the responsibility to make an ethical decision and takes the considered action. The counselor then assumes the responsibility for the consequences.

Much goes into making a sound ethical decision, and the process can be stressful, especially for new counselors. Various step-by-step models offer practical considerations for making a good decision. Kitchener and Anderson (2011) proposed an ethical decision-making model whose process highlights a critical evaluative level of moral reasoning. The model asks counselors to:

1. Pause and think about your response. Include how your beliefs and values influence your response.
2. Review the available information including the client diagnosis, presenting problem, and contextual information.
3. Identify possible options. Consult with colleagues to generate other possible options.
4. Consult the ethics code. If no single option emerges, continue with your evaluation.
5. Assess the foundational ethical issues. Assess the ethical questions and balance the principles involved in each option. Identify the option that is most justifiable from a moral point of view.
6. Identify legal concerns and agency policy.
7. Reassess options and identify a plan. Have you found an action that balances value over disvalue that respects individual rights?
8. Implement the plan and document the process. This may involve talking to the people involved.

Remley and Herlihy (2016) also reviewed a variety of ethical decision-making models, and based on this review, they described an ethical decision-making process that incorporates steps many of the models have in common. They proposed that counselors:

- Identify and define the problem. Take time to reflect and gather information. Examine the problem from several perspectives.
- Consider the principles and virtues. How do the moral principles apply? Rank them in the order of their priority in this situation. Consider the virtue ethics and the effect of your actions on your sense of moral self.
- Tune in to your feelings. How do your feelings impact your possible actions?
- Consult with colleagues or experts.
- Involve your client in the decision-making process.
- Identify desired outcomes. Brainstorm to generate new options.
- Consider possible actions. Think about the implications and consequences of each action for all concerned.
- Choose and act on your choice.

Virtue-Based Ethics and Ethical Decision Making

Virtue ethics starts with the assumption that professional ethics involve more than moral actions: they also involve traits of character or virtue (Corey, 2017; Remley & Herlihy, 2016). This perspective asks you to look at who you are rather than what you do (Stewart-Sicking, 2008). Principle ethics alone cannot account for why some people know the right thing to do but fail to do it. Principle and rule-bound ethics fail to address questions of moral character (Beauchamp & Childress, 2001; Fowers, 2005). Virtue ethics presumes that counselors and psychologists with good moral character will be better able to understand the moral dilemmas they face and make good decisions about them. Virtue ethics involves questions about "what a 'good person' would do in real life situations" (Pence, 1991, p. 249).

According to Kitchener and Anderson (2011), the virtues that are essential to counseling and psychology are:

- *Practical wisdom or prudence.* Prudence refers to the ability to reason well about moral matters and apply that reasoning to real-world problems in a firm but flexible manner. Fowers (2005) uses the term *practical wisdom*, which involves the components of moral perception of what is at stake, deliberation about what is possible, and reasoning among choices about what is the best course of action.
- *Integrity.* Integrity is a decided commitment to a set of moral or artistic values. To have integrity means we uphold standards even when upholding them might not be popular and may be difficult for other reasons.
- *Respectfulness.* Respectfulness implies that one considers others' wants or points of view. It involves giving moral recognition to some aspect of a person, such as racial background, gender, or disability, or even the law or social institutions.
- *Trustworthiness.* To trust someone means that we can rely on the person's character, truthfulness, and ability to get things done. We can count on the individual.
- *Care or compassion.* This is defined as a deep concern and empathy for another's welfare and sympathy or uneasiness with another's misfortune or suffering (Beauchamp & Childress, 1994).

A virtue-based approach to ethical decision making assumes there are certain ideals toward which one should strive. Virtues are character traits that enable one to be and act in ways that develop one's highest potential (Velasquez, Andre, Shanks, & Meyer, 1996). When practicing virtue-based ethical decision making, one asks the following kinds of questions:

- How can my values best show caring for my client in this situation (CCPA, 2007)?
- What decision would best define me as a person (CCPA, 2007)?
- What emotions and intuitions am I aware of when considering this decision (CCPA, 2007)?
- What course of action develops moral values (Velasquez et al., 1996)?
- What will develop character in myself and my community (Velasquez et al., 1996)?
- What course of action honors the trust my client has toward me?

Self-Tests After Resolving an Ethical Dilemma

After you have progressed through a systematic ethical decision-making process and come to an action plan, several self-tests may be considered.

The Test of Justice: Ask yourself if you would treat others the same way in this situation (CCPA, 2007).

The Test of Universality: Would you be willing to recommend this course of action to other counselors (CCPA, 2007)?

The Test of Publicity: Would you be willing to have this action headlined in the news (CCPA, 2007)?

The Test of Reversibility: Would you make this same choice if you were in the client's shoes (Remley & Herlihy, 2016)?

The Mentor Test: Consider someone you respect and trust and ask how they might solve the same ethical dilemma (Strom-Gottfried, 2008).

The Moral Traces Test: Are there lingering feelings of doubt or discomfort (Remley & Herlihy, 2016)?

Other sources for your reference are *A Practitioner's Guide to Ethical Decision-Making* (counselors can contact the ACA for a free copy of this document) and *Counselling Ethics: Issues and Cases* (counselors can contact the CCPA's national office).

Selected Ethical Issues for Consideration by Beginning Counselors

In this section, we focus on three ethical issues that are generating considerable reflection currently by counseling professionals or that are of special concern to you as a practicum or internship student. Our focus on these issues is not meant to diminish the importance of all other elements of ethical practice as described in the codes; however, the discussion here can prompt you to think further about the topics of: counseling culturally diverse clients, ensuring and managing issues related to self-care, and using technology in counseling.

Ethics of Counseling Culturally Diverse Clients

The importance of multicultural counseling appears in all ethical codes in the helping professions. The ACA *Code of Ethics* (2014), in particular, addresses the need for cultural competence in every section of the code. Starting with the preamble, the code identifies professional values on "honoring diversity and embracing a multicultural approach in the support of the worth, dignity and uniqueness of people within their social and cultural contexts" and "promoting social justice" (ACA, 2014, p. 3). Section A on the counseling relationship notes that counselors both explore their own cultural identities and those of their clients, including becoming aware of how differing cultural worldviews can affect the counseling process (ACA, 2014). In the same section, counselors are encouraged to advocate for social justice at the individual and societal level where appropriate. In all, Lee (2015) identified 26 standards in the 2014 code that address diversity issues. The strong presence of multicultural and social justice values woven through the ACA *Code of Ethics* underlies a widely held belief in the profession that multicultural and social justice counseling is based on the premise that all counseling is cross cultural (Remley & Herlihy, 2016). Highlighting this point, Ridley, Mollen, and Kelly (2011, p. 841) proposed that "counseling competence is multicultural competence" and that "competent counselors consistently incorporate cultural data into counseling."

Building Awareness

How can you develop multicultural counseling skills in your practicum and internship? To begin, re-examine and become aware of your own values, biases, and assumptions about human behavior. It is important to reflect on your own cultural conditioning and how it affects the personal beliefs values and attitudes you hold towards diverse populations. Similarly, it can be helpful to identify your cultural and racial identity and how that influences your approach to the counseling process (Sue & Sue, 2016). Engaging in this type of reflection can be uncomfortable, as it often brings one face-to-face with personal biases and assumptions. For some, recognizing the existence of white privilege or the dynamics of power and oppression in racial, gender, or socioeconomic interactions can trigger strong emotional reactions that might tempt them to avoid talking about these cultural issues.

However, this is where you are encouraged to bring openness, courage, and balanced reflection to bear on socially—and perhaps personally—challenging topics that are important to the counseling process.

Becoming Knowledgeable

Becoming knowledgeable about the cultural values, biases, and assumptions of the diverse groups of clients with whom you work is necessary for ethical practice. Use credible literature and personal experience to increase your knowledge of people who are culturally different from you. (Sue & Sue, 2016). For example, you might consider attending religious events from diverse religious practices, participating in events where you are a racial minority, paying attention to cultural norms related to gender relationships and dating practices, or reading materials that accurately depict non-western cultures and practices. It is important not to assume that Euroamerican values and practices are universal. When addressing cultural issues, it is also helpful to remember that culture is defined broadly and includes variables associated with marginalized groups in our society. Such groups as the disabled, LGBTQ individuals, older adults, religious groups, immigrants, and refugees regularly experience bias and discrimination from the larger society. A number of texts addressing the concerns of specific groups are available, as are workshops, seminars, and online courses.

As a way to help counselors conceptualize clients culturally and thus build informed knowledge bases about diverse clients, Sue (2001) proposed a tripartite model of personal identity. This model depicts personal identity as including individual, group, and universal elements that are arranged as three concentric circles. The inner-most circle is the individual level of personal identity. It refers to all of that which makes a person unique, including biological make-up and the array of shared and unshared life experiences in school and work environments, relationships with peers, and parental treatment, for example.

The next circle out from the center is the group-level aspect of identity, which refers to the social and cultural matrix of beliefs, values, rules, and social practices into which one is born. Group markers include race and gender, as well as things such as educational attainment, socio-economic status, mental status, geographic location, sexual orientation, ethnicity, and religion. Social, cultural, and political distinctions about group-level markers are made in most societies, and social distinctions based on group-level identity factors can influence how group members view themselves, as well as how they are viewed by others. The group-level aspect of identity also can influence the range of perceived choices and possibilities a person may see. A person usually is a member of more than one group and the salience he/she places upon one aspect of group identity over another can vary. Consider for a moment the groups in which you are a member and identify those which are most salient for you. How do your multiple referent group memberships influence your worldview? How have experiences of privilege or oppression affected you? Where do you fall on the power spectrum? Have you had life experiences where you have been a member of both dominant and non-dominant groups? Now, imagine what it might be like to work with a client whose cultural group memberships are different than your own or that have a different priority of group-factor salience. This kind of reflection helps counselors to realize that they may need to adjust their approach to best fit the client's cultural worldview.

Finally, the third and outer-most circle of Sue's identity model consists of elements at the universal level. These include human biological and physical similarities; birth, death, love, sadness, self-awareness, and the capacity for language. This level refers to those aspects of human being that are common to all people (Sue & Sue, 2016).

Psychology and counseling generally have focused on the individual level of identity or the universal level of identity and have placed less emphasis on the group level. Thus, issues of race, gender, sexual orientation, religion, etc. have been considered as add-ons rather than as having an equal role in understanding identity formation and worldview. This framework for understanding clients of diverse backgrounds equally considers individual, group, and universal influences of personal identity and can be quite useful as a foundation to building cultural competence.

Choosing Culturally Appropriate Strategies

Developing culturally appropriate skills and strategies completes the minimal requirements for culturally sensitive and ethical practice (Sue & Sue, 2016). Many traditional helping skills focus on the internal dynamics of the individual. The counselor can make an assumption that a client is free as an individual to be all that he/she may aspire to be. While this may be a suitable assumption for some clients, it is a value reflective of an individualistic culture and thus may be less suitable for clients whose group membership is collective in nature and emphasizes family or tribe over the individual. A client whose family and society are highly prized have a more circumscribed range of choices as a function of his/her group identity. For clients whose problems are related to oppression and discrimination, the counseling focus may need to shift to strategies that address the system in which the client functions. Helpful strategies for addressing systemic problems such as discrimination can include client advocacy, empowerment, and consultation.

We have previously stated that competent counselors consistently incorporate cultural data into their counseling. Including cultural data also has implications for the process of ethical decision making. The principles that are the basis of our profession's moral reasoning are not necessarily endorsed by all cultures. For example, the principle of *respect for autonomy* is grounded on an individualistic worldview, while clients from diverse cultures often make decisions in the context of family, tribe, group, or community. Consider, as well, the principle of *justice* and its significance when working with clients such as those of African American or Mexican origin whose problems can stem from discrimination, oppression, and marginalization. Counselors should be sensitive to the power differential between themselves and clients and should be careful not to assume that they know what is best for the client. *Beneficence* is best respected when clinical decisions are made with the client, not for the client.

Ethics scholars have suggested that integrating virtue ethics and principle ethics may be beneficial when counseling clients of diverse backgrounds (Herlihy & Watson, 2003). Virtue ethics recognizes the importance of cultural context and mutual respect in the counseling relationship. A transcultural integrative model for resolving ethical dilemmas (Garcia, Cartwright, Winston, & Borzuchowska, 2003) proposes that cultural data be considered in each step of the ethical decision-making process. Cultural issues to be considered include:

- Awareness of the counselor's own and the client's cultural identity.
- Determining whether resolutions being considered reflect the worldview of the counselor, client, or both.
- Considering the consequences of potential actions within the cultural worldview of persons involved.
- Anticipating cultural barriers such as bias, discrimination, stereotypes, and prejudices and developing culture specific counter measures (Remley & Herlihy, 2016).

As you progress through the practicum and internship experience, try to make every effort to develop your cultural expertise, as increasing your cultural competence will enhance your counseling effectiveness. Moreover, ethical counseling is widely viewed as requiring the incorporation of cultural data into the understanding of the counseling process and your clients' identities and worldviews.

Managing Issues Related to Self-Care

As you enter the practicum and internship, you will begin to use the most important instrument you have at your disposal for helping others: your own self. Given the dual professional and personal natures of counseling, it is important for students to accept the reality that their physical, mental, social, and emotional well-being is of utmost importance to ethical practice in the helping professions. Counseling is unlike other careers in which knowledge or skill competence alone can translate into job success. Because counselors are professionals who encounter *persons* in need of empathetic understanding, gentle challenges towards growth, and affirmation of change—and because we are not working with inanimate objects or things—we must be attentive to our own readiness to accept the responsibility of caring well for others in the ways that counselors do. Simply put, counselors and trainees alike have to ensure they are free from impairment when they actively work with clients. In its section on supervision, training, and teaching, the ACA *Code of Ethics* (2014, F.5.b) specifically notes that students "monitor themselves for signs of impairment from their own physical, mental, or emotional problems and refrain from offering or providing professional services when such impairment is likely to harm a client or others." If you are struggling with a significant impairment, it can translate into harm to clients, including inability to develop basic interpersonal skill competence, bias towards clients, judgementalism, and breach of professional boundaries, among other things.

Sometimes, it can be challenging for students in practicum and internship to get a sense of what is meant by personal well-being or what it means to be "free from impairment." It is not uncommon, for example, that students might not to want to acknowledge that some of their own past hurts, traumas, or even mental health illnesses are insufficiently addressed or re-emerge when they begin to see clients. Indeed, students in practicum and internship have a lot on the line as they begin with their site placements; they often are advanced in their programs and want to prove to themselves, their professors, their supervisors, and their clients that they are a fit for the profession. It can be quite unsettling for students in practicum or internship (or even at some point prior to these training components) to be informed by faculty or supervisors that there is concern over possible impairment (Jungers & Gregoire, 2013). When concerns arise, faculty and supervisor gatekeepers have the ethical responsibility to inform students and develop remediation plans intended to help them address areas of impairment (ACA, 2014, F.9). Sometimes, remediation plans include recommendations or requirements for individual counseling. Students should not take such recommendations as a critique of their personhood but should try to place them in a positive context: Counseling is not only for addressing problems, but it also is useful for personal growth. Indeed, some estimates suggest that 75% of counselors have themselves sought out counseling (Norcross & Guy, 2005). Being granted the privilege to move into practicum and internship means you also have the responsibility to engage in the habits and practices of ethical and virtuous counselors. This includes having the will and the courage to address areas of personal impairment and learn how to discern if and when an impairment is serious enough to warrant stepping back from clinical work until the area is addressed.

The Ethical Use of Distance Counseling, Technology, and Social Media

Once considered to exist on the fringes of clinical practice, the use of technology in counseling is an increasingly standard part of service delivery. As evidence of this reality, the most recent version of the ACA *Code of Ethics* (2014) added an entire section devoted to distance counseling, technology, and social media. Thus, counselors are expected to have a basic level of competence with using technology, be familiar with their state laws related to distance counseling, and thoughtfully reflect on the ethical implications of using technology when serving clients. Technology in counseling covers a broad range of practices from (a) the use of the telephone and related technologies, including texting; (b) the use of electronic mail and digital communications; (c) the practice of distance counseling, including its regulation by licensure boards; (d) the use of social media; (e) and the use of Web-based discussion groups for mental health professionals. We discuss some ethical considerations for each of these areas, while also recognizing that counselors who regularly incorporate technology into their work must keep abreast of changes and seek consultation as the rules, regulations, and codes of ethics cannot always keep pace with technological advances.

Telephones and Technologies Related to Telephone Use

Phones and related technologies are so often used that they might not even be thought of as technology. All professional codes of ethics hold the counselor responsible for safeguarding the privacy and confidentiality of the client and client information. Actions taken to safeguard confidentiality when using telephones and related devices include making certain that only the counselor hears or has access to voicemail. Any notes taken from phone messages should be treated as confidential and handled carefully. When contacting the client, check first with the client about how, where, when, if, and with whom they prefer messages to be left. When calling, identify yourself and state the message so that third persons will not hear anything clients would not want them to hear.

With the near universal use of cell and smart phones, text messaging is an extremely common form of communication, and there is much discussion about how to use text messages ethically with clients. Kaplan et al. (2017) recommended that texting should be addressed in the informed consent process in order to help establish appropriate counselor–client boundaries at the outset of therapy. For instance, they suggested that counselors clarify the hours during which they will respond to text and that they inform clients not to text in the event of an emergency because texts are not always seen immediately. Counselors also should keep in mind issues related to client confidentiality, especially how to ensure that clients cannot be identified in texts and how to limit personal information in texts. In addition, counselors who use text are strongly recommended to use an application that allows them to encrypt texts and e-mails (Kaplan et al., 2017).

Electronic Mail and Digital Communication

The use of electronic mail (e-mail) and other forms of digital communication are common. Although digital communications, especially e-mail, may seem secure because both parties use a password, it is easy to make errors and send messages to the wrong person. An additional challenge with digital communication is that it creates a record that is vulnerable to exposure. To address security issues, counselors are obliged to encrypt all communications of a therapeutic nature (National Board of Certified Counselors [NBCC], 2016). Similar to text messaging, if you use e-mail or other forms of digital communication, be extremely cautious about disclosing confidential information and warn clients about risks to confidentiality (NBCC, 2016). Include guidelines for digital communications in your written statement to indicate the time frame during which you typically will respond. Some professionals recommend that digital communication be used only for changing appointments or for notifying about an unexpected cancelation (Remley & Herlihy, 2016). Wheeler and Bertram (2008) reported that counselors have had complaints filed "based on an e-mail being sent to the wrong person, voice mail being inappropriately overheard, and computerized records landing in the wrong place" (p. 76).

Distance Counseling

Most professional codes of ethics now address distance counseling, which sometimes is referred to as online counseling, virtual counseling, internet counseling, and telehealth or telepsychology (Teufel-Prida, Raglin, Long, & Wirick, 2018). When providing these services, counselors must provide extensive informed consent information to clients prior to initiating counseling. Among other things, informed consent documents for distance counseling must include a statement of risks and benefits, confidentiality, procedures to use in an emergency when the counselor is unavailable, and possibility of technology failure during service delivery (ACA, 2014, H.2). Counselors who use technology-based services must first determine if clients are capable of engaging in distance counseling and whether or not it appropriately meets clients' needs (Cormier, 2016). Distance counseling services can be provided by e-mail only; by e-mail along with chat, telephone, or video services; or by video only. Videoconferencing appears to be an increasingly preferred method of delivering distance counseling, as it affords a visual component to therapy. Distance counseling presents some potential risks to client confidentiality, and, as mentioned, the client must be informed of the risks. Pope and Vasquez (2011) identified a series of questions to assess your use of digital media, especially confidentiality:

- Where is your computer? Who can see it or hear it? Is it secure from unauthorized access or theft?
- Is the computer protected from hackers? From malicious codes? From viruses?
- Is the computer password protected? Is confidential information encrypted?
- How are your confidential files deleted and stored?
- How do you make sure only the intended recipient receives confidential information?

It is important in distance counseling that the counselor can verify the identity of the client (ACA, 2014, H.3). Examples of verification methods include the use of code words or phrases. An additional consideration when providing distance counseling is that counselors must comply with the laws in the state or province in which the client resides, as well as the state in which the counselor resides (ACA, 2014, H.1). Of course, as a practicum or internship student, you will not yet be licensed; however, it is important to be aware of ethical and legal obligations around to whom services can be offered. Though not all states have rules and regulations that specifically address distance counseling, the general guideline is that a counselor must be licensed in the state in which the client resides in order to provide counseling to that client (Teufel-Prida et al., 2018). In summary, when practicing distance counseling, be certain to be knowledgeable about professional standards for practice. The ACA's *Code of Ethics* (2014) and the NBCC's *Policy Regarding the Provision of Distance Professional Services* (2016) are two excellent guidelines in this regard.

Social Media

Social media are used widely by adolescents and adults, and the range of options is increasing rapidly. There are some general principles that guide the use of social media. First, counselors are cautioned to avoid using social media to exchange confidential information and are recommended to inform clients about appropriate ways to contact them during the course of counseling (NBCC, 2016). Second, counselors are expected to respect clients' privacy, which, according to NBCC (2016, p. 4) includes "limit[ing] the use of" information obtained from social media. The ACA *Code of Ethics* (2014, H.6.c) recommends a stricter stance in protection of clients' privacy by obliging counselors not to gather information about clients on social media unless they are given consent to do so. Third, counselors are recommended to keep separate personal and professional social media accounts if they choose to have such accounts. Fourth, when using social media, a counselor must clearly define how he/she uses it in professional interactions and ought to have a policy on social media use that is shared with clients. In general, we advise that you do not accept clients as "friends" through any social media platform and that you do not accept current or former "friends" as clients. Students have been disciplined or dismissed from field sites due to inappropriate or unprofessional content social media sites or because they have allowed clients to be "friends" on these sites (Cormier, 2016). Finally, Kaplan, Wade, Conteh, and Martz (2011) provided a list of suggestions for the counselor who uses social media in professional interactions. They recommend that you:

- Create separate professional social media accounts and always use these accounts when interacting with clients professionally.
- Reserve your professional name (i.e., Dr. Jane Smith) for social media messages sent through this account.
- Use high-level privacy settings on your personal accounts.
- Be selective about what you post on your private accounts. Avoid potentially embarrassing names, pictures, or statements.
- If you choose to use instant messaging and Twitter with clients, provide them with a written policy about specific hours and anticipated response time to messages.
- Avoid searching for or making unsolicited visits to a client's social media pages.
- Check whether your agency, school, or institution has a policy on social media use and do not violate these rules (p. 6).

Web-Based Professional Discussion Groups

Counselors often use listservs or Web-based professional discussion groups to exchange ideas about professional practice or as a resource for consultation. Safeguarding client confidentiality remains a priority in these consultations. It is not sufficient to change only a client name when discussing such matters. You must ensure that any client data you share are fully disguised. If this is not possible, you must have a signed release from the client for that purpose (Remley & Herlihy, 2016).

Summary

Knowledge of the ethical issues presented by the authors in this chapter is critical for the establishment and maintenance of the counseling relationship. Knowledge of the ethical codes for counselors and psychologists ensures that the practitioner is well aware of the standards for conducting proper therapeutic activities. It is our hope that students will take the time to become familiar with the codes of their specific professional organizations before meeting with clients at their practicum and internship sites. This will ensure that their counseling practices will comply with the appropriate professional standards. We have provided material regarding ethical decision making, as well as some ethics issues, such as diversity issues, self-care, and the use of technology in counseling as these are areas to which the practicum/internship student must pay thoughtful attention.

References

American Counseling Association. (2014). *Code of ethics.* Alexandria, VA: Author.

American Psychological Association. (2017). *Ethical principles of psychologists and code of conduct.* Retrieved from www.apa.org/ethics/code/

American School Counselor Association. (2016). *Ethical standards for school counselors.* Alexandria, VA: Author.

Beauchamp, T. L., & Childress, J. P. (1994). *Principles of biomedical ethics* (4th ed.). Oxford: Oxford University Press.

Beauchamp, T. L., & Childress, J. P. (2001). *Principles of biomedical ethics* (5th ed.). Oxford: Oxford University Press.

Canadian Counselling and Psychotherapy Association (CCPA). (2007). *Code of ethics.* Retrieved from www.ccpa-accp.ca/_documents?CodeofEthics_en_new.pdf/

Canadian Psychological Association. (2017). *Canadian code of ethics for psychologists* (4th ed.). Ottawa, ON: Author.

Corey, G. (2017). *Theory and practice of counseling and psychotherapy* (10th ed.). Pacific Grove, CA: Brooks/Cole.

Corey, G., Corey, M. S., & Callahan, P. (2011). *Issues and ethics in the helping professions* (8th ed.). Belmont, CA: Brooks/Cole, Cengage.

Cormier, S. (2016). *Counseling strategies and interventions* (9th ed.). Upper Saddle River, NJ: Pearson.

Fowers, B. J. (2005). *Virtue and psychology: Pursuing excellence in ordinary practice.* Washington, DC: American Psychological Association.

Garcia, J. G., Cartwright, B., Winston, S. M., & Borzuchowska, B. (2003). A transcultural integrative model for ethical decision-making in counseling. *Journal of Counseling and Development, 81,* 268–277.

Gert, B. (2016). The definition of morality. In Edward N. Zalta (Ed.), *The Stanford encyclopedia of philosophy.* Retrieved from https://plato.stanford.edu/entries/morality-definition/

Herlihy, B., & Watson, Z. E. (2003). Cultural issues and multicultural competence in counseling. In F. D. Harper & J. McFadden (Eds.), *Culture and counseling: New Approaches* (pp. 363–378). Boston, MA: Allyn & Bacon.

Jungers, C., & Gregoire, J. (Eds.). (2013). *Counseling ethics: Philosophical and professional foundations.* New York, NY: Springer Publishing Company.

Kaplan, D. M., Francis, P. C., Hermann, M. A., Baca, G. E., Goodnough, S. H., & Wade, M. E. (2017). New concepts in the 2014 ACA code of ethics. *Journal of Counseling & Development, 95,* 110–120.

Kaplan, D. M., Wade, M. E., Conteh, J. A., & Martz, E. (2011). Legal and ethical issues surrounding the use of social media in counseling. *Counseling and Human Development, 43*(8), 1–10. Retrieved September 25, 2013 from www.counseling.org/docs/ethics/title

Kitchener, K. S., & Anderson, S. K. (2011). *Foundations of ethical practice, research, and teaching in psychology and counseling* (2nd ed.). New York, NY: Routledge/Taylor & Francis.

Kitchener, K. S., & Kitchener, R. F. (2008). Social science research ethics: Historical and philosophical issues. In D. M. Mertens & P. E. Ginsberg (Eds.), *Handbook of social science research ethics* (pp. 5–22). Thousand Oaks, CA: Sage.

Lee, C. C. (Ed.). (2015). Social justice and counseling across cultures. In B. Herlihy & G. Corey (Eds.), *ACA ethical standards casebook* (7th ed., pp. 155–162). Alexandria, VA: American Counseling Association.

Meara, N. M., Schmidt, L. D., & Day, J. D. (1996). Principles and virtues: A foundation for ethical decisions, policies, and character. *Counseling Psychologist, 24*(1), 4–77.

National Board of Certified Counselors. (2016). *Policy regarding the provision of distance professional services*. Retrieved from www.nbcc.org/Ethics

Norcross, J. C., & Guy, J. D. (2005). The prevalence and parameters of personal therapy in the United States. In J. D. Geller, J. C. Norcross, & D. E. Orlinsky (Eds.), *The psychotherapist's own psychotherapy: Patient and clinician perspectives* (pp. 165–176). New York, NY: Oxford University Press.

Pence, G. E. (1991). Virtue theory. In P. Singer (Ed.), *A companion to ethics* (pp. 249–258). Oxford: Blackwell.

Pope, K. S., & Vasquez, M. J. T. (2011). *Ethics in psychotherapy and counseling: A practical guide* (4th ed.). Hoboken, NJ: Wiley.

Remley, T. P., Jr., & Herlihy, B. (2016). *Ethical, legal, and professional issues in counseling* (5th ed.). Upper Saddle River, NJ: Pearson.

Ridley, C. R., Mollen, D., & Kelly, S. M. (2011). Beyond microskills: Toward a model of counseling competence. *Counseling psychologist, 39*, 825–864.

Seligman, L. (2004). *Diagnosis and treatment planning in counseling* (3rd ed.). New York, NY: Springer.

Sperry, L. (2007). *The ethical and professional practice of counseling and psychotherapy*. New York, NY: Pearson.

Stewart-Sicking, J. A. (2008). Virtues, values, and the good life: Alasdair MacIntyre's virtue ethics and its implications for counseling. *Counseling and Values, 52*, 156–171.

Strom-Gottfried, K. (2008). *The ethics of practice with minors: High stakes, hard choices*. Chicago, IL: Lyceum Books.

Sue, D. W. (2001). Multidimensional facets of cultural competence. In D. W. Sue & D. Sue (Eds.), *Counseling the culturally diverse: Theory and practice* (7th ed., pp. 48–51). Hoboken, NJ: Wiley.

Sue, D. W., & Sue, D. (2016). *Counseling the culturally diverse: Theory and practice* (7th ed.) Hoboken, NJ: Wiley.

Teufel-Prida, L. A., Raglin, M., Long, S. E., & Wirick, D. M. (2018). Technology-assisted counseling for couples and families. *The Family Journal: Counseling and Therapy for Couples and Families, 26*, 134–142. doi:10.1177/1066480718770152

Velasquez, M., Andre, C., Thomas Shanks, S. J., & Meyer, M. J. (1996). Thinking morally: A framework, for moral decision making. *Issues in Ethics, 7*(1). Retrieved from www.scu.edu/ethics/practicing/decision/thinking.html

Welfel, E. R. (2010). *Ethics in counseling and psychotherapy: Standards, research and emerging issues* (4th ed.). Pacific Grove, CA: Brooks/Cole.

Wheeler, A. M., & Bertram, B. (2008). *The counselor and the law* (5th ed.). Alexandria, VA: American Counseling Association.

CHAPTER 9

SELECTED TOPICS SURROUNDING LEGAL ISSUES IN COUNSELING

The law, as arbitrated through the court system, is society's attempt to ensure predictability, consistency, and fairness. Its purpose is to offer an alternative to private action in settling disputes. Legal issues are an important part of the day-to-day functioning of professional counselors. Almost all areas of counselor practice are affected by the law (Remley & Herlihy, 2016). Areas such as informed consent or disclosure statements; privacy, confidentiality, and privilege; handling of records; statutes regarding harm to self or others and the protection of minors and vulnerable others; and malpractice are all affected by the law. As Swenson (1997, p. 32) noted, "The question is not whether mental health professionals will interact with laws and legal professionals; it is *how* they will interact both now and in the future." Therefore, it is imperative that mental health professionals understand the legal system. In this chapter, we will review information on the law as it relates to mental health professionals. Elements of malpractice; privacy, confidentiality, and privilege; risk management; times when counselors must breach confidentiality; and client record keeping will be discussed.

The Law

Laws are the rules of a society that establish the basic principles for how people live together as a group (Remley & Herlihy, 2016). They should be viewed as dynamic, not as static. The law is not an entity that rigidly adheres to historically derived rules, but neither does it deny their relevance to current disputes. Legal principles derive from social interactions. At the same time, the law places a great deal of importance on precedence. As enforced through the legal system, the law can be seen as an instrument of concern by the state for the social well-being of the people. Its primary concerns are predictability, stability, and fairness; at the same time, the system must be sensitive to expansion and readaptation.

Classifications of the Law

Laws are classified as constitutional laws, statutes passed by legislatures, regulations, or case laws. The distinctions between these four classifications are explained as follows:

- *Constitutional laws* are those found in the US Constitution and in state constitutions.
- *Statutory laws* are those written by legislatures.

- Statutory laws may have enabling clauses that permit administrators to write *regulations* to clarify them. Once written, these regulations become laws. An important aspect of statuary laws is that the laws vary from state to state. Professional counselors have the responsibility to be informed of the state laws that relate to their scope of practice, just as they have the responsibility to be informed about the ethical codes and standards of practice that have been established for their profession.
- Finally, decisions by appeals courts create *case laws* for the people who reside in their jurisdictions. If a legal problem manifests itself and parties differ on how to solve it, they may go to a trial court. The decision made in the trial court is not published and does not become law. However, if lawyers do not believe the trial court (the lower court) interpreted the law correctly, they may bring their case to an appeals court (a higher court). The function of the appeals court is to determine whether the trial court applied the law correctly. The members of the appeals court publish the decision, and the majority decision becomes the law for that jurisdiction. The appeals court is then said to have set a precedent for that jurisdiction. *Case law* is the set of existing rulings that have made new interpretations of law and therefore can be cited as precedent. In the United States, all states (except Louisiana, which has adapted the French legal tradition) follow the English common law tradition. In the common law tradition, courts decide the law applicable to a case by interpreting statutes and applying precedents that record how and why prior cases have been decided.

Types of Laws

Functionally, we can define three types of law: civil law, criminal law, and mental health law (Johnston, Tarvydas, & Butler, 2016):

- *Civil law* is applicable, for the most part, to disputes between or among people. Losing the lawsuit usually means losing money. If a person fails to obey the stipulations made as an analogue to a civil lawsuit, he/she may be subject to a criminal charge called *contempt of court*. An example would be a mother or father who does not pay child support. *Tort law* is a body of rights, obligations, and remedies that is applied by courts in civil proceedings to provide relief to persons who have suffered from the wrongful acts of others. Each state has its own legislation (statuary laws) and accumulated case laws that can serve as the basis for malpractice suits against therapists and counselors (Pope & Vasquez, 2010).
- *Criminal law* is applicable to disputes between the state and people. Losing defendants often face a loss of liberty. The standard of proof is higher in a criminal case than in a civil case. Each state has its own set of criminal laws, usually set forth in the penal code.
- *Mental health law* regulates how the state may act regarding people with mental illnesses. These laws enact a permission from the state to protect people from serious harm to themselves or others. They allow the state to act as a guardian for those with mental disorders and to institutionalize them if necessary. Most experts believe mental health law is part of civil law.

The Steps in a Lawsuit

Laws are enacted to settle disputes that occur in society. They arise out of social interactions as members of society develop values that are necessary to the maintenance of order and justice. They come into being based on the common views and experiences of people in a society. They are antecedents to judgments regarding right and wrong. The person who claims to have been wronged is called the *plaintiff;* the person accused of committing the wrong is the *defendant.* The dispute is known as *a lawsuit.* A lawsuit proceeds through standard steps. Each step has serious legal consequences and rules that must be followed. It is important to remember that most lawsuits do not go to trial; instead, they are settled at an earlier stage.

First, the plaintiff files a complaint through a lawyer with a court in the appropriate jurisdiction. *Jurisdiction* is determined by geographical and substantive factors. Filing this complaint initiates the legal proceeding. Once the complaint is filed, the plaintiff must make a judicial effort to inform the defendant of his/her intentions (legal notice). This proceeding is called *due process.* The reason for this procedure is to allow the defendant to rebut the accusation. Once valid due process is accomplished, a *discovery process* is in order. At this point, the lawyers involved investigate the facts of the case. To obtain the facts, the lawyers may use a *subpoena.* The subpoena demands access to the facts and to the presence of witnesses at court hearings. On the basis of this information, the two sides may settle the dispute, or they may proceed to litigation. If the attorneys and clients decide to proceed with the lawsuit, the next step is to have *pretrial hearings.* At this step, the judge determines how the laws apply to the facts. The lawsuit may be settled at this point. "The general policy of most courts is to promote settlements and, in fact, disputants settle about 90% of all cases" (Swenson, 1997, p. 46). In the *trial phase*, each side presents evidence and attempts to discredit the evidence of the opponent. Ultimately, the lawsuit is decided by a judge or jury. If either party is dissatisfied with the verdict, he/she may claim that the law was not correctly applied and appeal to a higher court (Swenson, 1997).

Elements of Malpractice

As a legal term, *malpractice* describes complaints in which a professional is accused of negligence within a special relationship. The law of malpractice refers to torts. A *tort* is a wrongful act, injury, or damage (not including a breach of contract) for which a civil action can be brought. Malpractice involves professional misconduct and has been defined as

> Failure of one rendering professional services to exercise that degree of skill and learning commonly applied under all circumstances in the community by the average prudent reputable member of the profession with the result of injury, loss or damage to the recipient of those services or to those entitled to rely on them.
>
> (Black, 2004, p. 959)

The role of incompetency must be established in a malpractice lawsuit. It is not easy to prove that the counselor did not follow established practices. Although malpractice lawsuits have increased over the last decade, the total number of lawsuits is relatively small. Clients come to counseling with a reasonable expectation that the counselor has a legal obligation not to harm them. If clients believe they have been harmed by their counselor, they can file a malpractice lawsuit. The counselor is then obligated to defend himself/herself against the lawsuit before a judge or jury

Schwartz, Kelly, and Partlett (2010) identified the following elements that must be proven in order for the plaintiff to win a tort or malpractice claim involving counselors:

- The counselor had a duty to the client to use reasonable care in providing counseling services.
- The counselor failed to conform to the required duty of care.

- The client was injured.
- There was a reasonably close causal connection between the conduct of the counselor and the resulting injury (known as *proximate cause*).
- The client suffered an actual loss or was damaged.

Proximate cause is an important element because it must be proven that some other intervening event did not cause the injury. Few malpractice suits are filed against counselors because it is not easy to prove that a counselor deviated from accepted practices and that the counselor's negligence caused the harm that a client suffered.

Why Clients Sue

Unfortunately, we live in a litigious society, and counselors should not be naïve to the possibility that they might be sued by a client. Good relationships with clients, however, reduce the likelihood of lawsuits. Counselors should thus use their skills to create positive feelings between themselves and the clients they serve. People do not often want to sue someone whom they perceive is acting in their best interests.

Counselors are sued most often for sexual misconduct with clients. Counselors clearly are capable to decide whether or not to have sex with or engage in sexual acts a client. Pope and Vasquez (2010) reported on research into sexual misconduct with clients, its prevalence, and the harm done to clients. Self-report data indicates that approximately 7% of male counselors and 1.6% of female counselors reported sexual relationships with their current or former clients (Salisbury & Kinnier, 1996). It has been demonstrated that sexual relationships with counselors are extremely harmful to clients (Moleski & Kiselica, 2005). Because the harm done to clients is universally recognized, clients have a reasonable chance of winning their lawsuits. Both civil and criminal lawsuits can be filed. Victimized clients can allege malpractice, negligent infliction of emotional distress, battery, fraudulent misrepresentation, or breach of contract in their lawsuits (Jorgenson, 1995).

Counselor incompetence is the second most reported area of ethical complaints after dual relationships (i.e., sexual) with clients according to one survey of state licensure boards (Neukrug, Milliken, & Walden, 2001). Many lawsuits brought by clients alleging that they were harmed as clients focus on competence. The law demands a minimum level of competence, which is established through (a) completion of recognized academic preparation, (b) meeting the standard set by state licensing boards, and (c) completing the continuing education requirements to renew state licensing requirements. Competence can be characterized as existing on a continuum from gross negligence to maximum effectiveness. The law, academia, and the state identify minimum competencies. Voluntary national credentialing agencies seek to certify counselors who have distinguished themselves beyond the minimum in the field. Hughes (2014) has suggested that competence is comprised of knowledge, skills, attitudes, and values needed to provide effective counseling services to a specific client in a specific context. The ACA *Code of Ethics* expects that counselors "practice only within the boundaries of their competence" (ACA, C.2.a). Counselors could never be competent to offer counseling services in all areas of practice or to everyone who seeks their services. For example, counselors who counsel basically healthy clients who have difficulty coping with life transitions may not be qualified to counsel clients suffering from chronic psychotic disorders. The counselor is responsible to counsel clients who present with problems that he or she is qualified to treat.

The next leading reason that people sue revolves around situations in which clients attempt or complete suicide (Remley & Herlihy, 2016). Because blaming and anger are nearly universal reactions by family survivors, the mental health professional is particularly vulnerable. Today's counselors must know how to make assessments of a client's risk for suicide and must be able to defend their clinical decisions and actions at a later time (Linehan, Comtois, & Ward-Ciesielski, 2012). It is a legal requirement that counselors make assessments from an informed position and that they fulfill their obligations to a client in a manner comparable to what other reasonable counselors operating in a similar situation would have done (Remley & Herlihy, 2016).

Other reasons to sue involve the breaking of a contract and libel or slander. Breaking a contract is essentially the same as breaking a promise. The counselor's spoken and written word is an aspect of their duty to use reasonable care in providing counseling services. If the breach in spoken or written word causes damage or injury, the law may provide a monetary remedy. A client who is angry does not have to show negligence on the part of the mental health professional, only that the therapy did not achieve the purpose it was intended to achieve (Schwitzgebel & Schwitzgebel, 1980). Damages typically involve at least the cost of the therapy.

Injury to a person's reputation may occur when derogatory words or written statements are made to a third party about the person. Such injurious statements are called *defamation* of character: *Slander* is spoken defamation, and *libel* is written defamation. In a recent unpublished case, a trade school counselor made a public remark to the effect that a student had missed classes because she had a venereal disease contracted while working as a prostitute. In fact, the disease was the result of a rape. Because of stress related to gossip, the girl quit school, went into therapy, and sued the school district. The school settled the case, paying $50,000 in damages for the injury. The school also fired the counselor (Swenson, 1997). Mental health professionals should be extremely careful about information given in letters of recommendation, notes on educational records, or any other oral comments to students. Communication of an opinion, when it can be said to imply a false and damaging statement, could be judged as slanderous or libelous (*Milkovich v. Loraine Journal Inc.*, 1990). Other reasons for lawsuits brought against mental health professionals include inappropriate dual relationships, ineffective treatment, improper diagnosis, custody disputes, and breach of confidentiality (Pope & Vasquez, 2010).

Risk Management and the Counselor

Counseling, like many other professions, has some inherent risk of liability. Recognizing liability can be an asset that enables the counselor to examine carefully the level of risk in his/her decision-making processes in therapy. Risk management is an action practitioners can take that will reduce the risk of liability in the form of a lawsuit for malpractice and disciplinary action before the review board of an institution or an ethics challenge before a state licensing board or professional organization. According to Hackney (2000), a number of counselor actions can be helpful in minimizing liability risks:

1. *Competence:* Competence involves the counselor being aware of the limits of his/her training and not practicing outside the boundaries of his/her competence (Corey, Williams, & Moline, 1995). Taking on a client whose treatment and needs are beyond the counselor's skill level is both unethical and a major liability risk.
2. *Communication and attention:* Communicating and paying attention to the therapeutic relationship with clients help the counselor to minimize the risk of mistakes and misunderstanding

in the counseling process. Particularly important is the ongoing process of informed consent, which helps with the avoidance of client misunderstandings about therapy and with clients who have unrealistic expectations for treatment or who may be generally dissatisfied with the counseling received. The counselor must remain open to discussing these issues openly and honestly throughout the therapy process.

3. *Supervision and consultation:* Feedback from colleagues, supervisors, and consultants is invaluable in gaining insight into clinical problems of a legal or ethical nature. Establishing relationships with other mental health professionals before the need to consult arises is an important consideration. Active involvement in professional organizations can also be an excellent source of information on legal and ethical matters. According to Knapp and VandeCreek (2006), the very best step a counselor can take when faced with a difficult ethical decision or a legal question is to consult.

4. *Record keeping:* Record keeping is an axiom among practitioners in relationship to risk management; specifically, seasoned counselors often are heard saying if it is not written down, it did not occur. In an action against a mental health practitioner, accurate, contemporaneous records enhance the practitioner's testimony in a deposition or at trial (Woody, 2013). The pitfalls of overdocumentation and underdocumentation should be understood by the counselor. Overdocumentation includes irrelevant or sensitive material or observations that are disparaging of the client or others. Underdocumentation is the failure to document phone calls, significant events, decisions, and disclosures for informed consent and failure to obtain and review prior records. Documenting decisions or actions in your clinical case notes protects you in the case that such decisions or actions are questioned later (Mitchell, 2007).

5. *Insurance:* It goes without saying that obtaining liability insurance is an absolute practice essential. Counselors also need to understand their insurance policies, especially regarding exclusions, limits of liability, requirements to report claims, or circumstances that may give rise to a claim.

6. *Knowledge of ethics and relevant laws:* Familiarity with ethical and legal guidelines aids in the avoidance of liability claims and problems. The websites of the American Counseling Association (ACA), American Psychological Association (APA), Canadian Counselling and Psychotherapy Association (CCPA), and Canadian Psychological Association (CPA) frequently contain information about ethics, the law, and ethical decision making.

7. *Practitioner self-care:* The stress and tension generated by situations that present a potential for counselor liability necessitate that counselors address their own health and emotional well-being, which can help to ensure that they can maintain perspective and balance (Hackney, 2000).

Liability Insurance

All mental health professionals should purchase liability insurance before they begin practice. An occurrence-based policy covers incidents no matter when the claim is made, as long as the policy was in force during the year of the alleged incident. Thus, if a therapist is accused today of an infraction alleged to have occurred 2 years ago (when the policy was in effect), he/she is covered, even if the policy is not in force at present. A claims-made policy covers only claims made while the policy is in force. However, if a counselors previously had a claims-made policy, they may purchase tail-coverage insurance, which covers him/her if an alleged incident occurring during the period the policy was in effect is reported after the policy has expired.

Privacy, Confidentiality, and Privileged Communication

The client entering the counseling relationship has the expectation that thoughts, feelings, and information shared with the counselor will not be disclosed to others. The nondisclosure in the counseling relationship can be viewed from the vantage point of three separate concepts: privacy, confidentiality, and privilege. These three concepts are interrelated and are sometimes used interchangeably.

Privacy: Privacy is the broad concept that refers to the societal belief that individuals have a right to privacy. Although this right is not specifically stated in the US Constitution, it is derived from interpretations of the Fourth Amendment in the Bill of Rights. Individuals have the right to decide what information about them will be shared with or withheld from others (Remley & Herlihy, 2016). Privacy, when used in the context of counseling, is the "freedom or right of clients to choose the time, circumstances, and information others may know about them" (Corey et al., 1995, p. 163).

Confidentiality: Confidentiality applies to the relationship between counselors and clients. Confidentiality is an ethical responsibility and affirmative legal duty on the part of the counselor not to disclose client information without the client's prior consent. According to Welfel (2010), "confidentiality refers to an ethical duty to keep client identity and disclosures secret" (p. 116). The counselor's confidentiality pledge is the cornerstone of the trust that clients need in order to openly tell their stories and share their feelings. Any limitations to this promise of confidentiality must be identified at the outset before counseling begins. Remley and Herlihy (2016) provided a list of exceptions to confidentiality and privileged communication:

- when sharing information with subordinates or fellow professionals, when consulting with experts, when working under supervision, when coordinating client care, when using clerical assistance;
- when protecting someone who is in danger, when suspecting abuse or neglect of children or others with limited ability for self-care, when client poses a danger to others, when the client is suicidal, when the client has a fatal communicable disease and the client's behavior puts others at risk;
- when counseling multiple clients such as group counseling or couples and family counseling;
- when counseling minors; and
- when mandated by law.

Privilege: Privilege is a common law and statutory concept that protects confidential communication made within certain special relationships from disclosure in legal proceedings (Hackney, 2000). Privilege applies to the relationship between counselors and clients. Wigmore (1961) identified the requirements for a relationship to be privileged under the law:

1. The communication originates in a confidence that it will not be disclosed.
2. The element of confidentiality is essential to the relationship between the parties.
3. The relationship is one that, in the opinion of the community, ought to be fostered.
4. The injury to the relationship that would occur with disclosure of communication would be greater than the benefit gained for the correct disposal of the litigation.

Privileged communication is a legal concept. Privileged communication laws protect clients from having their confidential communication disclosed in a court of law without their consent

(Shuman & Weiner, 1982). Privileged communication is conferred by enacting a statute that grants privilege to a category of professionals and to those they serve. When a competent client presents for therapy, any disclosure he/she makes may be protected from legal disclosure. Such communication is considered privileged. The issue at hand is the conflict between the individual's right to privacy and the need of the public to know certain information. The client is considered the holder of the privilege, and he/she is the only one who can waive that right. Privileged communication is established by statutory law enacted by legislators. Client communication with a specified group of mental health professionals may be privileged in some states but not in others. Also, statutes may specify a wide range of exceptions to privileged communication. For instance, privileged communication laws are abrogated in all states by an initial report of child abuse.

Privileged communication is not absolute, and a wide range of exceptions to privilege exists (Glosoff, Herlihy, & Spence, 2000). In their research, Glosoff et al. (2000) studied the statutory codes in all 50 states and the District of Columbia and determined that exceptions to these concepts are numerous and varied across jurisdictions. However, they concluded that several categories of exceptions were found in 15% of the jurisdictions (see Glosoff et al., 2000, for a state-by-state listing). In addition, it is important to note that statutes and rules regulating privileged communication and its exceptions must be interpreted with caution because in some codes the rules are not readily apparent and existing statutes are continually modified. With these facts in mind, Glosoff et al. (2000) found the following nine categories of exceptions:

1. *When there is a dispute between client and counselor:* This is the most frequent exception and is found in 30 jurisdictions wherein clients filed complaints either in court or with licensing boards. In 30 jurisdictions, clients can be considered to have waived their privilege when they bring complaints of malpractice against their counselor(s).
2. *When the client raises the issue of mental condition in a court proceeding:* This was found in 21 jurisdictions, with 2 primary circumstances: (a) the individual raises the insanity defense in response to a criminal charge and (b) the individual claims in court that he/she has been emotionally damaged and the damage required him/her to seek mental health treatment.
3. *When the client's condition poses a danger to self or others:* This exception was found in 20 jurisdictions. Counselors who work with clients who pose a danger to self or others cannot rely solely on knowledge of statutory law. Case law may affect the status of their duty to warn and the requirement to breach confidentiality.
4. *Child abuse or neglect:* This exception was found in 20 jurisdictions. All states and US jurisdictions have mandatory child abuse and neglect reporting statutes of some type. Counselors must know the exact language of the statutes in their state because the laws vary significantly.
5. *Knowledge that a client is contemplating commission of a crime:* Seventeen jurisdictions waive privilege when the counselor knows that the client is contemplating the commission of a crime.
6. *Court-ordered examinations:* This exception was found in 15 jurisdictions. Communication made during ordered examinations is specifically exempted from privilege.
7. *Involuntary hospitalization:* Thirteen jurisdictions waive privilege when counselors participate in seeking the commitment of a client to a hospital.
8. *Knowledge that a client has been a victim of a crime:* Eight states waive privilege.
9. *Harm to vulnerable adults:* Eight jurisdictions waive privilege when the counselor suspects abuse or neglect of older people, adults with disabilities, residents of institutions, or other adults who are presumed to have limited ability to protect themselves (Glosoff et al., 2000).

It is crucial that you have knowledge of your state statutes to protect yourself and your client from breaches of privilege and confidentiality.

Release of Information

The essence of a counseling relationship is trust. Mental health professionals must protect the information they receive from clients. They must keep confidential communications secret unless a well-defined exception applies. Confidential information may be disclosed if the client (or the client's parent or legal representative) agrees and signs a consent form for such a disclosure. A consent to a waiver does not always have to be in writing, but it is best if it is. The client should be informed of any and all implications of the waiver.

When the Counselor Must Breach Confidentiality

As stated in the previous section on confidentiality, there are circumstances when a counselor is required, by law, to breach confidentiality. We have included the following information concerning the most frequently encountered circumstances when the counselor must make this difficult decision.

The Law and the Duty to Protect: The Suicidal Client

Counselors have an ethical duty to protect clients from harm to self. You must be prepared to take measures to prevent suicide attempts. Prevention measures begin with a risk assessment, and then, based on the level of danger, one must take action by involving a family member or significant other, by working with the client to arrange for voluntary hospitalization, or by initiating a process of involuntary commitment (Remley & Herlihy, 2016). Any of these actions involve a waiver of confidentiality and result in life disruption to the client. Counselors can be accused of malpractice for neglecting to take action to prevent harm, and they can be accused of malpractice for taking actions when there is no basis for doing so (Remley, Hermann, & Huey, 2003). Because of the standard of care to which counselors are held, the best action you can take is to consult with other mental health professionals who are similar to you. (Sommers-Flanagan, Sommers-Flanagan, & Lynch, 2001). The practicum/internship student should review again the literature regarding suicide risk assessment. We have included a section on harm to self in Chapter 10 of this text for your review and reference. Most practicum/internship sites already have in place guidelines for how to manage potentially suicidal clients. Speak with your field site supervisor to become informed of guidelines at your site, and follow them in consultation with your supervisor. No matter where you work as a counselor, you are likely to come into contact with individuals who might express suicidal thoughts. In situations where you must assess the potential risk of suicide, it is important that you document carefully. Counselors must know how to assess the risk for suicide, and they must be able to defend their decision at a later time. Remley and Herlihy (2016) have identified essential items to include in your documentation notes:

- what caused your concern (a referral from another person or something the client said);
- what you asked the client and his/her response;
- who you consulted, what you said, and how they responded; and

■ what interactions you had with any other person regarding the situation, from when you
became concerned until you completed your work regarding the situation.

The Law and the Duty to Warn: The Potentially Dangerous Client

Counselors are sometimes presented with a situation in which they must decide whether or not a
client has the potential to harm another person. If you determine that there is foreseeable danger
that a client may harm someone or someone's property, then you must take the necessary action to
prevent harm (Hermann & Finn, 2002). Ethical guidelines state that confidentiality does not apply
when you must protect clients or identified others from serious and foreseeable harm (ACA, 2014).
However, predicting with certainty whether a person is going to harm someone else is not possible.
The burden of deciding whether to breach confidentiality places the counselor in a complicated
situation that requires informed assessment practices and documented consultation with other
mental health professionals. You have both a legal requirement and an ethical duty to assess the
potential danger and to take action when you decide that violence is imminent. Is the client just
venting out of anger and frustration, or is he/she likely to act out in violence? Once you assess that
a client is dangerous and might harm someone, the law requires that you take action to prevent
harm and that the steps you take are the least disruptive ones possible (Rice, 1993). In addition
to the requirement to take steps to prevent harm, in most states you are also required to warn an
identifiable or foreseeable victim of a dangerous client. This duty to warn arose out of the *Tarasoff*
court case in California where the precedent was established that the therapist (in cases where serious danger to another was determined) "incurred an obligation to use reasonable care to protect
the foreseeable victim from such danger" (McClarren, 1987, p. 273). Decisions after the *Tarasoff*
case throughout the United States have interpreted the holding of the case in a variety of different
ways. The only state that has rejected the *Tarasoff* duty to warn is Texas (Remley & Herlihy, 2016).

When taking action to prevent harm, the counselor has a range of choices from the least to
the most intrusive. The least intrusive action would be to have the client promise not to harm
anyone. Other actions would be to notify family members to have them take responsibility to
keep the client under control, persuade the client to voluntarily commit to residential care, call
the police, or call the client periodically (Remley & Herlihy, 2016). In addition, you would need to
decide whether to warn intended victims, the police, or both. The steps identified for assessment,
consultation, and documentation in managing potentially suicidal clients would also be appropriate to managing the potentially dangerous client. We have included a section on the potentially
dangerous client in Chapter 10, where we review guidelines for assessing danger to others.

Mandatory Reporting: Suspected Child Abuse and Neglect

All states and US jurisdictions now have mandatory reporting statutes of some type regarding child
abuse and neglect. The statutes require that these situations be reported to the appropriate gov-
ernmental agency. In cases of child neglect, the statutes conclude that absolute confidentiality in
counseling must be broken out of the need to protect children. The statutes vary in their wording
from state to state, so it is necessary for counselors to check the exact language in the statute that
requires them to make reports. The United States Department of Health and Human Services (n.d.)
provides information regarding mandatory child abuse reporting statutes for each state and US
jurisdictions (www.childwelfare.gov/systemwide/laws_policies/state). The laws have clauses that

protect counselors who make reports in "good faith" so they can be protected from lawsuits by people who have been reported.

As in other situations where confidentiality is breached, counselors must exercise their professional judgment with several goals in mind. These include

1. maintaining, if possible, any counseling relationship with those involved;
2. expressing concern about the alleged victim before and after a report is made;
3. helping those involved deal with the process that follows the report; and
4. fulfilling their legal obligations (Remley & Herlihy, 2016).

Although reporting suspected abuse is a legal requirement, counselors must use their clinical judgment when they suspect that abuse is occurring. Perhaps the counselor has observed marks on the child, has observed behavior that indicates abuse, or has noticed something the child has said in the counseling session. Counselors must also consider the credibility of the alleged victim, the prevailing standards for discipline in the community, and information that is known about the alleged victim and the alleged perpetrator. Consult immediately with your supervisor when you have a suspicion that abuse is occurring. Before a report is filed, consult with your supervisor and colleagues and inform the appropriate administrator. Follow any procedures that are in place at the field site. Anytime a report is made, document the date and time that an oral report is made, the name of the person who took the report, and a written summary of what was said when the report was made.

Mandatory Reporting: Suspected Harm to Vulnerable Adults

Counselors have both an ethical and a legal duty to intervene when they suspect that a vulnerable adult is being harmed in some way. They have a duty to intervene to prevent the harm from continuing and to promote client welfare. Adults who might be considered vulnerable include developmentally disabled, severely mentally ill, elderly, and physically disabled persons. The elderly are the largest group of adults who are vulnerable to neglect and abuse. Types of elder abuse include physical abuse, sexual abuse, emotional abuse, financial exploitation, neglect, abandonment, and self-neglect (National Center on Elder Abuse, 2005). Neglect can be self-inflicted when elderly patients fail to take medication, skip meals, use alcohol to self-medicate for depression, and fail to maintain personal hygiene. Many states now have laws requiring reports of suspected abuse or neglect of vulnerable adults. All states have some form of legislation aimed at reducing elder maltreatment. In some ways, these statutes are similar to those regarding child abuse. However, not every state mandates that professionals report suspected abuse to authorities. Elder abuse reporting statutes usually allow older adults to refuse protective services if they do not want them (Welfel, Danzinger, & Santoro, 2000). Stetson University School of Law Center for Excellence in Elder Law (2014) provides information about specific laws regarding mandatory reporting of older and vulnerable adult abuse.

If, after careful analysis, you believe you must make a report, you must try to do this in a way that will not damage the counseling relationship. Consult your supervisor. Welfel et al. (2000) recommend that you involve the client in the reporting process, report only essential information to protect confidentiality to the extent possible, and follow up to make sure that needed services are being provided.

The Law and the Practice of Counselor–Client Confidentiality in Canada

Canadian students are referred to an article by Bryce and Mahaffy (2007). Topics covered include confidentiality, times when a counselor must breach confidentiality, counselor–client privilege, and Canada's private sector privacy legislation.

Managed Care and the Counselor

Managed mental health care rules and regulations have a significant impact on how counselors provide counseling services and often determine whether the services provided are reimbursable. Considerable debate has arisen over the effectiveness of mental health care. Managed care means that people are not given all the health care services that people want or that their providers want for them. Instead, health plan members are given the services that the health care plan company has determined are appropriate and necessary. The idea of managed care was that this approach to insurance would lead to lower costs to the company for health care by managing the care provided. However, as costs in health care have increased, so have the number of restrictions placed by insurers on reimbursement for mental health services (Cooper & Gottlieb, 2000). Most managed care companies require that mental health professionals assign a diagnosis from the *Diagnostic and Statistical Manual of Mental Disorders* (*DSM-5*) in order to qualify for reimbursement for services. The *DSM-5* contains a variety of diagnostic codes that are not reimbursable. Most companies limit in some way the diagnoses for which they will pay benefits. Some companies will not reimburse for V-code conditions, typical developmental transitions, adjustment disorders, or family or couples counseling (Remley & Herlihy, 2016). As a result, counselors struggle to meet the mental health needs of clients while at the same time recognizing the demands of managed care. The denial of services based on the *DSM-5* codes is widespread. As a result of these rules and regulations, many counselors are tempted to, and in some cases do, misdiagnose to get reimbursement. Their misguided efforts are an attempt to provide services for those clients who, without insurance reimbursement, would otherwise terminate therapy and, unfortunately, in some cases, to enhance the number of clients seen in therapy. Braun and Cox (2005) discussed the consequences of intentional misdiagnosis of mental disorders. They suggested that many counselors believe that it is in the client's best interest when they agree to intentionally misdiagnose mental status to receive reimbursement. They further stated that, by intentionally misdiagnosing clients' mental statuses, they abuse their position of power and break client trust because intentional misdiagnosis involves deceptive behavior. A review of the ACA, American Mental Health Counselors Association (AMHCA), and APA codes of ethics points to the fact that misdiagnosis is a violation of moral and legal standards and may also violate state and federal statutes. The misdiagnosis of a client's mental status for reimbursement is an ethical violation, as well as a violation of legal statutes. Intentional misdiagnosis of mental disorders for reimbursement is considered health care fraud (Infanti, 2000). The provisions of the 1986 False Claims Act, embodied in the US Code 31, chapter 37, subsection III, allow the government to investigate individuals (i.e., counselors) with the requisite knowledge who (a) submit false claims; (b) "cause" such claims to be submitted; (c) make or use false statements to get false claims paid (i.e., intentional misdiagnosing of mental disorders); or (d) "cause" false statements to be made or used (Braun & Cox, 2005, p. 430). Remember: The dilemma of attempting to counsel a client who otherwise could not afford treatment without reimbursement simply does not justify insurance fraud and the violation of professional ethics. Do not be tempted.

In addition to the problem of misdiagnosis, a variety of other significant issues need the counselor's thoughtful consideration when confronted with legal and moral issues. Braun and Cox (2005) suggested that counselors grapple with ethical and legal challenges involving the following:

1. *Informed consent:* Clients in the world of managed care may not know and understand their mental health benefits.
2. *Confidentiality:* Clients may be unaware that counselors can no longer ensure privacy of disclosure because managed care organizations may require client information for determining treatment and insurance reimbursement (Cooper & Gottlieb, 2000; Danzinger & Welfel, 2001).
3. *Client autonomy:* Under managed care, providers and types of treatment are often determined by policies and utilization reviews (Weinburgh, 1998).
4. *Competence:* Managed care organizations emphasize brief therapy models. When counselors have not received adequate training in brief therapy techniques and interventions, they may not be able to effectively provide services when a managed care organization limits counseling to only five sessions (Cooper & Gottlieb, 2000).
5. *Treatment plans:* The first task of mental health psychotherapy is to accommodate the treatment parameters of the benefit package.
6. *Termination:* The termination of counseling services may be imposed by managed care limitations (Cooper & Gottlieb, 2000).

As noted above, managed care often limits treatment options and the number of sessions allowed. Counselors must discuss this with clients in the beginning session as part of informed consent (Daniels, 2001). Counselors must also let clients know what information the managed care company requires the counselor to disclose and any implications of the diagnosis assigned. A particularly troublesome aspect of limiting the number of sessions is the issue of abandonment. Counselors have ethical obligations not to abandon or neglect clients and to assist in helping clients make appropriate arrangements to continue treatment when necessary (ACA, 2014, Standard A.12). Remley and Herlihy (2016) recommend several actions to protect counselors from legal liability:

- If needed services are denied, request additional services on behalf of the client. If the request is denied, file a written complaint.
- Instruct the client regarding the right to appeal to receive additional services.
- If patient is in crisis and cannot afford to pay you, continue services until care can be transferred to another facility that can provide care.

Client Records

Naturally, mental health professionals should keep records for each client. Records provide an excellent inventory of information for assisting the mental health professional in managing client cases. They also serve as documentation of a therapist's judgments, type of treatment, recommendations, and treatment outcomes. Therapists must also keep financial records. Financial records are necessary to obtain third-party reimbursement for the counselor or the client. The content of records may be defined by agency policy, state licensing laws, statutory laws, or regulation laws. Records may be read in open court; as a result, derogatory comments about clients should never be included.

In most jurisdictions, the paper or the device on which records are recorded belong to the agency, but the information on the paper or stored in the device belongs to the client. Clients can request copies of their records. Some jurisdictions limit access to records if such access is considered to be harmful to a client's mental health.

The evolving standard of practice is to keep records for seven years, although some suggest they should be kept forever. The appropriate regulatory agencies in one's jurisdiction should be consulted regarding record retention and disposition. The following are some types of information that should be kept in client records:

1. basic identifying information, such as the client's name, address, and telephone number (also, if the client is a minor, the names of parents or legal guardians);
2. signed informed consent for treatment;
3. history of the client, both medical and psychiatric, if relevant;
4. dates and types of services offered;
5. signature and title of the person who rendered the therapy;
6. a description of the presenting problem;
7. a description of assessment techniques and results;
8. progress notes for each date of service documenting the implementation of the treatment plan and changes in the treatment plan;
9. documentation of sensitive or dangerous issues, alternatives considered, and actions taken;
10. a treatment plan with explicit goals;
11. consultations with other professionals, consultations with people in the client's life, clinical supervision received, and peer consultation;
12. release of confidential information forms signed by the client; and
13. fees assessed and collected.

The keeping of clinical case notes is the record of most concern for clients because these notes often contain specific details the clients have disclosed about their concerns, as well as the counselor's clinical impressions. This is very sensitive and personal information about clients. Counselors must be aware of how often these notes are reviewed by clients, agencies, and the law. Counselors never know whether others will read their clinical notes. Therefore, counselors must assume that notes they write will become public information at some later time. There are two basic reasons to keep clinical case notes: to provide quality counseling services to clients and to document decisions you make regarding your actions as a counselor (Remley & Herlihy, 2016). The important decisions to document are when you take action to prevent harm (when you assess that a client is a danger to self or others), when you consult with other professionals regarding a client's situation, or when you make decisions a client may not like. If you decide to terminate counseling over a client's objection, advise a client to take some action he/she is reluctant to take, or limit a client's interactions with you outside of sessions, it is wise to document how and why you did this and the client's reactions. When you document such actions or decisions in case notes, you are doing this to protect yourself in case such decisions are later questioned by anyone else (Mitchell, 2007). Some situations where clear documentation is called for are if someone accuses the counselor of unethical or illegal behavior, a counselor reports suspected child abuse or determines a client is a danger to self or others, or a client who is being counseled is involved in legal proceedings. Questions about counselor action or inaction could be reviewed by an ethics panel, licensure board, or administrator or within a legal proceeding.

Summary

The legal issues addressed in this chapter were aimed at the major considerations necessary to ensure that counselors are able to protect both themselves and their clients from legal liability. It is important that all counselors and therapists have a complete understanding of the meaning of privacy, confidentiality, and privileged communication and the rights and responsibilities of helping professionals in legal situations. In addition, mental health professionals should be familiar with the steps in a lawsuit, the issue of negligence, and the elements of malpractice in an effort to avoid the liability that results from such claims. Important considerations that relate to the legal obligation to breach confidentiality in cases of harm to self or others, or suspected abuse of children and/or vulnerable adults, were detailed. Before beginning the practicum and internship experience, students will want to again familiarize themselves with the critical issues reviewed in this chapter.

References

American Counseling Association. (2014). *Code of ethics*. Alexandria, VA: Author.

Black, H. C. (2004). *Black's law dictionary* (8th ed.). St. Paul, MN: West.

Braun, S., & Cox, J. (2005). Managed mental healthcare: Intentional misdiagnosis of mental disorders. *Journal of Counseling and Development, 83*, 425–443.

Bryce, G. K., & Mahaffy, A. (2007). How private is private: A review of the law and practice of counsellor-client confidentiality in Canada and its exceptions. Paper presented at *Connecting With Our Clients: Counseling in the 21st Century, the Canadian Counselling Association National Conference*, Vancouver, BC. Retrieved from www.acadiau.ca/~rlehr/How20% Private20%is20%Private_pdf

Cooper, C. C., & Gottlieb, M. C. (2000). Ethical issues with managed care: Challenges facing counseling psychology. *Counseling Psychologist, 28*, 179–236.

Corey, G., Williams, G. T., & Moline, M. E. (1995). Ethical and legal issues in group counseling. *Ethics and Behavior, 5*(2), 161–183.

Daniels, J. A. (2001). Managed care, ethics and counseling. *Journal of Counseling and Development, 79*, 119–122.

Danzinger, P. R., & Welfel, E. R. (2001). The impact of managed care on mental health counselors: A survey of perceptions, practices, and compliance with ethical standards. *Journal of Mental Health Counseling, 23*, 137–151.

Glosoff, H. L., Herlihy, B., & Spence, E. B. (2000). Privileged communication and the counselor–client relationship. *Journal of Counseling and Development, 78*(4), 450–462.

Hackney, H. (2000). *Practice issues for beginning counselors*. Boston, MA: Allyn & Bacon.

Hermann, M. A., & Finn, A. (2002). An ethical and legal perspective on the role of counselors in preventing violence in schools. *Professional School Counseling, 6*, 46–54.

Hughes, G. (2014). *Competence and self-care in counseling and psychotherapy*. New York, NY: Routledge.

Infanti, M. C. (2000). Malpractice may not be your biggest risk. *RN, 63*(7), 67–71.

Johnston, S. P., Tardyvas, V. M., & Butler, M. (2016). Managing risk in ethical and legal situations. In M. Stebnicki & I. Marini (Eds.), *The professional counselor's desk reference* (2nd ed., pp. 61–68). New York, NY: Springer.

Jorgenson, L. M. (1995). Sexual contact in fiduciary relationships. In J. C. Gensiorek (Ed.), *Breach of trust: Sexual exploitation by health care professionals and clergy* (pp. 237–283). Thousand Oaks, CA: Sage.

Knapp, S., & VandeCreek, L. (2006). The ethics of advertising, billing and finances in psychotherapy. *Journal of Clinical Psychology: In Session, 64,* 613–625.

Linehan, M. M., Comtois, K. A., & Ward-Cielsielski, E. F. (2012). Assessing and managing risk with suicidal clients. *Cognitive and Behavioral Practice, 19,* 218–232.

McClarren, G. M. (1987). The psychiatric duty to warn: Walking a tightrope of uncertainty. *University of Cincinnati Law Review, 56,* 269–293.

Milkovich v. Loraine Journal Inc., 497 US 1 (1990).

Mitchell, R. W. (2007). *Documentation in counseling records: An overview of ethical, legal, and clinical issues* (3rd ed.). Alexandria, VA: American Counseling Association.

Moleski, S. M., & Kiselica, M. S. (2005). A continuum ranging from the destructive to the therapeutic. *Journal of Counseling and Development, 83,* 3–11.

National Center on Elder Abuse. (2005). *Fact sheet: Elder abuse prevalence and incidence.* Retrieved December 28, 2013 from www.ncea.aoa.gov/Resources/Publication/docs/FinalStatistics050331.pdf

Neukrug, E., Milliken, T., & Walden, S. (2001). Ethical complaints made against credentialed counselors: An updated survey of state licensing boards. *Counselor Education and Supervision, 41,* 57–70.

Pope, K. S., & Vasquez, M. J. T. (2010). *Ethics in psychotherapy and counseling* (4th ed.). Hoboken, NJ: Wiley.

Remley, T. P., Jr., & Herlihy, B. (2016). *Ethical, legal, and professional issues in counseling* (4th ed.). Upper Saddle River, NJ: Pearson.

Remley, T. P., Jr., Hermann, M. A., & Huey, W. C. (Eds.). (2003). *Ethical and legal issues in school counseling* (2nd ed.). Alexandria, VA: American School Counselors Association.

Rice, P. R. (1993). *Attorney-client privilege in the United States.* Rochester, NY: Lawyers Cooperative.

Salisbury, W. A., & Kinnier, R. T. (1996). Postdetermination friendship between counselors and clients. *Journal of Counseling and Development, 74,* 495–450.

Schwartz, V. E., Kelly, K., & Partlett, D. F. (2010). *Cases and materials on torts* (12th ed.). Westbury, NY: Foundation Press.

Schwitzgebel, R. L., & Schwitzgebel, R. K. (1980). *Law and psychological practice.* New York, NY: Wiley.

Shuman, D. W., & Weiner, M. F. (1982). *The psychotherapist-patient privilege: A critical examination.* Springfield, IL: Charles C. Thomas.

Sommers-Flanagan, R., Sommers-Flanagan, J., & Lynch, K. L. (2001). Counseling interventions with suicidal clients. In E. R. Welfel & R. E. Ingersoll (Eds.), *The mental health desk reference* (pp. 264–270). New York, NY: Wiley.

Stetson University School of Law Center for Excellence in Elder Law. (2014). *Guide to US state and mandatory reporting status and statutes.* Retrieved June 15, 2014 from www.stetson.edu/law/academics/elder/ecpp/statutory-updates.php

Swenson, L. C. (1997). *Psychology and law for the helping professions.* Pacific Grove, CA: Brooks/Cole.

Tarasoff v. Regents of the University of California, 13 Cal. 3d 177, 529 P. 2d 533, vacated, 17 Cal. 3d 425, 551 P. 2d 334 (1976).

United States Department of Health and Human Services. (n.d.). *The child welfare information gateway.* Retrieved June 15, 2014 from www.childwelfare.gov/systemwide/laws_policies/state

Weinburgh, M. (1998). Ethics, managed care and outpatient psychotherapy. *Clinical Social Work Journal, 26*(4), 433–443.

Welfel, E. R. (2010). *Ethics in counseling and psychotherapy: Standards, research and emerging issues* (4th ed.). Pacific Grove, CA: Brooks/Cole.

Welfel, E. R., Danzinger, P. R., & Santoro, S. (2000). Mandated reporting of abuse/maltreatment or older adults: A primer for counselors. *Journal of Counseling and Development, 78,* 284–293.

Wigmore, J. H. (1961). *Evidence in trials of common law* (vol. 8). Reviewed by John McNaughton. Boston, MA: Little Brown.

Woody, R. (2013). *Legal self-defense for mental health practitioners: Quality care and risk management strategy.* New York, NY: Springer.

CHAPTER 10

WORKING WITH CLIENTS IN CRISIS AND OTHER SPECIAL POPULATIONS

This chapter provides students with information critical to working with the special populations they will encounter most frequently in agencies and schools. The populations we will discuss include clients who have the potential to harm themselves, clients who have the potential to be a threat to others, abused children, sexual abuse victims, and clients who use or abuse substances. The chapter begins, however, with a review of basic crisis intervention and trauma-informed counseling concepts that can be used for case conceptualization and intervention. Forms for use with these client populations are included for the student's reference and use.

Understanding Crisis and Trauma

James and Gilliland (2017, p. 9) defined crisis as "the perception or experiencing of an event or situation as an intolerable difficulty that exceeds the person's current resources and coping mechanisms." Unless a person obtains relief, the crisis has the potential to cause severe affective, cognitive, and behavioral malfunctioning. However, with support, most people do have the capacity to bounce back to pre-crisis levels of functioning after a crisis-causing event.

Crises can unfold in various ways. Myer and Cogdal (2007) outlined four types of crisis-causing events, including developmental crises, existential crises, situational crises, and systemic crises. Developmental crises tend to emerge at marker moments or transitional periods in the life span and disrupt the typical flow of life events. For instance, a person who is just completing college or who is at the point of retirement may experience a crisis related to not knowing how to proceed next in life. Existential crises emerge with a person's reflection on his/her life; they have to do with how one puts meaning to life and how one evaluates his/her self-worth. An existential crisis can surface for people when they realize they have not fulfilled their dreams or desires in the realm of work and career, or people can experience an existential crisis when they realize they always wanted a family and are not capable of having children. Situational crises refer to the unforeseen circumstances that happen outside of the typical sequence of life events and overwhelm a person's coping mechanisms. These events include such things as having a child diagnosed with a life-threatening medical condition, being in a serious car accident, or finding out that one is being laid off from work. Finally, systemic crises are large-scale events that not only have an impact on the individuals most directly affected by the crisis but also have a ripple effect that touches the local and even global community (Myer & Moore, 2006). Examples of systemic crises include the 9/11 terrorist attacks, hurricanes, school shootings, and tornados.

A trauma tends to differ from a crisis with regard to the severity of the impact on human growth and functioning. Trauma is often characterized as a situation (one-time or continuous) that causes a person to feel an overwhelming sense of helplessness in the face of real physical or psychological threat, and it has the potential to upset a person's normal pathway to human development (Murray, Cohen, & Mannarino, 2013; Myer & Cogdal, 2007). Trauma victims can experience:

- persistent alterations in their beliefs about the world (e.g., most situations, even neutral ones, are believed to be fraught with danger);
- damage with regard to the ability to form healthy interpersonal relationships;
- altered neurological pathways;
- an overly developed threat-response system;
- flashbacks and nightmares; and
- difficulty in processing and regulating complex emotions (Curtois & Ford, 2013; Gentry, Baranowsky, & Rhoton, 2017; Lawson, Davis, & Brandon, 2013; Murray et al., 2013).

Trauma victims also may be prone to developing other psychological problems such as addictive or self-injurious behaviors.

Approaches to Crisis Intervention in the Community

The following sections review two models of crisis intervention that highlight tasks in crisis intervention. The first model was proposed by Kanel (2010), while the second was developed by James and Gilliland (2017). Both are useful for counselors who work in community settings.

The Kanel Model of Crisis Intervention

The ABC model of crisis intervention (Kanel, 2010) is a method of conducting very brief mental health interviews with clients whose functioning level has decreased following a psychosocial stressor. It is a problem-focused approach and is applied effectively within 4 to 6 weeks of the stressor. Kanel's (2010) model is designed around three specific stages: (a) developing and maintaining contact, (b) identifying the problem, and (c) developing coping strategies for the client. The following is a summary of the key points of the ABC model:

A. *Developing and maintaining contact:* Essential to the establishment of crisis intervention strategies is the development of rapport with the client. Thus, counselors need to be effective at employing basic attending skills learned early in their training programs. These skills include steady eye contact, appropriate body posture, vocal style, warmth, empathy, and genuineness. Skill in the use of open and closed questions and the skills of clarifying, reflecting, and summarizing are all used to develop and maintain contact with the person in crisis.

B. *Identifying the problem and therapeutic intervention:* By identifying the precipitating event, the counselor can gain information regarding the trigger(s) of the client's crisis. The actual cause of the crisis can vary from a recent event to an event that occurred several weeks or even months ago. The time of the event is important to determine. Kanel uses the following diagram to illustrate the process of crisis formulation:

Precipitating Event—Perception—Subjective Distress—Lowered Functioning

- *Perception of the event:* Perception suggests that how an individual views the stressful situation contributes to the development of a crisis. The meaning and assumptions the person makes about the crisis event serve to color and magnify the meaning for the client. Careful perception checking of the client's view of the precipitating event must be thoroughly considered.

- *Subjective distress:* This refers to the level of distress experienced by the client. Symptoms can affect academic, behavioral, occupational, social, and family functioning. Discussing the affected functional area(s) and the degree to which the crisis event affects them is crucial (Kanel, 2010).
- *Lowered functioning:* It is essential that pre- and post-levels of functioning are understood so that the counselor can ascertain the client's realistic level of coping and the severity of the crisis to the person.

C. *Developing coping strategies for the client:* The counselor assesses the past, present, and future coping behaviors of the client. Included in such an assessment are the client's unsuccessful coping strategies so that alternate approaches can be developed. Clients are encouraged to propose their own coping mechanisms in addition to those proposed by the counselor.

The James and Gilliland Model of Crisis Intervention

The following is a summary of the seven-task model of crisis intervention developed by James and Gilliland (2017):

1. *Predispositioning, engaging, and initiating contact:* The counselor needs to develop an understanding of the events that precipitated the crisis and the meaning that it has for the client. It is therefore essential that a helping relationship be established. The use of basic attending skills, sensitivity to cultural issues and values, and the counselor's calm and direct approach can help the client see that something is being done to alleviate the problem. Critical to this first task is introducing oneself, informing and clarify for the client what will occur in the crisis response process, and making genuine, caring contact.

2. *Exploring the problem and defining the crisis:* In conducting a crisis assessment, the counselor inquires about the event that precipitated the crisis, the meaning it has for the client, the support systems available to the client, and the level of functioning prior to the crisis. Coming to an understanding of what the crisis event was and how it is experienced by the client must be done within a culturally sensitive framework. In addition, determining what the client is feeling (rage, confusion, anger, hopelessness) can help the counselor understand the meaning of the crisis event for the client.

3. *Providing support:* Providing support involves continuing to assure the client that you, as the crisis helper, have a genuine interest in his/her well-being. Counselors, first and foremost, offer psychological support to people in crisis by expressing empathy and concern over their current situation. In addition, counselors can offer logistical, informational, and social support that helps clients meet their physical and social needs or that provides information necessary for making good decisions in the face of the crisis event (James & Gilliland, 2017). Offering social support involves connecting clients to those persons and systems in their life that will help during the crisis response and intervention process. Finally, in supporting clients, counselors must always assess for the threat of suicidal or homicidal behavior. Assessing how dangerous the client is to himself/herself or to others is a core task in crisis intervention. Suicidal ideation, homicidal ideation, danger from a third party, and fear of being harmed pose a serious risk to a client's physical or psychological safety (Myer, Lewis, & James, 2013).

It is essential that direct questioning focus on these possible responses to a crisis. By determining the client's risk for harm, the counselor can seek the support of family and friends, recommend hospitalization, or protect intended victims.

4. *Examining alternatives:* The counselor helps the client explore a variety of available options, especially because the client may feel as though there are no available options. It is not necessary to provide the client with a multitude of options; rather, it is more effective to discuss options that are reasonable, appropriate, and realistic.

5. *Planning in order to reestablish control:* In this practical step, the counselor must tenaciously hold the client's attention on one problem whose moderation will begin to restore equilibrium. The counselor attempts to get the client to look at possible alternatives or solutions. It is also helpful to elicit from the client pre-crisis coping strategies that can be modified. Specifically, the counselor helps the client identify concrete resources (e.g., people, organizations, etc.) that can be of assistance in relieving the crisis, and he/she provides some coping mechanisms, which may take the form of psychoeducation about what to expect during a crisis. Before ending the session, the counselor must assess the degree to which the client understands and can describe the action plan. It is important to remember that client ownership of the plan is crucial.

6. *Obtaining commitment:* The counselor demonstrates the need to carry out the action plan. Commitment should go well if the previous steps have been carried out successfully. Follow-up contact or telephone contact with the client will aid the counselor in determining the client's status, whether or not the action plan has been implemented, and the degree to which the client has progressed toward a resolution.

7. *Following up:* Finally, counselors who do crisis intervention follow up with clients about their action plans and their coping skills in the short term. Follow-up happens in the hours or days after the crisis and indicates to the client that the counselor is in touch with the gravity of the crisis event.

By reviewing just these two models, it may be clear that Kanel (2010) and James and Gilliland (2017) both include similar tasks that counselors undertake in the process of crisis response. Indeed, Myer et al. (2013) reviewed nine different models of crisis intervention in order to identify areas of similarity and difference in the various approaches to crisis counseling. They concluded that nearly all of the models recommended counselors to engage in three continuous activities: (a) assessing the crisis situation in order to gain a sense of how to tailor the response intervention, (b) ensuring safety, and (c) providing support. Likewise, all models described at least four focused tasks that include (a) creating an alliance with the client; (b) defining the problem at hand (e.g., What is the crux of the crisis?); (c) helping the client to regain a sense of control; and (d) following up after the intervention has been enacted. Myer and colleagues (2013) also noted that crisis intervention is best conceptualized as a group of clinical tasks that can unfold concurrently and repeatedly rather than as static stages. With this in mind, counselors do well to conceptualize crisis response more as a dynamic and fluid process than as a checklist of stages.

Approaches to Trauma Counseling

There is a growing interest among counseling professionals about how to work competently with clients who have suffered trauma. Moreover, in a professional counselor's career, he or she will almost invariably encounter clients who have lived through traumatic experiences. The following two sections provide a cursory overview of evidence-based treatments that have been shown to be effective when working with traumatized clients. We then will look at "key ingredients" to trauma approaches that cut across unique treatment strategies.

Evidence-Based Treatments

There is a large and expanding body of research related to evidence-based practices when working with trauma survivors from a multitude of circumstances, such as abusive family dynamics, exposure to community violence, and wartime violence. Interventions include:

- helping clients to repair early, insecure attachment styles that have persisted into adulthood and that were harmed due to abuse and maltreatment;
- motivating clients to stay in counseling (Lawson et al., 2013);
- applying cognitive-behavioral methods to help transform belief systems that the world is always (or nearly always) a dangerous place (Murray et al., 2013); and
- helping clients create concrete and specific safety plans when they feel threatened (Murray et al., 2013).

The Veterans Affairs and Department of Defense (2017) recommended treatment therapies with the most empirical backing, including prolonged exposure therapy, cognitive processing therapy, eye movement and desensitization and reprocessing (EMDR), narrative exposure therapy, and written narrative exposure. As the two most highly researched, we briefly describe prolonged exposure therapy (PE) and cognitive processing therapy (CPT) here.

Prolonged Exposure Therapy

Prolonged exposure therapy (PE) is one of several evidence-based approaches used to reduce the symptoms associated with post-traumatic stress disorder (PTSD; Hembree, Rauch, & Foa, 2003). One of the hallmarks of typical trauma response is that people mentally avoid thinking about or remembering the trauma event as a way of coping with memories of the painful or life-threatening situation. PE emerged from the school of cognitive-behaviorism and has the aim of helping clients gradually, and over time, approach the trauma situation and the feelings surrounding it. Two of the primary techniques used in PE are imaginal exposure and in vivo exposure. The process of PE involves first educating clients about the process of therapy so as to prepare them for what likely will be challenging and emotionally difficult work that purposefully engages the fear structure of the trauma (Hembree et al., 2003). Early on in the process, counselors teach clients breathing techniques that aid them in remaining calm and dealing with anxiety that often is stirred up during the exposure process. Breathing techniques ground clients physiologically and help them enter into a calming mental image. In the imaginal exposure component of the therapy, clients are asked to describe in detail and in the present tense the events of the trauma. Their descriptions are recorded so that they can listen to them in between sessions in order to increase the exposure to the events that they have been avoiding thinking about or feeling. In the in vivo component of therapy, clients are asked to create a list of the people, places, activities, and situations they tend to avoid as a result of the trauma. Clients are encouraged to gradually and regularly place themselves in these situations, again, as a way to undermine the avoidance coping mechanism that tends only to enhance their fears. Throughout the process of imaginal exposure and in vivo exposure, the counselor processes the client's feelings, assures the client of his or her safety, challenges the client to engage the process, and supports his or her progress.

Cognitive Processing Therapy

Cognitive processing therapy (CPT) is a psychosocial therapeutic intervention that is used to help adults restructure maladaptive cognitions that often emerge after a trauma (Held, Klassen, Brennan, & Zalta, 2018). Based on Albert Bandura's social cognitive theory of counseling, CPT helps people to address *stuck points* or the distorted beliefs about the trauma that negatively affect their emotions and behaviors. For example, many people who have been traumatized irrationally believe that they are morally accountable for the trauma event or that they could have prevented awful things from occurring to loved ones if only they had acted differently; this often leads to people to believe that they are bad people or even monsters. Such a belief can lead people to feeling depressed and chronically guilty when in fact they might be interpreting their power over the event through a biased view (e.g., the hindsight bias in which they hold themselves accountable for behavior during the trauma event based on information they had only after the event was over). Similarly, some people's view of the world becomes distorted after a trauma, and they begin to believe that the world is unsafe all of the time. CPT attempts to help people adjust their maladaptive beliefs to more appropriate beliefs about themselves and the world after the trauma, which often also has the effect of reducing excessive feelings of depression, guilt, betrayal, and self-blame (Held et al., 2018). Counselors using CPT often have to progress sensitively and empathetically with clients who even though they are encouraged to adopt more appropriate beliefs can find it difficult to let go of their irrational, negative beliefs. Affirming clients' while gently challenging their belief is recommended, as is patience with the process.

Cross-Cutting Ingredients for Effective Trauma Counseling

After years of research establishing which treatments are most effective in helping people who have experienced trauma, attention is more recently being paid to the factors that cut across all approaches and show effectiveness in helping reduce PTSD symptoms. Based on a review of data from the Veteran's Administration, the Department of Defense, and meta-analyses from various researchers, Gentry et al. (2017) identified active ingredients in evidence-based trauma counseling that are central to all approaches. These ingredients are highly recommended for inclusion in trauma counseling as they have been shown to improve trauma symptoms. They include:

- *Psychoeducation and cognitive restructuring*: Psychoeducation includes the counselor walking the client through the specific steps of the trauma counseling and answering questions from the client. Cognitive restructuring involves the many focused conversations in which the therapist challenges irrational (but common) beliefs about the self, world, and others that arise after a trauma event.
- *Therapeutic relationship and feedback informed treatment (FIT)*: Counselors who work with those who are traumatized must be able to remain calm and relaxed, regulate their own emotions, handle stress, and express empathy. They also are recommended to use FIT or intentional means (sometimes through computer programs) that allow them to gain the clients' regular impressions about their progress throughout the therapeutic process.

- *Self-regulation and relaxation*: Nearly all evidence-base treatments include ways to help the client manage their autonomic nervous system through relaxation techniques. Some include relaxation techniques, diaphragmatic breathing, and guided visualization.
- *Exposure or narrative*: Exposure is central to most trauma therapies and involves approaching the trauma event without over-stimulating the client. Likewise, many therapies involve helping the clients to develop new stories about the trauma event based on appropriate cognitions or interpretations of their own power over or role in the event.

Crisis Intervention and Trauma Response in Schools

Crisis and trauma prevention and response is recognized by now as critical to the safety and well-being of children across the country. Countless school shootings, natural disasters, and other incidences such as bullying and suicide have evidenced to the necessity of schools having plans in place for the physical and psychological health of all students. Not surprising, school counselors play a vital role in crisis and trauma response in their academic environments. In this section, we consider the emerging role of school counselors as trauma specialists; suggest some tasks in which they might engage at the level of crisis prevention, as well as offer school-wide recommendations for violence prevention; and review common reactions of children who have been exposed to violence or crisis.

School Counselor as Crisis and Trauma Specialist

In 2016, ASCA released a position statement calling for school counselors to practice as trauma-informed specialists. Grounded in research that suggests 46 million children are exposed to trauma or violence each year in the United States (Listenbee et al., 2012) and that those children are at risk for mental health problems, difficulties with relationships, and poor academic performance (Gerrity & Folcarelli, 2008), ASCA (2016b) urges counselors to be key players in developing a trauma-aware school environment. As such, school counselors must be knowledgeable of the impact of crisis and trauma on children, advocate for environments that actively promote safety, and identify and support students who have been victims of trauma. In addition, ASCA (2016b) recommends that school counselors who are trauma specialists:

- recognize signs of trauma in students,
- emphasize the importance of resilience in the face of trauma so that members of the school environment understand children's strengths and abilities to recover from crisis with appropriate support,
- avoid practices that would re-traumatize children,
- support an academic community grounded in social and emotional learning,
- promote policies and procedures that are trauma-sensitive,
- recognize how social media and technology can impact and magnify trauma for children and adults,
- encourage behavioral practices that are positive interventions and support and develop social and emotional learning, and
- provide information to parents and the community about how to support children in the event of a crisis or trauma.

Tasks of the School Counselor in Preventing and Responding to Crisis

School counselors can certainly apply the crisis intervention tasks described in the Kanel (2010) and James and Gilliland (2017) models when encountering students in crisis. However, because of their unique position in schools and because school counselors do not necessarily have one-to-one counseling relationships with all students, the focus and role of school counselors with respect to crisis response are somewhat different than for mental health counselors. In particular, school counselors play a role in preventing, intervening, and responding to crises that incite chaos and undermine the sense of safety and security within the entire school community (Allen et al., 2002; ASCA, 2013).

Citing best practices from the Idaho School Counselor Association, Riley and McDaniel (2000) discussed, first, how school counselors act as prevention specialists. Although counselors wear many hats in the schools in which they work, they increasingly play an important role in decreasing the likelihood of crisis and violence in schools by creating environments that are supportive and cohesive. To some extent, this means that they forge individual relationships with students, especially those who appear to be at high risk for becoming either a perpetrator or a victim of violence. Counselors may be called on to help assess the needs or risk levels of students who are identified as exhibiting early warning signs for violence or other types of crises. Thus, counselors themselves have to be familiar with the signs that precede violence among youths. In addition, ASCA (2013) specifically recommended school counselors to develop and implement anti-bullying, conflict resolution, and peer-mediation programs. In consultation with administrators, school counselors also can help schools partner with local law enforcement to have officers assigned to the building premises. These officers can be attentive to potential crisis and violence situations, as well as act as resources to school personnel. Finally, school counselors can petition to be on the school or school district crisis response team. Being familiar with district-wide response plans enables counselors to be an advocate for their own schools, students, and teachers.

Riley and McDaniel (2000) further recommended a set of tasks and roles for school counselors that involve them in intervening directly with students, as well as with parents, teachers, and school districts. They noted that, when working with students relative to crisis response, school counselors can work individually with students at risk (e.g., students who are the target of bullying) or with groups of students. When operating at the group level, school counselors can create classroom lessons and school programs that encourage mentoring and that discourage school violence; they also might lead counseling groups that help students to deal effectively with anger and emotions related to personal, social, and academic issues (ASCA, 2013). With regard to parents, school counselors can provide information or training on appropriate parenting and disciplining techniques, as well as act as a referral source for children who are struggling to be successful in the classroom and with peers. Working with parents and teachers to educate them about children's social and emotional needs, as well as their risk factors for committing violence, is a key part of intervening to reduce violence. At the systemic level, counselors can assist teachers, staff, and administration in handling students' discipline problems, as well as participate in the school district's crisis response team (Riley & McDaniel, 2000). Especially because of the increase in natural and manmade disasters, such as shootings and suicides that are occurring in and around schools, it is imperative that schools have plans in place to aid teachers, counselors, and all personnel in knowing what to do in the event of a crisis. Some responsibilities that fall to counselors on crisis teams include the following: organizing and providing counseling services to students in need, connecting and communicating with teachers and administrators, contacting parents and providing them with social support, canceling activities if needed, making connections with a feeder school in the event of crises, and coordinating follow-up care after a crisis. Sometimes, this involves making sure additional counselors are available to students on the school premises following a crisis event (Riley & McDaniel, 2000).

Practical Recommendations for Limiting School Violence

The following recommendations come from the National Association of School Psychologists (NASP, 2017) and are worth consideration by school counselors, who can play an important role in helping to implement these practices, though in reality all members of a school environment participate in preventing violence. School counselors, administrators, staff, and students can:

- create a safe and inviting school environment where all students are positively supported;
- engage students in taking responsibility for creating a positive and safe school atmosphere;
- ensure that all students know school codes of conduct and rules and that students are held accountable to those rules;
- encourage students to resist peer pressure to act negatively, violently, and irresponsibly;
- develop systems for students to report concerns for safety anonymously;
- limit, control, and monitor who has access to the school building;
- enlist volunteers or staff to monitor common areas such as parking lots, cafeterias, etc. for inappropriate or unusual behavior;
- develop a crisis plan and ensure that the school community is knowledgeable about the plan;
- hold crisis response drills regularly (e.g., drills regarding intruders or violent shooters);
- be a visible and welcoming presence at the school;
- review the safety and crisis response plan at least annually and use data to inform revisions to the plan; and
- plan trauma-informed lesson plans to be included in school curriculum (NASP, 2017).

Post-Crisis: Understanding Children's Responses

School counselors, as noted, play a role in preventing, responding to, and supporting students post-crisis. It is therefore critical that counselors be knowledgeable about trauma reactions in children. The American Academy of Experts in Traumatic Stress (2003) provided information about how crises affect children specifically and what counselors can do when they know or suspect that a student(s) has been exposed to a traumatic event. The following is a summary of the behavioral responses a school counselor might observe in children or learn about secondhand from parents during and after a crisis.

- *Regression in behavior:* Children may behave in ways more akin to those younger than themselves (e.g., sucking their thumb even if they have not used this form of comfort for some time, wetting the bed, or becoming clingy with trusted adults and parents).
- *Increase in fears and anxiety:* Children may respond to a crisis by appearing excessively afraid or worried about situations that do not normally cause anxiety, such as going to school alone or going to bed alone or in the dark.
- *Decreased academic performance and poor concentration:* Children may not be able to concentrate on or complete schoolwork as usual, especially if they are preoccupied with the crisis event or the fear caused by the event.

- *Increased aggression and oppositional behavior and decreased frustration tolerance:* Some children may show a disproportionate increase in aggressive behavior or, in adolescents, oppositional or defiant behaviors.
- *Increased irritability, emotional lability, and depressive feelings:* Children can show signs of depressed mood, lack of interest in the activities that previously were entertaining, and overall irritability.
- *Denial:* Children may deny or act as if a crisis or traumatic event such as a death of a parent, a beloved teacher, or a friend has not occurred. Although denial responses are as common in children as in adults, children may need help coming to terms with the reality of the crisis in gentle yet direct ways.

It is important to keep in mind that the reactions described above are typical responses to crises for children and adolescents and thus ought not be seen primarily as signs of psychological illness. Rather, they ought to be evaluated within the context of the crisis that occurred for the child or teenager.

The High-Risk Client: Understanding and Assessing Harm to Self

One of the most stressful experiences for mental health professionals in training involves helping people who pose a risk to their own safety and well-being. A question often asked by trainees is: What do I do when I have a client who wants to commit suicide? Meichenbaum (2005) noted that it is not unusual for counselors to work with suicidal clients over the course of their careers. Similarly, intern students who are placed in settings with highly stressed, chronically depressed, and under-resourced clients, as well as in placements such as inpatient hospitals, may be more likely than not to work with suicide-prone persons. The first part of this section introduces basic information about suicide, the suicidal client, and risk assessment with clients who pose a threat to their own lives.

Defining Suicide and Debunking Common Myths

We begin with a brief definition of suicide. Beauchamp (1985) talked about suicide this way:

- the person intentionally brings about his/her own death,
- the person is not coerced by others to take the action, and
- death is caused by conditions arranged by the person for the specific purpose of bringing about his/her own death.

Possibly because suicide is counter to natural instincts to persevere through even the most difficult of human situations (Joiner, 2010), there are many misconceptions about the act of suicide itself, as well as about people who commit suicide. Being aware of some of these myths is helpful for counselors so that they are better able to tailor their discussions with clients who are suicidal. Conversely, it is important for mental health professionals not to structure their clinical interventions around common misunderstandings about suicide in order to be of maximal benefit to clients and to ensure that they are not acting negligently with regard to their professional obligations. According to Joiner (2010), the following is a sample of some of those myths:

- Discussing suicide will cause the client to move toward doing it.
- Clients who threaten suicide don't do it.
- Suicide is an irrational and a selfish act.
- Persons who commit suicide are insane.
- Suicide runs in families—it is an inherited tendency.
- Once suicidal always suicidal.
- When a person has attempted suicide and pulls out of it, the danger is over.
- A suicidal person who begins to show generosity and share personal possessions is showing signs of renewal and recovery.
- Suicide is always an impulsive act.
- Suicide is an act of aggression or anger toward oneself.

Greene (1994) identified five additional myths surrounding childhood suicide:

- Children under the age of 6 do not commit suicide.
- Suicide in the latency years is extremely rare.
- Psychodynamically and developmentally, true depression is not possible in childhood.
- Children are cognitively and physically incapable of implementing a suicide plot successfully.

In the face of these many myths, it is important to keep in mind that most suicide attempts are expressions of extreme distress, not bids for attention (Captain, 2006; Joiner, 2010). Thus, Captain (2006) rightly noted that counselors should not be afraid to ask clients about suicidal thoughts. Most clients who are suicidal are relieved to talk about their feelings and to be assured that they are not out of the ordinary for thinking this way. Indeed, about a third of the population of people not in therapy has had suicidal thoughts (Meichenbaum, 2005).

Risk Assessment for Suicide

Unfortunately, suicide assessment can tend to be impressionistic and fail to consider pertinent information regarding a person's lethality. To guard against impressionistic evaluations of suicidal risk, it is helpful to review the research and the clinical data about suicide that outline the factors counselors ought to assess when they encounter a high-risk client. Joiner et al. (2007) noted that suicide can reliably be understood as involving (a) the desire to die, (b) the capacity to commit suicide, (c) the intent to harm oneself, and (d) buffers against self-harm. An effective suicide assessment addresses each of these areas.

Assessment Point 1: Desire to Die

The desire to die refers to a client's sense that life is simply not worth living and that he/she would be better off not alive. There is a strong psychological component to this factor that involves clients perceiving that they are a burden to others, as well as feeling hopeless and helpless with regard to their life situation. In assessing a client's desire to die, a counselor should inquire about the following (Joiner et al., 2007):

- the client's stated desire to die,
- the client's perceptions about being a burden to others in his/her life,

- the client's sense of hopelessness and helplessness (a depression screening can be helpful here),
- the client's feelings of being deeply alone, and
- the client's sense of being trapped by life circumstances with no way out.

Joiner et al. (2007) noted that, while the desire to die is always present in those who are suicidal, in itself this factor is not the most critical in determining whether or not a client is at high risk to die. The authors point out that many people have a wish to die but not every person is actually capable of committing the act. Thus, in the global assessment of risk, clients who desire to die but who do not have the capacity or intent to die are not at as high a risk as those with the latter two factors in place.

Assessment Point 2: Capacity to Commit Suicide

The second area that counselors want to assess for suicide relates to a person's actual ability to go through with the suicidal act (Joiner, 2005; Joiner et al., 2007; Rudd et al., 2006). To take one's life is not an easy task, and it involves both courage and desensitization to death and dying (Joiner, 2005). Joiner (2005) noted that the courage to commit suicide is not meant to be emulated or held up on a pedestal; rather, he noted that it speaks to the difficulty of actually overcoming the natural, inborn instinct to live. Overcoming the instinct to live can get eroded in repeated exposures to violence and death (including those that are experienced personally and those witnessed in others). To assess a person's capacity to die, Joiner et al. (2007) recommended asking clients about the following:

- the client's history of suicide attempts;
- the client's exposure to others' suicide attempts;
- the client's history or current participation in violence to others;
- the available means to kill oneself;
- the client's current substance use or current level of intoxication;
- the client's level of active symptoms of mental illness; and
- the client's expression of anger, rage, or agitation.

The presence of any or all of the above factors increases a person's capacity for suicide.

Assessment Point 3: Suicidal Intent

One of the most critical areas to assess with regard to suicide is a person's intent to commit the act (McGlothlin, Rainey, & Kindsvatter, 2005). Clients may have both a desire not to live and the ability to commit suicide, but if they do not have the intent or a specific plan to die, they are less likely to pursue their own deaths (Joiner et al., 2007). When counselors are assessing for a client's suicidal intent, they should consider the following points:

- The client is in the midst of an attempt to die or has a clear plan for how and when to die.
- The client has an identified means of taking his/her own life.
- The client has left important possessions to others.
- The client expresses the intention to die.

Assessment Point 4: Buffers Against Suicide

A suicide assessment should include not only the points of vulnerability that make a person desirous, capable, and intending of dying; it should also include an evaluation of the factors that mitigate against the suicide attempt. Buffers against suicide are the elements that protect people against death, provide points of hope, and indicate a will to continue living. When people can be reconnected to reasons to live, they will be less likely to follow through on suicidal intent, though it may not always directly decrease the risk level for suicide. Buffers for which counselors should assess include the following, as noted by Joiner et al. (2007):

- The client perceives he/she has immediate support available (e.g., in the person of the counselor, family, or friends).
- The client can identify a reason(s) to continue living and has a plan for the future.
- The client has core values that are strong.
- The client has a sense of purpose for life.
- The client is able to engage in the dialogue of the counseling session.

Evaluating Suicide Risk: Putting It All Together

The risk assessment model outlined by Joiner et al. (2007) and described above uses three levels of evaluation: high risk, moderate to high risk, and moderate to low risk.

- *High risk:* A client who is considered high risk has elements of the first three assessment points present; that is, the person has a desire to die, is capable of committing the suicidal act, and has the intent and/or a plan to die. In this instance, even the presence of buffers tends not to decrease risk, and a client with this presentation of factors should be aided in seeking immediate safety.
- *Moderate to high risk:* A client who is at moderate to high risk has a desire to die and also has either the capacity or the intent to die. In this case, the presence of buffers for safety can reduce the overall level of risk, and, conversely, the absence of any buffers can increase the risk level. When buffers against suicide are in place, a counselor may not need to recommend immediate action for the protection of a client's safety but likely will want to follow up and regularly monitor a client's risk and overall well-being. If buffers are not in place, immediate action to ensure a client's safety still may be needed.
- *Moderate to low risk:* A client has any of the three core elements of risk present, and the level of risk can be lessened by the presence of buffers for safety or elevated in the absence of such buffers.

Conducting a thorough risk assessment for suicide is part of competent clinical practice. However, Granello (2010) wisely pointed out that suicide assessment is as much about the process of conducting the risk assessment as it is about knowing the specific warning signs and risk factors for suicide. She identified numerous principles that guide the implementation of a suicide assessment. Specifically, she encouraged clinicians to keep in mind that assessment is unique to each person; an ongoing, collaborative, and complex process; responsive to warning signs; sensitive to cultural issues; reliant on clinical judgment; documented; errant on the side of caution; inclusive of tough questions; and a form of treatment itself.

Suicide Risk Assessment Instruments

The use of empirical evaluation can help ground suicide risk assessments. Suicide scales, checklists, and other psychological instruments can be helpful in determining suicidal risk (Granello, 2010; Klott, 2012). Empirical instruments are excellent resources for those who may be inexperienced in dealing with suicide. In addition, consultation and discussions with a more experienced supervisor, therapist, or treatment team help promote a multifaceted approach and decrease the probability of suicide resulting from flawed treatment interventions (Granello, 2010).

The Substance Abuse and Mental Health Services Administration recommended a five-step process in assessing suicide known as the Suicide Assessment Five Step Evaluation and Triage (SAFE-T) model. SAFE-T is based on best practice guidelines established by the American Psychiatric Association (2003) for assessing and treating suicide. Using this assessment tool, counselors first identify current risk factors for suicide; these can include a history of abuse, history of suicide attempts, diagnostic risk factors, history of family suicide attempts, and high level of impulsivity. Second, clinicians investigate with the client any potential protective factors that would mitigate against suicidal behavior, such as religious beliefs, positive relationships, and responsibility for children. Third, counselors inquire into suicidal thoughts, plans, behaviors, and overall intent. Fourth, clinicians must use their knowledge and experience in conjunction with the clinical interview to determine the level of risk that the client is facing with regard to suicide and, together with the client, make treatment decisions. Finally, all clinicians should document the details of the interview, the characteristics of risk, and interventions used to address risk. Fowler (2012) recommended that clinicians who use this or other assessment tools align themselves with the client and make a concerted effort to approach the process with concern and an attitude of curiosity (rather than authority). A collaborative style can help clients feel more at ease during the assessment and ultimately be more upfront about suicidal plans and intent.

Intervention and Planning

Listed below are some techniques generally recognized by therapists to facilitate the counseling process for suicidal clients:

- Listen intelligently, sensitively, and carefully to the client.
- Accept and understand the client's suicidal thoughts.
- Do not give false assurances such as "Everything is going to be all right."
- Be supportive.
- Assure the client of your availability.
- Be firm and caring at the same time.
- Do not use euphemisms. Ask direct questions such as "Would you like to kill yourself?" or "Are you thinking of killing yourself?" rather than using vague expressions.
- Bring out any ambivalence the client has. Try to increase his/her choices.
- If the client is in crisis, do not leave him/her alone.
- Intervene to find ways to dispose of any weapons the client has or encourage the client to make the weapon less easily accessible (e.g., having it locked in a safe rather than in a bedside table).
- Tell others, especially those who would be concerned and can help. (You have already informed the client of the limits of confidentiality.)
- Help the client identify and develop support systems, especially when in crisis.

- Trust your own judgment.
- Know the suicide hotline numbers.
- Be aware of commitment procedures in your area.

The above suggested actions are helpful to counselors in putting together an overall safety plan for clients who are suicidal. Students who are interested in reviewing a more comprehensive list of possible questions and active interventions are referred to Meichenbaum (2005).

Finally, students may have questions about the role and use of suicide contracts in the process of working with suicidal clients. Though many clinicians used to be in the habit of developing suicide contracts with their clients (that both suicidal clients and counselors would sign, acknowledging the client's agreement not to self-harm), these contracts are not strongly encouraged today (Rudd et al., 2006). Instead, counselors are urged to put together commitments to treatment (Rudd et al., 2006) or safety plans (Klott, 2012) that include a list of clients' and counselors' responsibilities and preferred actions in the event that clients are tempted to act on suicidal intentions. A safety plan can encourage clients to contact family members, walk away from stress-inducing circumstances, and utilize means of emotional regulation (Klott, 2012). However, even with the best-prepared plan for safety, some clients still may desire to act on suicidal intentions and will neither comply with the plan nor consent to hospitalization. In serious cases, counselors may be in the position to consider involuntary commitment to a treatment center. The procedures for commitment, whether voluntary or involuntary, vary a great deal from area to area, and laws on commitment procedures are different from state to state. Mental health professionals should be familiar with the legal aspects of commitment in their areas. A copy of a Suicide Consultation Form (Form 10.1) is included in the Forms section at the end of this book; students may use this form, in consultation with their supervisors, to facilitate their counseling of clients who are potentially harmful to themselves.

Ethical and Legal Mandates Relating to Danger to Self

Working with people who are suicidal has ethical and legal implications for counselors. All codes of ethics from well-established mental health professional associations clearly state that the welfare of clients is paramount in the clinical process. The following excerpts from the ASCA (2016a) and the ACA (2014) *Codes of Ethics* highlight the types of responses that are expected of school counselors and professional counselors in the case of clients who pose harm to themselves.

Professional School Counselors

According to the ASCA *Code of Ethics* (2016a), professional school counselors are expected to:

1. Inform parents/guardians and/or appropriate authorities when a student poses a serious and foreseeable risk of harm to self or others (ASCA, 2016a, A.9.a). School counselors are recommended to carefully deliberate and consult with other counseling professionals in determining risk, but they also are encouraged to err on the side of caution and inform concerned parties even if the risk appears remote.
2. Use risk assessments with caution. If risk assessments are used by the counselor, an intervention plan should be developed and in place prior to this practice (ASCA, 2016a, A.9.b). School counselors report risk assessments to parents even if the risk is minimal as it underscores the need to act on behalf of a child at risk.

3. Not release a student who is a danger to self or others until the student has proper and necessary support (ASCA, 2016a, A.9.c). In most cases, a counselor will contact a parent for support, but if a parent is not available, this might include contacting child protective services.
4. Report to parents/guardians and/or appropriate authorities when students disclose a perpetrated or perceived threat to their physical or mental well-being (ASCA, 2016a, A.9.d). The threats to well-being include various and all types of abuse, and counselors are expected also to follow the legal mandates of their states in making reports.

Professional Counselors

The ethical obligations for professional counselors working with clients at risk to harm themselves or others is laid out in the ACA *Code of Ethics* (2014) standard on confidentiality:

> The general requirement that counselors keep information confidential does not apply when disclosure is required to protect clients or identified others from serious and foreseeable harm or when legal requirements demand that confidential information must be revealed. Counselors consult with other professionals when in doubt as to the validity of an exception. Additional considerations apply when addressing end-of-life issues.
>
> (American Counseling Association, 2014, B.2.a.)

In addition to ethical responsibilities to do good by the client by protecting his/her bodily welfare in the instance of possible self-harm, the counselor also faces legal responsibilities around client suicidality. The mental health professional's special relationship with the client creates the context for the legal accountability for negligent malpractice with potentially suicidal persons. A therapist is assumed to possess superior knowledge and skills beyond those of the average person and may be considered by the courts to bear responsibility for the suicide of his/her client. The client's reliance on the counselor alone is enough to shift some of the weight of the responsibility for the client's actions to the mental health professional.

This was not always the case. In England, for example, toward the latter part of the 19th century, suicide was considered self-murder, and authorities buried the bodies of those who committed suicide at the side of the road with a stake through the heart (Bednar, Bednar, Lambert, & Waite, 1991). In contrast, today a mental health professional who does not take appropriate action to prevent a suicide can be held liable. At the same time, liability has not been found when apparently cooperative clients suddenly attempt suicide (*Carlino v. State*, 1968; *Dalton v. State*, 1970) or when an aggressive client does not reveal any suicidal symptoms (*Paridies v. Benedictine Hospital*, 1980). In determining liability, courts also must decide whether the recommendations of a mental health professional were followed. In one case, a hospital was found liable when the staff did not follow the psychiatrist's recommendations (*Comiskey v. State of New York*, 1979).

Liability may be imposed if a therapist is determined to be negligent in his/her treatment of a client. Negligence is found when the mental health professional does not perform his/her duties according to the standard of care for that particular profession. As a consequence, counselors should make as accurate an assessment of the danger as possible (based on the client interview, observation of client behavior, and review of the client's history); determine what action is reasonable, which may mean intensifying treatment, referring the client for a medication check, advising voluntary commitment, or authorizing involuntary commitment; and make sure the recommendation is followed.

Suicide Risk Assessment and Prevention in Schools

Suicide among American youths is cause of concern for counselors, who must not discount the possibility that young people can take their own lives. Gould, Shaffer, and Greenberg (2003) point out that 5.8% of deaths among children aged 10–14 are due to suicide. The American Association of Suicidology (2007) reported that, for youth aged 15–19, suicide is the third leading cause of death, which accounts for the loss of over 4,100 lives per year. Perhaps of greater concern is that actual cases are considered to be underreported (Barrio, 2007). The American Association of Suicidology (2007) also reported that for every completed suicide, youths make about 100–200 attempts. The tragedy of suicide is further complicated by the strong possibility that it can be prevented (Barrio, 2007). Professionals concur that most potential suicide victims want to be saved and often send out signals for help. Considering the magnitude of this problem, schools have a moral imperative to develop suicide prevention programs (Joe & Bryant, 2007).

Basics of Suicide Prevention Programs in Schools

School counselors have responsibility for the welfare and safety of students in their schools and therefore may be actively involved in creating and updating the school-based suicide prevention plan. This emphasizes the trauma-specialist perspective on school counseling called for by ASCA (2016b). Thinking globally about the welfare of students is necessary for counselors who act on behalf of hundreds of students at a time; for this reason, program-based prevention approaches are often the most accessible and effective in the school setting. The literature suggests that to be effective, school-based programs must be comprehensive and systematic and include strategies for suicide prevention, intervention, and postvention following a completed suicide (Miller, Eckert, & Mazza, 2009). Comprehensive and systematic programs also must be ongoing, intact, and continuously updated. Many researchers who have developed models of school-based programs share this position. A review of recent literature (e.g., Doan, LeBlanc, Roggenbaum, & Lazear, 2012) reveals the following components as those most often recommended for school-based adolescent suicide prevention and intervention programs:

- a written formal policy statement for reacting to suicide and suicidal ideation, as well as following up with postvention strategies;
- staff training and orientation for recognizing at-risk students, determining the level of risk, and knowing where to refer the student;
- "booster" trainings for teachers, staff, and personnel every 2–3 years to keep school personnel updated about suicide risk and risk assessment;
- mental health professionals on-site;
- a mental health team;
- information programs and prevention materials for distribution to parents;
- incorporation of suicide curriculum and education for students;
- psychological screening programs to identify at-risk students;
- prevention-focused classroom discussions;
- mental health counseling for at-risk students;
- development of peer support groups for students who are at risk;
- suicide prevention and intervention training for school counselors;
- postvention component in the event of an actual suicide;

- written statement describing specific criteria for counselors to assess the lethality of a potential suicide; and
- a written policy describing how the program will be evaluated.

Learning About and Responding to Potentially Suicidal Students

School-based mental health professionals may encounter suicide-related crisis situations in at least three different ways, each of which requires some specific guidelines. First, the student may attempt suicide on school premises. In this case, the counselor should refer to the school's policy regarding this intervention. Second, the student may disclose suicidal ideation directly to the counselor without having attempting suicide. When this happens, the counselor should assess lethality as the first level of response (steps for assessing risk are outlined in the next section) and consult the school's prevention and intervention plan. Third, peers may inform the counselor of a suicidal student. Seven out of ten students will tell a peer about suicidal ideation before telling anyone else. It is especially important to take this information seriously, conduct a risk assessment, and inform a student's parents of the concern in order to help the student receive appropriate care and to avoid acting negligently (Pate, 1992). In all cases, the ASCA *Code of Ethics* (2016a) should be consulted during the decision-making process. The following are some additional guidelines for action in each of the situations noted earlier:

1. *If a suicide attempt occurs on the premises*, involve appropriate school personnel, then notify the police and an ambulance service. Also notify the parents (or guardian). Let them know where their child is being taken. If the parents (or guardian) are not available, notify the next closest relative. See to it that the student receives proper medical and psychiatric care.
2. *If the student discloses suicidal ideation to you*, first consult your supervisor or another mental health professional. Go over the assessment of lethality with the student. This process will help you establish the standard of care. Call the parents (or guardian) and tell them to go to the appropriate psychiatric facility. Explain to the parents and the student that an evaluation or diagnosis does not necessarily mean commitment. If the parents resist this process, you may need to contact your local children and youth services for assistance. Be sure to contact the parents in the presence of the child, to eliminate the "he said—she said" phenomenon.
3. *If a peer tells you about another student's suicidal intent*, confront the student. If the student admits the suicidal ideation, follow the procedure outlined above. If the student denies the ideation, notify the parents (or guardian). Of course, you must inform the student about this disclosure.

Suicide Risk Assessment for Students

One of the elements of a suicide prevention program, as mentioned above, involves determining whether or not a student is at risk for attempting suicide. Appropriate intervention steps cannot be implemented until lethality is determined. In addition to the risk assessment procedures described in an earlier section (Joiner et al., 2007), the following process suggests actions that school teachers, counselors, and other personnel can take when a student is suspected of being suicidal (Pate, 1992):

1. *Ask directly during a session.* Ask the student, without hesitation, if he/she is thinking about killing himself/herself. If the student claims to have had suicidal ideation, the strength of the intent should be determined. Continue with the questioning.

2. *Ask if he/she has attempted suicide before.* If so, ask how many times attempts were made and when they were made. The more attempts, and the more recent the attempts, the more serious the situation becomes.
3. *Ask how the previous attempts were made.* If the student took aspirin, for example, ask how many. One? Six? Twenty? Then, ask about the consequences of the attempts. For example, was there medical intervention?
4. *Ask why.* Why did the student attempt suicide before? Why the suicidal thoughts now?
5. *Does the student have a plan?* Ask about the details. The more detailed the plan is, the more lethal it is. Does the student know when and how the attempt will be made? Assess the lethality of the method. This assessment is critical. Does the student have a weapon or access to one? Using a gun or hanging oneself leaves little time for medical help.
6. *Ask about the student's preoccupation with suicide.* Does he/she think about it only at home or during a particular incident—or does it go beyond all other activities?
7. *Ask about drug use.* Drug use complicates the seriousness of the situation because people tend to be less inhibited when under the influence of drugs. Although the student may deny drug use, try to get as much information as possible.
8. *Observe nonverbal actions.* Is the student agitated, tense, or sad? Is he/she inebriated? Use caution if the student seems to be at peace. This peaceful state may be the result of having organized a suicide plan, with completion being the next step.
9. *Try to gauge the level of depression.* A student may not be depressed because he/she is anxious about completing the plan.

Using the points outlined in this process will help in determining the level of suicide risk for a student. A low-risk student may have thoughts about suicide but has never attempted suicide in the past, does not have a plan, is not taking drugs, and is not preoccupied with the ideation. Most students at low risk will agree to the therapist's contacting their parents, which should be done.

A high-risk student has a plan but may or may not have attempted suicide in the past. Of course, a previous attempt is an important factor in assessing lethality, especially if the attempt was recent (Joiner, 2005). But counselors should remember that many first-time attempts are successful. The current situation must never be minimized. The plan of a high-risk student is usually detailed, and the ideation frequent. At this point, other people need to become involved, including the counselor's supervisor, principal, and school nurse.

Ideally, the school will have some type of suicide intervention policy. The goal in a high-risk situation is to have the student undergo a psychiatric evaluation as soon as possible, whether by voluntary or involuntary commitment. The student's parents must be notified. Although confidentiality laws vary from state to state, a counselor usually is not bound if the client intends to harm himself/herself or someone else (Moyer & Sullivan, 2008). It is absolutely imperative, however, that school counselors discuss confidentiality limits at the beginning of every client intake session.

The High-Risk Client: Potential Harm to Others

Working with clients who pose harm to others, like working with potentially suicidal clients, is an anxiety-provoking experience for seasoned counselors and for those in training. Mental health professionals become acutely aware of their own liability in such situations and thus must be prepared with regard to knowing about their professional obligations, being able to identify persons who pose a threat to others, and developing competence around assessing risk and determining an action plan for potentially dangerous clients. In this section, we look first at the issue of professional obligation (through the lens of the *Tarasoff* case) and then at the issues surrounding risk assessment.

The *Tarasoff* Case: The Events

Prosenjit Poddar was a graduate student at the University of California, Berkeley. In 1968, Poddar attended dancing classes at the International House in Berkeley, where he met a woman named Tatiana (Tanya) Tarasoff. This meeting quickly led to an obsessive, one-sided love affair. Poddar began harassing Ms. Tarasoff, calling and pestering her continually. He was consistently and repeatedly rebuffed by the young woman. In the summer of 1969, Tarasoff went to Brazil. When she returned, Poddar went to her home and again was rebuffed. Poddar drew a pellet gun and shot at her. Desperate, the young woman ran from the house, only to be chased down and caught by Poddar, who fatally stabbed her with a kitchen knife. This tragic chain of events unleashed some unforeseen and shocking consequences for mental health professionals. While Tarasoff was in Brazil, Poddar had sought help for depression at Cowell Memorial Hospital, an affiliate of the University of California, Berkeley. His intake interview was conducted by Dr. Stuart Gold, a psychiatrist, and his therapy was conducted by a psychologist, Dr. Lawrence Moore. In August 1969, Poddar told Dr. Moore he was going to kill Tarasoff when she returned from Brazil. Moore immediately consulted his supervisor, and they agreed that Poddar should be involuntarily committed. Dr. Moore called the police, who detained Poddar, but after questioning the man, police officials decided he was rational and released him. His freedom led directly to Tarasoff's death.

Implications of the Tarasoff *Case*

In late 1974, the California Supreme Court ruled there was cause for action for negligence against the therapist, the university, and the police for the failure to warn (*Tarasoff v. Regents of the University of California*, 1974). This case is commonly known as *Tarasoff I*. The court, apparently under pressure from various professional groups, agreed to a rehearing in 1976 (*Tarasoff v. Regents of the University of California*, 1976). This case is commonly known as *Tarasoff II*.

Whenever we mention the *Tarasoff* case throughout this book, we are citing *Tarasoff II*. In the court's final decision, presented in *Tarasoff II* on July 1, 1976, it set a new standard for therapists. The mandate was clear: "*Therapists who know or should know of patients' dangerousness to identifiable third persons have an obligation to take all reasonable steps necessary to protect the potential victims* [italics added]" (Appelbaum, 1985, p. 425).

Various writers on the subject of *Tarasoff* have defined the term *therapist* to include psychologists; counselors; child, marriage, and family therapists; and community mental health counselors. As Stone (cited in Waldo & Malley, 1992) noted,

> Many mental health professionals and paraprofessionals, including social workers, psychiatric social workers, psychiatric nurses, occupational therapists, pastoral counselors, and guidance counselors, provide some form of therapy. . . . How many of these millions of therapist–patient contacts each year are intended to be covered by the court's decision is unclear.

(p. 59)

What Tarasoff *Did Not Require*

Researchers have looked extensively at what the *Tarasoff* ruling requires and does not require of mental health professionals. VandeCreek and Knapp (1993) addressed this issue head on:

> Because the *Tarasoff* decision has been subject to so many misinterpretations, it is important to know what the *Tarasoff* court did *not* say. The court did not require psychotherapists to issue a warning every time a patient talks about an urge or fantasy to harm someone. On the contrary, the court stated that "a therapist should not be encouraged routinely to reveal such threats . . . unless such disclosure is necessary to avert danger to others" (*Tarasoff*, p. 347). Finally, the court did not specify that warning the intended victim was the only required response when danger arises; on the contrary, the court stated that the discharge of such duty may require the therapist to take one or more of various steps.
>
> (p. 6)

*Post-*Tarasoff

Since the *Tarasoff* trial, other courts have ruled that liability should not be imposed on the therapist if a victim was not identified (*Thompson v. County of Alameda*, 1980). However, other courts have ruled that the potential victim need only be foreseeably identifiable (*Jablonski v. United States*, 1983) or that the danger need only be foreseeable (*Hedlund v. Superior Court of Orange County*, 1983; *Lipari v. Sears Roebuck*, 1980). Mental health professionals have been found liable for not using prior patient records to predict violence (*Jablonski v. United States*, 1983) and for keeping inadequate records (*Peck v. The Counseling Service of Addison County*, 1985). A Florida appellate court ruled that *Tarasoff* should not be imposed because the relationship of trust and confidence, necessary for the therapeutic process, would be harmed if mental health professionals were required to warn potential victims (*Boynton v. Burglass*, 1991). According to Walcott, Cerundolo, and Beck (2001), the general movement of the courts in recent years has been to limit rather than expand *Tarasoff*.

Risk Assessment for Potentially Dangerous Clients

Walcott and his colleagues (2001) provided two basic guidelines for assessing danger in clients that would prompt the counselor to dispatch the duty to warn and protect others. First, counselors should determine if the client has a specific individual whom they wish to do harm, and, second, counselors need to assess the client's history of violence. If both a specific person is named and a history of violence is present, counselors would seem to have greater responsibility to warn and protect. Appelbaum (1985) also presented a model for fulfilling the *Tarasoff* obligation, urging that clinicians treating potentially dangerous patients undertake a three-stage process of risk assessment and action.

1. The first task, *assessment* of the client, has two components:
   a. First, the therapist must gather the data to evaluate the level of danger.
   b. Second, he/she must make a determination of dangerousness on the basis of that data.
2. The second task involves the clinician in *choosing a course of action* to protect potential victims when he/she has determined that a client is likely to be dangerous.

3. The third task entails the clinician *implementing decisions appropriately*. This task has two components:

   a. First, the therapist must take action to protect potential victims.
   b. Second, the counselor must monitor the situation on a continuing basis to assess the success or failure of the initial response, the likelihood that the patient will be violent, and the need for further measures (Appelbaum, 1985, p. 426).

Task I: Risk Assessment

Information needed to assess the level of danger can be found in the client's past and current history of behaviors, demographic factors, psychological diagnoses, and various other risk areas shown to increase the likelihood of violence. A thorough risk assessment should be gathered in the clinical interview. Otto (2000) pointed out that there are various means of risk assessment, including structured and clinical interviews, as well as assessment tools. Webster, Douglas, Eaves, and Hart (1997) authored the HCR-20, a tool for conducting a structured interview when evaluating violent behavior in clients. The HCR-20 aids the counselor in assessing historical factors, clinical factors, and risk-related factors that increase a client's likelihood for violence. Otto (2000) provided an excellent overview of areas to which counselors should attend when conducting a clinical risk assessment. He noted that there are demographic factors that increase likelihood of violence; for instance, people in their late teens to early 40s are more prone to commit violence than those younger or older. In addition, men tend to have a higher prevalence toward violent crimes and acts than do women. Otto (2000) also recommended that counselors assess the following areas, as they form a constellation of factors that increase risk:

- history of past violent or criminal behavior (this is one of the most reliable predictors of future violence) and start of violent behavior at an early age;
- history of and current use of substances;
- history of child abuse, maltreatment, or neglect;
- presence of a mental illness and presence of hallucinations in which the client hears a command to commit a violent act;
- perception that one is being threatened by others or outside forces;
- difficulty in dealing with life stressors;
- a disposition to be impulsive or respond angrily to stressors without thinking about options;
- presence of significant life stressors, such as financial stressors, unemployment, relationship difficulties, etc.; and
- lack of personal support systems.

The following questions and guidelines, based on the above-mentioned areas that increase risk of harm to others, can be used by counselors to help determine the potential for violent behavior:

1. Does the client have a history of violent behavior? Past violence is the best predictor of future violence.
2. Does the client have a history of violent conduct with a previous assessment or diagnosis of mental illness?
3. Does the client have a history of arrests for violent conduct?

4. Does the client have a history of threats associated with violent conflict?

5. Has the client ever been diagnosed with a mental disorder for which violence is a common symptom?

6. Has the client had at least one inpatient hospitalization associated with dangerous conduct, whether voluntary or involuntary?

7. Does the client have any history of dangerous conduct, apparently unprovoked and not stress related?

8. If the client has a history of dangerous conduct, how long ago was the incident? The more recent the dangerous behavior, the more likely it is that the behavior will be repeated.

9. If the client appears dangerous to someone else, document any threats, including clinical observations related to danger, and notify the person who might be harmed. Those acts that have a high degree of intent or intensity are most likely to recur.

10. Determine if any serious threats, attempts, or acts harmful to others have been related to drug or alcohol intoxication.

11. Ask the client direct and focused questions, such as "What is the most violent thing you have ever done?" and "How close have you come to becoming violent?" (Monahan, 1993, p. 244).

12. Use the reports of significant others. Often, family members can provide valuable information about a client's potential for violence. Again, ask direct questions, such as "Are you worried that your loved one is going to hurt someone?" (Monahan, 1993, p. 244).

13. Has the client threatened others?

14. Does the client have access to weapons?

15. What is the client's relationship to the intended victim(s)?

16. Does the client belong to a social support group that condones violence?

Task II: Selecting a Course of Action

Once the mental health professional has assessed the danger a client poses to others, he/she must decide what to do. Use the following guidelines to help form an action plan:

1. *If the danger does not seem imminent, keep the client in intensified therapy.* Deal with the client's aggression as part of the treatment. However, if the client does not adhere to the treatment plan—that is, if he/she discontinues therapy—the danger level should be considered higher.

2. *Invite the client to participate in the disclosure decision.* This process often makes the client feel more in control. It is also prudent to contact the third party in the presence of the client. This may limit paranoia over what has been communicated.

3. *Attempt environmental manipulations.* Medication may be initiated, changed, or increased. Have the client get rid of any lethal weapons.

4. *Keep careful records.* When recording information relevant to risk, note the source of the information (e.g., the name of the spouse); the content (e.g., the character of the threat and the circumstances under which it was disclosed); and the date on which the information was disclosed. Finally, include your rationale for any decisions you make.

5. *If warning a third party is unavoidable, disclose only the minimum amount necessary to protect the victim or the public.* State the specific threat, but reserve any opinions or predictions.

6. *Consult with your supervisor.* Agencies or schools should have a contingency plan for such problems that is derived in consultation with an informed attorney, an area psychiatric facility, and local police (Bernes & Bardick, 2007).

Task III: Monitoring the Situation

Counselors should constantly monitor any course of action to ensure that the objectives of the initial implementation are satisfied. Follow-up procedures should be scrupulously adhered to and well documented. The Harm to Others Form (Form 10.2), which can be used in the facilitation of the assessment and monitoring process, is included in the Forms section at the end of the book. Of course, because of the gravity of homicidal risk assessments, students should always participate in the assessment process with a supervisor present.

Clients' Past Criminal Acts

There is a substantial body of literature that addresses what counselors and mental health professionals should do when working with a client who has the potential to act on criminal intent. However, a less addressed issue relates to what to do in the case of a client revealing involvement in past crimes against others. Appelbaum and Meisel (1986) reported that therapists' legal obligations to report past criminal acts differ under state and federal laws. Under federal law, therapist obligations fall under a statute of "misprision of a felony." Appelbaum and Meisel (1986) noted these conditions as necessary to establish guilt for a misprision of a felony:

1. The principal committed and completed the felony alleged.
2. The defendant had full knowledge of the fact.
3. The defendant failed to notify authorities.
4. The defendant took an affirmative step to conceal the crime.

The mere failure to report the crime does not appear to meet the criteria of affirmative concealment. If the mental health professional is questioned by law enforcement officials, he/she must respond truthfully but is not obligated to break confidentiality; it does not appear that the mental health professional has an obligation to say anything at all. Few states have statutes addressing misprision of a felony. Most do require the reporting of gunshot wounds, child abuse, or other specified evidence of certain crimes. Walfish, Barnett, Marlyere, and Zielke (2010) examined the incidence of clients reporting past crimes to their therapists and found that it was not infrequent, which provides good reason for counselors to be familiar with their state laws regarding disclosure of past and unprosecuted crimes.

The Client Who Is Being Abused: Responding, Reporting, and Intervening

People who are victims of abuse can be of any age, race, ethnicity, educational level, and socioeconomic status. They clearly comprise a special population who are in crisis or prone to experience trauma. Intervening on behalf of persons who are being abused is critical in all instances. However, intervening on behalf of children who are being neglected, maltreated, or abused is critical because of the known deleterious effects of childhood maltreatment on normal human development. This section highlights the risk factors of childhood abuse, recommends a course of action for reporting child abuse, and also provides a list of suggested therapeutic approaches for working with adult survivors of childhood abuse.

According to the Children's Bureau, an affiliate of the United States Department of Health and Human Services (DHHS), approximately 3.4 million cases of child abuse were reported to child protective agencies in the United States during the year 2011 (US DHHS, 2011). In addition, it can be conservatively estimated that at least five students have been or will be reported as being possible victims of abuse in a typical teacher's classroom per year in the United States. Sadly, the Children's Bureau also reported that in 2011 an estimated 1,570 children died from abuse and maltreatment.

Child abuse is "an act of omission or commission causing intentional harm or endangerment to the child under age 18" (Bryant & Milsom, 2005, p. 63). Abuse is understood to include neglect, as well as physical, sexual, and emotional harm. Examples of abuse to which counselors must be alert include adults using children for their own sexual gratification, intentionally inflicting physical harm, or threatening or terrorizing a child in such a way that it harms the child's self-esteem. Neglect can be defined to include the failure to provide necessary food, care, clothing, shelter, supervision, or medical attention for a child (i.e., malnourished, ill-clad, dirty, without proper shelter or sleeping arrangements, lacking appropriate health care, unattended, lacking adequate supervision, ill and lacking essential medical attention; irregular or illegal absences from school; exploited, overworked, lacking essential psychological nurturing; abandonment). Neglect is the most often reported form of abuse and makes up about 78% of cases handled by child protective services (US DHHS, 2011). Physical abuse is a form of neglect that results in or could result in physical harm to a child (US DHHS, 2011). Forms of physical abuse include hitting, kicking, shaking, burning, strangling, and, in extreme cases, homicide. Just over 17% of all reported cases of abuse are categorized as physical abuse; this is the second most commonly reported form of abuse (US DHHS, 2011). Childhood sexual abuse is defined in various ways according to state laws, however, this type of abuse usually involves the perpetrator using a child for his or her own financial benefit or sexual gratification (US DHHS, 2011). Examples of sexual abuse include rape, molestation, incest, prostitution, and sexual exploitation in pornography. Psychological abuse refers to mental and emotional suffering related to hostile, punitive, and habitual verbal abuse. Examples of psychological abuse include things such as denigrating, humiliating remarks, ridiculing statements, and bullying such that a child feels threatened and in an ongoing state of hyper-arousal (Kenny, Fernandez, & Abreu, 2012).

Risk and Mediating Factors for Child Abuse

Kenny et al. (2012) provided an overview of the prevalence, risk factors, consequences, and mediating factors of childhood sexual abuse. Counselors should be knowledgeable about the following stressors that increase the likelihood that a child may be exposed to neglect, physical, sexual, and emotional abuse. Risk factors are not limited to, but, according to research, include:

- *Neglect*: poor parent-child relationships, parents perceiving their children as a burden, high stress levels in parents, history of anger in parents, poor self-concept on the part of parents, and financial problems.
- *Physical abuse*: lower socioeconomic status of parents, presence of chronic illness in the child, age of the child (those under age 4 are at greatest risk for physical abuse) (US DHHS, 2011), and parental history of being physically abused.
- *Sexual abuse*: gender (females are more often sexually abused than males), age (children aged 13–17 are at greatest risk for sexual abuse), presence of a substance-abusing father (for intra-familial sexual abuse), and presence of a substance-abusing mother (for extra-familial sexual abuse).

■ *Psychological abuse*: drug and alcohol abuse by a caregiver, presence of domestic violence, maternal depression, being raised in a single-parent household, and the caregiver's own history with emotional abuse.

Mediating factors are environmental or intrapersonal strengths that help children to cope with and lessen the impact or consequences of neglect and abuse. Being familiar with mediating factors when working with abuse victims can aid counselors because knowledge of these factors can help them prioritize the in which to support and intervene. Cicchetti and Rogosch (2009) found that important intrapersonal resources for neglect and physical abuse victims were self-esteem, an ability to be self-reliant, an ability to regulate one's emotions, and an adaptable personality. An ability to be optimistic about the future also is important. Mediating factors for childhood sexual abuse include strong family support, immediate response and treatment for the abuse, and a supportive maternal relationship upon revelation of the abuse (Goodyear-Brown, Fath, & Myers, 2012).

Legal Issues Related to Reporting Child Abuse

Mandated reporters usually are professionals who interact with children in the course of their work. The federal Child Abuse Prevention and Treatment Act (US Department of Health and Human Services, 2003) requires that sexual, physical, and psychological exploitation of children be reported. *Any circumstance that indicates serious harm or threat to a child's welfare must be reported.* Confidentiality and privileged communication are not legal reasons for failing to report abuse. The laws against child abuse supersede the laws of privilege and the ethical mandates of confidentiality (Lambie, 2005). Thus, it is critical that counselors are familiar with the laws in their state that govern their responses to child abuse. State laws can vary with regard to the threshold required to trigger a report to child protective services agencies (Marshall, 2012). For example, some states require that counselors make a report if they suspect that abuse has occurred, while other states have laws that oblige a report if the clinician suspects abuse has occurred or *is likely to occur* (Marshall, 2012). In addition, states have varying definitions of what constitutes abuse, and definitions differ with regard to the specificity of how abuse is delimited. For example, the states of Georgia and Washington are the only ones that do not include psychological abuse in their statutes on child abuse (US Department of Health and Human Services, 2009). It is helpful to keep in mind that, if the abuse is reported in good faith, most states do not allow retribution; that is, the mental health professional cannot be sued for defamation of character even if the abuse report is unfounded. Most states do not have a statute of limitations on child abuse cases, unless the abuse was reported previously and the charges were dismissed. This suggests that mental health professionals must report abuse that occurred many years ago. Counselors may be liable in civil lawsuits for failure to report suspected abuse, though no criminal cases have come against counselors in this regard (Lambie, 2005).

Making a Report Related to Child Abuse

Therapists who decide to file a child abuse report typically do so by calling the appropriate social service agency. They must file a written report subsequent to the call. A caseworker will be assigned to the case by the child protective services agency. If the caseworker finds probable evidence that neglect or abuse has occurred, he/she refers the case to a law enforcement agency. At that point, the state either begins a criminal prosecution or takes civil action. If someone other than a parent or caretaker accuses a parent of sexually abusing a child, authorities may initiate both criminal and civil proceedings simultaneously (Bryant & Milsom, 2005). It should be noted that one difficulty in making a report of suspected child abuse is that clinicians may be obliged even if the child does not want the report made and even if the mental health professional does not feel it is in the best interest of the child to do so (Sikes, Remley, & Hays, 2010). Marshall (2012) pointed out that the decision-making process around reporting can be tricky and demands nuanced development of clinical skills. For example, she noted that clinicians will have to determine, in the instance of emotional abuse, the level of abuse that is occurring and consider that evaluation in deciding whether or not to make a report. A clinician will have to assess if the actions on the part of a parent or caregiver are the result of poor, underdeveloped, but nonmalicious parenting skills that can be addressed therapeutically or if the style of interaction with the child is consistently harmful and pernicious enough to constitute abuse. A Child Abuse Reporting Form (Form 10.3) is included in the Forms section. This asks the counselor to record basic information required to make an initial call to the authorities and to file a formal written report. The Child Abuse Reporting Form shows the required information a counselor needs to have prior to filing a report of child abuse.

Interviewing Children Who May Have Been Sexually Abused

Counselors working with young children on possible sexual abuse must be aware that the language, cognition, and logic systems of children are different from those of adults; in other words, children are not miniature adults. A child's vocabulary is much more limited, which means that children understand much more than they can say. Counselors must learn specific interviewing techniques and clinical skills to work with young children (Mart, 2010). For instance, the use of pronouns, double negatives, and compound sentences should be avoided in the interview. Instead, the counselor should focus on familiar events, for example, "Did this take place after your birthday or before your birthday?"

Children remember what happened, but their causal connections are not the same as those of adults. If they have been sexually abused, they may think (indeed, they most often do) that they caused the abuse or even wanted it. Thus, counselors should carefully assess the developmental level and capabilities of their young clients before interviewing them. For example, Berliner and Lieb (2001) suggested assessing younger children's cognitive ability to distinguish between the truth and a falsehood by using concrete examples and questions. In addition, children often are afraid they will no longer be loved; are guilty, ashamed, and afraid they will get into trouble; and may even fear harm or death (their own or others') if the sexual abuse is disclosed.

Before the Interview

It is not possible to predetermine how long the interview should be. The ideal time is one that allows the truth of the matter to purge itself. The counselor should have information pertinent to the history of the case before starting the interview. Information such as the child's name, nicknames, family members' names, and when and where the disclosure was made will contribute to the counselor's efficacy before and during the interview.

Interviewing the Child

The main ingredient for veracity in an interview is the introduction of support and rapport (Mart, 2010). Berliner and Lieb (2001) suggested that a clinical interview of a child who may be a victim of abuse should begin with a good deal of relationship building. The counselor should spend some time getting to know the child by asking about his/her hobbies, schoolwork, things a child likes to do, favorite teacher or subject in school, and so on. It is also important that the therapist appear to be on the same level as the child. This requires an atmosphere that is comfortable. The counselor should be able to make eye contact with the child. Eye contact is essential when communicating to a child that he/she is not at fault and that what happened was hurtful. It is important to remember that the effects of sexual abuse are pervasive and emotionally difficult for the rest of the child's life. After establishing some rapport, the interviewer may want to get a sense of the child's level of development related to episodic memory, or memory for events that have taken place in his/her life. Asking the child to talk about a recent school happening or a holiday, for example, can give the counselor some insight into how developed the child's ability to accurately recall the details of life events is. In the course of the interview, the counselor will want to transition the conversation to the critical issue of abuse at hand. The interviewer can do this by beginning to ask the child to speak about his/her home environment (e.g., who lives at home with the child?) and then asking the child if he/she knows why the interview is taking place. Focused and open-ended questions about the incident(s) of concern eventually must be addressed. For example, the interviewer might say, "I heard that something happened to you. Tell me from the beginning to the end what happened." Supporting a child emotionally and responding to displays of distress is of utmost importance during an interview (Berliner & Lieb, 2001).

The interviewer must not overreact to any statements the child makes. Some interviews may include interested third parties. The third party may even be the perpetrator or someone from whom the child is keeping a secret. Third parties should be directed to go to the side of the room, where they are not directly part of the interview. The therapist should arrange the parties so that eye contact is not possible between the child and adult. Above all, third parties must be instructed that they are not to be part of the interview.

Counselors must be careful not to ask leading questions. Brainer, Reyna, and Brandse (1996) reported how easy it was to implant memories of events that never happened in 5- to 8-year-old children by suggestion alone. What is more, the implanted false memories often were remembered in more detail than real memories. The biggest danger in examinations of potential sexual abuse is the interviewer who asks leading questions. Questions should be specific; most important, they should not suggest an answer. A question such as "Is it true your Uncle John did this to you?" is leading and may put pressure on the child to answer affirmatively. Likewise, if the child says, "Uncle John touched me," an appropriate response would be "Where did Uncle John touch you?" Asking "Did he touch you on your private parts?" is, again, leading the child. Finally, counselors should be careful to remember that what they conceptualize as sexual abuse may not be experienced in that way by a child, and thus, questions that assume distress on the part of the child may not fit a child's understanding of sexuality or abuse (Mart, 2010; Freidrich et al., 2001). Interviewing children is a clinical art form; mental health professionals who conduct such interviews should receive considerable supervised training in this area; thus, students should not conduct such interviews on their own without receiving training and supervision.

Counseling the Sexually Abused

There are many ways to counsel people who have a history of childhood sexual abuse. Depending on the level, intensity, and type of abuse a client experienced, counselors may be advised to take a trauma-informed approach that draws on some of the evidence-based treatments for trauma, including those from the cognitive-behavioral school. It is always important to create a therapeutic environment that is safe and that allows for the disclosure of the abuse events. Indeed, Edwards and Lambie (2009) emphasized positive regard, genuineness, and empathy as key components to helping survivors feel comfortable with the counseling process. Harrison (2001, pp. 91–92) discussed several considerations for therapy specifically with sexual abuse survivors. These should be kept in mind alongside the goal of diminishing trauma-related symptoms that might be present:

1. On the basis of statistics, survivors of sexual abuse are probably telling the truth, so the counselor begins treatment with each client by adopting this assumption.
2. It is not the survivor's fault in any way. The responsibility for the assault or abuse rests solely with the perpetrator.
3. The counselor's initial goal is to help the survivor regain a sense of personal control. He/she has had personal power taken away in a manner that affected him/her emotionally, physically, and spiritually.
4. Secondary goals of therapy include building self-esteem; moving toward autonomy; and training in coping skills, anger management, and assertive skills aimed at prevention of sexual abuse in the future.

Harrison (2001) further suggested an expansive list of dos and don'ts of therapy. The list was compiled from various sources, including the Minnesota Coalition Against Sexual Assault (1994) and Slavik, Carlson, and Sperry (1993).

1. Do ensure a safe environment and presence in sessions. If it appears that the abuse is ongoing, enlist help from the appropriate social service agencies to remove the client from an abusive environment.
2. Do return a sense of control by encouraging clients to solve problems, elicit new choices, and then trust their own judgments to arrive at their own decisions. Also distinguish between then, when the client felt helpless during the sexual abuse, and now.
3. Do not minimize the client's experience. A client once said that a previous therapist's reaction had been to say, "Well, at least he didn't beat you up when he raped you."
4. Do listen to, support, acknowledge, and validate feelings.
5. Do not be a caretaker or rescuer.
6. Do not operate based on the myths about sexual abuse, and educate clients, especially about the prevalent myth (or cognitive distortion) that victims are to blame for the sexual abuse.
7. Do trust the healing and support process, and ask a client to do so, reminding him/her that the time frame will vary for each individual.
8. Do model setting boundaries, for example, by starting and stopping sessions on time.
9. Do be aware of your own blind spots and question your assumptions. Don't assume that the perpetrator was of the opposite sex or that the act involved penetration.
10. Don't judge or use a patronizing manner. Many clients who have been sexually abused have later become very sexually active, some involved in group sex, pornography, and prostitution. If you see yourself as on the same plane as your client, then you will not be patronizing. Many clients verbalize that they take little or no enjoyment in sex, even with a caring partner, yet they feel obligated to perform sexual acts.
11. Do confer with colleagues and practice self-care.

12. Do listen with a calm interest about the sexual assault or abuse when the client is ready to discuss it.
13. Do accept unconditionally the client's ambivalent feelings about discussing the abuse.
14. Do see clients as capable of new ways of thinking, feeling, and acting and expect them to be competent and creative.
15. Do not see clients as fragile, although they may act as if they are.
16. Do help clients get in touch with unexpressed anger to combat depression, and teach them how to make choices about using their anger constructively rather than destructively.
17. Do help clients to redefine themselves apart from their role relationships and to explore fears about potential role changes.
18. Do encourage clients to nurture themselves, and reframe this self-focus as essential to healing, not as selfish.
19. Do be specific in giving positive feedback (Slavek et al., 1993, pp. 113–114).

The Client Who Is Dealing With Addiction

In this final section, we look at the issue of addiction, which is likely to be an issue that nearly every mental health professional will encounter whether or not he/she works in a specifically designated addictions treatment facility. We include information about clients dealing with addiction in this chapter as they often present in a state of crisis when they seek counseling. The information provided below relates primarily to recovery from addiction to a substance (e.g., alcohol or drugs). However, there is growing evidence for the existence of process addictions for which the counselor should be prepared, such as gambling addiction, sexual addiction, and the like.

Understanding Addiction

Until recently, conceptualizations of substance abuse generally adhered to the categories of use, abuse, and dependence, which suggested that people either had an addiction or they did not. Abuse was conceptualized as the mild form of addiction, while dependence was conceptualized as the more severe occurrence of addiction (American Psychiatric Association, 2013b). Current conceptualizations of substance addiction are that it occurs along a continuum, a view advocated by the American Psychiatric Association (2013a) in the *Diagnostic and Statistical Manual of Mental Disorders* (5th ed.; *DSM-5*). Not everyone who uses substances is addicted, and moreover, clinicians are increasingly recognizing the developmental aspects of addiction. People are not necessarily seen as either having an addiction or not but are viewed as moving along a path toward greater and greater disordered use of substances or behaviors when their use of substances or behaviors has ongoing adverse effects. In addition, alcohol and drug addiction is often conceived of as a disease that over time causes changes in the person's body, mind, and behavior, and the individual is unable to control his/her use of substances despite the harm that it causes. The chronicity and relapsing of the disease means that an addiction may persist or reappear over the course of an individual's life (Breshears, Yeh, & Young, 2004).

Diagnosing Alcohol and Drug Use

The *DSM-5* (American Psychiatric Association, 2013a) recognizes ten classes of drugs for which qualified practitioners and supervised interns can make the diagnosis of addiction; it also includes criteria for diagnosis of gambling addiction, as there is a growing body of evidence that some of the same behavior patterns and symptoms associated with substance use are similarly associated with excessive gambling. There are two broad categories of diagnosis in the *DSM-5* that deal with substance-related addiction: substance-induced disorders and substance use disorders. Substance-induced disorders emerge as a result of use and include intoxication, withdrawal, and substance-induced mental illness, such as depression, anxiety, psychosis, and sleep disorders. Substance use disorders involve sets of behavioral, cognitive, emotional, social, psychological, and physiological responses to use that are problematic for a user; in addiction, these symptoms tend to persist even though they are negative. The *DSM-5* (American Psychiatric Association, 2013a) describes a person with substance use disorder as having a pathological relationship to his/her substance of choice, and any number of symptoms can be present with this type of relationship. For example, clients may desire to stop using their substance of choice but be incapable of doing so; they may have cravings for their drug of choice and concurrently need more and more of the drug to be satisfied; they may spend an inordinate amount of time thinking about or trying to obtain the substance; they may experience many social consequences such as loss of a job or divorce; and they may engage in risky behaviors in the effort to obtain the substance.

When making a diagnosis, it is important to remember that the *DSM-5* (American Psychiatric Association, 2013a) considers substance use as part of a continuum. Therefore, it has collapsed the two diagnostic categories of substance abuse and dependence (as outlined in former editions of the *DSM*) into a single disorder known as substance use disorder, for which clinicians will indicate a mild or moderate form after conducting a clinical assessment (American Psychiatric Association, 2013b). According to the American Psychiatric Association (2013b), the former categories of abuse and dependence were not always clear to clinicians and clients, and the association stated that the single diagnostic category of substance use disorder is a better reflection of clients' experiences (American Psychiatric Association, 2013b). We recommend that students make a careful review of the diagnostic criteria and categories as outlined in the *DSM-5* and seek supervision before engaging in diagnosis and treatment of substance-related disorders.

What Is Treatment?

A number of alcohol and drug treatment models are used successfully, and treatment can include a variety of services and activities. Levels of treatment can range from outpatient, day treatment, and short- and long-term residential programs to inpatient hospital-based programs. Prior to beginning treatment, some individuals require detoxification and stabilization. Other individuals may need outreach services to help overcome barriers to treatment. Treatment may involve a single service or a combination of therapies and services. The following is a partial list of treatment services:

- assessment and treatment planning;
- prescription of certain drugs, such as Antabuse for alcohol dependence or methadone and buprenorphine for heroin addiction (Arias & Kranzler, 2008);
- crisis intervention;
- case management to coordinate among the treatment providers;
- individual and group counseling and psychotherapy;
- alcohol and drug abuse recovery programs;
- medical assessment and care;
- diet, physical exercise, spiritual practices, and other nontraditional programs;

- self-help groups or 12-step programs; or
- trauma-specific services or other mental health services.

The duration of treatment can range from weeks to years. The type, length, and intensity of treatment are determined by the severity of the addiction; type of drugs used; support systems available; personality; and other behavioral, physical, or social problems of the addicted person. It is important to think about treatment as management of a lifelong disease such as diabetes or high blood pressure rather than as crisis intervention such as emergency treatment for a broken leg. The treatment plan should be developed based on information gathered in the substance abuse assessment process (Breshears et al., 2004).

The National Institute on Drug Abuse ([NIDA], 2012) has developed a number of research-based treatment principles that are important to the recovery process:

- No single treatment is appropriate for all individuals. Treatment and services should be matched to the person's problems and needs.
- Treatment needs to be readily available.
- Effective treatment attends to multiple needs of the individual, not just to his/her drug use.
- Medical, psychological, social, vocational, and legal problems must be addressed in addition to substance addiction.
- Remaining in treatment for an adequate period of time is critical for effectiveness.
- Treatment does not need to be voluntary to be effective. Court-ordered treatment, an employment mandate, or family insistence can increase treatment entry, retention, and success.
- Possible drug use during treatment must be monitored continuously. Monitoring can help reduce the desire to use and provide early warning of use if a slip or relapse occurs.
- Recovery from drug addiction can be a long-term process and frequently requires multiple episodes of treatment.

What Is Recovery?

Treatment does not equal recovery. Treatment is an important part of recovery, but recovery is much more than obtaining sobriety. Recovery is a process of making lifestyle changes to support healing and to regain control of one's life. Recovery involves being accountable and accepting responsibility for one's behavior. It is the process of establishing and reestablishing patterns of healthy living. Former addicts talk about being "in recovery" as opposed to having "recovered," because recovery is viewed as an ongoing process.

Stages of Recovery

There are different stages of recovery. A person who has been drug free for a week and one who has been drug free for a year experience different issues. Recovery is complicated. It may be helpful to view recovery as a developmental process. The developmental model of recovery describes stages and tasks as part of recovery:

- *Transition:* The person recognizes that his/her attempts to control substance use are not working.
- *Stabilization:* The person goes through physical withdrawal and begins to regain control of his/her thinking and behavior.

- *Early recovery:* The person changes addictive behaviors and develops relationships that support sobriety and recovery.
- *Mid-stage recovery:* The person builds a more effective lifestyle and repairs lifestyle damage that occurred during substance use.
- *Late-stage recovery:* The person examines his/her childhood, family patterns, and beliefs that supported a dysfunctional lifestyle, and the person learns to grow and recover from childhood and adult trauma.
- *Maintenance:* The person learns to cope in a productive and responsible way without reverting to substance use.

Counseling Recommendations for Clients With Addiction

It is important for counselors who work with clients who have a substance use disorder to adopt an objective and factual approach to assessment interviews. As many clients enter treatment for substance-related problems because of external pressures (i.e., family, employers, the legal system), the counselor must convey an impression that he/she is an ally to the client in addressing his/her problems (Burrow-Sanchez, 2006). In asking assessment questions, the counselor should use objective criteria as a guideline and proceed in a nonjudgmental and matter-of-fact way. In addition, it is helpful to work with a client's resistance to counseling, rather than to confront it outright, especially in the beginning of a clinical relationship. Initial interviewing goals include establishing a flow of information and disclosure about the client's level of motivation for treatment and obtaining the necessary information to formulate an objective impression. Many counselors find that motivational interviewing (MI) is an excellent approach to assessing investment in the recovery process and an effective overall approach to working with clients with an addiction problem (Miller & Rollnick, 1991; Miller & Rollnick, 2002).

The counselor should relay the results of the assessment interview to the client in the same objective fashion and emphasize that the assessment is based on the information the client provided and on data from assessment instruments. This process may help the client work though treatment resistance as well as reinforce the therapeutic alliance. Below are some general guidelines for working with substance-abusing clients:

1. *Understand the emotional role the substance of choice plays for the client.* A central challenge for the counselor is to identify the client's rationale for using a mood-altering substance. Almost invariably that rationale has an affective base (i.e., substance use to avoid or escape negative situations or to acquire a desired affective state). Once the affective motivation is established, the counselor can undertake treatment to develop adaptive coping responses. Therapists should be cautious in immediately addressing traumatic issues if the client has had only a brief period of abstinence or if affect tolerance or modulation appears tenuous.

2. *Identify the internal and external triggering events for substance cravings and impulses.* Substance-using impulses are often precipitated by events that may or may not be evident to the client. The counselor needs to detect the internal (i.e., thoughts, feelings, memories, attitudes) and external (i.e., interpersonal conflicts, social isolation, interpersonal/existential losses) antecedents for the client's substance use impulses and cravings. Helping the client identify these triggers when they occur allows him/her to implement substance-avoidance behaviors. Once substance triggers are identified, specific plans for coping with them can be constructed.

3. *Confront internal versus external locus of control regarding substance-using behaviors.* Many substance-abusing clients rationalize their substance use by either relinquishing responsibility for control ("I can't help it") or externalizing control over their behavior ("My boss makes me use—he's so demanding"). The counselor must confront the client by reflecting that he/she ultimately chooses to use a substance regardless of the circumstances. Once clients accept this reality, controlling the impulses to use becomes a treatment focus.

4. *Challenge substance dependence—reinforcing cognitions (i.e., beliefs and thinking styles).* Many substance-abusing clients present belief systems that reinforce chemical dependency ("Without my crack, I can't deal with life" or "I need a drink to control myself"). The counselor should challenge such maladaptive cognitions.

5. *Help the client learn and apply abstaining behaviors.* Coping with cravings and impulses is a vital therapeutic goal. A useful resistance skill is for the client to focus on previous negative consequences of substance use when he/she experiences cravings or impulses. This technique shifts the psychological focus from the desired and expected immediate mood-altering effect to the association of the substance with emotionally negative events. This technique of "thinking the craving through" can divert clients from impulsiveness and make them aware of adaptive options. Counselors should review with clients the distinctions between thinking, feeling, and doing (physical action).

6. *Practice therapeutic rather than antagonistic confrontation.* As treatment engagement on the part of the client is critical, the counselor must be careful not to confuse confrontation with intolerance. Therapeutic confrontation occurs when the counselor presents the client with concrete examples of clinical material representative of the disorder. Therapeutic confrontation is based on objective data or behavior that the client presents, not on a conflict of personal values. Attempts to impose guilt or shame on the client increase the potential for treatment dropout.

7. *Establish healthy developmental goals.* An important part of counseling substance-abusing clients is addressing the frequent developmental disturbances that accompany maladaptive patterns of substance use (dropping out of school, getting fired from jobs, having family disruptions, etc.). Part of the treatment plan should include a return (perhaps gradually) to normal and productive functioning. Frustration and anxiety tolerance may be a central focus, depending on the severity and duration of psychosocial disturbances.

A Substance Abuse Assessment Form (Form 10.4) is included in the Forms section at the end of the book. This form provides questions for the intern to use when working with substance-abusing clients.

Preventing Relapse

Relapse, or the full-blown use of drugs or alcohol after a period of non-use, is a typical experience in long-term recovery and should be anticipated in the same way that relapse occurs with the management of other chronic diseases or illnesses (Burrow-Sanchez, 2006; NIDA, 2012). Behaviorally, relapse prevention can be seen as one set of operationalized target behaviors implemented and practiced consistently over time that results in another set of targeted undesired behaviors being discontinued. Below are some general framework suggestions for an operationalized psychoactive substance relapse prevention program:

1. *Help the client identify high-risk situations.* High-risk situations may include attending social events where substance use is prominent or spending time at places where substances are

readily available. Being aware of high-risk situations alerts the client to consider avoidance or to apply specific behavior plans for increasing controls to maintain abstinence (Witkiewitz & Marlatt, 2004).

2. *Help the client make necessary lifestyle changes and relationship modifications.* The client must gain awareness of specific lifestyle behaviors (theft, prostitution, drug sales, etc.) that are specifically related to the substance-using pattern. Often, the client must change those behavior patterns to maximize the prognosis for abstinence. Likewise, specific relationships that reinforce substance use must be confronted, modified, or even discontinued until the client has gained sufficient behavioral and impulse controls to withstand the influence of others who advocate substance use.

3. *Reduce access to psychoactive substances.* A strategic component of relapse prevention is reducing access to psychoactive substances. This may occur by removing psychoactive substances from the client's residence, eliminating routine purchases of substances (alcohol), or identifying specific places (high-risk situations) where substances are readily available or promoted.

4. *Address any underlying psychopathology.* Untreated psychiatric disorders (or psychopathology) constitute one of the most common reasons for psychoactive substance relapse (NIDA, 2012). Mood, anxiety, or personality disorders or other forms of psychopathology that persist into the abstinence period should be formally evaluated and treated. Using simultaneous combination treatments (psychotherapy, pharmacotherapy, family therapy, and self-help groups) may be most advantageous.

5. *Help the client rebound from a relapse.* Relapses happen; in specific patient subtypes (i.e., severe personality disorders, untreated mood or anxiety disorders), they may be common. The counselor must be clinically prepared for relapse and assure the client that a relapse should not be viewed fatalistically but rather as a mistake with the current treatment focus. Relapses can be used as restarting points in treatment if therapeutic engagement is maintained.

Summary

This chapter addressed the concepts of crisis and trauma in counseling and discussed some of the special populations who are identified as having experienced crisis or trauma, including clients who are harmful to themselves or others, abused clients, survivors of sexual abuse, and substance-abusing clients. Counselors often encounter such clients in schools and standard therapeutic settings, and the student will likely work with them throughout the internship. Thus, it is important that interns familiarize themselves with the issues that can arise in therapy and the special considerations that must be made when determining appropriate interventions. The intervention strategies and clinical forms provided were designed to assist the counselor or therapist in the treatment and reporting of critical client data.

References

Allen, M., Burt, K., Bryan, E., Carter, D., Orsi, R., & Durkan, L. (2002). School counselors' preparation for and participation in crisis intervention. *Professional School Counseling, 6,* 96–103.

American Academy of Experts in Traumatic Stress. (2003). *Teacher guidelines for crisis response.* Retrieved from www.schoolcrisisresponse.com/teacherguidelines.pdf

American Association of Suicidology. (2007). *Youth suicide fact sheet.* Retrieved from http://211big bend.net/PDFs/YouthSuicideFactSheet.pdf

American Counseling Association. (2014). *Code of ethics*. Alexandria, VA: Author.

American Psychiatric Association. (2003). *American Psychiatric Association Practice Guideline for the assessment and treatment of suicidal behaviors*. Arlington, VA: Author.

American Psychiatric Association. (2013a). *Diagnostic and statistical manual of mental disorders* (5th ed.). Washington, DC: Author.

American Psychiatric Association. (2013b). *Substance-related and addictive disorders*. Washington, DC: Author. Retrieved from www.psychiatry.org/practice/dsm/dsm5

American School Counselor Association. (2013). *The school counselor and safe schools and crisis response*. Alexandria, VA: Author.

American School Counselor Association. (2016a). *Ethical standards for school counselors*. Alexandria, VA: Author.

American School Counselor Association. (2016b). *The school counselor and trauma-informed practice*. Alexandria, VA: Author.

Applebaum, P. S. (1985). *Tarasoff* and the clinician: Problems in fulfilling the duty to protect. *American Journal of Psychiatry, 142*(4), 425–429.

Applebaum, P. S., & Meisel, M. A. (1986). Therapists' obligations to report their patients' criminal acts. *Bulletin of the American Academy of Psychiatry and the Law, 14*(3), 221–229.

Arias, A. J., & Kranzler, H. R. (2008). Treatment of co-occurring alcohol and other drug use disorders. *Alcohol Research & Health, 31*, 155–167.

Barrio, C. A. (2007). Assessing suicide risk in children: Guidelines for developmentally appropriate interviewing. *Journal of Mental Health Counseling, 29*, 50–66.

Beauchamp, T. L. (1985). Suicide: Matters of life and death. *Suicide and Life-Threatening Behavior, 24*(2), 190–195.

Bednar, R. L., Bednar, S. C., Lambert, M. J., & Waite, D. R. (1991). *Psychology with high-risk clients: Legal and professional standards*. Pacific Grove, CA: Brooks/Cole.

Berliner, L., & Lieb, R. (2001). *Child sexual abuse investigation: Testing documentation methods*. Olympia, WA: Washington State Institute for Public Policy. Retrieved from www.wsipp.wa.gov/rptfiles/PilotProjects.pdf

Bernes, K. B., & Bardick, A. D. (2007). Conducting adolescent violence risk assessments: A framework for school counselors. *Professional School Counselor, 10*, 419–427.

Boynton v. Burglass, No. 89–1409, Fla. Ct. App., 3d Dist. (September 24, 1991).

Brainer, C. J., Reyna, C. F., & Brandse, E. (1996). Are children's false memories more persistent than their true memories? *Psychological Science, 6*(6), 359–364.

Breshears, E. M., Yeh, S., & Young, N. K. (2004). *Understanding substance abuse and facilitating recovery: A guide for child welfare workers*. Rockville, MD: US Department of Health and Human Services, Substance Abuse and Mental Health Services Administration.

Bryant, J., & Milsom, A. (2005). Child abuse reporting by school counselors. *Professional School Counselor, 9*, 63–71.

Burrow-Sanchez, J. (2006). Understanding adolescent substance abuse: Prevalence, risk factors, and clinical implications. *Journal of Counseling & Development, 84*, 283–290.

Captain, C. (2006). Is your patient a suicide risk. *Nursing, 36*(8), 43–47.

Carlino v. State, 294 N.Y.S.2d 30 (1968).

Cicchetti, D., & Rogosch, F. A. (2009). Adaptive coping under conditions of extreme stress: Multilevel influences on the determinants of resilience in maltreated children. In E. A. Skinner & M. J. Zimmer-Gembeck (Eds.), *Coping and the development of regulation*. New Directions for Child and Adolescent Development, 124 (pp. 47–59). San Francisco, CA: Jossey-Bass.

Comiskey v. State of New York, 418 N.Y.S.2d 233 (1979).

Curtois, C. A., & Ford, J. D. (2013). *Treatment of complex trauma: A sequenced, relationship-based approach*. New York, NY: Guilford.

Dalton v. State, 308 N.Y.S.2d 441 (App. Div. 1970).

Doan, J., LeBlanc, A., Roggenbaum, S., & Lazear, K. A. (2012). *Suicide prevention guidelines: Issue brief 5*. Tampa, FL: University of South Florida, College of Behavioral and Community Sciences, Louis de la Parte Florida Mental Health Institute, Department of Child & Family Studies (FMHI Series Publication #218–5 Rev 2012).

Edwards, N., & Lambie, G. (2009). A person-centered counseling approach as a primary therapeutic support for women with a history of childhood sexual abuse. *Journal of Humanistic Counseling, Education, and Development, 48*, 23–45.

Fowler, J. C. (2012). Suicide risk assessment in clinical practice: Pragmatic guidelines for imperfect assessments. *Psychotherapy, 49*, 81–90.

Freidrich, W. N., Fisher, J. L., Dittner, C. A., Acton, R., Berliner, L., & Butler, J., (2001). Child sexual behavior inventory: Normative, psychiatric, and sexual abuse comparisons. *Child Mal-treatment, 6*, 37–49.

Gentry, E. J., Baranowsky, A. B., & Rhoton, R. (2017). Trauma competency: An active ingredients approach to treating posttraumatic stress disorder. *The Journal of Counseling & Development, 95*, 279–287.

Gerrity, E., & Folcarelli, C. (2008). *Child traumatic stress: What every policymaker should know*. Durham, NC and Los Angeles, CA: National Center for Child Traumatic Stress.

Goodyear-Brown, P., Fath, A., & Myers, L. (2012). Child sexual abuse: The scope of the problem. In Paris Goodyear-Brown (Ed.), *Handbook of child sexual abuse: Identification, assessment, and treatment* (pp. 3–28). Hoboken, NJ: Wiley Press.

Gould, M. S., Shaffer, D., & Greenberg, T. (2003). The epidemiology of youth suicide. In R. King & A. Apter (Eds.), *Suicide in children and adolescents* (pp. 1–40). New York, NY: Cambridge University Press.

Granello, D. H. (2010). The process of suicide risk assessment: Twelve core principles. *Journal of Counseling & Development, 88*, 363–370.

Greene, D. B. (1994). Childhood suicide and myths surrounding it. *Social Work, 39*, 230–233.

Harrison, R. (2001). Application of Adlerian principles in counseling survivors of sexual abuse. *Journal of Individual Psychology, 57*(1), 91–101.

Hedlund v. Superior Court of Orange County, 669 P. 2d 41, 191 Cal. Rptr. 805 (1983).

Held, P., Klassen, B. J., Brennan, M. B., & Zalta, A. K. (2018). Using prolonged exposure and cognitive processing therapy to treat veterans with moral injury-based PTSD: Two case examples. *Cognitive and Behavioral Practice, 25*, 377–390.

Hembree, E. A., Rauch, S. A., & Foa, E. B. (2003). Beyond the manual: The insider's guide to prolonged exposure therapy for PTSD. *Cognitive and Behavioral Practice, 10*, 22–30.

Jablonski v. United States, 712 F.2d 391 (9th Cir. 1983).

James, R. K., & Gilliland, B. E. (2017). *Crisis intervention strategies* (8th ed.). Belmont, CA: Brooks/Cole.

Joe, S., & Bryant, H. (2007). Evidence-based suicide prevention screening in schools. *Children & Schools, 29*, 219–227.

Joiner, T. E. (2005). *Why people die by suicide*. Cambridge, MA: Harvard University Press.

Joiner, T. E. (2010). *Myths about suicide*. Cambridge, MA: Harvard University Press.

Joiner, T. E., Kalafat, J., Draper, J., Stokes, H., Knudson, M., & Berman, A. (2007). Establishing standards for the assessment of suicide risk among callers to the national suicide prevention lifeline. *Suicide and Life-Threatening Behavior, 37*, 353–365.

Kanel, K. (2010). *A guide to crisis intervention*. Belmont, CA: Brooks/Cole.

Kenny, M. C., Fernandez, L., & Abreu, R. (2012). Child maltreatment: Incidence, consequences, and mediating factors. In R. Turner & H. Rogers (Eds.), *Child abuse: Indicators, psychological impact, and prevention* (pp. 1–25). New York, NY: Nova Science Publishers.

Klott, J. (2012). *Suicide and psychological pain: Prevention that works*. Eau Claire, WI: Premier Publication and Media.

Lambie, G. W. (2005). Child abuse and neglect: A practical guide for professional school counselors. *Professional School Counseling, 8*, 249–258.

Lawson, D. M., Davis, D., & Brandon, S. (2013). Treating complex trauma: Critical interventions with adults who experienced ongoing trauma in childhood. *Psychotherapy, 50*, 331–335.

Lipari v. Sears Roebuck, 497 F. Supp. 185 (D. Neb. 1980).

Listenbee, R. L., Torre, J., Boyle, G., Cooper, S. W., Deer, S. Durfee, D. T., . . . Taguba, A. (2012). *Report of the Attorney General's national task force on children exposed to violence*. US Department of Justice. Retrieved from http://www.justice.gov/defendingchildhood/cev-rpt-full.pdf

Marshall, N. A. (2012). A clinician's guide to recognizing and reporting parental psychological maltreatment of children. *Professional Psychology: Research and Practice, 43*, 73–79.

Mart, E. G. (2010). Common errors in the assessment of allegations of child abuse. *Journal of Psychiatry and Law, 38*, 325–343.

McGlothlin, J. M., Rainey, S., & Kindsvatter, A. (2005). Suicidal clients and supervisees: A model for considering supervisor roles. *Counselor Education and Supervision, 45*, 134–146.

Meichenbaum, D. (2005). 35 years of working with suicidal patients: Lessons learned. *Canadian Psychology, 46*, 64–72.

Miller, D. N., Eckert, T. L., & Mazza, J. J. (2009). Suicide prevention programs in the school: A review and public health perspective. *School Psychology Review, 38*, 168–188.

Miller, W. R., & Rollnick, S. (1991). *Motivational interviewing: Preparing people to change addictive behavior*. New York, NY: Guilford Press.

Miller, W. R., & Rollnick, S. (2002). *Motivational interviewing: Preparing people for change* (2nd ed.). New York, NY: Guilford Press.

Minnesota Coalition Against Sexual Assault. (1994). *Training manual*. Edina, MN: Author.

Monahan, J. (1993). Limiting therapist exposure to *Tarasoff* liability: Guidelines for risk containment. *American Psychologist, 48*, 242–250.

Moyer, M., & Sullivan, J. (2008). Student risk taking behaviors: When do school counselors break confidentiality? *Professional School Counselor, 11*, 236–245.

Murray, L. K., Cohen, J. A., & Mannarino, A. P. (2013). Trauma-focused cognitive behavioral therapy for youth who experience continuous traumatic exposure. *Peace and Conflict: Journal of Peace Psychology, 19*, 180–195.

Myer, R. A., & Cogdal, P. (2007). Crisis intervention in counseling. In J. Gregoire & C. M. Jungers (Eds.), *The counselor's companion: What every beginning counselor needs to know* (pp. 550–566). Mahwah, NJ: Erlbaum.

Myer, R. A., Lewis, J. S., & James, R. K. (2013). The introduction of a task model for crisis intervention. *Journal of Mental Health Counseling, 35*, 95–107.

Myer, R. A., & Moore, H. B. (2006). Crisis in context theory: An ecological model. *Journal of Counseling & Development, 84*, 139–147.

National Association of School Psychologists. (2017). *School violence prevention: Brief facts and tips*. Retrieved from www.nasponline.org/resources-and-publications/resources/school-safety-and-crisis/school-violence-prevention

National Institute on Drug Abuse (NIDA). (2012). *Principles of drug addiction treatment: A research-based guide.* Retrieved from www.drugabuse.gov/sites/default/files/podat_1.pdf

Otto, R. (2000). Assessing and managing violence risk in outpatient settings. *Journal of Clinical Psychology, 56,* 1239–1262.

Paridies v. Benedictine Hospital, 431 N.Y.S.2d 175 (App. Div. 1980).

Pate, R. H. (1992, Summer). Are you liable? *American Counselor, 10,* 23–26.

Peck v. The Counseling Service of Addison County, 499 A.2d 422 (Vt. 1985).

Riley, P. L., & McDaniel, J. (2000). School violence, prevention, intervention, and crisis response. *Professional School Counselor, 4,* 120–125.

Rudd, M. D., Berman, A. L., Joiner, T. E., Jr., Nock, M. K., Silverman, M. M., & Mandrusiak, M. (2006). Warning signs for suicide: Theory, research, and clinical implications. *Suicide and Life-Threatening Behavior, 36,* 255–262.

Sikes, A., Remley, T. P., & Hays, D. G. (2010). Experiences of school counselors during and after making suspected child abuse reports. *Journal of School Counseling, 8,* 30.

Slavik, S., Carlson, J., & Sperry, L. (1993). An Adlerian treatment of adults with a history of childhood sexual abuse. *Individual Psychology, 49*(2), 111–131.

Tarasoff v. Regents of the University of California, 13 Cal. 3d 177, 529 P. 2d 533 (1974), vacated, 17 Cal. 3d 425, 551 P. 2d 334 (1976).

Tarasoff v. Regents of the University of California, 113 Cal. Rptr. 14, 551 P. 2d 334 (Cal. 1976).

Thompson v. County of Alameda, 614 P. 2d 728 (Cal. 1980).

US Department of Health and Human Services. (2003). *The child abuse prevention and treatment act.* Retrieved from www.acf.hhs.gov/sites/default/files/cb/capta2003.pdf

US Department of Health and Human Services, Administration for Children and Families, Administration on Children, Youth and Families, Children's Bureau. (2009). *Definitions of child abuse and neglect: Summary of state laws.* Washington, DC: US Government Printing Office.

US Department of Health and Human Services, Administration for Children and Families, Administration on Children, Youth and Families, Children's Bureau. (2011). *Child maltreatment.* Retrieved from www.acf.hhs.gov/sites/default/files/cb/cm11.pdf#page=69

VA/DOD clinical practice guideline for the management of posttraumatic stress disorder and acute stress disorder. (2017). www.healthquality.va.gov/guidelines/MH/ptsd/VADoDPTSDCPGFinal012418.pdf

VandeCreek, L., & Knapp, S. (1993). *Tarasoff and beyond: Legal considerations in the treatment of life-endangering patients* (Rev. ed.). Sarasota, FL: Professional Resource Press.

Veterans Affairs and Department of Defense. (2017). *VA/DOD Clinical practice guideline for the management of posttraumatic stress disorder and acute stress disorder.* Retrieved from www.healthquality.va.gov/guidelines/MH/ptsd/

Walcott, D. M., Cerundolo, P., & Beck, J. C. (2001). Current analysis of the *Tarasoff* duty: An evolution towards the limitation of the duty to protect. *Behavioral Sciences and the Law, 19,* 325–343.

Waldo, S., & Malley, P. B. (1992). *Tarasoff* and its progeny: Implications for school counselors. *School Counselor, 40,* 56–63.

Walfish, S., Barnett, J. E., Marlyere, K., & Zielke, R. (2010). "Doc, there's something I have to tell you": Patient disclosure to their psychotherapist of unprosecuted murder and other violence. *Ethics & Behavior, 20,* 311–323.

Webster, C. D., Douglas, K. S., Eaves, D., & Hart, S. D. (1997). *HCR-20: Assessing risk for violence* (Version 2). Burnaby, BC: Mental Health, Law, and Policy Institute, Simon Fraser University.

Witkiewitz, K., & Marlatt, G. A. (2004). Relapse prevention for alcohol and drug problems: That was Zen this is Tao. *American Psychologist, 59,* 224–235.

CHAPTER 11

CONSULTATION IN THE SCHOOLS AND MENTAL HEALTH AGENCIES

Consultation has become one of the most sought-after services rendered by counselors in mental health agencies and in schools. The practice was born out of the Mental Health Act of 1962 and Gerald Caplan's (1970) seminal work *The Theory and Practice of Mental Health Consultation*, which provided a solid basis for understanding and implementing mental health consultation. In the school systems, a formal consultation role for counselors arose in the late 1970s as they started branching out from one-to-one relationships to working with teachers and caretakers, who then worked with student-clients (Baker, 2000). Consultation is a way counselors can use their knowledge and skills to support a variety of professionals who play a role in facilitating the healthy emotional, psychological, academic, and career development of clients or students. Given the importance of consultation in the mental health clinician's range of duties, this chapter aims to provide students with a basic understanding of consultation in schools and mental health agencies.

What Is Consultation?

The expansion of consultation as a mental health service has led to a diversity of views on what consultation actually is (Gravois, 2012). Caplan (1970), who provided some of the earliest perspectives on consultation, viewed it as a collaborative process between two professionals who each have their own area of expertise. Adding more specificity, Ohlsen (1983) defined consultation as an activity in which a professional helps another person with regard to a third person or party (e.g., a student or a client). Kirby (1985) described consultation in terms of its relationship conditions: (a) the consultation relationship is voluntary, (b) the focus of attention is on the problem situation as articulated by the consultee(s), (c) the consultant typically is not part of the organizational system in which he or she is consulting, and (d) the consultant's expertise is sufficient to facilitate change. Finally, Dougherty (2005, p. 11) suggested that consultation is a process in which "a human service professional assists a consultee with a work-related (or caretaking-related) problem with a client system, with the goal of helping both the consultee and the client system in some specified way."

In trying to define consultation, early authors (e.g., Alpert, 1977; Caplan, 1970) also offered differing viewpoints about the focus of consultation and its distinctive qualities. In particular, they were concerned about whether consultation was a direct or an indirect service. Prior to the advent of consultation as a professional practice, counselors traditionally were involved in direct, therapeutic service to clients. By the 1980s, however, attention began to focus on how mental health specialists could provide indirect, preventive care to clients and not just remedial interventions, which often are equated with direct counseling services (Erchul, 2011; Neukrug, 2012). The emphasis on counselors as prevention specialists that emerged in the 1980s is still strong today, and it is clear that consultation has evolved into a unique, indirect service requiring counselors to assist *other* professionals who have direct responsibility for the welfare of clients or students (Crothers, Hughes, & Morine, 2008).

One of the most salient implications of consultation as an indirect approach to intervention and prevention is that providers have to ensure that role confusion around counseling and consultation does not hamper service delivery. Consultation differs from therapy in that the consultant typically does not assume the full responsibility for the final outcome of consultation. The consultant's role is to develop and enhance the role of the consultee, which is in contrast to counseling, where the focus is on the personal improvement of the client. The consultant must remember that the relationship established with the consultee is not primarily therapeutic in nature. Rather, the consultant serves in the capacity of collaborator and facilitator to assist the consultee in performing his/her duties in a more productive and effective manner (Sears, Rudisill, & Mason-Sears, 2006).

Types of Mental Health Consultation

Caplan (1970) identified four types of consultation that are still relevant to its current practice. These types feature prominently in the literature and continue to frame contemporary research studies in consultation (O'Kane, Barkway, & Muir-Cochrane, 2012). They are:

- *Client-centered case consultation:* A consultee has difficulty in dealing with the mental health aspects of one of his/her clients and calls in a specialist to advise on the nature of the difficulties and on how the consultee's work difficulty relates to the management of a particular case or group of cases. The consultant makes an assessment of the client's problem and recommends a course of action.
- *Program-centered administrative consultation:* The consultant is invited by an administrator to help with a current problem of program development, with some predicament in the organization of an institution, or with planning and implementation of organizational policies, including personnel policies. The consultant is expected to provide feedback to the organization in the form of a written report.
- *Consultee-centered case consultation:* The consultee's work problem relates to the management of a particular client, and he/she invokes the consultant's help to improve handling of the case. The consultant's primary focus is on clarifying and remedying the shortcomings in the consultee's professional functioning that contribute to the present difficulties with the case about which he/she is seeking help. This type of interaction is distinguished from supervision in that the consultant does not usually have an ongoing, long-term relationship with the consultee in the way that a supervisor might.
- *Consultee-centered administrative consultation:* The consultant helps the administrative staff of an organization deal with current problems in organizational policies. The focus of attention is the consultee's work difficulties and attempts to help improve his/her problem-solving skills (Caplan, 1970).

Characteristics of Mental Health Consultation

As noted, mental health consultation has become an increasingly important part of prevention and intervention approaches in the helping fields and in school settings (Gilliam, Maupin, &

Reyes, 2016; O'Kane et al., 2012; Vuyk, Sprague-Jones, & Reed, 2016). Though the way in which consultation is applied in different settings can vary, many of the core characteristics of mental health consultation are the same. Caplan (1970) identified the following core traits of mental health consultation:

1. Mental health consultation is a method for use between two professionals in respect to a lay client or a program of such clients.
2. The consultee's work problem must relate to (a) a mental disorder or personality idiosyncrasies of the client, (b) the promotion of mental health in the client, or (c) interpersonal aspects of the work situation.
3. The consultant has no administrative responsibility for the consultee's work or professional responsibility for the outcome of the client's case.
4. The consultee is under no compulsion to accept the consultant's ideas or suggestions.
5. The basic relationship between the two is coordinate. No built-in hierarchical authority tension exists.
6. The coordinate relationship is fostered by the consultant's usually being a member of another profession and coming into the consultee's institution from the outside.
7. Consultation is usually given as a short series of interviews that take place in response to the consultee's awareness of a current need for help with the work problem.
8. Consultation is not expected to continue indefinitely.
9. A consultant has not pre-determined a body of information that he/she intends to impart to a particular consultee.
10. The twin goals of consultation are to help the consultee improve his/her handling or understanding of the current work difficulty and to increase his/her capacity to master future problems of a similar type.
11. The aim is to improve the consultee's job performance, not his/her well-being.
12. Consultation does not focus overtly on the personal problems and feelings of the consultee; however, the consultant is sensitive to how they factor into the disturbance of task functioning.
13. Consultation is usually only one of the professional functions of a specialist, even if he/she is formally titled "consultant."
14. Mental health consultation is a method of communication between a mental health specialist and other professionals (Caplan, 1970).

With the evolution of mental health consultation over the past 40 years, at least a couple of nuances have to be noted with regard to Caplan's original conceptualization of consultation. First, Caplan (1970) primarily viewed the consultant as having a base of operations that was outside of or external to the consultee's work setting. However, in today's practice, mental health consultants are frequently in-house or internal employees and staff members who have specialized training that is brought to bear on the issues with which the whole organization grapples (Caplan, Caplan, & Erchul, 1994; Crothers et al., 2008; Erchul, 2011). This is especially true in the case of school counselors, who often may find that they are wearing the consultant hat in their interactions with teachers and administrators looking for better ways to work with students. School counselors also often act as consultants to their own colleagues with regard to specialized issues, such as training and implementation of crisis response and prevention plans and suicide intervention policies. Caplan et al. (1994) suggested that it is difficult for an in-house consultant to act freely when he/she is an employee of the system where the consultation is taking place. Factors such as organizational hierarchies can affect how consultees view the consultant and the information he/she has to offer. The practice of internal consultation led to a second, related change to Caplan's original conceptualization. With the increased use of insider consultants, it has become clear that consultees working with consultants from within their own systems may not be as free as first thought to reject the advice or recommendations from in-house consultants (Caplan et al., 1994). When consultants are themselves members of the system for which they are consulting and own responsibility for the outcomes of their own recommendations, they may not find it easy to permit the consultee the freedom to reject their expert views (Caplan et al., 1994).

Because the use of in-house consultants is not without challenges, especially regarding the consultee's freedom to accept or reject advice from the consultant, Caplan and his colleagues (1994) proposed that, in the instance of internal consultation, it may be more appropriate to talk not about consultation but about collaboration. In collaboration, the specialist-collaborator and consultee share responsibility for the general outcome of the client, and the specialist-collaborator takes on the primary responsibility for the mental health–related elements of the case. The specialist-collaborator is seen as a fully participating team member acting as a hands-on clinician or advisor and making the best use of his/her specialized diagnostic and remedial skills to improve the mental health outcomes of the case. The consultant is expected to direct consultees' attention to salient aspects of the case in order to lead to positive outcomes. Also, in collaboration, the consultee-collaborator does not have the same freedom to accept or reject advice from the consultant as happens when an outside consultant is being used. Rather, the consultee is obliged to follow the best possible course of action to improve the client's condition (Brown, Pryzwansky, & Schulte, 2011).

Cook and Friend (2010) pointed out that in school settings the concept of collaborative consultation (or just simply collaboration) began to emerge in the 1980s as a way to empower teachers, especially special education teachers, to advocate for the needs of children with disabilities. These authors point out that collaboration is comparable to consultation, though with much more emphasis on professionals acting as partners who all have the same goal of meeting children's needs. Often, in schools, counselors, psychologists, and social workers can take on the role of consultant working in a nonhierarchical way to help teachers, for example, to better understand the behavioral, academic, and psychological needs of their students and prompt their overall success in the school environment (Crothers et al., 2008).

Assumptions Behind and Metaphors for Consultation

There are a number of metaphors and assumptions on which the practice of consultation is based. Schein (1969, 1990, 1997) focused on the need for the helper or consultant to understand the assumptions he/she brings to the consultation relationship. The basic components and major assumptions of the purchase-of-expertise model, doctor–patient model, and process consultation model are outlined here.

The Purchase-of-Expertise Model

The purchase-of-expertise model generally suggests that one seeks out a consultant for his/her special expertise or knowledge and is willing to pay for that knowledge through the practice of consultation. It makes the following assumptions:

1. The client has to have made a correct diagnosis of what the real problem is.
2. The client has identified the consultant's capabilities to solve the problem.

3. The client must communicate what the problem is.
4. The client has thought through and accepted all the implications of the help that will take place (Rockwood, 1993).

The purchase-of-expertise model enables clients to remove themselves from the problem, relying on the skills and expertise of the consultant to fix the problem.

The Doctor–Patient Model

The doctor–patient model also focuses on content and assumes that the diagnosis of and prescription for the problem solution rest solely in the hands of the consultant. It is characterized as follows:

1. The client has correctly interpreted the organizational assumptions and knows where the "sickness" is.
2. The client can trust the diagnosis.
3. The person or group defined as such will provide the necessary information to make the diagnosis.
4. The client will understand and accept the diagnosis, implement the prescription, and think through and accept the consequences.
5. The client will be able to remain healthy after the consultant leaves.

The Process Consultation Model

The process consultation model focuses on how problems are solved in a collaborative effort. It can be characterized as follows:

1. The nature of the problem is such that the client not only needs help in making a diagnosis but would also benefit from participating in the making of the diagnosis.
2. The client has constructive intent and some problem-solving abilities.
3. Ultimately, the client is the one who knows what form of intervention or solution will work best in the organization.
4. When the client engages in the diagnosis and then selects and implements interventions, there will be an increase in his/her future problem-solving abilities.

Process consultation is systematic in that it accepts the goals and values of the organization as a whole and attempts to work with the client within those values and goals to jointly find solutions that will fit within the organizational system (Rockwood, 1993). Finally, Schein (1997) recommended eight principles that can guide process consultants in their work with clients, including aiming to make every contact helpful to the client, using every interaction with the client to unearth information about the client and the system, and being honest about what is unknown about the client or system so as to be able to learn about the client more directly and fully.

Cultural Issues in Consultation

Helping professionals of all specialties, including consultation, have become increasingly aware of the impact of cultural diversity on their practices (Kirmayer, Guzder, & Rousseau, 2014). Behring and Ingraham (1998) sent a call to the field of consultation to incorporate cultural awareness and practices into consultation. They defined multicultural consultation as "a culturally sensitive and indirect service in which the consultant adjusts the consultation services to address the needs and cultural values of either the consultee, or client, or both" (Behring & Ingraham, 1998, p. 58). For all types of consultation, Behring and Ingraham recommended that consultants be aware of their own cultural values and biases and how they are different from those of their consultees. Furthermore, in multicultural consultation, consultants consider how culture can affect the communication style of both themselves and the consultees and, therefore, directly affect the process and outcome of consultation. Olivos, Gallagher, and Aguilar (2010) discussed the impact of cultural and linguistic diversity on consultation and collaboration in a school setting. They noted that families who are not part of the majority (i.e., white, European, middle-class) culture and who have children with special needs may not have equal access to services as those families who are members of the dominant culture. Olivos et al. (2010) suggested that consultants or collaborators ensure that culturally diverse families (a) have full access to the school and to those (e.g., teachers, administrators, counselors, etc.) who serve students; (b) feel empowered in the collaboration process so that they know how and to whom to express concerns related to their children; (c) know all of the information that is pertinent to decisions being made on behalf of their children and are free to offer their input on the decision-making process; and (d) are familiar with the general education teachers in addition to special education teachers so that parents can consult them about their child's needs. Given the complexities involved in being culturally competent, consultants are encouraged to become knowledgeable about their consultee's cultural background and look for ways to account for cultural differences.

School Consultation

In mental health consultation, the consultation models focus on a work problem and the consulting relationship facilitates a problem-solving process. With regard to consultation in schools, Schmidt (2003) stated, "School counselors use consultation in a broader context that includes educational, information and problem solving relationships" (p. 176). He went on to frame the school consultation process as a triadic relationship between the counselor-consultant; the consultee (student, teachers, parents, etc.); and a situation with a third party or an external situation (prevention, development, remediation). Crothers et al. (2008) similarly noted that consultants who intervene in schools work with professional personnel, such as principals and teachers, to aid them in bettering their skills so that they can serve students and their families in the best possible ways.

When the focus of consultation is helping schools prevent problems, educational or informational consultation is implemented. Counselors often use large group instruction for parents, students, and teachers to give information or teach new skills. This kind of educational consultation does not include evaluation and thus aims instead at asking questions and sharing opinions. These consulting activities differ from direct counseling because the goal is to remedy a situation that is external to the relationships between the consultant and the consultee. Informational consulting situations occur when students, parents, and teachers have a need regarding community and school resources, career and educational materials, or other referrals. In other words, the counselor has contacts in the community and knowledge of resources where the consultee can get needed information.

Kurpius and Fuqua (1993) outlined four generic modes of consulting that identify the different roles counselors take on when performing consulting functions in schools. The first role is "expert." In this role, counselors either provide answers to problems by giving expert information to parents, students, and teachers or use direct skills to fix the problem. The second role is the "prescriptive role," in which the counselor collects information, makes a diagnosis, and recommends solutions. The third role is that of "collaborator," where the counselor works in partnership with consultees to define concerns and develop strategies to change or improve an external situation. The consulting role of collaborator assumes an equal relationship among participants to facilitate change. This role is often used when consulting with students, parents, and teachers as well as with administrators and other professionals. The collaborative role can be more broadly defined when it includes the initiation and formation of collegial relationships with a variety of educational, medical, and other professionals who provide auxiliary services to school populations. These alliances benefit all parties concerned as they work to create circumstances that facilitate the healthy development of children. They also ensure the availability of outside services for students, parents, and teachers who interact with school counselors (Schmidt, 2003). The fourth mode in the Kurpius and Fuqua (1993) framework is that of "mediator." As mediator, the counselor facilitates conflict resolution between two or more persons or between persons and an outside situation. The goal is to find common ground and compromise.

Baker (2000) proposed basic consulting competencies for school counselors as proceeding through stages parallel to those proposed in Egan's (2010) three-stage helping paradigm for problem-solving counseling. Egan's paradigm has been restated for consulting stages in Table 11.1, and the word *consultee* was used where the word *client* was used in the original counseling model.

Baker (2000) proposed the basic skills of a comprehensive consulting model in the context of the three stages of identification/clarification, goal setting/commitment, and action. In the identification/clarification stage of consulting, an opening interview is held. The skills used in this consulting interview are the same skills counselors use in an initial client interview: strategies that encourage sharing, identifying, and clarifying. Next, the counselor-consultant invites the consultee to share tier-targeted problems while establishing a facilitative working alliance. As the problem is clarified, the consultant determines the mode of consulting that fits the problem: expert, prescriptive, collaborative, or mediator. The consultant clarifies the problem as he/she understands it, explains his/her understanding of the consultee's motives, and negotiates the role the consultant will take.

The second stage of goal setting/commitment follows. Implicit in proceeding to this stage is the decision to consult. Assuming this decision is made, further exploration of the problem issues and possible solutions is undertaken. Basic challenging skills of information sharing, immediacy, and confrontation are brought in at this stage. If consultants are using the collaborative mode, brainstorming of hypotheses and solutions follows. As many hypotheses and solutions as possible are identified without analysis. In the prescriptive mode, consultants explain their treatment plans and then brainstorm who will implement them. When solutions have been identified, alternatives are evaluated using workability, reasonability, and motivation as criteria. Sometimes,

Table 11.1 Brief Stages and Goals of Consultation

Stage	Goal
I	The consultee's problem situation and unused opportunities are identified and clarified.
II	Hopes for the future become realistic goals to which the consultee is committed.
III	Strategies for reaching goals are devised and implemented.

more information about the problem is needed before final goals can be established. A shift occurs as the consultant encourages and supports the consultee's understanding of and commitment to the goal.

The final stage in this consulting process is action strategies. The consultee may need help with the final decision making. Depending on the mode of consulting, counseling for rational thinking may apply, or competence enhancement regarding child and adolescent development or classroom management skill training may be deemed appropriate. When mediation is the appropriate mode selected, counselors respond directly to requests from two or more parties to facilitate a mutual agreement or reconciliation. Basic counseling skills, challenging skills, and knowledge of interpersonal communication are requisite skills for mediation. Mediation can be between student and parent, student and student, student and teacher, teacher and administrator—any two parties engaged in the educational endeavor. As with any counseling process, reluctance, and/or resistance can be handled using the same skills as those used in counseling interactions (Baker, 2000).

Consulting processes also include a closing phase. Consulting goals that have been established provide the criteria for whether the expected results have occurred. Consultees can also give feedback about their satisfaction with the consulting process and, upon reflection, make suggestions about how things could have been more helpful (Baker, 2000).

In addition to the modes of consultation proposed by Kurpius and Fuqua (1993) and Baker (2000), Gravois (2012) suggested that consultation in schools has three primary dimensions: focus, function, and form. The school-based consultant first has to define who the recipient of the consultation services is or, in other words, who is the focus of services. Gravois (2012) noted that in school settings the focus tends to lie primarily on teachers, students, or the school system itself. In defining the function of school-based consultation, Gravois (2012) proposed that consultation can have the aim of primary, secondary, or tertiary prevention and that consultants need to clarify in which area the consultation will be applied. Last, this model considers form to be the means through which consultation services are provided. The form of consultation includes provision of services through individuals, groups, or teams who are capable of having an impact on the identified consultation focus and issues.

In the 21st century, school counselors are faced with ever-increasing responsibilities on the job. At-risk students, reintegration of special students, and the job of coordinating the school and community services are but a few of the added responsibilities of the school counselor. The American School Counselors Association's (2003) national model advocates that the school counseling program be established as an integral component in the academic mission of the school, with academic development, personal development, and career development as the foci. An outline of a comprehensive school counseling program for the state of Alabama (Alabama Department of Education, 2003) identified consultation as a counselor's role in implementing a guidance curriculum in responsive services and in systems support. Other articles propose that the counselor expand the educational consulting role to include peer facilitator training, counselor–teacher consultation to plan and implement a guidance curriculum, the training and coordination of teacher advisory programs, and others (Dahir, Sheldon, & Valiza, 1998; Myrick, 1997). It is not a leap to conclude that the consulting role for school counselors may become equal to the counseling practice role as the American School Counselors Association model is adopted by more school systems.

Consultation Models and Practices in Schools

In this section, we look at models of consultation that have been proposed for use in school settings. The first model (Clemens, 2007) uses developmental counseling and therapy as a conceptual framework and is meant to aid counselors who consult with teachers, parents, and students in the school setting. The second model, developed by Kahn (2000), draws on solution-focused therapy as its backdrop. The third model, from Truscott et al. (2012), is a school-based model that is explicitly consultee centered (i.e., teacher centered) and draws on the theories of positive psychology and self-determination. The final set of school-based mental health consultation practices we describe are part of an emerging evidence-base for early-childhood intervention aimed at addressing child-hood mental health problems within schools.

Developmental Counseling and Therapy-Based Consultation

Clemens's (2007) model of consultation for school counselors draws on the work of Ivey, Ivey, Myers, and Sweeney (2005), who recommended a developmental approach to counseling that they call developmental counseling and therapy (DCT). DCT uses Piaget's insights into cognitive development in order to help counselors assess the way in which clients perceive and make meaning of their world. The four cognitive modalities identified by DCT are sensorimotor, concrete, formal-operational, and dialectic/systemic. Clients and consultees who operate from a sensorimotor modality tend to focus on the emotional component of their experience as they relay it to the counselor/consultant. Those who are concrete in their thinking style often speak about their experience in a linear fashion, emphasizing cause-and-effect elements of their experiences. Formal-operational thinkers tend to highlight patterns of thinking and behaving in their accounts of their needs. Finally, dialectic/systemic thinkers also talk about patterns, but they focus on the types of interactions between systems and groups that seem typical (Clemens, 2007). Each cognitive modality has its benefits and limitations, and Clemens (2007) suggested that it is the consultant's job to help consultees (such as stressed teachers) expand their use of multiple modalities in thinking about the issue for which they are seeking consultation. Thus, one goal of the consultation process using DCT is to aid the consultee in using more than one cognitive modality so that the consultee can perceive the situation of concern from a different and more helpful point of view. She recommended using the following questions to prompt thinking in the four cognitive styles identified in DCT consultation:

Sensorimotor

- What are you seeing and hearing?
- What does the classroom look like? Describe in detail.
- Who else is present?
- What are they doing?
- Where are you in the room?
- What are you feeling?
- Where are you feeling X in your body (Clemens, 2007, p. 355)?

Concrete

- Can you think of a specific example?
- Tell me what happened just before the student did X.
- What happened just after the student did X?
- What did you do or say?

- How did you feel?
- So when you did Y, then the student did X and you felt Z (Clemens, 2007, pp. 355–356)?

Formal-Operational

- Is this a pattern for the student/teacher?
- Does this happen a lot in your classroom?
- What are the exceptions to these patterns?
- What are you saying to yourself when this type of situation occurs?
- How do you act or respond (Clemens, 2007, p. 356)?

Dialectic/Systemic

- What purpose do you think the student's behavior is serving?
- How do you think the student learned this way of acting in the classroom?
- How did you learn your way of responding to this pattern of behavior?
- What else might be impacting your response to this particular situation?
- What is the rule or the cognition that guides your response?
- What are the limitations of that rule (Clemens, 2007, p. 356)?

In proposing the above questions, Clemens (2007) cautioned that school counselors should clarify whether or not a teacher is seeking consultation for themselves when they approach the counselor with a student issue. She also noted that counselors must be able to accurately assess a teacher's cognitive style in order to be helpful.

Solution-Focused Consultation

A second model of consultation in the schools is Kahn's (2000) solution-focused consultation approach. According to Kahn, a solution-focused model is an appropriate fit for the school environment because the objectives of education, like this consultation approach, tend to be future oriented, positive, and goal directed. Several steps characterize Kahn's (2000) model, all of which are grounded in the assumption that the consultant and consultee are collaborators in trying to resolve the issue at hand. The process begins when the consultant (usually the school counselor) asks the consultee (a teacher, parent, or administrator) to identify strengths he/she brings to the consultation relationship. Directing the consultee to consider strengths and resiliencies reflects the solution-focused consultant's belief that language is formative and helps play a role in coming to a resolution of the problem (Kahn, 2000). After encouraging the consultee to use positive language throughout the process, both parties attend to goal setting, which typically happens early on in the relationship so that little time is spent ruminating about the problem. The consultant helps the consultee to describe the actions he/she wants to see take place (rather than what should not be happening) and also helps to motivate the consultee to participate fully in the process if he/she is somewhat complacent about seeking help.

After establishing goals for the consultation relationship, the consultant and consultee reflect on any prior workable solutions that the consultee has used for the issue needing to be resolved or any exceptions to the problem of which he/she is aware. This focus emphasizes the solution-centered consultant's beliefs that the consultee has the ability to resolve the issue and that the issue can be successfully addressed and managed. Looking at exceptions to the problem helps the consultant and consultee to ready themselves for the next step in the process, which is to decide on a seemingly workable solution to the consultation issue. Kahn (2000) suggested that consultants ask specific and concrete questions such as "Which solution seems most doable given the resources of the student, the student's family, the school, etc.?" and "In the solution, who is doing what and when and where?" Finally, Kahn (2000) proposed that school-based consultants compliment their consultees in order to highlight their dedication and motivation to change.

Positive Psychology Approaches to Consultation

A third model of school-based consultation was developed by Truscott and his colleagues (2012) and is known as Exceptional Professional Learning (EPL). This model focuses its attention primarily on the consultee, which usually means its focus is on helping teachers. The EPL model assumes that by aiding teachers to create productive learning environments and implement effective learning practices, the consultant is indirectly helping students, who are seen as the recipients of services. The EPL approach is grounded in theories such as positive psychology (Seligman & Csikszentmihalyi, 2000) and self-determination theory (Ryan & Deci, 2000). In brief, some of the goals of EPL consultation are:

- encouraging social atmospheres that foster strengths;
- shifting teacher attention away from struggling students to using proven teaching practices; and
- viewing teachers as autonomous professionals who are empowered to make decisions they believe in (Truscott et al., 2012).

In practice, the EPL model takes up the following tasks (Truscott et al., 2012):

- *Gaining entry into the system:* Generally, this means that consultants focus first on developing authentic relationships with consultees in the school system.
- *Selecting and implementing projects:* The consultant and consultees together determine which areas of focus are of greatest need in their ability to do their jobs effectively; in essence, the consultant conducts a needs assessment.
- *Identifying consultee competencies:* The consultant helps the consultees to identify their existing areas of strength and competencies as relevant to the needs that have emerged.
- *Building knowledge:* The consultant helps to build consultee knowledge about the consultation area of focus by leading presentations, implementing new skills, and practicing those with consultees.
- *Assessing and responding:* Consultants and consultees evaluate the effectiveness of the consultation projects and interactions.

Emerging Evidence-Based Approaches to Consultation in Schools

Extensive research suggests that children with severe behavioral and mental health problems that emerge during pre-school and the early years of elementary school are at risk for academic failure, expulsion, difficulty with peer socialization, and a number of other problems that can limit their potential for life-long success (Gilliam et al., 2016). Often, children with such behavioral problems have already been exposed to some type of adversity or toxic stress, including abuse or neglect, lack of stable parenting, and transitions between foster homes (Perry & Conners-Burrow, 2016). Nationally and internationally, there is widespread recognition—including at the political levels—that efforts must be made for early-childhood interventions that reduce childhood expulsion from school.

Early Childhood Mental Health Consultation (ECHMC) has been recognized as an emerging evidence-based approach to preventing children from being retained or asked to leave school because of serious problem behaviors (Gilliam et al., 2016; O'Kane et al., 2012). ECHMC is a collaborative process among mental health professionals; school personnel, such as teachers and school staff; and family members that aims at identifying, preventing, and treating mental health problems of young children (Vuyk et al., 2016). It is not a direct counseling service. Rather, mental health consultants work with school staff and teachers to train them on how to manage poor classroom behaviors and to promote social and emotional awareness and skills in children. The training that consultants offer can be manualized or less formalized. The common objective across all forms of ECMHC, however, is to assist teachers and family members (when possible) to become better skilled at meeting children's needs. This can include being able to identify a need, to adjust physical spaces, or to build skills of a whole classroom of children around how to respond to a child with poor behaviors (Perry & Conners-Burrow, 2016). Mental health consultants thus are increasingly viewed as playing a key role in furthering school teachers' and other personnel's capacity to reduce risk levels for children with problem behaviors and poor social skills.

General Guidelines for Consultation

The stages of consultation outlined by numerous authors (e.g., Kurpius & Fuqua, 1993) have been adapted here and serve as guidelines for the development of a consultation plan. To some extent, these guidelines are reflected in many consultation models (for example, reflections of these steps are seen in the EPL school consultation approach described briefly above). At the same time, Tindal, Parker, and Hasbrouck (1992) found that stage descriptions of consultation are not necessarily reflective of the practice of consultation in every instance and should be applied flexibly.

Preentry

Preentry is considered part of the consultation process because it enables the consultant to assess the degree to which he/she is the proper fit for the consultation situation. Preentry is the preliminary stage when the consultant forms a conceptual foundation to work from and through the process of self-assessment and is able to articulate to self and others who he/she is and what services he/she can provide (Neukrug, 2012; Truscott et al., 2012). Kurpius and Fuqua (1993) suggested that throughout this self-assessment and reflective process, consultants should understand their beliefs and values, understanding how individuals, families, programs, organizations, or systems cause, solve, or avoid problems. Furthermore, Kurpius and Fuqua (1993) maintained that in the preentry stage it is essential for consultants to conceptualize the meaning and operation of consultation to themselves and be ready to do the same with their consultees or consultee system. To this end, the following questions are often helpful:

- What models, processes, theories, and paradigms do you draw on to conceptualize your model of helping?
- How do you define consultation to the consultee or consultee system?

- Do you see the process of consultation as triadic (consultant, consultee, client) or didactic (consultant and client)?
- When is having a vision, looking into the future, and planning a better intervention than cause-and-effect problem solving?

Entry Into the System

The consultant's entry into the system is a crucial step in determining the success or failure of consultation efforts. Several tasks characterize formal entry into the system. For the external consultant, entry usually begins with the exploration of the match between the organization's needs and the consultant's skills. Discussions between the consultant and members of the organization center around descriptive information about the organization, its needs, and desired outcomes. The consultant's skill, style of consultation, and plan for how consultation efforts can be implemented in the setting are discussed and negotiated. Once the parties have agreed that consultation is indeed needed, the process proceeds to the negotiation of an informal or formal contract. The formulation of a contract follows the consultant's defining of his/her function and role in the system. A clear understanding of the specific duties and functions of the consultant must be presented to personnel involved in the consultation effort (Truscott et al., 2012; Brown et al., 2011). Negotiating a contract with key personnel serves to ensure that the highest level of administrators participate in the consultation process and helps to facilitate a smooth transition into the system. The formal discussion of the contract should include the following:

- goals or intended outcomes of consultation,
- identity of the consultee,
- confidentiality of service and limits of confidentiality,
- time frame (How long will the service be provided to the organization? To the individual consultee?),
- times the consultant will be available and ways to contact him/her,
- procedures for requesting to work with the consultant,
- the possibility of contract renegotiation if change is needed,
- fees (if relevant),
- consultant's access to different sources and types of information within the organization, and
- the person to whom the consultant is responsible (Brown et al., 2011).

Orientation to Consultation

Orientation to consultation requires the consultant to communicate directly with key personnel in the system. Initially, the consultant, in establishing a working relationship, must discuss the roles the consultant and consultees will play in the process. This enables all parties to share in the expression of their needs and preferences and creates an atmosphere of open communication. Typical questions addressed in the orientation include the following:

- What are the consultant's expectations about consultation?
- What roles will the consultant and consultee assume in the consultative effort?
- What are the boundaries of the consultant's interventions?

- What are the ethical concerns of the consultee?
- What are the guidelines of confidentiality?
- How long will the consultation take?
- What are the procedures governing the gathering of data?
- What are the guidelines for the giving and receiving of feedback?
- What are the procedures used in the assessment of the consultation plan?

Problem Identification

Once the consultant and consultee have oriented themselves to the process of consultation, the consultant needs to identify the problem(s) to be addressed (Neukrug, 2012). A first step in problem identification is to meet with the consultee to gather appropriate data. Problem identification begins with establishing goals and objectives to be accomplished in consultation. Specific outcomes to be expected and the format for assessing outcomes are discussed. For example, questions to be considered might include the following:

- What are your general concerns about the problem?
- What needs to be accomplished to overcome your concerns?
- What role will the consultee play in overcoming the problem?
- What aspects of the consultee's problem are most distressing?

Consultation Intervention

Having defined the problem and reviewed the data gathered with the consultee, the consultant proceeds with the development of a specific intervention plan. The plan will include the establishment of objectives, the selection of strategies to be implemented, and the assessment procedures to be followed (Neukrug, 2012). Bergan and Kratochwill (1990) suggested the following four-point outline as part of implementing a consultation plan:

1. *Make sure the consultee and consultant agree on the nature of the problem:* Problem identification during the consultation process is critical to the overall success of consultation and sets the stage for the establishment of the consultant–consultee relationship. During the process, the consultant's main priority is to assist the consultee in identifying and clarifying the main problem that is experienced by the client. According to Baker (2000), the skills and techniques of focusing, paraphrasing, setting goals, and showing empathy and genuineness are particularly valuable at this problem identification stage. These skills assist in the development of a plan based on authenticity and collaborative commitment between the consultant and consultee.

2. *Complete either the setting and intrapersonal analysis or the skills analysis:* One role of the consultant is to help the consultee to accurately estimate the importance of situations, as well as to develop self-efficacy expectations regarding performance. Once performance of a productive behavior has been completed, self-evaluation based on reasonable standards must occur. These processes can be facilitated through modeling and feedback to the consultee. Often, motivation can be enhanced by reminding the consultee about the possible positive outcomes of consultation, helping to set goals that correspond with his/her own standards and developing situations that will build confidence that he/she can perform the skills needed to solve the problem (Brown et al., 2011).

3. *Design a plan to deal with the identified problem:* Once the problem has been identified, the consultant and consultee work to establish realistic goals—the objectives of the consortium effort. Setting realistic expectations for the outcomes of consultation implies communication about and knowledge of environmental consultee constraints. Furthermore, successful consultation requires consultees who are knowledgeable of the consultation process. Without this understanding, discordant expectations between consultant and consultee frequently will lead to resistance (Kilburg, 2010). Unless consultees actively contribute during consultation interactions, they often will be frustrated by recommendations that are inconsistent with their own thinking, will feel little psychological ownership of treatment plans, and will fail to expand their own professional skills. This agreement to and acceptance of the objectives of the consultation plan must be ensured before consultation interventions can be planned. The selection of intervention strategies should rest with the consultee (Cook & Friend, 2010). The consultee's involvement in the selection process will raise the client's awareness of the problem and should enhance motivation by engaging clients in goal setting and evaluation. The major issue in selecting intervention strategies is their appropriateness to the setting and the amount of time needed to monitor strategies.

4. *Make arrangements for follow-up sessions with the consultee:* Successful termination of consultation includes the need on the part of the consultant to express an openness to work with the consultee again with other presenting problems. In addition, the collection of data from the consultee on the outcomes of change efforts can document effective consultation and justify its use in professional practice (Neukrug, 2012).

Assessing the Impact of Consultation

The success or failure of consultation interventions is determined by assessing the degree to which the results are congruent with the specific objectives. Data for making this determination come from the observations that began during the entry process and have continued throughout the consultation process. Brown et al. (2011) suggested that steps in the evaluation process are as follows:

1. *Determine the purpose(s) of the evaluation:* The extent to which consultees provide or gather data affects their involvement at this point. The opportunity to make choices that will affect the time that needs to be directed to evaluation as well as the types of information that are collected will contribute to ownership of the evaluation. A major issue to be considered is the confidentiality of the information to be presented.

2. *Agree on measurements to be made:* The consultant and consultee must agree on methods and procedures of measurement. Measures must specifically address the objective and goals of the intervention plan.

3. *Set a data collection schedule:* The consultant and consultee must agree on a formalized calendar of data collection. The method of collection, the tasks assigned to each party, and the method for summarizing and reporting data are discussed.

4. *Develop a dissemination plan:* The dissemination plan, which includes the format in which data are reported, needs to be carefully considered by both parties. Issues surrounding the reporting of data, the individuals to whom data are reported, and the confidentiality of the data are agreed on and follow a pre-determined plan of action.

5. *Concluding consultation:* The termination of the consultation process is as important as the initial entry into the system. An imperative step is for the consultant to act in a culturally

competent fashion with regard to the disengagement process, as well as to provide the consultee with an open invitation to seek further assistance as the need arises (Dougherty, Tack, Fullam, & Hammer, 1996). Follow-up of consultation activities ensures that the consultant and consultee have the opportunity to measure the effects of the process over time. The degree to which the termination process is perceived as a smooth transition can determine whether consultation services will be sought in the future.

Resistance to Consultation

Resistance in consultative relationships can happen as in any other human relationship. Kilburg (2010) noted that consultants must put concerted effort into developing trust with the consultee in order to have a positive outcome and to help reduce the potential for resistance in the process. Various authors have discussed different manifestations of organizational resistance as noted below:

1. *The desire for systems maintenance:* The entrance of the consultant into the system requires the system to adapt to new input that drains energy and threatens the system (Crothers et al., 2008; Gilman & Gabriel, 2004). To avoid this pitfall, the consultant should be careful not to threaten existing roles or challenge others' jobs or role definitions. The simpler the consultant's entry and the less change in structure, tone, process, or product it entails, the easier it will be for the consultant to avoid resistance based on system maintenance.
2. *The consultant as the outsider:* The consultant is viewed as an alien in the organization and is treated with suspicion. The consultant should become familiar with the institution's history, mission, philosophy, and procedures and increase his/her availability to and contact with the staff to reduce outsider status.
3. *The desire to reject the new as nonnormative:* There is often a desire to maintain the status quo by conforming to existing norms in the organization. The consultant must guard against tampering with time-honored programs, processes, and procedures. Consultant sensitivity to organizational vulnerability is essential.
4. *The desire to protect one's turf or vested interests:* The consultant must recognize that his/her presence is often viewed as an intrusion on the consultee's area of interest or professional responsibility. Involving the consultee in the process tends to lessen the resistance (Crothers et al., 2008).
5. *Being so close to a problem that one loses perspective:* Consultees sometimes can feel as if they have invested so much energy and thought into a client or student that they are hesitant to engage consultation because they cannot see how new approaches will aid the problem or because their view of the client or student is distorted by continuous close contact (Hylander, 2012).

Similarly, some specific variables can increase resistance to consultation. For example, the less time and resources needed to implement interventions, the greater the acceptance. Gonzales, Nelson, Gutkin, and Shwery (2004) proposed that, when the costs of consultation and its potential required outcomes outweigh the perceived benefits, consultees (especially teachers) may resist the process. Discordant expectations between consultant and consultees will frequently lead to resistance. Finally, Maital (1996) discussed resistance as emerging when consultees, such as parents who are seeking consultation for their children, lose objectivity and find it difficult to implement a plan of action created by a consultant.

Contracting and the Forces of Change in the Organization

Kurpius and Fuqua (1993) suggested that an understanding of the cycles of change and the forces of change within the organization is helpful in gaining a better understanding of the problems and the culture surrounding the problems in the organization. Stages of change include the following:

1. *Development:* Help is needed at an early stage of a new problem or program.
2. *Maintenance:* Things are becoming stagnant and falling behind, needing help to improve. This stage shows signs of consultee desire and motivation for change.
3. *Decline:* Things are worse, and consultees recognize that they cannot solve the problem. Consultees may want a quick fix and have high expectations for the consultant.
4. *Crisis:* Consultees or consultee system is desperate for help. The consultant may look for dependency first, but it is important that consultees understand that their situation and the investment need to return to a stable state.

The forces of change within the system need to be understood for consultation to proceed. When the system is closed to change and internal forces vary between being for and against change, there is usually little opportunity for change to occur. When the system recognizes that change is needed but forces for and against change are balanced, progress is possible but slow moving. When the forces for change are external to the members who prefer not to change, one can expect a high degree of conflict and slow change. Finally, when the members recognize the need for help and all want help to improve, then the best chance for successful helping occurs (Kurpius & Fuqua, 1993).

These models can serve as a test of the feasibility of the consultant's effort and the type of contract the consultant will implement. The formal discussion of the contract between the consultant and the consultee should include a number of critical questions to be answered before a contract is developed and implemented. According to Remley (1993), consultation contracts should do the following:

1. clearly specify the work to be completed by the consultant,
2. describe in detail any work products expected from the consultant,
3. establish a time frame for the completion of the work,
4. establish lines of authority and the person to whom the consultant is responsible,
5. describe the compensation plan for the consultant and the method of payment, and
6. specify any special agreement or contingency plans agreed on by the parties.

Remley (1993) suggested that some individuals complain that written contracts are too legalistic and signify distrust between the consultant and the consultee. Consultation is a business arrangement and should be entered into in a businesslike fashion. By reducing to written form agreements that have been reached by the parties, misunderstandings can be identified and resolved before further problems arise.

Summary

Consultation in schools and mental health agencies is a highly sought-after skill, and one with which counseling and psychotherapy interns should become familiar. In this chapter, the models and methods of consultation were presented to provide the student with an overview of the ways to organize and establish consultative relationships. The differences between mental health consultation and school consultation have been discussed, along with critical issues such as resistance. Systems and integrative approaches to consultation were chosen as representative samples of consultation strategies, and guidelines for consulting in the school were presented.

References

Alabama Department of Education. (2003). The revised comprehensive counseling and guidance model of Alabama public schools. In D. C. Cobia & D. A. Hendeson (Eds.), *Handbook of school counseling* (p. 48). Upper Saddle River, NJ: Pearson Education.

Alpert, J. L. (1977). Some guidelines for school consultation. *Journal of School Psychology, 15,* 308–319.

American School Counselors Association. (2003). ASCA national model: A framework for school counseling programs. *Professional School Counseling, 6*(3), 54–58.

Baker, S. B. (2000). *School counseling for the twentieth century* (3rd ed.). Upper Saddle River, NJ: Prentice Hall.

Behring, S. T., & Ingraham, C. L. (1998). Culture as a central component of consultation: A call to the field. *Journal of Educational and Psychological Consultation, 9,* 57–72.

Bergan, J. R., & Kratochwill, T. R. (1990). *Behavior consultation and therapy.* New York, NY: Plenum.

Brown, D., Pryzwansky, W. B., & Schulte, A. C. (2011). *Psychological consultation and collaboration: Introduction to theory and practice.* Upper Saddle River, NJ: Pearson.

Caplan, G. (1970). *The theory and practice of mental health consultation.* New York, NY: Basic Books.

Caplan, G., Caplan, R., & Erchul, W. P. (1994). Caplanian mental health consultation: Historical background and current status. *Consulting Psychology: Practice and Research, 46,* 2–12.

Clemens, E. (2007). Developmental counseling and therapy as a model for school counselor consultation with teachers. *Professional School Counselor, 10,* 352–359.

Cook, L., & Friend, M. (2010). The state of the art of collaboration on behalf of children with special needs. *Journal of Educational and Psychological Consultation, 20,* 1–8.

Crothers, L. M., Hughes, T. L., & Morine, K. A. (2008). *Theory and cases in school-based consultation: A resource for school psychologists, school counselors, special educators, and other mental health professionals.* New York, NY: Routledge.

Dahir, C. Q., Sheldon, C. B., & Valiza, M. J. (1998). *Vision into action: Implementing the national standards for school counseling program.* Alexandria, VA: American School Counseling Association.

Dougherty, A. M. (2005). *Psychological consultation and collaboration in school and community settings* (4th ed.). Pacific Grove, CA: Brooks/Cole.

Dougherty, A. M., Tack, F. E., Fullam, C. B., & Hammer, L. A. (1996). Disengagement: A neglected aspect of the consultation process. *Journal of Educational and Psychological Consultation, 7,* 259–274.

Egan, G. (2010). *The skilled helper: A problem management approach to helping* (9th ed.). Pacific Grove, CA: Brooks/Cole.

Erchul, W. P. (2011). School consultation and response to intervention: A tale of two literatures. *Journal of Educational and Psychological Consultation, 21,* 191–208.

Gilliam, W. S., Maupin, A. N., & Reyes, C. R. (2016). Early childhood mental health consultation: Results of a statewide random-controlled evaluation. *Journal of the American Academy of Child and Adolescent Psychiatry, 55,* 754–761.

Gilman, R., & Gabriel, S. (2004). Perceptions of school psychological services by educational professionals: Results from a multi-state survey pilot study. *School Psychology Review, 33,* 271–286.

Gonzales, J. E., Nelson, J. R., Gutkin, T. B., & Shwery, C. (2004). Teacher resistance to school-based consultation with school psychologists: A survey of teacher perceptions. *Journal of Emotional and Behavioral Disorders, 12,* 30–37.

Gravois, T. A. (2012). Consultation services in schools: A can of worms worth opening. *Consulting Psychology Journal: Practice and Research, 64,* 83–87.

Hylander, I. (2012). Conceptual change through consultee-centered consultation: A theoretical model. *Consulting Psychology Journal: Practice and Research, 64,* 29–45.

Ivey, A. E., Ivey, M. B., Myers, J. E., & Sweeney, T. J. (2005). *Developmental counseling and therapy: Promoting wellness over the lifespan.* Boston, MA: Lahaska.

Kahn, B. B. (2000). A model of solution-focused consultation for school counselors. *Professional School Counselor, 3,* 248–254.

Kilburg, R. R. (2010). Executive consulting under pressure: A brief commentary on some timeless issues. *Consulting Psychology Journal: Practice and Research, 62,* 203–206.

Kirby, J. (1985). *Consultation: Practice and practitioner.* Muncie, IN: Accelerated Development.

Kirmayer, L. J., Guzder, J., & Rousseau, C. (Eds.). (2014). *Cultural consultation: Encountering the other in mental health care.* New York, NY: Springer.

Kurpius, D. J., & Fuqua, D. R. (1993). Fundamental issues in defining consultation. *Journal of Counseling and Development, 71,* 598–600.

Maital, S. L. (1996). Integration of behavioral and mental health consultation as a means of overcoming resistance. *Journal of Educational and Psychological Consultation, 7,* 291–303.

Myrick, R. D. (1997). *Developmental guidance and counseling: A developmental approach.* Minneapolis, MN: Educational Media.

Neukrug, E. (2012). *The world of the counselor: An introduction to the counseling profession.* New York, NY: Brooks/Cole.

Ohlsen, M. M. (1983). *Introduction to counseling.* Itasca, IL: F. E. Peacock.

O'Kane, D., Barkway, P., & Muir-Cochrane, E. (2012). Understanding child mental health consultation from the perspective of primary health care professionals. *Neonatal, Paediatric, and Child Health Nursing, 15,* 2–9.

Olivos, E. M., Gallagher, R. A., & Aguilar, J. (2010). Fostering collaboration of culturally and linguistically diverse families of children with moderate to severe disabilities. *Journal of Educational and Psychological Consultation, 20,* 28–40.

Perry, D. F., & Conners-Burrow, N. (2016). Addressing early adversity through mental health consultation in early childhood settings. *Family Relations: Interdisciplinary Journal of Applied Family Studies, 65,* 24–36.

Remley, T. P. (1993). Consultation contracts. *Journal of Counseling and Development, 72,* 157–158.

Rockwood, G. F. (1993, July/August). Edgar Schein's process versus content consultation models. *Journal of Counseling and Development, 71,* 636–638.

Ryan, R. M., & Deci, E. L. (2000). Self-determination theory and the facilitation of intrinsic motivation, social development, and well-being. *American Psychologist, 55,* 68–78.

Schein, E. H. (1969). *Process consultation.* Reading, MA: Addison-Wesley.

Schein, E. H. (1990). Organizational culture. *American Psychologist, 45,* 109–119.

Schein, E. H. (1997). The concept of "client" from a process consultation perspective: A guide for change agents. *Journal of Organizational Change Management, 10,* 202–216.

Schmidt, J. J. (2003). *Counseling in schools: Essential services and comprehensive programs* (4th ed.). Boston, MA: Allyn & Bacon.

Sears, R., Rudisill, J., & Mason-Sears, C. (2006). *Consultation skills for mental health professionals.* Hoboken, NJ: Wiley.

Seligman, M. E. P., & Csikszentmihalyi, M. (2000). Positive psychology: An introduction. *American Psychologist, 55*, 5–14.

Tindal, G., Parker, R., & Hasbrouck, J. E. (1992). The construct validity of stages and activities in the consultation process. *Journal of Educational and Psychological Consultation, 3*, 99–118.

Truscott, S. D., Kreskey, D., Bolling, M., Psimas, L., Graybill, E., & Albritton, K. (2012). Creating consultee change: A theory-based approach to learning and behavioral change processes in school-based consultation. *Consulting Psychology Journal: Practice and Research, 64*, 63–82.

Vuyk, M. A., Sprague-Jones, J., & Reed, C. (2016). Early childhood mental health consultation: An evaluation of effectiveness in a rural community. *Infant Mental Health Journal, 37*, 66–79. doi:10.1002/imhj.21545

CHAPTER 12

LOOKING AHEAD TO A CAREER IN PROFESSIONAL COUNSELING

The practicum and internship are the most complex and rich learning experiences in a training program for counselors and other related mental health professionals. The internship, in particular, is meant to give students a taste of what it is like to take on the roles and responsibilities of entry-level practitioners. Upon completion of internship, most students are nearing graduation and contemplating the next steps of their career development. In this final chapter, we offer information about how to move from being a practicum and internship student to becoming a professional counselor who sustains a years-long career in the field. Related information about licensure may also be found in Chapter 1.

The First Steps Towards Licensure

Because counseling is a profession regulated by licensure and certification boards, there are certain evidences of competence and accomplishment a new graduate has to present to a board in order to meet its minimum qualifications for non-independent and independent licensure or certification. Practicing as a licensed or certified professional is a privilege one must earn, not a right that is granted upon completion of a degree program (Bernard & Goodyear, 2014). Recognizing that one practices counseling as a privilege earned is a mindset novice professionals have to embrace, and it sets the tone for one's career. Thus, it is important that counseling professionals do not lose sight of the fact that, at its heart, a career in counseling is a career of service built upon a person's disposition of care for others, ongoing skill mastery, and sufficiently broad body of knowledge to meet the needs of diverse groups of clients. Concretely, the entry-level evidences of knowledge and skill competence that most boards require of applicants include: transcripts indicating a qualifying graduate degree; a passing score on a licensure or certification exam; a background check; a laws and rules exam that reviews the state or province's rules and regulations for professional counselors; and, for independent licensure, completion of a minimum number of supervised hours by a board-approved supervisor.

Licensure Law

Counselor licensure laws are not the same from state to state, and therefore, it is important that counseling students take the time to become familiar with the licensure laws in the region in which they plan to practice. For example, states vary with regard to the scope of practice granted to professional counselors (Remley & Herlihy, 2016). Some states have an expansive scope that allows for independent diagnosis and treatment of clients, including psychological testing, while others have laws that do not permit unsupervised diagnosis of mental and emotional disorders even by an independently licensed counselor. Other important distinctions surround the kind of graduate degrees that are acceptable to a board. The number of states that now require its applicants for licensure to hold a CACREP-accredited degree is slowing increasing. Conversely, other states allow applicants to have a counseling or related professional degree (e.g., master's degree in psychology, marriage and family therapy, rehabilitation counseling, or art therapy) from a program without a specialized accreditation. Most states require a minimum of 60 credit hours from a planned educational program to qualify for licensure. Finally, students will want to become familiar with their chosen state's licensure structure. For instance, some states have a single license that is granted only after the applicant for licensure completes a minimum number of supervised hours in the field under a board-approved supervisor. Other states have a two-tiered system. States that use the two-tier system grant a non-independent license or an associate license first. Applicants qualify for the non-independent license primarily on the basis of having an acceptable degree and a passing score on a licensure exam. The independent license in the two-tiered system is granted after all training supervision hours have been completed. New graduates are strongly advised to become familiar with their state's licensure structure and steps to independent licensure, as they may be required to garner certain board approvals throughout the licensure process. For example, some states will not award even the associate license until the applicant provides the board with the name and credentials of a clinical supervisor acceptable to the board or a supervision plan.

Licensure and Certification Exams

As noted in Chapter 1, the two most commonly used licensure and certification exams for counselors are the National Counselor Exam (NCE) and the National Clinical Mental Health Counselor Exam (NCMHCE). Both of these have been created and are updated by the National Board for Certified Counselors (NBCC). Strictly speaking, the NCE and the NCMHCE exams are used to qualify individuals for national counselor certification. However, every state has adopted one or the other—and in some cases both—of the exams as part of their licensure process. Students who are enrolled in a CACREP-accredited program can qualify to sit for the exams prior to graduation. The program faculty are responsible for coordinating the exam with the NBCC, and it can be offered either on or off campus. Students who are not enrolled in a CACREP-accredited program can be approved to take an exam either through their licensing board or directly through the NBCC. If a student registers for an exam through the NBCC and wants to use the exam results to qualify for dependent or independent licensure, he/she will have to request that the scores of the exam be sent to the licensing board of choice. An exam result is good for five years, which is an incentive for a new counselor to complete all state-licensure requirements, especially supervised experience, within that time period.

The NCE and the NCMHCE are separate exams with differing formats; each is intended to test for different sets of knowledge and skills. The NCE, which is used by the majority of states for counselor licensure, is a 200-question multiple-choice exam that tests for knowledge, skills, and abilities relevant to professional counseling practice (NBCC, 2018). The knowledge domains on the NCE cover each of the eight core-content areas established by CACREP; additionally, there are questions that pertain to contemporary work behaviors. The work domain questions are created through a job analysis of counselors' current work experiences (NBCC, 2018). The NCMHCE tests for a counselor's ability to gather appropriate information, analyze clinical data, conceptualize cases, problem solve, and diagnose and treat clinical cases accurately. The format of the exam is based around ten clinical cases divided into at least five sections that involve the test-taker answering questions related to information gathering and decision making (NBCC, 2018). The NCMHCE is not created to text for basic comprehension of knowledge, as is the NCE; rather, it tests for clinical skill. For whichever exam you need to take for licensure purposes, we highly recommend that you review for the test. There are numerous study guides available for both exams; some are in print format, while others are electronic (online) or offered in an in-person workshop. Investing in preparation time is helpful because the exams are used as gatekeeping tools for the next steps in your career development.

Securing a Supervisor for Post-Graduate Training Supervision

Post-graduate training supervision is supervision that happens after one completes an academic degree program and is employed in a counseling agency or related work setting. Like training supervision in the practicum and internship, post-graduate training supervision is intended to enhance the professional skills and functioning of the counselor, as well as ensure the protection of clients' welfare (Borders & Brown, 2005). Training supervision is not the same as work or administrative supervision, which focuses on work-related performance management issues.

We have already noted that each state and province has its own laws, rules, and regulations that govern counselor licensure and practice. Broadly speaking, state licensure laws are more similar than they are dissimilar. However, for the new professional who is not independently licensed the differences sometimes can have significant implications for one's ability to achieve licensure, especially if the new professional moves from one state to another prior to becoming independently licensed.

One of the areas requiring careful thought and research is that of securing a supervisor to oversee one's post-graduate training supervision. New graduates who are working in the field first should ensure that their training supervisor has the appropriate supervisory credentials according to their state rules and regulations. It is fundamentally the supervisee's responsibility to find and secure an acceptably credentialed supervisor. Unfortunately, new professionals sometimes assume that they are receiving supervision from an individual who is board-approved only to realize partway through the collection of hours that the supervision will not be able to be used due to having an unapproved supervisor. Some states provide lists of approved supervisors; others require that supervisors have a specific supervision endorsement as part of their professional credential and title (for example, LPCC-S or the Licensed Professional Clinical Counselor with a Supervisory designation). We strongly recommend that you investigate your state rules and regulations on supervisor qualifications prior to engaging in post-graduate training supervision.

Because each state has the right to establish its own laws governing training supervision, there is not a national standard for clinical supervisor qualifications. Many states require counselors to be supervised by independently licensed counselors with a minimum number of years of experience plus training in clinical supervision. However, this is not exclusively the case. For instance, some states allow a portion (even up to half) of post-graduate training supervision to be provided by a mental health professional who is not a licensed counselor. A counselor's training supervisor thus may be an independently licensed counselor, social worker, marriage and family therapist, psychologist, or psychiatrist. Bernard and Goodyear (2014) note the advantages and disadvantages of receiving training supervision from a person with a different professional identity than your own. On a practical level, and in terms of entry into the profession, the new counselor should be aware that not all training-supervision hours collected in one state prior to independent licensure may be transferable to another state. For example, a counselor might be working in a state that allows up to half of training supervision hours to be provided by a non-counselor (e.g., a social worker). If that counselor moves prior to independent licensure to a state that requires its licensees to be supervised only by counseling professionals, that counselor may have to re-accumulate supervision hours if they are not acceptable to the board. Usually, once a counselor is independently licensed and has an established record of practice in the field, the training supervision is a less important component of having one's license endorsed from state-to-state. We recommend that you carefully consider the credentials of your training supervisor and keep a record of his/her resume. One cannot always predict or control life changes and opportunities, but being informed of some of the possible challenges to licensure in the area of supervision, at least early in one's career, can help to smooth the transition.

Longevity in the Profession

Completing an academic program of study in counseling, including a practicum and internship; securing a first job as a mental health professional; passing a licensure exam; and working under post-graduate clinical supervision for at least a couple years are all hurdles that must be overcome successfully before one can begin to feel like an established professional counselor. Becoming an established—or at least a licensed—professional is an accomplishment that happens relatively early on in one's career (on average, 2 to 3 years post-graduation if one is working full-time in the field). However, most people who complete a counseling program intend to engage in clinical work for the long-term. Looking into the horizon of one's career, it is helpful to reflect, therefore, on what enhances longevity in the helping professions.

Self-Care, Wellness, and Burnout

We discussed in Chapter 8 the need for counselors-in-training to be in tune with their own personal areas of growth, wounds, and hurts before entering into (and while completing) the practicum and internship experience. The ACA *Code of Ethics* (2014) focus on self-care is a way to obligate students and professionals not to engage with clients or certain client populations when there is the potential for impairment. At the same time, the code's standards on self-care indicate a value within the profession on its practitioners' own well-being. Sustaining professional excellence over years of service requires that each one of us takes the time, and finds the means, to care for ourselves, as well as for our clients. Being other-centered and service oriented is a virtue, but it must be balanced by a certain amount of self-interest, self-focus, and healthy boundaries.

A commonly used term in the helping field is burnout, which has been described as a state of depersonalization, emotional fatigue, and a sense of uselessness to clients (Lawson, 2007). New professionals are cautioned not to be naïve about the risks to burnout, especially because the stresses of working with others who are under-resourced, troubled, or needy in any variety of ways are quite real. Compounding the challenges of working with people who demand a high level of emotional as well as psychological attention are factors such as stressed organizational systems, unsupportive peers, and long hours that also can contribute to burnout (Maslach, 2003). Finally, counselors often evaluate their own success by the client's ability or will to change, which is an unfair and incomplete measure of one's competence because it fails to account for the important factors of client motivation and autonomy. These factors are outside of the counselor's control and must not be overly emphasized in the evaluation of professional achievement.

Recommendations for Sustaining Personal and Professional Excellence

Skovholt and Ronnestad (2001) conducted an investigation into the experiences of career formation among counselors. Their participants represented professionals from all phases of development, including students in training to become counselors to professionals who worked 40 or more years in the field. Not only did their work distill fascinating themes of career-long counselor development milestones, but they also were able to glean pieces of wisdom about how to sustain oneself in a helping profession for decades of work. Based on their research findings, we offer the following recommendations for enhancing longevity and staving off burnout:

1. *Maximize experiences of personal success:* Focus on areas of client change within your own control, such as being prepared for sessions and being knowledgeable about client issues rather than define success solely as client change.
2. *Create an individualized plan for development:* Be open to learning at all times from various professional sources and be willing to reinvent yourself to add vigor to the work.
3. *Reflect and create a plan for self-awareness:* Find moments to introspect and reflect on your professional self, your work, and personal life.
4. *Create a work environment that promotes growth:* Gather a group of professional peers and supervisors who will support and mentor you and provide honest feedback.
5. *Minimize professional losses:* Try to ensure that as much as possible an opportunity for termination with clients is made and acknowledge the impact of not having closure.
6. *Focus on personal health and wellness:* Find time to spend with the people who add meaning to your life and to engage the activities that are personally enjoyable (Skovholt & Ronnestad, 2001).

There is no one right way to work skillfully and with a sense of joy and interest in the counseling profession across a life span. However, we hope that these recommendations, coupled with your own interests and creative approaches to self-care will help you to move from a fruitful practicum and internship experience to a lifetime of meaningful encounters and clinical successes as a professional counselor.

References

American Counseling Association. (2014). *Code of ethics.* Alexandria, VA: Author.

Bernard, J. M., & Goodyear, R. K. (2014). *Fundamentals of clinical supervision* (5th ed.). Upper Saddle River, NJ: Pearson.

Borders, L. D., & Brown, L. L. (2005). *The new handbook of counseling supervision.* Mahwah, NJ: Lahaska.

Lawson, G. (2007). Counselor wellness and impairment: A national survey. *Journal of Humanistic Counseling, Education, and Development, 46,* 20–34.

Maslach, C. (2003). *Burnout: The cost of caring.* Cambridge, MA: Malor Books.

National Board of Certified Counselors. (2018). *Examinations.* Retrieved from www.nbcc.org/Exams

Remley, T. P., Jr., & Herlihy, B. (2016). *Ethical, legal, and professional issues in counseling* (5th ed.). Upper Saddle River, NJ: Pearson.

Skovholt, T. M., & Ronnestad, M. H. (2001). The long, textured path from novice to senior practitioner. In T. M Skovholt (Ed.), *The resilient practitioner: Burnout prevention and self-care strategies for counselors, therapists, teachers, and health professionals* (pp. 25–54). Boston, MA: Allyn & Bacon.

APPENDICES

PSYCHIATRIC MEDICATIONS

Traditionally, counselor training programs have not focused on psychopharmacology as a major content area of training. Philosophical as well as ethical issues regarding the use of medications are contributing factors in the lack of training in this area.

Unfortunately, today's counselors in both schools and agencies are confronted with the fact that a portion of their clientele may be taking medications or is in need of medication to function more effectively. It is therefore critical that counselors have at least a rudimentary understanding of the types of medications commonly prescribed and their uses in treating mental health issues. Counselors are expected to consult and cooperate with other mental health professionals in the treatment of clients. Familiarity with medications is especially helpful in understanding the pharmacological treatment regimens prescribed for clients by physicians and psychiatrists.

The following listing of medications, used in the treatment of mental health issues, is provided for the purposes of

- providing interns in schools and agencies with a listing of common psychotropic medications used in the treatment of mental disorders;
- familiarizing the intern with basic pharmacological terms, symbols, and definitions;
- providing interns with suggested readings to help in their understanding of psychopharmacological treatment; and
- encouraging interns to learn more about the use and abuse of medications.

The number and types of medications used for the treatment of mental health issues are vast. The following is a representative sampling of the more commonly used medications in the United States.

Antidepressant Medications

All antidepressants have similar effects, and most have different side effects. About 50% of patients will respond to the medications with some symptom reduction within the first several days to week of treatment. Remission of symptoms is harder to achieve and may take 8 to 12 weeks. Those patients who do not achieve remission of symptoms are more likely to relapse back into depression and are at an increased risk of suicide (Wegman, 2012).

There are six classes of antidepressant medications on the US drug market:

- cyclics,
- selective serotonin reuptake inhibitors (SSRIs),
- serotonin and norepinephrine reuptake inhibitors (SNRIs),
- norepinephrine reuptake inhibitors (NRIs),
- monoamine oxidase inhibitors (MAOIs), and
- atypical antidepressants.

Cyclics

Tricyclic antidepressants (TCAs): This includes tricyclics and tetracyclics, which have similar chemical structures. TCAs are 65% to 75% effective in relieving the somatic features associated with depression. The cyclics are effective treatments for depression and were used primarily from the 1950s through the 1990s. Unfortunately, they can have serious side effects. They can be dangerous in overdose and can increase the sedative effects of alcohol and cause life-threatening heart rhythm disturbances when taken in overdose (Smith, 2012).

Trade Name	Generic Name	Daily Dosage
Anafranil	clomipramine	150–200 mg
Desyrel	trazodone	150–400 mg
Elavil	amitriptyline	100–200 mg
Norpramin	desipramine	150–300 mg
Pamelor	desipramine	75–150 mg
Sinequan	doxepin	150–300 mg
Tofranil	imipramine	100–200 mg

Note: See Wegman (2012).

Selective Serotonin Reuptake Inhibitors (SSRIs)

SSRIs, a second-generation antidepressant, have fewer side effects than TCAs and monoamine oxidase inhibitors (see below). Generally, SSRIs cause less weight gain and less sedation and hypotension than TCAs. In addition, SSRIs are less lethal when taken in overdose.

Trade Name	Generic Name	Daily Dosage
Celexa	citalopram	20–80 mg
Lexapro	escitalopram	10–40 mg
Luvox	fluvoxamine	100–400 mg

Trade Name	Generic Name	Daily Dosage
Paxil	paroxetine	20–50 mg
Prozac	fluoxetine	10–80 mg
Sarafem	fluoxetine	20–80 mg
Viibryd*	vilazodone	10–40 mg
Zoloft	sertraline	50–200 mg

Note: SSRI/atypical.

Serotonin and Norepinephrine Reuptake Inhibitors (SNRIs)

These are considered dual action antidepressants that show slightly more effective results for treating major depression than SSRIs.

Trade Name	Generic Name	Daily Dosage
Cymbalta	duloxetine	20–80 mg
Effexor	venlafaxine	75–350 mg
Effexor XR	venlafaxineXR	75–350 mg
Pristiq	venlafaxine	75–350 mg

Norepinephrine Reuptake Inhibitors (NRIs)

NRIs are noted for providing an energy boost as well as for decreasing distractibility and improving the attention span. *Strattera* (atomoxetine) is pharmacologically considered an antidepressant but is approved by the Food and Drug Administration for the treatment of attention deficit—hyperactivity disorder. *Remeron* (mirtazapine) helps with the anxiety and sleep problems common to depression.

Monoamine Oxidase Inhibitors (MAOIs)

MAOIs were first developed in the 1950s and today are rarely used. MAOIs are indicated for some patients who are unresponsive to other antidepressants. Because of their side-effects profile and a potential for serious interactions with other drugs and food, MAOIs are no longer used as a first drug of choice when treating depression (Buelow, Hebert, & Buelow, 2000).

Trade Name	Generic Name	Daily Dosage
Emsam	selegiline	patch 6–12 mg
Nardil	phenelzine	10–30 mg
Parnate	tranylcypromine	10–30 mg

Atypical Antidepressants

Trade Name	Generic Name	Daily Dosage
Aplenzin	bupropion(Hbr)	174–522 mg
Remeron	mirtazapine	15–45 mg
Oleptro	trazodone ER	150–300 mg
Symbyax	olanzapine/fluoxetine	6 mg olanzapine/25 mg fluoxetine
Viibryd*	vilazodone	10–40 mg
WellbutrinSR	bupropionSR	150–300 mg
WellbutrinLA	bupropionLA	150–300 mg

Antianxiety Medications

Anxiolytics or Minor Tranquilizers

Benzodiazepines (BDZs): BDZs are a group of structurally related compounds that have sedative properties. Because of the greater safety margin of BDZs, their use has, for the most part, replaced the use of barbiturates, a more dangerous class of sedatives (Buelow et al., 2000). BDZs are often the treatment of choice for anxiety. While BDZs are popular and widely used, the risk of dependence is significant. They can also be dangerous when used in overdose, particularly when combined with alcohol. Their use should be monitored. When discontinued, their dose should be reduced slowly, over days, weeks, or even months, to prevent withdrawal symptoms (Wegman, 2012). These medications are often used with SSRIs in the treatment of panic attacks. Antianxiety medication is not indicated for obsessive-compulsive disorder, which is typically treated with higher doses of serotonin antidepressants (SSRIs) in combination with cognitive behavioral therapy.

Trade Name	Generic Name	Daily Dosage
Ativan	lorazepam	1–10 mg
Klonopin	clonazepam	0.25–1.5 mg
Librium	chlordiazepoxide	20–40 mg
Valium	diazepam	20–40 mg
Xanax	alprozolam	0.5–1.5 mg

Antianxiety Agents Other Than Benzodiazepines

Trade Name	Generic Name	Daily Dosage
Atarax	hydroxyzine	100–400 mg
Buspar	buspirone	15–30 mg
Vistaril	hydroxyzine pamoate	100–400 mg

Mood-Stabilizing Medications

These medications are used primarily for the treatment of bipolar disorder.

Lithium (Lithobid) is considered as a first-line agent in the treatment of acute mania and hypomania as well as for the maintenance treatment of bipolar I and II. It is safe and effective when closely monitored. Therapeutic doses can be close to toxic, and consequently blood levels must be carefully monitored. Other medications used in the treatment of bipolar disorders are the anticonvulsants and the atypical antipsychotics.

Anticonvulsant Medications Used in the Treatment of Bipolar Disorder

Trade Name	Generic Name	Daily Dosage
Depakote	divalproex	750–3000 mg
Lamictal	lamotrigine	100–200 mg
Tegretol	carbamazepine	600–1200 mg
Topamax	topiramate	200–400 mg

In addition to the mood stabilizers and the anticonvulsant medications, all second-generation antipsychotic medications have been approved for the treatment of bipolar mania. However, most are not effective in bipolar depression with the exception of Seroquel and Abilify. Traditional antidepressants have little, if any, advantage in the treatment of bipolar depression (Wegman, 2012).

Antipsychotic Medications

The modern era for the treatment of psychotic disorders began in the early 1950s when Thorazine was found to be an effective treatment for schizophrenia. All antipsychotic medications block dopamine receptors in the central nervous system. But, because of their actions on the neurotransmitter systems, there can be many side effects. When the medications are effective the patient feels relaxed and less fearful, and thought distortion and mood may also improve (Wegman, 2012). These medications induce in schizophrenia a "neuroleptic state" that is characterized by decreased agitation, aggression, and impulsiveness, as well as a decrease in hallucinations and delusions and, generally, less concern with the external environment (Buelow et al., 2000, p. 66). Antipsychotic medications fall into two main categories: the older conventional agents and the newer atypical agents.

Conventional Agents

The first antipsychotic medication on the US drug market was Thorazine in 1952. This was followed by several others. However, these first-generation medications are no longer considered agents of choice. These conventional agents fell out of favor because of the neurological side effects and because 20% of adult schizophrenics are unresponsive to these conventional medications (Wegman, 2012).

Trade Name	Generic Name	Daily Dosage
Haldol	haloperidol	1–40 mg
Mellaril	thioridazine	150–800 mg
Moban	molindone	20–225 mg
Navane	thiothixene	10–60 mg
Prolixin	fluphenazine	3–45 mg
Stelazine	trifluoperazine	2–40 mg
Thorazine	chlorpromazine	60–800 mg

Atypical Antipsychotic Agents

The atypicals are not a single homogeneous class of drugs. They carry a lower risk of neurological side effects and tardive dyskinesis. All of the atypicals are approved for use with bipolar mania, but effectiveness varies depending on symptomatic circumstances.

Trade Name	Generic Name	Initial Dosage
Abilify	aripiprazole	10–15 mg
Clorazil	clozapine	300–600 mg
Fanapt	iloperidone	12–24 mg
Geodon	ziprasidone	120–160 mg
Invega	paliperidone	3–12 mg
Risperdal	risperidone	2 mg/divided/bid
Saphris	asenapine	10–20 mg
Symbyax	olanzapine/fluoxetine	5–20 mg
Seroquel	quetiapine	100–150 mg
Zyprexa	olanzapine	5–20 mg

Special Populations: Psychopharmacological Treatments for Children and Adolescents

Disorder	Medications
Major depression	SSRIs
Bipolar disorder	Lithium, Depakote, Risperdal, Abilify

Schizophrenia	Risperdal, Abilify, Zyprexa, Seroquel
Obsessive-compulsive disorder	Luvox, Zoloft
Separation anxiety disorder	Buspar, Vistaril, SSRIs
Attention-deficit/hyperactivity disorder (ADHD)	RitalinLA, AdderallXR, Daytrana, Vyvanse, WellbutrinSR/LA, Intuniv
Psychotic disorder	Seroquel, Zyprexa

These lists of medications are offered to provide an overview of medications currently used in treatment and are not intended to be used prescriptively. The information reflects currently accepted practice, but any recommendations must be held up against individual circumstances at hand. These lists of medications were adapted from the following sources. Miller's (2009) book is particularly helpful to use with patients.

References

Buelow, G., Hebert, S., & Buelow, S. (2000). *Psychotherapists resource on psychiatric medications: Issues of treatment and referral.* Belmont, CA: Wadsworth.

Miller, F. (2009). *My mental health medication workbook.* Eau Claire, WI: PESI.

Smith, T. (2012). *Psychopharmacology: What you need to know about psychiatric medications.* Eau Claire, WI: CMI Education.

Wegman, J. (2012). *Straight talk on mental health medications.* Eau Claire, WI: Premier Publishing & Media.

APPENDIX II: FORMS

Form 2.1: Practicum Contract

This agreement is made on _____ by and between_____

(date)   (field site)

and _____. The agreement will be effective for a period

(university program)

from _____ to _____ for _____ per week for _____.

(starting date)   (ending date)   (number of hours)   (student name)

Purpose

The purpose of this agreement is to provide a qualified graduate student with a practicum experience in the field of counseling or psychology.

The University Program Agrees

1. to assign a university faculty liaison to facilitate communication between university and site;
2. to provide the site prior to placement of the student the following information:

   a. a profile of the student named above, and
   b. an academic calendar that shall include dates for periods during which student will be excused from field supervision;

3. to notify the student that he/she must adhere to the administrative policies, rules, standards, schedules, and practices of the site;
4. that the faculty liaison shall be available for consultation with both site supervisors and students and shall be immediately contacted should any problem or change in relation to student, site, or university occur; and
5. that the university supervisor is responsible for the assignment of a fieldwork grade.

The Practicum Site Agrees

1. to assign a practicum supervisor who has appropriate credentials, time, and interest for training the practicum student;
2. to provide opportunities for the student to engage in a variety of counseling activities under supervision and for evaluating the student's performance (suggested counseling experiences included in the "Practicum Activities" section);
3. to provide the student with adequate work space, telephone, office supplies, and staff to conduct professional activities;
4. to provide supervisory contact that involves some examination of student work using audio or video recordings, observation, and/or live supervision; and
5. to provide written evaluation of student based on criteria established by the university program.

The Practicum Student Agrees

1. to obtain transportation to and from the site;
2. to schedule and attend weekly supervision sessions with on-site supervisor and attend weekly supervision sessions with faculty supervisors;
3. to adhere to the ethical guidelines of the American Counseling Association *Code of Ethics;* and
4. to adhere to the policies and procedures, rules, and standards of the placement site.

Within the specified time frame,_____ (site supervisor) will be the primary practicum site supervisor. The training activities (checked below) will be provided for the student in sufficient amounts to allow an adequate evaluation of the student's level of competence in each activity.

_____ (faculty liaison) will be the faculty liaison with whom the student and practicum site supervisor will communicate regarding progress, problems, and performance evaluations.

Practicum Activities

1. Individual counseling/psychotherapy
   Personal/social nature
   Occupational/educational nature

2. Group counseling/psychotherapy
   Co-leading
   Leading

3. Intake interviewing
   Taking social history information

4. Testing
   Administration
   Analysis
   Interpretation of results

5. Report writing
   Record keeping
   Treatment plans
   Treatment

6. Consultation
   Referrals
   Professional team collaboration

7. Psychoeducational activities
   Parent conferences
   Outreach

8. Career counseling

9. Individual supervision

10. Group or peer supervision

11. Case conferences or staff meetings

12. Other (please list) _____
    _____
    _____

Practicum site supervisor _____ Date _____

Student _____ Date _____

Faculty liaison _____ Date _____

Form 2.2: Internship Contract

This agreement is made this_____ day of_____, by and between

_____ (hereinafter referred to as the

AGENCY/INSTITUTION/SCHOOL) and _____

(hereinafter referred to as the UNIVERSITY). This agreement will be effective for a period from

_____to_____ for student_____.

Purpose

The purpose of this agreement is to provide a qualified graduate student with an internship experience in the field of counseling/therapy.

The UNIVERSITY Shall Be Responsible for the Following:

1. Selecting a student who has successfully completed all of the prerequisite courses and the practicum experience.
2. Providing the AGENCY/INSTITUTION/SCHOOL with a course outline for the supervised internship counseling that clearly delineates the responsibilities of the UNIVERSITY and the AGENCY/INSTITUTION/SCHOOL.
3. Designating a qualified faculty member as the internship supervisor who will work with the AGENCY/INSTITUTION/SCHOOL in coordinating the internship experience.
4. Notifying the student that he/she must adhere to the administrative policies, rules, standards, schedules, and practices of the AGENCY/INSTITUTION/SCHOOL.
5. Advising the student that he/she should have adequate liability and accident insurance.

The AGENCY/INSTITUTION/SCHOOL Shall Be Responsible for the Following:

1. Providing the intern with an overall orientation to the agency's specific services necessary for the implementation of the internship experience.
2. Designating a qualified staff member to function as supervising counselor/therapist for the intern. The supervising counselor/therapist will be responsible, with the approval of the administration of the AGENCY/INSTITUTION/SCHOOL, for providing opportunities for the intern to engage in a variety of counseling activities under supervision and for evaluating the intern's performance. (Suggested counselor/therapist experiences are included in the course outline.)
3. Providing areas for conducting counseling sessions and for doing paperwork. Provisions will be made to ensure that students have the ability to meet course requirements for internship, especially regarding direct service hours with clients.

The STUDENT Shall Be Responsible for the Following:

1. Obtaining transportation to and from the site.
2. Scheduling and attending weekly supervision sessions with on-site supervisor and attending weekly supervision sessions with faculty supervisors.

3. Adhering to the ethical guidelines of the American Counseling Association's *Code of Ethics*.
4. Adhering to the policies and procedures, rules, and standards of the placement site.

Equal Opportunity

It is mutually agreed that neither party shall discriminate on the basis of race, color, nationality, ethnic origin, age, sex, or creed.

Financial Agreement

Financial stipulations, if any, may vary from one AGENCY/INSTITUTION/SCHOOL to another. If a financial stipulation is to be provided, the agreement is stipulated in a separate agreement and approved by the intern, the AGENCY/INSTITUTION/SCHOOL, and the UNIVERSITY.

Termination

It is understood and agreed by and between the parties hereto that the AGENCY/INSTITUTION/SCHOOL has the right to terminate the internship experience of the student whose health status is detrimental to the services provided to the patients or clients of the AGENCY/INSTITUTION/SCHOOL. Furthermore, it has the right to terminate the use of the AGENCY/INSTITUTION/SCHOOL by an intern if, in the opinion of the supervising counselor/therapist, such person's behavior is detrimental to the operation of the AGENCY/INSTITUTION/SCHOOL and/or to patient or client care. Such action will not be taken until the grievance against any intern has been discussed with the intern and with UNIVERSITY officials.

The names of the responsible individuals at the two institutions charged with the implementation of the contract are as follows:

_____   _____
Internship supervisor at the UNIVERSITY   Agency supervising counselor/therapist at the AGENCY/INSTITUTION/SCHOOL

In witness whereof, the parties hereto have caused this contract to be signed the day and year first written above.

_____   _____
AGENCY/INSTITUTION/SCHOOL   Witness
(Administrator)

_____   _____
UNIVERSITY (Representative)   Witness

Form 2.3: Student Profile Sheet

Directions: The student counselor is to submit this form in duplicate to the field site.

Practicum Student Counselor/Psychologist

Name _____

Address _____

_____

Telephone: (home) _____

(office) _____

Date _____

I hold the degree of _____ from

_____ and have completed the following

courses as part of the _____ (degree)

program, with a major in _____

from _____.

Psychology of Human Development _____   Tests and Measurements _____

Diagnosis and Treatment _____   Personality Development_____

Counseling Skills _____   Career Development _____

Intro to Counseling _____   Legal and Ethical Issues _____

Theories of Counseling _____   Process and Techniques of
Group Counseling _____

Multicultural Counseling _____

Other (please specify) _____

_____

_____

Professional and Nonprofessional Work Experience _____

_____

_____

Form 2.4: Student Practicum/Internship Agreement

Directions: Student is to complete this form in duplicate and submit a copy of this agreement to the university practicum supervisor or internship coordinator.

1. I hereby attest that I have read and understood the American Psychological Association, the American Counseling Association, or other appropriate professional association's *Code of Ethics* and will practice my counseling in accordance with these standards. Any breach of these ethics or any unethical behavior on my part will result in my removal from practicum/internship and a failing grade, and documentation of such behavior will become part of my permanent record.
2. I agree to adhere to the administrative policies, rules, standards, and practices of the practicum/internship site.
3. I understand that my responsibilities include keeping my practicum/internship supervisor(s) informed regarding my practicum/internship experiences.
4. I understand that I will not be issued a passing grade in practicum/internship unless I demonstrate the specified minimal level of counseling skill, knowledge, and competence and complete course requirements as required.
5. I understand I must obtain proper clearances (e.g., child abuse clearance, criminal background checks) or health tests (e.g., TB test) as required by the program and/or my site prior to the start of practicum and internship.
6. I understand that my placement site is subject to the approval of the program faculty.

Signature _____

Date _____

Form 3.1a: Parental Release Form: Secondary School Counseling

_____ school district offers short-term individual counseling and group counseling to students as the need arises. Parents/guardians or school staff may refer students for counseling, or students may request counseling. These counseling services are provided by_____, the school counselor, or _____ , the counseling intern. Should it be determined that more extensive services are needed, it is the parent's responsibility, with the assistance of the counselor, to arrange outside counseling or psychiatric services.

School counseling services are short-term services aimed to enhance the education and socialization of students within the school community. Trust is a cornerstone of the relationship between the counselor and student. Information shared by the student will be kept confidential except in certain situations in which ethical responsibility limits confidentiality. You will be notified if:

1. The student reveals information about hurting himself/herself or someone else.
2. The student or someone else may be in physical danger.
3. A court order is received directing disclosure of information.

We encourage you to contact us whenever you have a question, input, or concern.

The counseling intern is an advanced-level master's degree student in the Department of _____ at _____University. The University requires that the counseling sessions conducted by the counseling intern be audio/video recorded for confidential supervision purposes. Personal identifying details will be deleted, and the recording will be reviewed by the supervisor and peer members of the supervision group to review the counseling practice of the intern. The recording will be destroyed after the supervision review. Supervision requires that ethical standards regarding confidentiality be followed.

Student's name _____

By signing this form, I give permission for my child to receive counseling services during the 20___ school year. I understand that anything my child shares is confidential except in the above-mentioned cases.

Parent/guardian_____   Date_____

I do _____ do not ____ give permission for the recording of sessions for confidential supervision purposes.

Form 3.1b: Elementary School Counseling Permission Form

Short Form

We, the parents of _____ , acknowledge and approve of our child being seen by the elementary school counselor or counselor intern. The counselor may engage our child in any counseling services deemed appropriate in encouraging positive educational and social development.

We understand that that the intern is an advanced-level graduate student in the Department of _____ at _____ University and will audio/video record counseling sessions for supervision purposes. The recording will be reviewed by the University supervisor and peer group members of the supervision seminar to evaluate the intern's counseling practice. The recording will be destroyed after supervision. Supervision requires following confidentiality standards established in the professional code of ethics.

_____

Parent signature

_____

Date

OR

We, the parents of _____ , acknowledge but do not give our permission for our child to be seen by the elementary school counselor or counseling intern to receive counseling services. We decline the offer of services at this time but reserve the opportunity to reconsider services at a later date.

_____

Parent signature

_____

Date

Form 3.2: Client Permission to Record Counseling Session for Supervision Purposes

I,_____, give my permission for the counseling intern,_____
_____to audio/video record my counseling sessions_____ (fill in date or inclusive dates if over a period of time). [If client is under 18, change wording to "record the counseling sessions with my child" and fill in child's name.] I understand that the counseling intern at _____ Agency is an advanced-level master's degree student in the Department of _____ at _____University. The University requires that the counseling sessions conducted by the counseling intern be audio/video recorded for confidential supervision purposes. Personal identifying details will be deleted, and the recording will be reviewed by the supervisor and peer members of the supervision group to review the counseling practice of the intern. The recording will be destroyed after the supervision review. Supervision requires that ethical standards regarding confidentiality be followed.

_____ Name of agency supervisor

_____ Name of university supervisor

_____   _____

Client's signature   Date

_____

Parent/guardian signature

Form 3.3: Initial Intake Form

Name_____ Date _____

Address _____ City_____ State_____ Zip _____

Telephone (home) _____ (work) _____ (cell) _____

Counselor's name _____ Date _____

Identifying Information

Age _____ Date of birth____/____/____ Place _____

Sex: Male _____ Female _____ Height _____ ft._____ in. Weight _____lbs.

Race: White _____ Black _____ Asian _____ Hispanic _____ Other _____

Marital status: M _____ S _____ D _____ W _____ Sep _____

If married, spouse's name_____ Age _____

Occupation (client) _____ Employer _____

Occupation (spouse) _____ Employer _____

Referral source: Self _____ Other _____

Name of referral source _____

Address of referral source _____

Treatment History (General)

Are you currently taking medication? Yes _____ No _____

If yes, name(s) of the medication(s) _____

Dosage of medication(s) _____

Provider of medication(s) _____

Have you received previous psychiatric treatment? Yes _____ No _____

If yes, name provider _____

Dates of service _____ Location _____

Reason for termination of treatment _____

Presenting problem or condition (current) _____

Presenting factors (contributors) _____

Symptoms (describe) _____

_____

Acute _____ Chronic _____

Family History (General)

Father's name _____ Age _____ Living _____ Deceased _____

Occupation _____ Full-time _____ Part-time _____

Mother's name _____ Age _____ Living _____ Deceased _____

Occupation _____ Full-time _____ Part-time _____

Brother(s)/sister(s)

Name _____ Age _____ Living _____ Deceased _____

Name _____ Age _____ Living _____ Deceased _____

Name _____ Age _____ Living _____ Deceased _____

Educational History (General)

	Name of Institution	*Location*	*Dates*	*Degree*
Secondary				
College				
Trade				
Graduate				

Employment History (General)

Title/Description	*From When to When*	*Full- or Part-Time*

Form 3.4: Psychosocial History

Directions: Practicum/internship students should review/complete this form prior to the initiation of therapy and after completion of the Initial Intake Form.

I. Identifying Information

Name _____ Age _____

Address _____ Date of birth _____

Phone _____ Cell phone _____ Marital status _____

II. Presenting Problem/Complaint

Nature of complaint? _____

_____

When did the problem begin? (date of onset) _____

How often does it occur? (be specific) _____

How does it affect your daily functioning? _____

_____

Are there events, situations, and person(s) that precipitate it? _____

_____

Symptoms:

Acute (describe) _____

_____

Chronic (describe) _____

_____

Previous treatment (list by whom, outcome, and reason(s) for termination of treatment)_____

_____

_____

_____

Medical:

Physician's name _____

Treatment dates from _____ to _____

Describe _____

Psychiatric:

Therapist's name _____

Treatment dates from _____ to _____

Substance use _____

_____

III. Developmental History

Pregnancy _____

_____

Delivery _____

_____

Infancy (developmental milestones) _____

_____

Middle childhood (developmental milestones) _____

_____

Young adulthood (developmental milestones) _____

_____

IV. Family History

Where were you born and raised? _____

What culture/ethnic group do you identify with? _____

What is your primary language? _____

Parent (names, ages, occupations) _____

_____

Were your parents married?   Yes _____ No _____

Do they remain married?   Yes _____ No _____

If divorced, how were you affected by it? _____

_____

Who was primarily responsible for your upbringing? _____

Describe the relationship between your parents _____

_____

Describe your relationship with your parents _____

_____

Do you feel supported by your family? Explain _____

_____

Do you feel loved in your family? Explain _____

_____

Describe how love was expressed in your family _____

_____

Who was the disciplinarian in your family? _____

_____

How was discipline handled? _____

_____

Were you physically, verbally, or emotionally abused in any way? _____

_____

Describe your best memory _____

_____

Describe your worst memory _____

_____

V. Educational/Occupational History

Education (highest grade achieved) _____

Describe your school performance _____

_____

Did you take any special classes? Explain _____

_____

Did you have any special needs?_____

_____

Do you have adequate reading skills?　　　Yes_____　No_____

Do you have adequate math skills?　　　Yes_____　No_____

Occupational

Have you served in the military? _____

When and where did you serve? _____

What was your rank? _____

Describe your duties _____

Usual occupation _____

Present status: Employed? _____ Unemployed? _____ Full time _____ Part time _____

Job satisfaction: Good _____ Fair _____ Poor _____

Estimate the number of jobs that you have held _____

Longest continued employments (dates) _____

Reason(s) for leaving? Explain _____

_____

What impact does your present concern have on your employment?

None _____ Terminated _____ Absenteeism _____ Tardiness _____ Laid off _____

Poor work performance _____ Conflict with fellow workers _____

Conflict with employer _____

VI. Health History

Childhood diseases (list) _____

_____

Surgeries? _____

_____

Current health (describe) _____

_____

Family health (grandparents, parents, children) _____

_____

Current medications (prescribed and over the counter). List _____

_____

_____

_____

Do you have any chronic medical problems? _____

_____

Do you have any bio-medical problems requiring medical monitoring? _____

_____

VII. Relationship History

Single _____ Married _____ Separated _____ Divorced _____ Widowed _____

Common law_____ Years married? _____

Number of children (names and ages) _____

_____

_____

Problems, stressors in the relationship? Explain _____

_____

Your perception of sexual relationship (attitudes/behavior) _____

_____

_____

Have you ever been physically or emotionally abused in the relationship?

_____

_____

VIII. Additional Information

Information that has not been covered that you feel is an important consideration in your treatment (explain, be specific) _____

_____

_____

Form 3.5: Case Notes

These case notes are confidential and must be kept in a secure place under the control of the counselor.

Counselor's name _____ Agency/school _____

CLIENT IDENTIFYING DATA

Client's ID _____ Age _____ Sex _____

Date of session _____ Session number _____

Recording: Audio _____ Video _____

Presenting/current concern (Subjective)

_____

_____

_____

Key issues addressed

_____

_____

_____

Summary of the session (Objective)

_____

_____

_____

Diagnostic impression(s) and interventions (Assessment)

_____

_____

_____

Client progress/setbacks (Current internal/external dynamics that support or inhibit change)

_____

_____

_____

Action to be taken (Plan)

_____

_____

Counselor's comments

_____

_____

_____

Supervisor's comments

_____

_____

_____

Date _____   Counselor's signature _____

Date _____   Supervisor's signature _____

Form 3.6: Weekly Schedule/Practicum Log

Day of Week	Location	Time	Practicum Activity	Comment
_____	_____	_____	_____	_____
_____	_____	_____	_____	_____
_____	_____	_____	_____	_____
_____	_____	_____	_____	_____
_____	_____	_____	_____	_____
_____	_____	_____	_____	_____
_____	_____	_____	_____	_____
_____	_____	_____	_____	_____
_____	_____	_____	_____	_____
_____	_____	_____	_____	_____
_____	_____	_____	_____	_____
_____	_____	_____	_____	_____
_____	_____	_____	_____	_____
_____	_____	_____	_____	_____
_____	_____	_____	_____	_____
_____	_____	_____	_____	_____
_____	_____	_____	_____	_____
_____	_____	_____	_____	_____

Student counselor name _____

Week beginning _____   Ending _____

Total hours of direct service _____   Indirect service _____

Site supervisor signature _____   Date _____

Form 3.7: Monthly Practicum Log

Directions

1. Record the dates of each week at the site where indicated.
2. Record the total number of hours per week for each activity under the appropriate column.
3. Total the number of hours for the week at the bottom of the week's column.
4. At the end of the month, total the hours spent in each activity by adding the hours across each activity; indicate the total in the monthly totals column.
5. Get the supervisor's signature. Keep this in your file to be submitted to the university internship coordinator at the completion of the internship.

Activities	Week 1 From: To:	Week 2 From: To:	Week 3 From: To:	Week 4 From: To:	Monthly Totals
Intake interview*					
Individual counseling*					
Group counseling*					
Family counseling*					
Consulting/intervention*					
Psychoeducation/guidance*					
Community work					
Career counseling*					
Report writing					
Case conference					
Program planning					
Testing/assessment					
Individual supervision					
Other					
Weekly totals					
Total direct contact*					

Note:* Indicates direct contact.

Intern's name _____

Supervisor's signature and date _____

Form 4.1: Mental Status Checklist

Appearance and Behavior

	Check If Applies	Circle	Therapist's Comments
1. Posture	Normal _____	Limp, rigid, ill at ease	_____
2. Gestures	Normal _____	Agitated, tics, twitches	_____
3. Grooming	Neat _____	Well groomed,	_____
		disheveled,	_____
		meticulous	_____
		Dirty, careless,	_____
4. Dress	Casual _____	inappropriate,	_____
	Formal _____	seductive	_____
5. Facial expression	Appropriate __	Poor eye contact, dazed, staring	_____
6. Speech			_____
a. Pace	Normal _____	Retarded, pressured, blocking	_____
b. Volume	Normal _____	Soft, very loud, monotone	_____
c. Form	Logical _____	Illogical, rambling,	_____
	Rational _____	incoherent, coherent	_____
d. Clarity	Normal _____	Garbled, slurred	_____
e. Content	Normal _____	Loose, associations, rhyming, obscene	_____

Attention/Affect/Mood

	Check If Applies	Circle	Therapist's Comments
1. Attention	Normal _____	Short span, hyper,	_____
	Alert _____	alert, distractible	_____
2. Mood	Normal _____	Elated, euphoric,	_____
		agitated, fearful,	_____
		hostile, sad	_____
3. Affect	Appropriate __	Inappropriate,	_____
		shallow, flat,	_____
		intense	_____

Perception and Thought Content

	Check If Applies	*Description*
1. Hallucination	_____	_____
a. Auditory	_____	_____
b. Visual	_____	_____
c. Tactile	_____	_____
d. Gustatory	_____	_____
e. Olfactory	_____	_____

2. Delusion

a. Paranoid	_____	b. Persecutor	_____
c. Grandiose	_____	d. Reference	_____
e. Control	_____	f. Thought	_____
g. Broadcasting	_____	h. Insertion	_____
i. Thought withdrawal	_____		

3. Illusions

a. Visual _____

b. Auditory _____

Describe _____

_____

4. Other derealization

a. Phobias	_____	b. Obsessions	_____
c. Compulsions	_____	d. Ruminations	_____

Describe _____

_____

5. Suicide/homicide

Ideation _____ Plans _____

Describe _____

_____

Orientation   Oriented × 3   Yes _____   No _____

Disoriented to: Time _____   Place _____   Person _____

Judgment   Intact _____   Impaired _____

Describe _____

_____

Concentration/Memory

1. Memory   Intact _____   Impaired _____
2. Immediate recall   Good _____   Poor _____
3. Reversals   Good _____   Poor _____
4. Concentration   Good _____   Poor _____

Abstract Ability

1. Similarities   Good _____   Poor _____   Bizarre _____
2. Absurdities   Recognized _____   Not recognized _____
3. Proverbs   Appropriate _____   Literal _____   Concrete _____   Bizarre _____

Insight   Good _____   Fair _____   Poor _____   Absent _____

Form 4.2: Elementary School Counseling Referral Form

Please complete and return this confidential referral form to me. The form should be closed in a sealed envelope and placed in my office mailbox. Do not duplicate.

To: _____ School Counselor _____ Date _____

Priority

Low (schedule when available); High (as soon as possible); Emergency (see now)

Student's name and grade _____

Referred by _____

Please check any behaviors of concern that you have observed:

☐ aggression   ☐ academics

☐ dramatic change in behavior   ☐ homework completion

☐ bullying—victim   ☐ study skills

☐ bullying—bully   ☐ organizational skills

☐ daydreams/fantasizes   ☐ impulsive

☐ poor peer relationships   ☐ always tired

☐ poor social skills   ☐ inattentive

☐ family concerns (illness, divorce)   ☐ disruptive

☐ suspected abuse   ☐ worried/anxious

☐ cries easily/often for age   ☐ scared

☐ self-image/self-confidence   ☐ sadness

☐ personal hygiene   ☐ withdrawn/shy

☐ lying   ☐ depressed

☐ stealing   ☐ defiant

☐ grief and loss   ☐ difficulty making friends

☐ other

Explanation: _____

_____

_____

_____

_____

Best time to pull child from class: 1st choice _____   2nd choice _____

I recommend this child for individual counseling _____; small group counseling _____.

Thank you for taking the time to share this information with me.

Form 4.3: Secondary School Counseling Referral Form

Please complete this confidential counseling referral form, place it in a sealed envelope, and place it in the mailbox of the counselor to whom you are making the referral. Do not duplicate.

Date referral received _____

Counselor's name _____

Student's name and grade _____

Referred by _____

Priority:

Low (schedule when available)   High (as soon as possible)   Emergency (see now)

Have you had a discussion with the child's parent(s) regarding this referral? Yes or no

Student's Present Functioning (as you perceive it)

	Excellent	Above Average	Average	Below Average	Poor
Self-directed learner					
Attention span					
Quality of writing					
Self-image					
Attitude toward authority					
Peer relationships					
Works well with others					
Completes assignments					
Follows classroom rules					

Please check any behaviors of concern that you have observed or have knowledge of:

☐ academic	☐ tardiness
☐ absences	☐ depression
☐ anger/aggression	☐ family issues (illness, divorce)
☐ truancy	☐ stress/anxiety
☐ suicidal thoughts	☐ health/hygiene
☐ peer relationships	☐ student/teacher issues
☐ boyfriend/girlfriend issues	☐ student/parent issues
☐ dramatic change in behavior	☐ hurts/cuts self
☐ sexuality issues	☐ child neglect/abuse
☐ dropout risk	☐ work habits/organization
☐ grief/loss	☐ withdrawn
☐ bullying—victim	☐ substance abuse
☐ bullying—bully	☐ other

Special skills, talents, or competencies this student has _____

_____

Reason for referral (based on your observations) _____

_____

Signature _____   Date _____

Position _____

Form 4.4: Therapeutic Progress Report

Date _____

Therapist's name _____

Therapist's phone _____

Client's name/ID _____

Client's age _____ Sex _____

Sessions to date with client _____

(dates from/to and total number)

Client's presenting complaint

_____

_____

_____

Therapeutic summary

_____

_____

_____

Methods of treatment

_____

_____

_____

Duration of treatment

_____

_____

_____

Current status

_____

_____

_____

Treatment recommendations

_____

_____

_____

_____

Therapist's signature   Supervisor's signature

Form 5.1: Counseling Techniques List

Directions

1. First, examine the techniques listed in the first column. Then, technique by technique, decide the extent to which you use or would be competent to use each. Indicate the extent of use or competency by circling the appropriate letter in the second column. If you do not know the technique, then mark an "X" through the "N" to indicate that the technique is unknown. Space is available at the end of the techniques list in the first column to add other techniques.

2. Second, after examining the list and indicating your extent of use or competency, go through the techniques list again and, in the third column, circle the theory or theories with which each technique is appropriate. The third column, of course, can be marked only for those techniques with which you are familiar.

3. The third task is to become more knowledgeable about the techniques that you do not know—the ones marked with an "X." As you gain knowledge relating to each technique, you can decide whether you will use it and, if so, with which kinds of clients and under what conditions.

4. The final task is to review the second and third columns and determine whether techniques in which you have competencies are within one or two specific theories. If so, are these theories the ones that best reflect your self-concept? Do those techniques marked reflect those most appropriate, as revealed in the literature, for the clients with whom you want to work?

Extent of Use Key

N = None   M = Minimal   A = Average   E = Extensive

Theory for Technique Key

Ad = Adlerian (Adler, Dreikurs)   Ge = Gestalt (Perls)

Be = Behavioral (Skinner, Bandura, Lazarus)   PC = Person Centered (Rogers)

CBT = Cognitive behavioral (Beck, Ellis, Meichenbaum)   Ps = Psychodynamic (Freud, Erikson)

Ex = Existential (May, Frankl)   Re = Reality (Glasser, Wubbolding)

FS = Family systems (Bowen, Satir, Minuchin)   SF = Solution focused (Berg, de Shazer)

Technique	Extent of Use	Theory for Technique
ABC model	N M A E	Ad Be CBT Ex FS Ge PC Ps Re SF
Acceptance	N M A E	Ad Be CBT Ex FS Ge PC Ps Re SF
Accurate empathic understanding	N M A E	Ad Be CBT Ex FS Ge PC Ps Re SF
Analysis of resistance	N M A E	Ad Be CBT Ex FS Ge PC Ps Re SF
Analysis of transference	N M A E	Ad Be CBT Ex FS Ge PC Ps Re SF
Analyze cognitive triad	N M A E	Ad Be CBT Ex FS Ge PC Ps Re SF
Analyze defense mechanisms	N M A E	Ad Be CBT Ex FS Ge PC Ps Re SF

Technique	Extent of Use	Theory for Technique
Analyzing cognitive distortions	N M A E	Ad Be CBT Ex FS Ge PC Ps Re SF
Assertiveness training	N M A E	Ad Be CBT Ex FS Ge PC Ps Re SF
Assignment of tasks	N M A E	Ad Be CBT Ex FS Ge PC Ps Re SF
Avoid focus on symptoms	N M A E	Ad Be CBT Ex FS Ge PC Ps Re SF
Behavioral tasks	N M A E	Ad Be CBT Ex FS Ge PC Ps Re SF
Bibliotherapy	N M A E	Ad Be CBT Ex FS Ge PC Ps Re SF
Birth order	N M A E	Ad Be CBT Ex FS Ge PC Ps Re SF
Boundary setting	N M A E	Ad Be CBT Ex FS Ge PC Ps Re SF
Bridging compliments to tasks	N M A E	Ad Be CBT Ex FS Ge PC Ps Re SF
Change faulty motivation	N M A E	Ad Be CBT Ex FS Ge PC Ps Re SF
Change focused questions	N M A E	Ad Be CBT Ex FS Ge PC Ps Re SF
Change maladaptive beliefs	N M A E	Ad Be CBT Ex FS Ge PC Ps Re SF
Changing language	N M A E	Ad Be CBT Ex FS Ge PC Ps Re SF
Clarify personal views on life and living	N M A E	Ad Be CBT Ex FS Ge PC Ps Re SF
Classical conditioning	N M A E	Ad Be CBT Ex FS Ge PC Ps Re SF
Cognitive homework	N M A E	Ad Be CBT Ex FS Ge PC Ps Re SF
Cognitive restructuring	N M A E	Ad Be CBT Ex FS Ge PC Ps Re SF
Commitment to change	N M A E	Ad Be CBT Ex FS Ge PC Ps Re SF
Communication analysis	N M A E	Ad Be CBT Ex FS Ge PC Ps Re SF
Communication training	N M A E	Ad Be CBT Ex FS Ge PC Ps Re SF
Compliments	N M A E	Ad Be CBT Ex FS Ge PC Ps Re SF
Confrontation	N M A E	Ad Be CBT Ex FS Ge PC Ps Re SF
Co-therapy	N M A E	Ad Be CBT Ex FS Ge PC Ps Re SF
Detriangulation	N M A E	Ad Be CBT Ex FS Ge PC Ps Re SF
Disputing irrational beliefs	N M A E	Ad Be CBT Ex FS Ge PC Ps Re SF
Dramatization	N M A E	Ad Be CBT Ex FS Ge PC Ps Re SF
Dream analysis	N M A E	Ad Be CBT Ex FS Ge PC Ps Re SF
Dreamwork	N M A E	Ad Be CBT Ex FS Ge PC Ps Re SF
Early recollections	N M A E	Ad Be CBT Ex FS Ge PC Ps Re SF
Empty chair	N M A E	Ad Be CBT Ex FS Ge PC Ps Re SF
Enactments	N M A E	Ad Be CBT Ex FS Ge PC Ps Re SF
Encouragement	N M A E	Ad Be CBT Ex FS Ge PC Ps Re SF
Exaggeration exercise	N M A E	Ad Be CBT Ex FS Ge PC Ps Re SF
Examine source of present value system	N M A E	Ad Be CBT Ex FS Ge PC Ps Re SF
Examining automatic thoughts	N M A E	Ad Be CBT Ex FS Ge PC Ps Re SF
Exception questions	N M A E	Ad Be CBT Ex FS Ge PC Ps Re SF

Technique	Extent of Use	Theory for Technique
Experiential learning	N M A E	Ad Be CBT Ex FS Ge PC Ps Re SF
Experiments	N M A E	Ad Be CBT Ex FS Ge PC Ps Re SF
Explore quality world	N M A E	Ad Be CBT Ex FS Ge PC Ps Re SF
Explore subjective reality	N M A E	Ad Be CBT Ex FS Ge PC Ps Re SF
Exposing faulty thinking	N M A E	Ad Be CBT Ex FS Ge PC Ps Re SF
Family constellation	N M A E	Ad Be CBT Ex FS Ge PC Ps Re SF
Family-life chronology	N M A E	Ad Be CBT Ex FS Ge PC Ps Re SF
Finding alternative interpretations	N M A E	Ad Be CBT Ex FS Ge PC Ps Re SF
Flooding	N M A E	Ad Be CBT Ex FS Ge PC Ps Re SF
Focus on choice	N M A E	Ad Be CBT Ex FS Ge PC Ps Re SF
Focus on personal responsibility	N M A E	Ad Be CBT Ex FS Ge PC Ps Re SF
Focus on present problems	N M A E	Ad Be CBT Ex FS Ge PC Ps Re SF
Focus on what client can control	N M A E	Ad Be CBT Ex FS Ge PC Ps Re SF
Formulate first-session task	N M A E	Ad Be CBT Ex FS Ge PC Ps Re SF
Foster social interest	N M A E	Ad Be CBT Ex FS Ge PC Ps Re SF
Free association	N M A E	Ad Be CBT Ex FS Ge PC Ps Re SF
Genogram	N M A E	Ad Be CBT Ex FS Ge PC Ps Re SF
Genuineness	N M A E	Ad Be CBT Ex FS Ge PC Ps Re SF
Guided imagery	N M A E	Ad Be CBT Ex FS Ge PC Ps Re SF
Hypothesizing systemic roots of problems	N M A E	Ad Be CBT Ex FS Ge PC Ps Re SF
Identify and define wants and needs	N M A E	Ad Be CBT Ex FS Ge PC Ps Re SF
Identify basic mistakes	N M A E	Ad Be CBT Ex FS Ge PC Ps Re SF
Immediacy	N M A E	Ad Be CBT Ex FS Ge PC Ps Re SF
Internal dialogue	N M A E	Ad Be CBT Ex FS Ge PC Ps Re SF
Interpersonal empathy	N M A E	Ad Be CBT Ex FS Ge PC Ps Re SF
Interpretation	N M A E	Ad Be CBT Ex FS Ge PC Ps Re SF
In vivo exposure	N M A E	Ad Be CBT Ex FS Ge PC Ps Re SF
Keep therapy in the present	N M A E	Ad Be CBT Ex FS Ge PC Ps Re SF
Lifestyle assessment	N M A E	Ad Be CBT Ex FS Ge PC Ps Re SF
Logotherapy	N M A E	Ad Be CBT Ex FS Ge PC Ps Re SF
Maintain analytic framework	N M A E	Ad Be CBT Ex FS Ge PC Ps Re SF
Making the rounds	N M A E	Ad Be CBT Ex FS Ge PC Ps Re SF
Miracle question	N M A E	Ad Be CBT Ex FS Ge PC Ps Re SF
Natural consequences	N M A E	Ad Be CBT Ex FS Ge PC Ps Re SF
Negative reinforcement	N M A E	Ad Be CBT Ex FS Ge PC Ps Re SF
Objective empathy	N M A E	Ad Be CBT Ex FS Ge PC Ps Re SF

Technique	Extent of Use	Theory for Technique
Objective interview	N M A E	Ad Be CBT Ex FS Ge PC Ps Re SF
Observational tasks	N M A E	Ad Be CBT Ex FS Ge PC Ps Re SF
Operant conditioning	N M A E	Ad Be CBT Ex FS Ge PC Ps Re SF
Plan for acting	N M A E	Ad Be CBT Ex FS Ge PC Ps Re SF
Positive reinforcement	N M A E	Ad Be CBT Ex FS Ge PC Ps Re SF
Progressive muscle relaxation	N M A E	Ad Be CBT Ex FS Ge PC Ps Re SF
Psychoeducation	N M A E	Ad Be CBT Ex FS Ge PC Ps Re SF
Recognizing and changing unrealistic negative thoughts	N M A E	Ad Be CBT Ex FS Ge PC Ps Re SF
Reflection of feeling	N M A E	Ad Be CBT Ex FS Ge PC Ps Re SF
Reframing	N M A E	Ad Be CBT Ex FS Ge PC Ps Re SF
Rehearsal exercise	N M A E	Ad Be CBT Ex FS Ge PC Ps Re SF
Reject transference	N M A E	Ad Be CBT Ex FS Ge PC Ps Re SF
Reorientation	N M A E	Ad Be CBT Ex FS Ge PC Ps Re SF
Reversal exercise	N M A E	Ad Be CBT Ex FS Ge PC Ps Re SF
Scaling questions	N M A E	Ad Be CBT Ex FS Ge PC Ps Re SF
Sculpting	N M A E	Ad Be CBT Ex FS Ge PC Ps Re SF
Self-evaluation	N M A E	Ad Be CBT Ex FS Ge PC Ps Re SF
Self-monitoring	N M A E	Ad Be CBT Ex FS Ge PC Ps Re SF
Shame-attacking exercises	N M A E	Ad Be CBT Ex FS Ge PC Ps Re SF
Social skills training	N M A E	Ad Be CBT Ex FS Ge PC Ps Re SF
Staying with the feeling	N M A E	Ad Be CBT Ex FS Ge PC Ps Re SF
Stress inoculation training	N M A E	Ad Be CBT Ex FS Ge PC Ps Re SF
Subjective empathy	N M A E	Ad Be CBT Ex FS Ge PC Ps Re SF
Subjective interview	N M A E	Ad Be CBT Ex FS Ge PC Ps Re SF
Systematic desensitization	N M A E	Ad Be CBT Ex FS Ge PC Ps Re SF
Unbalancing	N M A E	Ad Be CBT Ex FS Ge PC Ps Re SF
Unconditional positive regard	N M A E	Ad Be CBT Ex FS Ge PC Ps Re SF

Note: *Adapted from Hollis, Joseph W. (1980). Techniques used in counseling and psychotherapy. In K. M. Dimick and F. H. Krause (Eds.), *Practicum manual in counseling and psychotherapy* (4th ed., pp. 77–80). Muncie, IN: Accelerated Development. Theories and techniques listed have been updated and drawn from Corey, G. (2013). *Theory and practice of counseling and psychotherapy* (9th ed.). Belmont, CA: Brooks/Cole.

Form 6.1: Self-Assessment of Counseling Performance Skills

Purposes: To provide the trainee with an opportunity to review levels of competency in the performance skill areas of basic helping skills and professional procedural skills.

To provide the trainee with a basis for identifying areas of focus for supervision.

Directions: Circle a number next to each item to indicate your perceived level of competence.

Basic and Advanced Helping Skills	*Poor*		*Average*		*Good*
1. Ability to demonstrate active attending behavior	1	2	3	4	5
2. Ability to listen to and understand nonverbal behavior	1	2	3	4	5
3. Ability to listen to what client says verbally, noticing mix of experiences, behaviors, and feelings	1	2	3	4	5
4. Ability to understand accurately the client's point of view	1	2	3	4	5
5. Ability to identify themes in client's story	1	2	3	4	5
6. Ability to identify inconsistencies between client's story and reality	1	2	3	4	5
7. Ability to respond with accurate empathy	1	2	3	4	5
8. Ability to ask open-ended questions	1	2	3	4	5
9. Ability to help clients clarify and focus	1	2	3	4	5
10. Ability to balance empathic response, clarification, and probing	1	2	3	4	5
11. Ability to assess accurately severity of client's problems	1	2	3	4	5
12. Ability to establish a collaborative working relationship with client	1	2	3	4	5
13. Ability to assess and activate client's strengths and resources in problem solving	1	2	3	4	5
14. Ability to identify and challenge unhealthy or distorted thinking or behaving	1	2	3	4	5
15. Ability to use advanced empathy to deepen client's understanding of problems and solutions	1	2	3	4	5
16. Ability to explore the counselor–client relationship	1	2	3	4	5
17. Ability to share constructively some of own experiences, behaviors, and feelings with client	1	2	3	4	5
18. Ability to summarize	1	2	3	4	5
19. Ability to share information appropriately	1	2	3	4	5
20. Ability to understand and facilitate decision making	1	2	3	4	5
21. Ability to help clients set goals and move toward action in problem solving	1	2	3	4	5
22. Ability to recognize and manage client reluctance and resistance	1	2	3	4	5
23. Ability to help clients explore consequences of the goals they set	1	2	3	4	5

Basic and Advanced Helping Skills	*Poor*		*Average*		*Good*
24. Ability to help clients sustain actions in direction of goals	1	2	3	4	5
25. Ability to help clients review and revise or recommit to goals based on new experiences	1	2	3	4	5
26. Ability to open the session smoothly	1	2	3	4	5
27. Ability to collaborate with client to identify important concerns for the session	1	2	3	4	5
28. Ability to establish continuity from session to session	1	2	3	4	5
29. Knowledge of policy and procedures of educational or agency setting regarding harm to self and others, substance abuse, and child abuse	1	2	3	4	5
30. Ability to keep appropriate records related to counseling process	1	2	3	4	5
31. Ability to end the session smoothly	1	2	3	4	5
32. Ability to recognize and address ethical issues	1	2	3	4	5
33. Ability to integrate privacy practices and informed consent into initial session	1	2	3	4	5

Trainee's signature _____

Supervisor's signature _____

Date _____

Form 6.2: Self-Awareness/Multicultural Awareness Rating Scale

KEY   1 = low—lack competence in this practice
        2 = low average—some competence in this practice but need to improve
        3 = average—adequate competence in this practice
        4 = high average—competence level is more than adequate in this practice
        5 = high—perform extremely well in this practice

Directions: Read each of the statements below and indicate the extent to which this applies to your counseling practice using the 1 through 5 key above.

_____ 1.   I explore how my personal attitudes can impact my clients.

_____ 2.   I understand how my family background impacts my activities and relationships.

_____ 3.   I understand how my early family experiences may trigger a reaction to my client's concerns.

_____ 4.   I am aware of and can avoid imposing my own needs on clients.

_____ 5.   I reflect on my own dynamics following a counseling session, particularly when I have strong emotional reactions or am uncomfortable with my client's emotional reactions.

_____ 6.   I reflect on my own dynamics following a counseling session, particularly when I have a strong negative judgment about my client's thoughts, feelings, and behaviors.

_____ 7.   I understand countertransference and am aware of how my unresolved personal issues and conflicts can be projected onto my clients.

_____ 8.   I am aware of my own biases and prejudices. This includes issues of gender, sexual orientation, poverty, privilege, and authority relationships.

_____ 9.   I pay attention to the worldview of my client and how it may be different from mine.

_____10.   I understand and am aware of how my own culture may impact my counseling relationships.

_____11.   I understand how my religious values, political values, and family values impact my counseling relationships.

_____12.   I can broach cultural issues with my client and discuss issues of diversity.

_____13.   I am involved with cultures of people different from me.

_____14.   I help clients make decisions that are congruent with their own worldview.

_____15.   I help clients define goals that are consistent with their life experiences and cultural values.

Review your ratings on the above items. Pay particular attention to items rated 1 or 2 as they may indicate areas of focus needed in this skill area.

Form 6.3: Directed Reflection Exercise on Supervision

Respond to the following questions or directives using one or two sentences.

1. Describe your anxiety level about being supervised.
2. What are your concerns about being evaluated?
3. What is your internal dialogue about your counseling practice (i.e., I'm really bad at this, I need a lot of back-up, I'll never be good enough, I'm very self-conscious)?
4. Describe your current level of confidence as a counselor.
5. What kind of structure and support do you hope for in supervision (a great deal, a moderate amount, a back-up)?
6. Describe the extent to which you feel dependent on your supervisor.
7. Describe what you need from your supervisor in the teacher role? The counselor role? The consultant role?
8. What areas of your counseling practice may need the most focus initially?
9. What is your comfort level for self-disclosing personal history as it relates to your work with clients?
10. How difficult would it be for you to give feedback to your supervisor about the supervisor–supervisee relationship?

Review your answers to the question and directives. You may want to discuss some of these questions with your peers in group supervision. Perhaps your peers could add additional questions to the list? Reviewing your answers can help you clarify your goals related to your developmental level in the supervision process.

Form 6.4: Supervisee Goal Statement

Directions: The student should complete this and provide a copy for your individual and/or group supervisor at the beginning of supervision. This will assist you in forming the supervision contract with your supervisor. The goal statements can be updated as appropriate when current goals are met and your contract is revised.

Student name _____

Supervisor name _____

Date submitted _____

Counseling Performance Skills

_____

_____

_____

_____

Cognitive Counseling Skills

_____

_____

_____

_____

Self-Awareness/Multicultural Awareness

_____

_____

_____

_____

Developmental Level

_____

_____

_____

_____

Form 6.5: Recording Critique Form

Student counselor's name _____

Client ID_____ No. of session _____

Brief summary of session content:

_____

_____

_____

Intended goals:

_____

_____

_____

Comment on positive counseling behaviors:

_____

_____

_____

Comments on areas of counseling practice needing improvement:

_____

_____

_____

Concerns, observations, or comments regarding client dynamics:

_____

_____

_____

Plans for further counseling with this client:

_____

_____

_____

Recording submitted to _____

Date _____

Form 6.6: Peer Rating Form

Purposes

1. To provide the trainee with additional sources of feedback regarding skill development.
2. To provide the rater with the opportunity to increase knowledge and recognition of positive skill behavior.

Directions

1. The trainee submits this sheet to be completed by peers who review the trainee's recordings in the group supervision class. The particular skills the counselor is working on are identified by the counselor trainee. All ethical guidelines regarding confidentiality must be followed for this recording review process, and the recording should be destroyed after the supervision session.
2. The peer writes remarks on all recordings reviewed, rating performance on the targeted skill behavior.
3. The information is cumulative to aid in review of progress.

Counselor's name _____

Targeted skills (to be identified by counselor) _____

_____

_____

_____

Remarks (based on all recordings reviewed during the week) _____

_____

_____

_____

Signature of rater _____

Date _____

Form 6.7: Interviewer Rating Form

Rating of a Counseling Session Conducted by a Student Counselor*

Client's identification _____

Student counselor's name _____

Check one:

___ Audio recording ___ Video recording ___ Observation ___ Other (specify) _____

Signature of supervisor or observer _____

Date of interview_____

Directions: Supervisor or peer of the student counselor circles a rating for each item and as much as possible provides remarks that will help the student counselor in his/her development.

Specific Criteria

Rating
(best to least)
Remarks

1. Opening: Was opening unstructured, friendly, and pleasant? Any role definition needed? Any introduction necessary?   5 4 3 2 1

2. Rapport: Did student counselor establish good rapport with client? Was the stage set for a productive interview?   5 4 3 2 1

3. Interview responsibility: If not assumed by the client, did student counselor assume appropriate level of responsibility for interview conduct? Did student counselor or client take initiative?   5 4 3 2 1

4. Interaction: Were the client and student counselor really communicating in a meaningful manner?   5 4 3 2 1

5. Acceptance/permissiveness: Was the student counselor accepting and permissive of client's emotions, feelings, and expressed thoughts?   5 4 3 2 1

6. Reflections of feelings: Did student counselor reflect and react to feelings, or did the interview remain on an intellectual level?   5 4 3 2 1

7. Student counselor responses: Were student counselor responses appropriate in view of what the client was expressing, or were responses concerned with trivia and minutia? Meaningful questions?   5 4 3 2 1

8. Value management: How did the student counselor cope with values? Were attempts made to impose counselor values during the interview?   5 4 3 2 1

9. Counseling relationship: Were student counselor–client relationships conducive to productive counseling? Was a counseling relationship established?   5 4 3 2 1

10. Closing: Was closing initiated by student counselor or client? Was it abrupt or brusque? Any follow-up or further interview scheduling accomplished?   5 4 3 2 1

11. General techniques: How well did the student counselor conduct the mechanics of the interview?   5 4 3 2 1

A. Duration of interview: Was the interview too long or too short? Should interview have been terminated sooner or later?

B. Vocabulary level: Was student counselor vocabulary appropriate for the client?

C. Mannerisms: Did the student counselor display any mannerisms that might have adversely affected the interview or portions thereof?

D. Verbosity: Did the student counselor dominate the interview, interrupt, override, or become too wordy?

E. Silences: Were silences broken to meet student counselor needs, or were they dealt with in an effectual manner?

Comments for student counselor assistance: Additional comments that might assist the student counselor in areas not covered by the preceding suggestions.

Form 7.1: Supervision Contract

Purpose: The purpose of the supervision is to monitor client services provided by the supervisee and to facilitate the professional development of the supervisee. This ensures the safety and well-being of our clients and satisfies the clinical supervision requirements of _____ University and _____ school/agency.

Supervisor's Responsibilities

- The supervisor agrees to provide face-to-face supervision to the supervisee for 1 hour per week at a regularly scheduled time for the fall/spring practicum/internship semester as required by _____ University.
- The supervisor will complete forms required by the University concerning hours, completion, verification, and evaluation of the supervisee's practicum/internship and make appropriate contact with the University liaison concerning supervisee's progress.
- The supervisor will make a recommendation as to the student's grade, but responsibility for the final grade rests with the University.
- The supervisor will review audio recordings, case notes, and other written documents; do live observations; and co-lead groups as part of the supervision format.
- The supervision sessions will focus on professional development, teaching, mentoring, and the personal development of the supervisee.
- Skill areas will include counseling performance skills and professional practices, cognitive counseling skills, self-awareness/multicultural awareness, and developmental level in supervision.
- The supervisor will provide weekly formative evaluation, document supervision sessions, and provide summative evaluations based on mutually agreed-on supervision goals. Evaluation will be offered within the skill categories listed above and use evaluation instruments recommended by the University program.
- The supervisor will practice consistent with accepted ethical standards.

Supervisee's Responsibilities

- Uphold the American Counseling Association/Canadian Counseling and Psychotherapy Association *Code of Ethics*.
- Prepare for weekly supervisions by reviewing audio recordings and framing concerns for focus of the supervision session.
- Be prepared to discuss and justify the case conceptualization made and approach and techniques used.
- Reflect on your own personal dynamics and any multicultural issues that may surface in your sessions.
- Review any ethical dimensions that may be important in your sessions.
- Contact supervisor immediately in any crisis situations involving harm to self or others or abuse of a child, vulnerable adult, or elder.
- Keep notes regarding the supervision sessions.
- Provide the supervisor with audio/video recordings to be reviewed prior to the supervision session.

GOAL 1: _____

    Objective 1: _____

    Objective 2: _____

    Objective 3: _____

GOAL 2: _____

    Objective 1: _____

    Objective 2: _____

    Objective 3: _____

GOAL 3: _____

    Objective 1: _____

    Objective 2: _____

    Objective 3: _____

GOAL 4: _____

    Objective 1: _____

    Objective 2: _____

    Objective 3: _____

Supervisor signature and date _____

Supervisee signature and date _____

Form 7.2: Supervisor Notes

Supervisor name _____

Supervisee name _____

_____

Session #

Supervisee concerns _____

Date _____

Supervision intervention/strategies/recommendations _____

_____

_____

_____

Supervisor observation of counselor's skill level _____

_____

Session #

Supervisee concerns _____

Date _____

Supervision intervention/strategies/recommendations _____

_____

_____

_____

Supervisor observation of counselor's skill level _____

_____

_____

Supervisor signature and date _____

Form 7.3: Supervisee Notes on Individual Supervision

The supervisee should keep brief notes summarizing the weekly supervision session.

For supervision from _____ to _____ .

_____

Session insights and/or comments _____

(Dates) _____

_____

_____

_____

_____

Session insights and/or comments _____

(Dates) _____

_____

_____

_____

_____

Session insights and/or comments _____

(Dates) _____

_____

_____

_____

_____

Session insights and/or comments _____

(Dates) _____

_____

_____

_____

_____

Session insights and/or comments _____

(Dates) _____

_____

_____

_____

_____

_____   _____
Supervisee's signature and date   Supervisor's signature and date

Form 7.4: Supervisor's Formative Evaluation of Supervisee's Counseling Practice

Name of student counselor _____

Identifying code of client _____

Date of supervision _____or period covered by the evaluation _____

Directions: The supervisor, following each counseling session that has been supervised or after several supervisions covering a period of time, circles a number that best evaluates the student counselor on each performance at that point in time.

General Supervision Comments	Poor		Adequate		Good	
1. Demonstrates a personal commitment in developing professional competencies	1	2	3	4	5	6
2. Invests time and energy in becoming a counselor	1	2	3	4	5	6
3. Accepts and uses constructive criticism to enhance self-development and counseling skills	1	2	3	4	5	6
4. Engages in open, comfortable, and clear communication with peers and supervisors	1	2	3	4	5	6
5. Recognizes own competencies and skills and shares these with peers and supervisors	1	2	3	4	5	6
6. Recognizes own deficiencies and actively works to overcome them with peers and supervisors	1	2	3	4	5	6
7. Completes case reports and records punctually and conscientiously	1	2	3	4	5	6

The Counseling Process	Poor		Adequate		Good	
8. Researches the referral prior to the first interview	1	2	3	4	5	6
9. Keeps appointments on time	1	2	3	4	5	6
10. Begins the interview smoothly	1	2	3	4	5	6
11. Explains the nature and objectives of counseling when appropriate	1	2	3	4	5	6
12. Is relaxed and comfortable in the interview	1	2	3	4	5	6
13. Communicates interest in and acceptance of the client	1	2	3	4	5	6
14. Facilitates client expression of concerns and feelings	1	2	3	4	5	6
15. Focuses on the content of the client's problem	1	2	3	4	5	6
16. Recognizes and resists manipulation by the client	1	2	3	4	5	6
17. Recognizes and deals with positive affect of the client	1	2	3	4	5	6
18. Recognizes and deals with negative affect of the client	1	2	3	4	5	6
19. Is spontaneous in the interview	1	2	3	4	5	6
20. Uses silence effectively in the interview	1	2	3	4	5	6
21. Is aware of own feelings in the counseling session	1	2	3	4	5	6
22. Communicates own feelings to the client when appropriate	1	2	3	4	5	6
23. Recognizes and skillfully interprets the client's covert messages	1	2	3	4	5	6
24. Facilitates realistic goal setting with the client	1	2	3	4	5	6

25. Encourages appropriate action-step planning with the client	1	2	3	4	5	6
26. Employs judgment in the timing and use of different techniques	1	2	3	4	5	6
27. Initiates periodic evaluation of goals, action-steps, and process during counseling	1	2	3	4	5	6
28. Explains, administers, and interprets tests correctly	1	2	3	4	5	6
29. Terminates the interview smoothly	1	2	3	4	5	6

The Conceptualization Process	*Poor*		*Adequate*		*Good*	
30. Focuses on specific behaviors and their consequences, implications, and contingencies	1	2	3	4	5	6
31. Recognizes and pursues discrepancies and meaning of inconsistent information	1	2	3	4	5	6
32. Uses relevant case data in planning both immediate and long-range goals	1	2	3	4	5	6
33. Uses relevant case data in considering various strategies and their implications	1	2	3	4	5	6
34. Bases decisions on a theoretically sound and consistent rationale of human behavior	1	2	3	4	5	6
35. Is perceptive in evaluating the effects of own counseling techniques	1	2	3	4	5	6
36. Demonstrates ethical behavior in the counseling activity and case management	1	2	3	4	5	6

Additional comments and/or suggestions: _____

_____

_____

_____

Date _____ Signature of supervisor _____

or peer _____

My signature indicates that I have read the above report and have discussed the content with my site supervisor. It does not necessarily indicate that I agree with the report in part or in whole.

Date _____ Signature of student counselor _____

Form 7.5: Supervisor's Final Evaluation of Practicum Student

Supervisor name and signature _____

Supervisee name and signature _____

Date _____

Directions: The supervisor will indicate the degree to which the supervisee has demonstrated competency in each of the following areas by indicating 3 for exceeds expectations, 2 for meets expectations, or 1 for does not meet expectations. This completed form will be given to the faculty group supervisor to be considered as part of the final practicum grade.

_____ Consistently demonstrates the use of basic and advanced helping skills

_____ Has the ability to appropriately use additional theory-based techniques consistent with at least one theoretical framework

_____ Demonstrates skill in opening and closing sessions and managing continuity between sessions

_____ Demonstrates knowledge and integration of ethical standards into practice

_____ Has cognitive skills of awareness, observation, and recognition of relevant data to explain some client dynamics

_____ Writes accurate case notes, intake summaries, and case conceptualizations

_____ Recognizes how several of his/her personal dynamics may impact a client and the counseling session and demonstrates sensitivity to cultural differences

_____ Demonstrates moderate to low levels of anxiety and moderate to low levels of dependency on supervisor direction during supervision sessions

Additional comments and suggestions:

_____

_____

_____

_____

Form 7.6: Supervisor's Final Evaluation of Intern

Please indicate your evaluation of the intern on the following competencies using the following rating scale:

1 = low (lacks competency)

2 = low average (possesses competency but needs improvement)

3 = average (possesses adequate competency)

4 = high average (performance level more than adequate)

5 = high (performs extremely well)

Counseling Performance Skills

_____ 1. Uses basic and advanced counseling techniques.

_____ 2. Opens and closes sessions smoothly, incorporates privacy and informed consent information, and manages transitions between sessions.

_____ 3. Develops a therapeutic relationship with a wide variety of clients.

_____ 4. Appropriately uses theory-based techniques consistent with personal guiding theory.

_____ 5. Responds and intervenes appropriately in crisis situations.

_____ 6. Recognizes ethical dilemmas and follows a consistent ethical decision-making process.

_____ 7. Practices in a manner consistent with the American Counseling Association's *Code of Ethics* standards.

Cognitive Counseling Skills

1. Demonstrates competencies in

_____ Assessment

_____ Case conceptualization

_____ Goal setting

_____ Treatment planning

_____ Record keeping and case notes

_____ 2. Practices using a personal guiding theory of counseling.

_____ 3. Conceptualizes cases accurately.

_____ 4. Develops appropriate goals as a result of conceptualization.

_____ 5. Identifies key themes relevant to the client.

_____ 6. Identifies key factors maintaining client problems.

_____ 7. Moves clients toward achieving mutually formed goals.

Self-Awareness/Multicultural Awareness

_____ 1. Examines transference/countertransference issues as related to clients.

_____ 2. Examines personal values as related to work with clients.

_____ 3. Recognizes how elements of culture impact the client's view of the counseling process.

_____ 4. Demonstrates the qualities of openness, flexibility, and emotional stability.

_____ 5. Communicates an understanding of each client's worldview as perceived by the client and develops goals consistent with client's worldview.

_____ 6. Identifies and examines multicultural elements related to assessment, goal setting, and intervention strategies.

Developmental Level in Supervision

_____ 1. Comes to supervision prepared and open to receiving feedback.

_____ 2. Identifies appropriate priorities for the work in supervision.

_____ 3. Functions with appropriate autonomy and knows when to consult.

_____ 4. Demonstrates self-confidence in the role of counselor.

_____ 5. Comfortably integrates all elements of practice when receiving supervision.

_____ 6. Demonstrates reflective thinking when reviewing a case.

In comparison with other counselors at this stage in their development, how would you rate this person?

1	2	3	4	5	6	7	8	9
Clearly				Like			Clearly	
deficient				others			excellent	

Comments _____

_____

_____

_____   _____

Supervisor   Supervisee

Date _____

Form 7.7: Evaluation of Intern's Practice in Site Activities

Directions: The site supervisor is to complete this form in duplicate. One copy is to go to the student; the other copy is sent to the faculty liaison. The areas listed below serve as a general guide for the activities typically engaged in during counselor training. Please rate the student on the activities in which he/she has engaged using the following scale:

A = Functions extremely well and/or independently

B = Functions adequately and/or requires occasional supervision

C = Requires close supervision in this area

NA = Not applicable to this training experience

Training Activities

_____ 1. Intake interviewing

_____ 2. Individual counseling/psychotherapy

_____ 3. Group counseling/psychotherapy

_____ 4. Testing: Administration and interpretation

_____ 5. Report writing/documentation

_____ 6. Consultation with other professionals or parents/family

_____ 7. Psychoeducational activities

_____ 8. Career counseling

_____ 9. Family/couple counseling

_____ 10. Case conference or staff presentation

_____ 11. Other

Additional Comments

Please use the additional space for any comments that would help us evaluate the student's progress. Student may comment on exceptions to ratings, if any.

_____

_____

_____

_____

_____

_____   _____

Student name   Supervisor signature

Site _____   Date _____

Form 7.8: Client's Assessment of the Counseling Experience

Counselor'sname _____

Date _____

Directions: Please read the following statements and place a check next to the ones that accurately describe your counseling experience with this counselor.

_____ I got the help that I needed with my concerns.

_____ I was satisfied with the relationship I had with my counselor.

_____ I received help with concerns that were in addition to my original concerns.

_____ I feel much better now compared to how I was feeling when I started counseling.

_____ The counseling helped me understand myself better.

_____ I would gladly return to this counselor if I wanted help with another concern.

_____ I would recommend this counselor to a friend.

_____ My counselor was competent and skilled.

_____ My counselor put me at ease right away.

_____ My counselor understood and was sensitive to my feelings and my situation.

_____ I didn't feel free to talk about all my concerns with my counselor.

_____ Counseling helped me see a number of things I could do to change and improve my situation.

_____ The counselor asked questions and made comments that made it easy for me to talk about my concerns.

_____ I felt I could not get my story across and that I couldn't get the counselor to understand me.

_____ I felt I could be honest and talk about my feelings and thoughts and behaviors openly.

_____ I would prefer to work with a counselor who has a different approach to counseling.

Thank you for completing this form. Your feedback will be very helpful.

Form 7.9: Supervisee Evaluation of Supervisor**

Directions: The student counselor is to evaluate the supervision received. Circle the number that best represents how you, the student counselor, feel about the supervision received. After the form is completed, the supervisor may suggest a meeting to discuss the supervision desired.

Name of practicum/internship supervisor _____

Period covered: From _____ to _____

	Poor		Adequate		Good	
1. Gives time and energy in observations, recording processing, and case conferences.	1	2	3	4	5	6
2. Accepts and respects me as a person.	1	2	3	4	5	6
3. Recognizes and encourages further development of my strengths and capabilities.	1	2	3	4	5	6
4. Gives me useful feedback when I do something well.	1	2	3	4	5	6
5. Provides me the freedom to develop flexible and effective counseling styles.	1	2	3	4	5	6
6. Encourages and listens to my ideas and suggestions for developing my counseling skills.	1	2	3	4	5	6
7. Provides suggestions for developing my counseling skills.	1	2	3	4	5	6
8. Helps me understand the implications and dynamics of the counseling approaches I use.	1	2	3	4	5	6
9. Encourages me to use new and different techniques when appropriate.	1	2	3	4	5	6
10. Is spontaneous and flexible in the supervisory sessions.	1	2	3	4	5	6
11. Helps me define and achieve specific concrete goals for myself during the practicum experience.	1	2	3	4	5	6
12. Gives me useful feedback when I do something wrong.	1	2	3	4	5	6
13. Allows me to discuss problems I encounter in my practicum/internship setting.	1	2	3	4	5	6
14. Pays appropriate amount of attention to both my clients and me.	1	2	3	4	5	6
15. Focuses on both verbal and nonverbal behavior in me and in my clients.	1	2	3	4	5	6
16. Helps me define and maintain ethical behavior in counseling and case management.	1	2	3	4	5	6
17. Encourages me to engage in professional behavior.	1	2	3	4	5	6
18. Maintains confidentiality in material discussed in supervisory sessions.	1	2	3	4	5	6

_____

Notes: * This form was designed by two Purdue graduate students based on material drawn from *Counseling Strategies and Objectives*, by H. Hackney and S. Nye (1973). Englewood Cliffs, NJ: Prentice Hall. Printed by permission from Harold Hackney, PhD.

* This form originally was printed in chapter 10 of the *Practicum Manual for Counseling and Psychotherapy*, by K. Dimick and F. Krause (Eds.) (1980). Muncie, IN: Accelerated Development.

19. Deals with both content and affect when supervising.	1	2	3	4	5	6
20. Focuses on the implications, consequences, and contingencies of specific behaviors in counseling and supervision.	1	2	3	4	5	6
21. Helps me organize relevant case data in planning goals and strategies with my client.	1	2	3	4	5	6
22. Helps me to formulate a theoretically sound rationale of human behavior.	1	2	3	4	5	6
23. Offers resource information when I request or need it.	1	2	3	4	5	6
24. Helps me develop increased skill in critiquing and gaining insight from my counseling recordings.	1	2	3	4	5	6
25. Allows and encourages me to evaluate myself.	1	2	3	4	5	6
26. Explains his/her criteria for evaluation clearly and in behavioral terms.	1	2	3	4	5	6
27. Applies his/her criteria fairly in evaluating my counseling performance.	1	2	3	4	5	6

Additional Comments and/or Suggestions

_____

_____

_____

_____

My signature indicates that I have read the above report and have discussed the content with my supervisee. It does not necessarily indicate that I agree with the report in part or in whole.

_____

Supervisee's signature and date

Form 7.10: Site Evaluation Form

Directions: The student completes this form at the end of the practicum and/or internship. This should be turned in to the university supervisor or internship coordinator as indicated by the university program.

Name _____ Site _____

Dates of placement _____ Site supervisor _____

Faculty liaison _____

Rate the following questions about your site and experiences with the following scale:

A. *Very satisfactory*   B. *Moderately satisfactory*   C. *Moderately unsatisfactory*   D. *Very unsatisfactory*

1. _____   Amount of on-site supervision
2. _____   Quality and usefulness of on-site supervision
3. _____   Usefulness and helpfulness of faculty liaison
4. _____   Relevance of experience to career goals
5. _____   Exposure to and communication of school/agency goals
6. _____   Exposure to and communication of school/agency procedures
7. _____   Exposure to professional roles and functions within the school/agency
8. _____   Exposure to information about community resources
9. _____   Rate all applicable experiences that you had at your site:

     _____   Report writing
     _____   Intake interviewing
     _____   Administration and interpretation of tests
     _____   Staff presentation/case conferences
     _____   Individual counseling
     _____   Group counseling
     _____   Family/couple counseling
     _____   Psychoeducational activities
     _____   Consultation
     _____   Career counseling
     _____   Other

10. _____   Overall evaluation of the site

Comments: Include any suggestions for improvements in the experiences you have rated *moderately unsatisfactory* (C) or *very unsatisfactory* (D). _____

_____

_____

_____

Form 7.11: Weekly Internship Log

Directions: Fill in the number of hours spent in each activity for each day at your internship site. Activities with an * are those activities that are counted as direct contact hours.

Week of: From _____ to_____

Activity	Monday	Tuesday	Wednesday	Thursday	Friday	Total
Individual counseling*						
Group counseling*						
Family/couple counseling*						
Career counseling*						
Intake interview*						
Consulting with professionals or parents*						
Crisis intervention/referral*						
Psychoeducation/guidance*						
Testing/assessment						
Documentation						
Program/case planning						
Case conference						
Professional development						
Other/please list						
Individual supervision/site						
Group supervision						
Total direct contact hours*						
Total indirect contact hours						
Total hours						

_____   _____
Student signature and date   Supervisor signature and date

Form 7.12: Summary Internship Log

Directions: Fill in the dates of each week of internship where indicated. Fill in the total number of hours spent in each activity for the week indicated. Indicate the total number of hours spent in direct contact with clients (activity indicated by *). Total the hours spent in indirect contact. Then, indicate the total of all hours where indicated at the bottom of the form. Hours in supervision are not included in total hours.

Activity Week> Dates>	1	2	3	4	5	6	7	8	Total
Individual counseling*									
Group counseling*									
Couple/family counseling*									
Career counseling*									
Intake interview*									
Consulting with professionals/parents*									
Testing/assessment									
Crisis intervention/ referrals*									
Psychoeducation/guidance*									
Documentation/report writing/grant preparation									
Program/case planning									
Case conference									
Professional development									
Other/please list									
Individual supervision/site									
Group supervision									
Total direct contact hours									
Total indirect contact hours									
Total hours									

_____
Student signature and date

_____
Supervisor signature and date

Form 10.1: Suicide Consultation Form

Directions: Student will complete this form when working with a potentially suicidal client. The student will take this information to his/her supervisor for consultation, collaborate on a treatment plan, and place in client's file.

Part I

Name of institution _____

Intern's name _____ Supervisor's name _____

Supervisor's professional degree _____

Supervisor is licensed in _____ Supervisor is certified in _____

Client's name _____ Client's age _____

If the client is a minor, has the parent signed a consent form? _____

When was the counseling initiated? Month _____ Day _____ Year _____

Where was counseling initiated? _____

Number of times you have seen this client _____

Part II

Check the presenting symptoms often associated with a suicidal client.

Client is between the ages of 14 and 19. Yes _____ No _____

Client is depressed. Yes _____ No _____

If yes, include a description of the client's depressive behavior:

_____

_____

Has a previous attempt of suicide occurred? Yes_____ No_____

If yes, how long ago was the attempt? _____

Is the client abusing alcohol? Yes _____ No _____

If yes, how much does he/she drink? _____

_____

Is the client abusing some other substance? Yes _____ No_____

If yes, what other substance? _____

_____

Is rational thinking lost? Yes _____ No _____

If yes, explain how this behavior is manifested: _____

_____

_____

_____

Does the client have little social support? Yes _____ No _____

How does the client spend his/her time? _____

_____

_____

Does the client have an organized suicide plan? Yes _____ No _____

If yes, what is the plan? _____

_____

_____

_____

If there is a plan, does it seem irreversible, for example, gunshot?

Yes_____ No_____

Is the client divorced, widowed, or separated? Yes _____ No_____

Is the client physically sick? Yes_____ No _____

If yes, describe the symptoms: _____

_____

_____

Does the client have sleep disruption? Yes_____ No_____

If yes, describe the disruption: _____

_____

_____

_____

_____

Has the client given his/her possessions away? Yes_____ No_____

Does the client have a history of previous psychiatric treatment or hospitalization?

Yes _____ No _____

If yes, describe for what the client was hospitalized: _____

_____

_____

_____

Does the client have anyone near him/her to intervene? Yes_____ No_____

Does the client seem agitated? Yes _____ No _____

If yes, describe the client's behavior: _____

_____

_____

Part III

Describe and summarize your interactions with the client. What are his/her basic problems? What is your goal with the client? What techniques are you using?

_____

_____

_____

_____

Describe your supervisor's reaction to the problem:

_____

_____

_____

_____

_____
Supervisor's signature

What are your plans for the client? _____

_____

_____

_____

Form 10.2: Harm to Others Form

Directions: Student completes the form prior to supervisory sessions and records supervisor's comments and reactions; student and supervisor then sign the completed form. The student should keep the form in his/her confidential records.

1. Student's name _____

   Client's name _____

2. Number of times the client has been seen _____

3. Dates client has been seen _____

   _____

Client's presenting problem _____

_____

_____

Risk Assessment[1]

Does the client have any of the following characteristics, traits, or current life circumstances? (Check yes for all that apply.)

	Yes	No
History of previous violence toward others (e. g., hitting, slapping, punching, stabbing, etc.)	☐	☐
History of violence at a young age	☐	☐
Relationship instability	☐	☐
Employment instability or problems	☐	☐
Substance use history	☐	☐
Current use of substances	☐	☐
Mental illness diagnosis	☐	☐
Presence of psychopathology	☐	☐
Maladjustment early in life (e.g., problems in school, problems with peers)	☐	☐
Diagnosis of a personality disorder	☐	☐
Lacking in insight into the mental disorder	☐	☐
Active symptoms of the mental disorder	☐	☐
Negative perceptions toward authority or those trying to intervene to help	☐	☐
History of impulsive behaviors	☐	☐
Access to means of lethality (e.g., weapons, guns, knives, etc.)	☐	☐
History of being unresponsive to treatment	☐	☐
Presence of current life stressors	☐	☐
Lack of support	☐	☐

---

[1] Items for the checklist are adapted from C. D. Webster, K. S. Douglas, D. Eaves, & S. D. Hart (1997), HCR-20 risk assessment for violence (Version 2). Burnaby, Canada: Mental Health, Law, and Policy Institute, Simon Fraser Institute.

Additional Clinical Assessment Areas for Risk

4. What did the client do or say to make the counselor concerned that he/she could represent a "harm to others"? _____

_____

_____

_____

5. Describe the client's history of violence or criminal behavior _____

_____

_____

_____

6. Have you consulted the client's case notes/treatment records for such a history? _____

_____

7. Does the client have a history of child abuse and maltreatment? If yes, briefly describe:

_____

_____

_____

8. Does the client have a history of substance abuse? Describe the client's history and current use of substances? _____

_____

_____

_____

_____

9. Is the client experiencing hallucinations (auditory or visual), and does the client perceive that his/her life is being threatened? Describe: _____

_____

_____

_____

_____

_____

10. What is the client's history of dealing with stress? Describe his/her level of impulse control, reactivity to stressful situations, and history of acting without thinking: _____

_____

_____

_____

_____

_____

_____

11. What stressors is the client currently facing, and does he/she have any support in dealing with them? (Stressors can be relational, related to work, finances, housing, etc.) _____

_____

_____

_____

_____

_____

12. Was a specific victim(s) named? _____

13. If the victim was not named, what was the relationship of the client to the victim? _____

_____

14. If the victim was not named, did the counselor suspect who the person was? _____

_____

15. Was a clear threat made? If yes, what threat? _____

16. Is serious danger present? For example, does the client have access to victims and to weapons and the setting in which to commit violence? _____

_____

_____

17. Is the danger believed to be imminent? _____

If so, why? _____

_____

_____

If not, why not? _____

_____

_____

18. Supervisor's reaction/advice? _____

_____

_____

19. What plan of action is to be taken? _____

_____

_____

_____

Student's signature

_____

Supervisor's signature

_____

Date of conference

Form 10.3: Child Abuse Reporting Form

Counselor trainee and position _____

Date and time _____

Alleged perpetrator_____ DOB _____

Address _____

Alleged victim _____ DOB _____

Address _____

Information obtained from_____ DOB _____

Address _____

Relationship to alleged perpetrator _____

Relationship to alleged victim _____

Brief description of incident or concern _____

_____

_____

Incident(s) ongoing? _____ Or specific date _____

Reported to immediate supervisor on _____

Supervisor's name and position _____

Reported to children and youth services on _____ Time _____

Children and youth worker's name _____

Alleged perpetrator aware of report?   Yes _____ No _____

Alleged victim aware of report?   Yes _____ No _____

Alleged perpetrator in counseling?   Yes _____ No _____

If so, where? _____

Alleged victim in counseling?   Yes_____ No _____

If so, where? _____

Results _____

_____

Counselor trainee's signature _____

Field supervisor's signature _____

cc: Client's file, Agency file

Form 10.4: Substance Abuse Assessment Form

Directions: Student asks the client the specific questions addressed on the form as a way to make a clinical assessment of the level of severity of use and abuse of substances in the client's life.
   The completed form is kept in the student's confidential file.

1. What substances do you or have you used? _____

_____

_____

_____

2. How long have you used (beginning with experimentation)? _____

_____

_____

_____

3. How often are you high in a week? _____

_____

_____

_____

4. How many of your friends use? _____

_____

_____

_____

5. Are you on medication? _____

_____

6. Do you have money for chemicals? How much? _____

_____

7. How much do you spend for drugs or alcohol in a month? _____

_____

8. Who provides if you are broke? _____

_____

_____

9. Have you ever been busted (police, school, home, DWIs)? _____

_____

10. Have you lost a job because of your use? _____

_____

_____

11. What time of day do you use? _____

_____

_____

12. Do you use on the job or in school? _____

_____

_____

13. Does it take more, less, or about the same amount of the substance to get you high? _____
_____
_____

14. Have you ever shot up? What substance? Where on your body? _____
_____
_____

15. Do you sneak using? How do you do it? _____
_____
_____
_____

16. Do you hide things? _____
_____

17. Do you have rules for using? What are they? How did they come about? _____
_____
_____
_____

18. Do you use alone? _____
_____

19. Have you ever tried to quit? How often have you tried to quit and not been able to? _____
_____
_____

20. Have you had any withdrawal symptoms? _____
_____
_____
_____

21. Have you lost your "good time highs"? _____
_____
_____

22. Have you ever thought about suicide? _____
_____
_____

23. Do you mix your chemicals when using? _____
_____
_____

24. Do you ever shift from one chemical to another? Yes _____ No _____
What happened that made you decide to shift? _____
_____
_____
_____

25. Do you avoid people who don't use? _____
_____
_____

26. Do you avoid talking about your drug or alcohol use? _____
_____
_____

27. Have you done things when using that you are ashamed of? Yes _____ No _____
What happened? _____
_____
_____
_____

28. Who is the most important person in your life, including yourself? _____
_____
_____

29. How are you taking care of him/her? _____
_____
_____

30. On a scale of 1 (*low*) to 10, how is your life going? _____
Explain_____

31. Are there any harmful consequences you are aware of in your chemical use other than those
touched upon? _____
_____
_____
_____

32. Do you think your chemical is harmful to you? Yes _____ No _____
Do you think you have a chemical problem? Yes _____ No _____
Explain _____
_____
_____

_____
Student's signature

_____
Client's signature

_____
Supervisor's signature

_____
Date

INDEX

Note: Page numbers in *italic* indicate a figure. Page numbers in **bold** indicate a table.

abandonment 169
ABC model of crisis intervention 176–177
Abilify (aripiprazole) 247–249
abstract ability, client mental status assessment and 55
abuse 198–204; child 164, 166–167, 198–204; drug/ substance 204–209 (*see also* addiction); elder 167; examples of 199; neglect 164, 166–167, 199–200
ACA *see* American Counseling Association
academic performance, decrease in response to crisis 183
acceptance: in acceptance and commitment therapy (ACT) 91; in mindfulness techniques 89
acceptance and commitment therapy (ACT) 90–91
accountability, treatment plan and 73
accreditation, advantages of 5
accreditation standards for practicum and internship 4–7; CACEP 6–7; CACREP/CORE 6; MPCAC 7
ACT (acceptance and commitment therapy) 90–91
action, in stages of change model 72
active listening 37
AdderallXR 249
addiction 204–209; counseling recommendations for clients with 207–208; diagnosing alcohol and drug use 204–205; gambling 205; relapse, preventing 208–209; treatment 205–206; understanding 204
addictions counseling, CACREP standards and 51
addictions counselor, NBCC specialty certification for 8
ADHD (attention-deficit/hyperactivity disorder), treatment of 249
Adler, Alfred **77**
administrative supervision 116
adolescents: psychopharmacological treatments of 248–249; school-based suicide prevention and intervention programs 191–192; *see also* children
affect, client mental status assessment and 54
affirmative concealment of a crime 198
aggression, in children's response to crisis 184
alcohol use: diagnosing 204–205; treatment 205–206
Alcohol Use Disorders Identification Test (AUDIT) 55
alertness, client mental status assessment and 54
Allport, Gordon **78**
alprozolam (Xanax) 246

American Academy of Experts in Traumatic Stress 183
American Association of Marriage and Family Therapy 9, 140
American Association of Pastoral Counselors Therapy 140
American Association of Suicidology 191
American Counseling Association (ACA): *Code of Ethics* 18, 28, 31, 115, 123, 140–144, 147, 150–153, 160, 168, 189–190, 238; educational standards 4; practicum site ethical guidelines 16; *Practitioner's Guide to Ethical Decision-Making, A* 147; website 141, 162
American Mental Health Counselors Association (AMHCA): code of ethics 18, 168; website 141
American Psychiatric Association 60
American Psychological Association (APA): code of ethics 143, 168; Commission on Accreditation (APA-CoA) 5; practicum site ethical guidelines 16; website 141, 162
American School Counselor Association (ASCA) 181–182, 191, 222; code of ethics 140–141, 189–190, 192; *Ethical Standards for School Counselors* 18, 46; website 141
AMHCA *see* American Mental Health Counselors Association
amitriptyline (Elavil) 244
Anafranil (clomipramine) 244
anecdotal notes, in school counseling 45–46
antianxiety medications 246–247
anti-bullying programs 182
anticonvulsant medications 247
antidepressant medications 243–246; atypical antidepressants 246; cyclics 244; monoamine oxidase inhibitors (MAOIs) 245; norepinephrine reuptake inhibitors (NRIs) 245; selective serotonin reuptake inhibitors (SSRIs) 244–245; serotonin and norepinephrine reuptake inhibitors (SNRIs) 245
antipsychotic medications 247–248
anxiety: children's response to crisis 183; practicum experience and 25–26
anxiolytics 246
APA-CoA (American Psychological Association Commission on Accreditation) 5
Aplenzin (bupropion) 246
appearance, client mental status assessment and 54

aripiprazole (Abilify) 247–249, 248
ASCA *see* American School Counselor Association
asenapine (Saphris) 248
asking for help 27
assessment 51–67; behavioral 64–65; CACREP standards 51; case conceptualization 60–63; of client progress 64–67; client's mental state 54–55; as collaborative process between counselor and client 51; components to data-gathering and hypothesis-testing process of 64; continuous 64–65, 130; cultural factors and 144; evaluation in group supervision of internship 112–113; evaluation in group supervision of practicum 108–109; evaluation of counseling performance in individual supervision 130–133; gathering family history data 52–53; gathering personal history data 53–54; goals of 56–58; impact of consultation 229–230; initial 52–55; midpoint and summative evaluation in internship 132–133; midpoint and summative evaluation in practicum 130–132; notes after each counseling session 65–66; obtaining information from others 55; prioritizing problems of clients 56; processes and categories for assessing client problems 56–58; qualitative activities 64–65; review of client's records 64; risk assessment for potentially dangerous clients 195–198; risk assessment for suicide 185–188; sharing information with the client 63–64; structured 55; suicide risk 185–188; wellness model of mental health 57
assessment interview 56, 207
assistance, seeking 28
associate licensure 236
Association for Counselor Education and Supervision (ACES) 123
Association for Multicultural Counseling and Development website 141
Atarax (hydroxyzine) 246
Ativan (lorazepam) 246
atomoxetine (Strattera) 245
attending 37, 51, 98, 141, 176–177
attention: client mental status assessment and 54; liability and 161–162; to the present, in mindfulness techniques 89
attention-deficit/hyperactivity disorder (ADHD), treatment of 249
atypical antidepressants 246
audio recordings *see* recording sessions
AUDIT (Alcohol Use Disorders Identification Test) 55
autonomy: developmental models and 120; managed care and 169; respect for 142–143, 149
awareness, in mindfulness techniques 89

Bandura, Albert **78**, 180
barbiturates 247
Beck Anxiety Inventory (BAI) 55
Beck Depression Inventory II (BDI-II) 55
beginning statements, poor 107
beginning the practicum experience 25–29; becoming part of the team 28–29; confidence 26; consulting 28–28; finding appropriate technique 27; saying the wrong thing 26–27; tips 25–26; trusting yourself 27–28
behavior, client mental status assessment and 54

behavioral assessment 64–65
behavioral charts 98
behavioral problems, children with 225–226
behavior change, solution-focused therapy and 85
behaviorism, traditional 88
being present, in acceptance and commitment therapy (ACT) 91
beneficence 142–143, 149
benzodiazepines 247
Best Practices in Clinical Supervision (ACES) 123
bias, hindsight 180
bipolar disorder, treatment of 247–248
blind spots, identification of 37
blocking, group counseling skill 42
board certification 7–8
borderline personality disorder 91
boundaries, counselor-client 151
breach notification rule, HIPAA 30
breach of contract 159, 161
breath, focusing on 88–89
breathing techniques 179
brief therapies 85–88; cognitive restructuring therapy 87–88; coping skills brief therapy 88; managed care and 169; rational emotive behavior therapy 88; solution-focused brief therapy 85–86; strategic solution-focused therapy 86–87
buffers against suicide 187
bupropion (Aplenzin) 246
bupropionLA (WellbutrinLA) 246, 249
bupropionSR (WellbutrinSR) 246, 249
burnout 238–239
Buspar (buspirone) 246, 249
buspirone (Buspar) 246, 249

CACEP *see* Canadian Council on Accreditation of Counselling Education Programs
CACREP *see* Council for the Accreditation of Counseling and related Education Programs
Canada: demographics of clients 18; health information privacy 30; practice of counselor-client confidentiality in 168; regulation of practice of counseling 9
Canadian Certified Counsellor (CCC) 8
Canadian Council on Accreditation of Counselling Education Programs (CACEP) 3, 5–7; group supervision requirement 110; practicum/internship contracts 20; standards for initial and final practicum 6–7
Canadian Counselling and Psychotherapy Association (CCPA) 5–6, 8; code of ethics 18, 141, 143; *Counselling Ethics: Issues and Cases* 147; group supervision requirement 110; internship hours 133; practicum/internship contracts 20; practicum site ethical guidelines 16; website 141, 162
Canadian Professional Counsellors Association (CPCA): membership levels 8; Registered Professional Counsellor (RPC) 8
Canadian Psychological Association (CPA): code of ethics 141, 143; practicum site ethical guidelines 16; website 141, 162
Caplan, Gerald 215
carbamazepine (Tegretol) 247
care, as a virtue 146

career: licensure 235–238; longevity 238–239; recommendations for sustaining personal and professional excellence 239; wellness and burnout 238–239

case conceptualization 60–63; assignments in group supervision in internship 110; models 61–63

case conceptualization models 61–63; categories of information found in case formulation methods 61; integrative model 63; inverted pyramid model 62–63; linchpin model 61–62

case formulation 61; *see also* case conceptualization

case law 158

case notes 66, 170

Case Notes Form 46, 66

case presentation 105

CCC (Canadian Certified Counsellor) 8

CCPA *see* Canadian Counselling and Psychotherapy Association

Celexa (citalopram) 244

certification: codes of ethics 141; exams 236–237; *see also* counselor certification

Certified Rehabilitation Counselor (CRC) 8

change: in organizations 231; stages of change model 71–72; strategies and dialectical behavior therapy (DBT) 91

child abuse 164, 166–167, 198–204; counseling sexually abused children 202–204; defined 199; examples of 199; interviewing sexually abused children 201–202; legal issues related to reporting 200–201; making a report related to 200–201; mediating factors 200; risk factors 199–200; statistics 198–199

Child Abuse Prevention and Treatment Act 200

Child Abuse Reporting Form 201–202

children: abuse 164, 166–167, 198–204; behavioral problems 225–226; psychopharmacological treatments of 248–249; suicide 185, 191; trauma reactions in 183

Children's Bureau 198–199

chlordiazepoxide (Librium) 246

chlorpromazine (Thorazine) 247, 248

citalopram (Celexa) 244

civil law 158

clarifying 37, 97

clearances 16

client advocacy 149

client-centered consultation 216

client observation 37, 98

Client Permission to Record Counseling Session for Supervision Purposes 34–35

client population, of placement site 17–19

client records 169–170; *see also* record keeping

clients: counselor performance rating by 133; dangerous 166, 193–198

Client's Assessment of the Counseling Experience form 133

clinical case notes 43; *see also* progress notes

Clinical Member Status, American Association for Marriage and Family Therapy 9

clinical mental health counseling, CACREP standards and 51

clinical mental health counselor, NBCC specialty certification for 8

clinical supervision 116

clinical supervision process 123–130

clomipramine (Anafranil) 244

clonazepam (Klonopin) 246

Clorazil (clozapine) 248

closed questions 107

closing sessions 37–40, 98

clozapine (Clorazil) 248

Code of Professional Ethics for Rehabilitation Counselors website 141

codes of ethics 18, 28, 31, 123, 125; as aspirational 140; competence and 160; confidentiality 151, 190; distance counseling 151–152; ethical decision making and 142–145; functions of 139; on impairment 150; informed by schools of philosophical ethics 140; multicultural counseling 147; national and regional 140; policing role of 140; self-care and 238; similarities across disciplines and specialties 141–142; suicidal clients 189–190; websites for 140

cognitive-behavioral model 119

cognitive behavioral therapy 88; behavioral charts 98; mindfulness-based cognitive therapy (MBCT) 90

cognitive counseling skills 98, 101, 112–113, 131

cognitive diffusion, in acceptance and commitment therapy (ACT) 91

cognitive processing therapy (CPT) 180

cognitive restructuring therapy 87–88, 180

cognitive styles 223–224; concrete 223–224; dialectic/systemic 224; formal-operational 224; sensorimotor 223

collaboration: building 35; consultation and 218; how to approach 28–29; peer 106–108; in school consultation 221; supervisor-supervisee relationship 116

collaborative mental health service teams 58

commentator role in triadic supervisor method 121–122

Commission for Rehabilitation Counselor Certification 141

commitment 189, 190, 195

committed action, in acceptance and commitment therapy (ACT) 91

common law 158

communication: digital 151–152; liability and 161–162; privileged 163–164

compassion, as a virtue 146

competence: boundaries of 144, 160–161; components of 160; ethical codes and 141; informed consent and 31; lawsuits and counselor incompetence 160; liability and 161; licensure and 235; minimum competencies 160; skills that suggest to client 98

competencies: practicum 110; for school counselors 221

complainant client, in solution-focused therapy 85, 86

concentration: client mental status assessment and 54; poor in response to crisis 183

conceptualization, focus in discrimination model 121

concrete cognitive style 223–224

confidence: building 27; skills that suggest to client 98; in your training 26

confidentiality: of assessment 55; breach 165–167; codes of ethics 151, 190; digital communication

151–152; distance counseling 152; as ethical duty 163; ethics and 139, 141, 144; exceptions to 163–167, 190, 200; explaining to client 38; group supervision 103; informed consent and 33–34; limits to 32, 141; managed care and 169; practice of counselor-client confidentiality in Canada 168; progress notes 44; release of information 165; school counseling 34, 45–46; social media 153; in Supervisor Informed Consent and Disclosure Statement 125; telephones 151; trust 163; waiver of 165; web-based professional discussion groups 151, 153

conflict resolution program 182

confrontation 37, 208

confusion, in developmental models 120

consent, informed see informed consent

constitutional law 157

consultant, supervisor role in discrimination model 120–121

consultation 215–232; action strategies 222; assessment of impact 229–230; assumptions behind and metaphors for 218–219; characteristics of mental health 216–218; client-centered 216; collaboration 218; consultee-centered administrative 216; consultee-centered case 216; contract 227, 231; cultural issues in 219–210; definitions 215; doctor-patient model 219; educational 220, 222; expectations for outcomes of, setting 229; forces of change in organizations 231; goals 217, **221**, 221–222, 229; guidelines for 226–229; as indirect service 215–216; informational 220; internal 217–218; intervention 228–229; interview 217; minimizing liability risks 162; models and practices in schools 222–226; multicultural 220; peer consultation in group supervision 106–108; process consultation model 219; program-centered administrative 216; purchase-of-expertise model 218–219; relationship conditions 215; resistance to 230; in schools 220–226; seeking 28; as strategy for addressing systemic problems 149; suspicion of child abuse 167; types of 216

consultation guidelines/steps 226–229; consultation intervention 228–229; entry into the system 227; orientation to consultation 227–228; preentry 226–227; problem identification 228

consultee-centered administrative consultation 216

consultee-centered case consultation 216

contact person, practicum site 19

contemplation, in stages of change model 72

contempt of court 158

content in groups 42

contract 20–21; breach of 159, 161; consultation 227, 231; suicide 189; supervision 125–127

coping questions 86

coping responses, for substance use 207–208

coping skills brief therapy 88

coping strategies, developing client 177–178

CORE (Council on Rehabilitation Education) 3, 5–6, 8

Council for the Accreditation of Counseling and related Education Programs (CACREP) 3–8; CACREP-accredited degree 236; Certified Rehabilitation Counselor (CRC) 8; group supervision requirements 97, 109–110; internship hours 133; NCE and 236; practicum/internship contracts 20; program assessment processes 133; standards and assessment 51; standards for practicum and internship 6, 132; triadic supervision 121

Council on Rehabilitation Education (CORE) 3, 5–6, 8

counseling, definition of 3–4

counseling performance: evaluation of performance in individual supervision 130–133; skills 97–98, 100–101, 131

counseling philosophy, in informed consent document 33

Counseling Techniques List 76, 84, **80–84**, 100

Counselling Ethics: Issues and Cases (CCPA) 147

counselor: development sequence 128–130; licensure 9; supervisor role in discrimination model 120–121; see also professional counselor

counselor certification 7–9; board certification 7–8; Canadian Certified Counsellor (CCC) 8; Certified Rehabilitation Counselor (CRC) 8; Clinical Member Status, American Association for Marriage and Family Therapy 9; National Certified Counselor (NCC) 7–8; NBCC specialty certification 8; Registered Professional Counsellor (RPC) 9; specialty certification 8

counselor-in-training, supervision of developing 128–130

course requirements, practicum 26

cover letter 19

CPA see Canadian Psychological Association

CPCA see Canadian Professional Counsellors Association

CPT (cognitive processing therapy) 180

cravings, for substance use 207–208

crime: criminal acts, client's past 198; exceptions to privileged communication 164

criminal background check 16

criminal law 158

crisis: children's reaction to 183–184; definition 175; developmental 175; existential 175; process of crisis formulation 176–177; situational 175; systemic 175; types 175

crisis intervention 176–178; ABC model of 176–177; continuous activities for 178; focused tasks for 178; James and Gilliland model of 177–178; Kanel model of 176–177; school counselor tasks in preventing and responding to crisis 182–183; in schools 181–184; seven-task model of 177–178

crisis stage of change in organizations 231

cultural awareness, consultation and 220

cultural competence 18–19, 99; building awareness 147–148; building knowledge 148–149; choosing culturally appropriate strategies 149–150; consultation 220

cultural diversity skills, demonstration of 111

culture: codes of ethics and 142; cultural issues in consultation 219–210; culturally appropriate goals 72; ethics of counseling culturally diverse clients 147–150; factors in using assessment and diagnostic tools 143–144; supervision and 119; transcultural integrative model for resolving ethical dilemmas 149; treatment plan and 75; variables of 18

current life situations, assessing client's 57
customer client, in solution-focused therapy 85, 86
cyclics 244
Cymbalta (duloxetine) 245

dangerous clients 166, 193–198; client's past criminal acts 198; risk assessment for potentially 195–198; *Tarasoff* case 166, 194–195
danger to self 189–190; *see also* suicide
DAP (data, assessment, plan) format 44
Daytrana 249
DBT (dialectical behavior therapy) 91
DCT (developmental counseling and therapy) 223–224
death: desire for 185–186; *see also* suicide
decision making *see* ethical decision making
decline stage of change in organizations 231
defamation of character 161
defendant, lawsuit 159
defensiveness 117
delegating, group counseling skill 42
demographics of United States and Canada 18
denial, children's response to crisis 184
denial of services 168–169
Depakote (divalproex) 247, 248
depression: antidepressant medications 243–246; increase in children's response to crisis 184; student suicide and 193; treatment of bipolar disorders 247
descriptive metaphor 111
desipramine (Norpramin, Pamelor) 244
desire to die 185–186
Desyrel (trazodone) 244
development: principles regarding 11; reflected in the learning process 12; reflected in the program structure 11–12; reflected in the supervisor interaction 12
developmental counseling and therapy (DCT) 223–224
developmental crisis 175
developmental level: evaluation of 131; skills 99–101
developmental models 119–120
development stage of change in organizations 231
diagnosis: for alcohol and drug use 204–205; in counseling 58–60; determination in treatment plan development 75; in informed consent document 33–34; intentional misdiagnosis of mental disorders 168; managed care 168; *other specified and unspecified designation* 60; subtypes and specifiers 59
Diagnostic and Statistical Manual of Mental Disorders (DSM) 51, 58–60, 168; addiction 204–205; codes and classification 60; crosswalking to ICD-10-CM codes 60; ordering by classification 59; *other specified disorder* 60; subtypes and specifiers 59; treatment plan development and 74–75; *unspecified disorder* 60
dialectical behavior therapy (DBT) 91
dialectic/systemic cognitive style 224
diazepam (Valium) 246
digital communication 151–152
dignity, respect for 143
Directed Reflection Exercise on Supervision form 100

directives 37, 98
discovery process 159
discrepancies, identification of 37
discrimination 142–143, 149
discrimination model 120–121
discussion groups, web-based professional 151, 153
dispositions suited to running groups 42–43
distance counseling 151–152
distorted beliefs, addressing 180
distress, subjective 177
divalproex (Depakote) 247, 248
diversity: codes of ethics and 142, 147; consultation and 219–220; ethics of counseling culturally diverse clients 147–150; field site client population 18–19; supervision and 119; *see also* culture
doctor-patient model 219
documentation: case notes 170; internship hours 133–134; practicum hours 132; risk management 162; of suicidal clients 165–166; suicide risk assessment 188; suspicion of child abuse 167
do no harm 27, 142
dopamine receptor blockers 247
"Do something different" principle 86–87
doxepin (Sinequan) 244
drug use: diagnosing 204–205; suicide and 193; treatment 205–206
DSM-5 see Diagnostic and Statistical Manual of Mental Disorders (DSM)
dual relationship 141, 161
due process 159
duloxetine (Cymbalta) 245
duty to protect 165–166
duty to warn 166
dysfunctional behaviors 107–108

Early Childhood mental Health Consultation (ECMHC) 226
early recovery, stage of recovery 207
EARS (elicit, amplify, reinforce, and start again) 86
EBP (evidence-based practices) 144
EBTs *see* evidence-based therapies
educational consultation 220, 222
Effexor (venlafaxine) 245
Effexor XR (venlafaxineXR) 245
elder abuse 167
electronic mail (e-mail) 151–152
Elementary School Counseling Referral Form 55
Ellis, Albert **78**, 88
EMDR (eye movement and desensitization and reprocessing) 179
emergency, mental health 33
emotional abuse 201
emotional liability, in children's response to crisis 184
emotions, observing client's 65
empathy 29; in consultation process 228; conveying 37; in crisis intervention 177; in trauma counseling 180–181; as a virtue 146
empowerment 149
empty chair technique 98
Emsam (selegiline) 245
encouraging 37, 98
EPL (Exceptional Professional Learning) 225

Erikson, Erik 77
escitalopram (Lexapro) 244
ethical codes *see* codes of ethics
ethical decision making 142–147; cultural data and 149–150; models 145; principle-based ethics 142–145; process 145; self-tests after resolving ethical dilemmas 146–147; virtue-based ethics 145–146
ethical dilemmas 143–144; self-tests after resolving 146–147; transcultural integrative model for resolving 149
ethics 139–154; area for regular consideration 143–144; confidentiality and 139, 141, 144; of counseling culturally diverse clients 147–150; definitions 139–140; exceptions to confidentiality 163–167; intentional misdiagnosis of mental disorders 168; knowledge required for licensing and certification 139; mandates relating to danger to self 189–190; principle-based 142–145, 149; reasons to be ethically informed counselor 139; rule-bound 145; self-care, managing issue related to 150; virtue-based 145–146, 149
euphemisms, avoiding 188
evaluating suicide risk 187
evaluation: consultation interventions 229; of counseling performance in individual supervision 130–133; of counselor trainees in a specialization 132–133; disclosure in Supervisor Informed Consent and Disclosure Statement 125; of internship in group supervision 112–113; midpoint and summative evaluation in internship 132–133; midpoint and summative evaluation in practicum 130–132; of practicum 108–109; *see also* assessment
Evaluation of Intern's Practice in Site Activities form 133
events-based model 121
evidence-based approaches to school consultation 225–226
evidence-based practices (EBP) 144
evidence-based therapies (EBTs) 65, 84, 88–91; acceptance and commitment therapy (ACT) 90–91; counseling sexually abused children 202; dialectical behavior therapy (DBT) 91; mindfulness-based cognitive therapy (MBCT) 90; mindfulness-based stress reduction (MBSR) 89–90; mindfulness-based therapy (MBT) 88–89; trauma counseling 179–181
exams, licensure and certification 236–237
Exceptional Professional Learning (EPL) 225
exception questions 86
existential crisis 175
existentialists **79**
exposure, in trauma counseling 181
eye movement and desensitization and reprocessing (EMDR) 179

face-to-face interview 19
facilitating, group counseling skill 42
failure to warn 194
False Claims Act 168
false memories, implanted 202
family: forms of 53; history data, gathering 52–53
Family Education Rights and Privacy Act 45

Fanapt (iloperidone) 248
fear: children's response to crisis 183; doing/saying wrong thing 26–27
feedback 37, 98; about supervisor 133; administrative 116; from clients of supervisee 133; clinical supervision 116; directed 107; in supervision 130; from supervisor 116–117, 121–122, 125
feedback informed treatment (FIT) 180
fidelity 142–143
field site: credentials of 16; negotiating placement 19–21; orientation and 21; role and function of student 21–22
field site selection: checklist of questions to be researched and answered before selection 10; choosing appropriate 25; criteria for 16–19; guidelines 15–16; negotiating placement 19–21; student say in 15; timing of 16
field site selection criteria 16–19; client population 17–19; professional affiliations of site 16; professional practices of site 16–17; professional staff and supervisor 16; site administration 17; theoretical orientation of the site and supervisor 17; training and supervision values 17
financial records 169
first client, preparing to meet with 29–35
FIT (feedback informed treatment) 180
fluoxetine (Prozac, Sarafem) 245
fluphenazine (Prolixin) 248
fluvoxamine (Luvox) 244, 249
focused observations, in peer consultation 108
focused solution development 85
focusing 37, 228
forces of change in organizations
formal-operational cognitive style 224
formative evaluation: disclosure in Supervisor Informed Consent and Disclosure Statement 125; evaluation of counseling performance in individual supervision 130; of internship 113; of practicum 108
fraud, health care 168
freedom of choice 142
Freud, Sigmund **77**
Fromm, Eric **78**
frustration, decreased tolerance for in response to crisis 184

gambling addiction 205
genuineness 35, 43, 97, 176, 203, 228
Geodon (ziprasidone) 248
Gestalt therapy 98
goal development, in treatment plan development 74
goals: consultation 217, **221**, 221–222, 229; effectiveness of setting 73; elements to consider when identifying 72; emphasis as student progresses in practicum 101, *102*; initial 73; internship 132; outcome 72, 75; process 72, 75; of psychodynamic supervision 119; setting in counseling 71–73, 228; in solution-focused therapy 85; stages of change model and 71–72; statement in supervision contract 125–127; Supervisee Goal Statement 100–101; supervision 125–127, 129; treatment plan and 74; types of 72–73

Gold, Stuart 195
graduate student supervisors 6
graduation from an accredited program, advantages
    of 5
group counselor, effective 41
group dynamics 41–42
group identity 148–149
groups: content in 42; dispositions suited to running
    42–43; observing existing 40–41; preparing to lead
    your first 40–43; process in 42; proposing and
    developing 41; skills to practice implementing
    when running 42; things to know about running
    41–42; tips for co-leading 43
group supervision 97–113; activities in 106–108;
    assignments in internship, typical seminar
    110–111; concepts in 101–103; confidentiality
    103; course objectives and assignments in group
    practicum 105–106; defined 111; evaluation of
    internship in 112–113; evaluation of practicum
    in 103, 108–109; in internship 109–113; models
    in internship 111–112; peer consultation
    106–108; in practicum 103–109; recordings
    103, 104; requirements 97, 103, 109–110; self-
    assessment 103
group supervision models in internship 111–112;
    structured group supervision model (SGS) 112;
    structured peer group supervision model (SPGS)
    111–112

Haldol (haloperidol) 248
haloperidol (Haldol) 248
harm 27, 142; exceptions to privileged
    communication 164; malpractice and 159–160; to
    others 193–198; potentially dangerous client 166;
    to self 165, 184–193; taking action to prevent 166;
    to vulnerable adults 167
hatha yoga 89
HCR-20 tool 196
Health Insurance Portability and Accountability Act
    (HIPAA) 29–30, 34, 44, 59
hearing, pretrial 159
help, asking for 27
helping skills 36–37, 97–98
highest-priority problem, identification in strategic
    solution-focused therapy 87
high-risk client: potential harm to others 193–198;
    understanding and assessing harm to self 184–193
HIPPA see Health Insurance Portability and
    Accountability Act
history: gathering family history data 52–53;
    gathering personal history data 53–54
humanistic-relational model 119
hydroxyzine (Atarax) 246
hydroxyzine pamoate (Vistaril) 246

ICD (International Classification of Diseases) 58–60
Idaho School Counselor Association 182
identity: group 148–149; tripartite model of personal
    identity 148; verification of client identity 152
"If it works, do more of it" principle 86–87
iloperidone (Fanapt) 248
imaginal exposure 179
imipramine (Tofranil) 244
immediacy 37

impairment 150
implanted false memories 202
implementation of consultation plan 228–229
impulses, for substance use 207–208
indirect service, consultation as 215–216
individualized learner plan 126
Individual Student Contact Sheet form 46
individual supervision 115–134; evaluation of
    counseling performance in 130–133; internship 129
individual supervision models and methods
    118–123; developmental models 119–120;
    discrimination model 120–121; integrated
    developmental models 119–120; models grounded
    in psychotherapy theory 119; process models
    120–121; triadic method 121–123
informational consultation 220
information release 165
informed consent 29, 31–35; codes of ethics 31;
    distance counseling 152; elements of 31–32;
    group supervision 103; initial session and 39;
    liability risks 162; managed care and 169; sample
    informed consent and disclosure statement 32–34;
    in supervision 123–125
Initial Intake Form 40
initial session with client 35–40; assessment
    information gathered prior to 52–55; closing
    39–40; helping skills 36–37; intake summary 40;
    objectives of 36; pretherapy intake information
    40; structured and unstructured interviews 36;
    structuring 38–39; three-stage structured, solution-
    focused approach 36–37
inner voice, trusting 27–28
insight, client mental status assessment and 55
instincts, trusting 27–28
instinct to live, overcoming 186
insurance 16; coverage and diagnosis 58; ICD code
    requirements 59; informed consent and 31, 34;
    liability 162; managed care 168–169
intake interview 52, 56
intake questionnaire 52
intake summary 40
integrated developmental models 119–120, 129
integration, in developmental models 120
integrative model 63
integrative paper, internship assignment 110–111
integrity 143, 146
internal consultation 217–218
International Classification of Diseases (ICD) 58–60
internet counseling 152
internship: goals 132; group supervision in 109–113;
    individual supervision 129; midpoint and
    summative evaluation in 132–133; practicum
    competencies 110; successful completion of
    113; transitioning to 109; see also practicum and
    internship
internship hours: CACREP/CORE guidelines 6;
    documenting 133–134; MPCAC guidelines 7
interpersonal dynamics, in counseling situation 119
interpretation 37
intervention(s): consultation 228–229;
    developmental models and 120; evidence-based
    treatments 179–181; focus in discrimination
    model 120; school suicide intervention policy
    193; skills 132; suicide counseling intervention

and planning 188–189; in trauma counseling 179–181; *see also* treatment plan
intervention creation, in treatment plan development 75
interview(s): assessment 56, 207; consultation 217; guidelines for initial 36; intake 52, 56; motivational interviewing 207; preparing for 19; questions to ask during 20; questions typically asked during 19–20; semi-structured 36; sexually abused children 201–202; stages 36–37; structured 36; unstructured 36
Interviewer Rating Form 107
Intuniv 249
Invega (paliperidone) 248
inverted pyramid model 62–63
in vivo exposure 179
involuntary commitment 164–165, 189, 190, 195
irritability, in children's response to crisis 184
issue-specific skills 98

James and Gilliland model of crisis intervention 177–178
judgment, client mental status assessment and 54
Jung, Carl **77**
justice: ethical principle 142–143; principle of 149; social 147; test of 146

Kanel model of crisis intervention 176–177
Kelly, George **77**
Klonopin (clonazepam) 246

labeling emotions 88–89
Lamictal (lamotrigine) 247
lamotrigine (Lamictal) 247
late-stage recovery 207
law(s) 140, 157–171; case 158; civil 158; classifications of 157; common 158; constitutional 157; criminal 158; duty to protect 165–166; duty to warn 166; licensure 235–236; limits to confidentiality 141; mental health 158; practice of counselor-client confidentiality in Canada 168; privilege and 163–164; purpose of 157; statutory 157–158; suspected child abuse and neglect 166–167; suspected harm to vulnerable adults 167; tort 158; types of 158; *see also* legal issues
lawsuits: malpractice 158–160; reasons for 160–161; steps in 158–159
learning process, development reflected in 12
legal issues 157–171; client's past criminal acts 198; confidentiality breach 165–167; liability insurance 162; malpractice, elements of 159–160; managed care and 168–169; mandates relating to danger to self 189–190; privacy, confidentiality, and privileged communication 163–165; record keeping 169–170; reporting child abuse 200–201; risk management 161–162; *Tarasoff* case 166, 194–195; *see also* law
Lexapro (escitalopram) 244
liability: client suicide and 190; failure to report suspected abuse 200; potentially dangerous clients 193–195
liability insurance 162
liability risks 161–162
libel 161

Librium (chlordiazepoxide) 246
Licensed Professional Clinical Counselor with Supervisory designation (LPCC-S) 237
licensure 9–10; associate 236; codes of ethics 141; distance counseling 151; evidence of knowledge and skill competence 235; exams 236–237; first steps toward 235–238; structure 236
licensure laws 235–236
life span model 120
Likert scale 132
linchpin model 61–62
linking, group counseling skill 42
listening sequence of open and closed 37, 98
listening to clients 27
lithium (Lithobid) 247, 248
Lithobid (lithium) 247, 248
locus of control, regarding substance-using behavior 208
logical consequences 37, 98
longevity, career 238–239
long-term memory, client mental status assessment and 55
lorazepam (Ativan) 246
LPCC-S (Licensed Professional Clinical Counselor with Supervisory designation) 237
Luvox (fluvoxamine) 244, 249

maintenance: stage of change in organizations 231; stage of recovery 207; in stages of change model 72
major depression, treatment of 248
maladaptive beliefs, adjusting 180
maladaptive cognitions 208
malpractice: elements of 159–160; insurance 16; lawsuits 158–160; potentially suicidal persons 190
malpractice suits 139
managed care 31, 34, 58, 84, 168–169
mandatory reporting: suspected child abuse and neglect 166–167; suspected harm to vulnerable adults 167
mantra 89
marginalization 149
Maslow, Abraham **78**
MAST (Michigan Alcohol Screening Test) 55
Masters in Psychology and Counseling Accreditation Council (MPCAC) 3, 5, 7
MBCT (mindfulness-based cognitive therapy) 90
MBSR (mindfulness-based stress reduction) 89–90
MBT (mindfulness-based therapy) 88–89
mediation, in school consultation 222
medications 243–249; antianxiety 246–247; antidepressants 243–246; antipsychotic 247–248; for children and adolescents 248–249
Mellaril (thioridazine) 248
mental health, wellness model of 57
Mental Health Act 215
mental health consultation *see* consultation
mental health law 158
mental state, assessment of client's 54–55
mental status categories of assessment 54–55
Mental Status Checklist 54
mental status examination, in initial assessment 54
mentor test 146
metaphor, descriptive 111

Michigan Alcohol Screening Test (MAST) 55
microskills training model 37, 98
midpoint evaluation: in internship 132–133; in practicum 130–132
Midpoint Narrative Evaluation of a Practicum Student 130–131
mid-stage recovery 207
mindfulness 88, 91
mindfulness-based cognitive therapy (MBCT) 90
mindfulness-based stress reduction (MBSR) 89–90
mindfulness-based therapy (MBT) 88–89
minimization 108
Minnesota Coalition Against Sexual Assault 203
minor tranquilizers 247
miracle question 86, 98
mirtazapine (Remeron) 245, 246
misdiagnosis 168
misprison of a felony 198
Moban (molindone) 248
molindone (Moban) 248
monitoring client in therapy 65
Monthly Practicum Log 46, 48, 132
mood, client mental status assessment and 54
mood-stabilizing medications 247
Moore, Lawrence 195
morality 139–140
moral traces test 146
motivation: in consultation process 228; developmental models and 120; dialectical behavior therapy (DBT) 91; for substance use 207
motivational interviewing 207
multicultural awareness: evaluation of 131; skills 99, 101, 111
multicultural competency 18–19, 37
multicultural consultation 220
multicultural counseling: building awareness 147–148; building knowledge 148–149; choosing culturally appropriate strategies 149–150; ethics of counseling culturally diverse clients 147–150; transcultural integrative model for resolving ethical dilemmas 149
multiple relationship 141

NAADAC-The Association for Addiction Professionals website 141
Nardil (phenelzine) 245
narrative, in trauma counseling 181
narrative exposure therapy 179
narrative therapy **79**
National Association of School Psychologists (NASP) 183
National Board of Certified Counselors (NBCC) 7–8; code of ethics 141; exams 236–237; *Policy Regarding the Provision of Distance Professional Services* 152; specialty certification 8; website 141
National Career Development Association 9, 141
National Certified Counselor (NCC) 7–8
National Clinical Mental Health Counseling Exam (NCMHCE) 7–9, 236–237
National Counselor Exam for Licensure and Certification (NCE) 7–8, 236–237
National Institute on Drug Abuse 206
Navane (thiothixene) 248
NBCC *see* National Board of Certified Counselors

NCC (National Certified Counselor) 7–8
NCE (National Counselor Exam for Licensure and Certification) 7–8, 236–237
NCMHCC (National Clinical Mental Health Counseling Exam) 7–9, 236–237
negative thinking 90
neglect 164, 166–167; defined 199; mediating factors 200; risk factors 199
negligence: client suicide and 190; failure to warn 194
nonmaleficence 142–143
nonprofessional relationship 141
Norpramin (desipramine) 244
notes: after each counseling session 65–66; case notes 66, 170; progress 43–45
Notice of Privacy Practices (NPP) 30

objective construction, in treatment plan development 74–75
objective information 44
objectives: consultation 229; supervision 127
observer role in triadic supervisor method 121–122
obsessive-compulsive disorder, treatment of 249
olanzapine (Zyprexa) 248, 249
olanzapine/fluoxetine (Symbyax) 246, 248
Oleptro (trazodone ER) 246
online counseling 152
opening sessions 37, 98
operationalized psychoactive substance relapse prevention program 208–209
oppression 54, 147–149
organizations: forces of change in 231; internal consultation 217–218; resistance to consultation 230; stages of change in 231
orientation: client mental status assessment and 54; field site 21
outcome goals 72, 75
overdocumentation 162

Paiget, Jean 223
paliperidone (Invega) 248
Pamelor (desipramine) 244
panic attacks, treatment of 246
paraphrasing 37, 98, 228
Parental Release Form 34
Parent Contact Log form 46
parents resistance to consultation 230
Parnate (tranylcypromine) 245
paroxetine (Paxil) 245
patronizing 203
patterns and connections, pointing out 37
Paxil (paroxetine) 245
peer consultation in group supervision 106–108; benefits of 106–107; dysfunctional behaviors, identification of 107–108; guidelines for activities 107; peer critique of recordings 107; structured peer group supervision model (SPGS) 108
peer-mediation programs 182
Peer Rating Form 107
perception, client mental status assessment and 54
performance skills 97–98, 100–101, 108
personal history data, gathering 53–54
personal identity, tripartite model of 148
Personal Information Protection and Electronics Documents Act 30

personalization, focus in discrimination model 121
personal theory of counseling: developing 76, 129; identifying your theory and technique preferences 76, 84, **80–84**
phases of practicum and internship 11–12; development reflected in the learning process 12; development reflected in the program structure 11–12; development reflected in the supervisor interaction 12
phenelzine (Nardil) 245
PHI (protected health information) 30
phone messages 151
physical abuse: defined 199; mediating factors 200; risk factors 199
placement, negotiating 19–21
plaintiff 159
Policy Regarding the Provision of Distance Professional Services (NBCC) 152
positive language, use of 224
positive psychology approaches to consultation 225
post-graduate training supervision 237–238
post-modernists **79**
post-traumatic stress disorder (PTSD) 179–180
power, of supervisors 116–117
practical wisdom 146
practicum: competencies 110; group supervision in 103–109; midpoint and summative evaluation in 130–132; starting the practicum 25–48
practicum and internship: accreditation standards for 4–7; phases of 11–12; requirements 5; site selection 15–19
practicum evaluation: formative 108; in group supervision 108–109; summative 108–109
practicum hours: CACEP guidelines 7; CACREP/CORE guidelines 6; documenting 132
Practitioner's Guide to Ethical Decision-Making, A (ACA) 147
precontemplation, in stages of change model 71
preentry step, in consultation process 226–227
premature advice or problem solving 108
preparation, in stages of change model 72
pre-practicum considerations 10–11
presenting issues, intake interview and 52
present moment, in mindfulness techniques 89
present with the client, being 27
pretherapy intake information 40
pretrial hearing 159
primary problem, clarification of 87
principle-based ethics 142–145, 149
Pristiq (venlafaxine) 245
privacy: HIPAA rule 30; informing clients of 29; right to 163; social media 153
privilege 45–48, 163
privileged communication 163–164; exceptions to 163–164, 200; legal issues 163–164
probes 37, 56, 107
problem complexity, client assessment and 57–58
problem definition, in treatment plan development 74
problem identification step in consultation process 228
problem solving, premature 108
procedural skills 37–38, 98
process consultation model 219
process goals 72, 75

process in groups 42
process models 120–121
professional counseling team, becoming part of 28–29
professional counselor: professionalization of counseling 3–4; steps to becoming 4
professional development sequence 128–130
professional functioning, domains of 120
professional skills 98
program-centered administrative consultation 216
program structure, development reflected in 11–12
progress: assessment of 64–67; of practicum students 115; questions in examining treatment effectiveness 66; reporting therapeutic progress 66–67
progress notes 43–45; content of 44; DAP format 44; SOAP format 44–45
Prolixin (fluphenazine) 248
prolonged exposure therapy 179–180
protected health information (PHI) 30
protecting, group counseling skill 42
proximate cause 160
Prozac (fluoxetine) 245
prudence 146
psychiatric medications *see* medications
psychodynamic model 119
psychodynamic supervision 119
psychoeducation 180
psychological abuse: defined 199; risk factors 199
psychological associate 10
psychological flexibility 90–91
psychologists: competencies for 132; licensure 9–10
psychopathology: client assessment and 57; relapse prevention and 209
Psychosocial History form 40, 52, 55
psychosocial history questionnaire 52
psychotherapy: overview of theories of **77–79**; supervisors 115
psychotic disorders, treatment of 247, 249
PTSD (post-traumatic stress disorder) 179–180
publicity, test of 146
purchase-of-expertise model 218–219

qualitative assessment activities 64–65
questions: closed 107; considered when reviewing theories 76; coping 86; dysfunctional behaviors 107; effective questioning 51; examining treatment effectiveness 66; exception 86; excessive 107; leading 202; listening sequence of open and closed 37, 98; miracle 86, 98; why 107
quetiapine (Seroquel) 248, 249

rapport, building 35
rational emotive behavior therapy 88
recent memory, client mental status assessment and 55
Recording Critique Form 103, *104*
recording sessions 17, 20, 84; critique form 103, *104*; group supervision 103; individual supervision and 121, 124, 126–128, 130; informed consent and 34–35; peer critique of 107–108, 112; supervision session and 128, 130
record keeping 43–48, 169–170; electronic 43; potentially dangerous clients 197; risk management 162; school counselor 45–48

Record of All Students Seen form 46
records: client request for copies 170; financial 169; Health Insurance Portability and Accountability Act (HIPAA) and 29–30, 34, 44; retention and disposition of 170; types of information kept in 170
recovery: description of 206; preventing relapse 208–209; stages of 206–207
recycling, in stages of change model 72
reflecting feelings 37, 97–98
reflection of meaning 37
reflective model 120
reflective skills 99
reframing 37
Registered Professional Counsellor (RPC) 9
regression in behavior 183
regulations 158
relapse: preventing 208–209; in stages of change model 72
relaxation, in trauma counseling 181
release of information 165
Remeron (mirtazapine) 245, 246
reputation, injury to
requirements, practicum 26
resistance: client assessment and 58; to consultation 230; to supervision 119
respectfulness 146
responsibility to society 143
responsible caring 143
restorying 37
résumé 19
reversibility, test of 146
risk assessment for potentially dangerous clients 195–198
risk assessment for suicide 185–188; assessment instruments 188; buffers against suicide 187; capacity to commit suicide 186; desire to die 185–186; evaluating suicide risk 187; for students 192–193; suicidal intent 186
risk management 161–162
Risperdal (risperidone) 248, 249
risperidone (Risperdal) 248, 249
RitalinLA 249
Rogers, Carl 79
role of practicum/internship student 21–22
role taking, in peer consultation 108
RPC (Registered Professional Counsellor) 9
rule-bound ethics 145

SAFE-T (Suicide Assessment Five Step Evaluation and Triage) model 188
safety plan, for suicidal client 189
Saphris (asenapine) 248
Sarafem (fluoxetine) 245
saying the wrong thing 26–27
schemas, internal built by client 87
schizophrenia, treatment of 247, 249
school consultation 220–226; collaborative consultation 218; focus, function, and form dimensions 222; models and practices 222–226; overview 220–222; stages and goals of 221, 221–222
school consultation models and practices 222–226; developmental counseling and therapy (DCT) 223–224; evidence-based approaches 225–226;

Exceptional Professional Learning (EPL) 225; positive psychology approaches 225; solution-focused consultation 224–225
school counselors: brief therapies 84; competencies 221; confidentiality guidelines 34; consultation 217–218; consulting competencies 221; as crisis and trauma specialist 181; diagnosis in counseling 58; ethical and legal mandates relating to danger to self 189–190; informed consent and confidentiality guidelines 33–34; NBCC specialty certification 8; potentially suicidal students 192; record keeping 45–48; responsibilities of 222; roles of 220–222; state certification 9; suicide risk assessment for students 192–193; tasks in preventing and responding to crisis 182–183
schools: crisis intervention and trauma response 181–184; suicide intervention policy 193; suicide risk assessment and prevention 191–193
school violence: practical recommendations for limiting 183; preventing and responding to crisis 182–183
secondary relationship 141
Secondary School Counseling Referral Form 55
security rule, HIPAA 30
sedatives 247
selective serotonin reuptake inhibitors (SSRIs) 244–245, 248, 249
selegiline (Emsam) 245
self as context, in acceptance and commitment therapy (ACT) 91
self-assessment: counseling student's 129; in group supervision 103, 105–106; in skill areas 100
Self-Assessment of Counseling Performance Skills form 108
self-awareness: enhanced by peer consultation 107; evaluation of 131; plan for 239; skills 99, 101
Self-Awareness/Multicultural Awareness Rating Scale form 100
self-care: career longevity and 238; managing issue related to 150; practitioner 162
self-determination theory 225
self-disclosure 37–38, 98
self-evaluation in consultation process 228
self-regulation, in trauma counseling 181
semi-structured interviews 36
sensorimotor cognitive style 223
separation anxiety disorder, treatment of 249
Seroquel (quetiapine) 247–249, 249
serotonin and norepinephrine reuptake inhibitors (SNRIs) 245
sertraline (Zoloft) 245, 249
setting: CACEP guidelines 7; CACREP/CORE guidelines 6; MPCAC guidelines 7
seven-task model of crisis intervention 177–178
sexual abuse: counseling the sexually abused 202–204; dos and don'ts of therapy 203–204; interviewing sexually abused children 201–202; mediating factors 200; myths about 203; risk factors 199
sexual misconduct 160
sexual relationships 160
SGS (structured group supervision) model 112
shadowing 21
shared meaning, between supervisor and supervisee 117

Sinequan (doxepin) 244
single-focus form, in triadic supervisor method 122
site *see* field site
Site Evaluation Form 133
site supervisors 6, 16–17, 21
situational crisis 175
skill areas: cognitive counseling skills 98, 101; counseling performance skills 97–98, 100–101; developmental level 99–101; identifying 97–100; self-assessment in 100–101; self-awareness/multicultural awareness skills 98–99, 101
skills: attending 176–177; basic and advanced counseling 97–98; case formulation 61; cognitive counseling 131; cognitive counseling skills 98, 101, 112–113; consultation 221–222, 228; counseling performance 37, 97–98, 100–101, 108, 131; cultural diversity 111; developmental level 99–101; dysfunctional 107; helping 36–37, 97–98; identifying counseling skill areas 97–100; interpersonal influence 98; interventions 132; issue-specific 37, 98; microskills training model 37, 98; mulicultural-awareness 99, 101, 111; multicultural counseling 147; procedural 37–38, 98; professional 98; recommended levels for transitioning to internship 109; self-assessment of 129; self-awareness 99, 101; theory-based techniques 98
Skinner, B.F. **78**
slander 161
SNRIs (serotonin and norepinephrine reuptake inhibitors) 245
SOAP (subjective, objective, assessment, plan) format 44–45
social cognitive theory of counseling 180
social justice 147
social media 151, 153
social support, in crisis intervention 177–178
software, case management 43
solution-focused consultation 224–225
solution-focused therapy 85–86, 98; goal setting 73; strategic 86–87
solution scenario, in strategic solution-focused therapy 87
specialist-collaborator 218
specifiers, disorder 59
SPGS (structured peer group supervision) model 108, 111–112
split-focus form, in triadic supervisor method 122
SSRIs (selective serotonin reuptake inhibitors) 244–245
stabilization, stage of recovery 206
stages of change model 71–72
stagnation, in developmental models 120
starting the practicum 25–48; first client, preparing to meet with 29–35; groups 40–43; initial session with client 35–40; therapeutic alliance, establishing 35; *see also* beginning the practicum experience
state licensure for counselors and psychologists 9–10
statutory law 157–158
Stelazine (trifluoperazine) 248
strategic solution-focused therapy 86–87
Strattera (atomoxetine) 245
structured assessment 55

structured group supervision model (SGS) 112
structured interviews 36
structured peer group supervision model (SPGS) 108, 111–112
structuring initial session with client 38–39; confidentiality 38; opening comments 38
structuring therapeutic relationship: five-step process 38–39; initial contact 38
stuck points, addressing 180
student counselor role 21–22
subjective information 44
subpoena 159
Substance Abuse and Mental Health Services Administration 188
Substance Abuse Assessment Form 208
substance addiction *see* addiction
substance-induced disorders 205
substance use disorders 205, 207–209; *see also* addiction
subtypes, disorder 59
suicidal and homicidal risk, intake interview and 52
suicidal ideation/thoughts: asking clients about 185; asking student about 192–193; prevalence of 185; student disclosure of 192
suicidal intent 186
suicide 184–193; buffers against 187; capacity for 186; children 185, 191; counseling intervention and planning 188–189; definition of 184; duty to protect 165–166; evaluating risk 187; lawsuits and 161; myths about 184–185; prevalence of 191; risk assessment for 185–188
Suicide Assessment Five Step Evaluation and Triage (SAFE-T) model 188
Suicide Consultation Form 189
suicide contract 189
suicide risk assessment and prevention schools 191–193; learning about and responding to potentially suicidal students 192; suicide prevention programs, basics of 191
summarizing 37, 97–98
Summary Internship Log 133
summative evaluation: disclosure in Supervisor Informed Consent and Disclosure Statement 125; evaluation of counseling performance in individual supervision 130–133; in internship 132–133; of internship 112–113; in practicum 130–132; of practicum 108–109
supervisee: evaluation of site experience 133; evaluation of supervisor 133; sources of discomfort 117
Supervisee Evaluation of Supervisor form 133
Supervisee Goal Statement 100–101
supervision: administrative 116; clinical 116, 123–130; contract 125–127; of developing counselor-in-training 128–130; evaluation of counseling performance in individual supervision 130–133; feedback in 130; goal emphasis as student progresses during practicum *102*; goals 125–127, 129; individual 115–134; informed consent 123–125; lousy 117–118; minimizing liability risks 162; post-graduate training 237–238; psychodynamic 119; purposes of 115; role-modeling process and *102*; structured group supervision model (SPGS) 112; structured peer

group supervision model (SPGS) 108, 111–112; student anxiety concerning 118–119; supervisor-supervisee relationship 116–117; thought-based approaches to 117; *see also* group supervision

Supervision Contract 125–127

supervision sessions 128, 130

Supervisor Informed Consent and Disclosure Statement 123–125

supervisors 6, 16–17; awareness of class requirements 26; CACEP guidelines 7; CACREP/CORE guidelines 6; credentials of 16; development reflected in the supervisor interaction 12; evaluation of internship in group supervision 112–113; evaluation of practicum in group supervision 108–109; field site orientation 21; gatekeeper duties of 133; for post-graduate training supervision 237–238; role and function in practicum and internship 115; as role models 115; roles in discrimination model 120–121; seeking assistance of 28; shadowing 21; supervisee's evaluation of 133; supervisor-supervisee relationship 116–117; theoretical orientation of 17; university 103, 112, 115, 121, 125, 132, 134

Supervisor's Final Evaluation of Intern form 132

Supervisor's Final Evaluation of Practicum Student form 132

Supervisor's Formative Evaluation of Supervisee's Counseling Practice form 130

Support Group form 46

Symbyax (olanzapine/fluoxetine) 246, 248

sympathy, as a virtue 146

systemic crisis 175

systemic models 119

systems approach to supervision model 121

Tarasoff case 166, 194–195; events of 194; implications of 194; ruling requirements 195

teacher supervisor role in discrimination model 120–121

technology 151–152

Tegretol (carbamazepine) 247

telehealth 152

telephones 151

telepsychology 152

terminating sessions *see* closing sessions

tests, in assessment process 55

text messages 151

theories of counseling: overview of **77–79**; questions to consider when reviewing 76

The Theory and Practice of Mental Health Consultation (Caplan) 215

theory-based techniques 98

therapeutic alliance: establishing 35; informed consent and 32

Therapeutic Progress Report form 67

therapeutic progress reports 66–67

therapist, as defined by *Tarasoff II* 194

thioridazine (Mellaril) 248

thiothixene (Navane) 248

third wave cognitive behavioral approaches 84, 88–91

Thorazine (chlorpromazine) 247, 248

thought content, client mental status assessment and 54

thought processes, client mental status assessment and 54

time: amount for sessions 38; planning your practicum 26

Tofranil (imipramine) 244

Topamax (topiramate) 247

topiramate (Topamax) 247

tort 159

tort law 158

transference 117

transition, stage of recovery 206

transitioning to internship 109

tranylcypromine (Parnate) 245

trauma 175–176; children's reaction to 183–184; victim experiences 176

trauma counseling 178–181; cognitive processing therapy (CPT) 180; cross-cutting ingredients for effective 180–181; evidence-based treatments 179–181; prolonged exposure therapy 179–180

trauma-informed approach to counseling sexually abused children 202

trauma-informed specialists, school counselors as 181

trauma response in schools 181–184

trazodone (Desyrel) 244

trazodone ER (Oleptro) 246

treatment: for alcohol and drug use 205–206; medications 243–249; *see also* intervention(s)

treatment goals *see* goals

treatment plan: broad-brush approach 75; counselor-client process approach 75; developing 73–75; guiding principles for use in preparation 75; phases of therapy 74; roles in the counseling process 73–74; solution-focused therapy and 85

treatment recommendations, in therapeutic progress reports 67

triadic method of supervision 121–123

trial phase 159

tricyclic antidepressants (TCAs) 244

trifluoperazine (Stelazine) 248

triggering events, for substance use 207

tripartite model of personal identity 148

trust: confidentiality 163; consultation and 230; fidelity and 142; between supervisor and supervisee 117

trusting yourself and your inner voice 27–28

trustworthiness 146

underdocumentation 162

United States Department of Health and Human Services 166, 198

universality, test of 146

unstructured interviews 36

utterances, dysfunctional 107

Valium (diazepam) 246

values, in acceptance and commitment therapy (ACT) 91

V-code conditions 168

venlafaxine (Effexor, Pristiq) 245

venlafaxineXR (Effexor XR) 245

veracity 143

videoconferencing 151

video recordings *see* recording sessions

Viibryd (vilazodone) 245, 246

vilazodone (Viibryd) 245, 246
violence: harm to others 193–198; practical recommendations for limiting school violence 183; preventing and responding to crisis 182–183
virtual counseling 152
virtue-based ethics 145–146, 149; described 145; ethical decision making 146; virtues essential to counseling 146
visitor client, in solution-focused therapy 85, 86
Vistaril (hydroxyzine pamoate) 246, 249
voicemail 151
vulnerable adults, harm to 167
Vyvanse 249

web-based professional discussion groups 151, 153
Weekly Internship Log 133
Weekly Schedule/Practicum Log 46, *47*, 48, 132
well-being, personal 150, 238
WellbutrinLA (bupropionLA) 246, 249

WellbutrinSR (bupropionSR) 246, 249
wellness model of mental health 4, 57
"What's the Trouble" principle 86–87
white privilege 147
why questions 107
wisdom, practical 146
working alliance 38, 100, 116–117, 119, 221
World Health Organization, ICD use by 59
World Health Organization Disability Assessment Schedule (WHODAS) 59
written narrative exposure 179

Xanax (alprozolam) 246

Z codes 59
ziprasidone (Geodon) 248
Zoloft (sertraline) 245, 249
Zung Self-Rating Anxiety Scale 55
Zyprexa (olanzapine) 248, 249